THE NEGRO IN INDIANA
BEFORE 1900

THE NEGRO IN INDIANA BEFORE 1900

A Study of a Minority

BY

EMMA LOU THORNBROUGH

Published in association with
THE INDIANA HISTORICAL BUREAU

INDIANA UNIVERSITY PRESS
Bloomington and Indianapolis

First Indiana University Press Edition 1993

© 1985 by the Indiana Historical Bureau

The paper used in this publication meets the minimum requirements of American National Standard for Information Sciences—Permanence of Paper for Printed
Library Materials, ANSI Z39.48-1984.

Manufactured in the United States of America

Library of Congress Cataloging-in-Publication Data

Thornbrough, Emma Lou.
  The Negro in Indiana before 1900 : a study of a minority / by Emma Lou Thornbrough.
    p.   cm.
  "Published in association with the Indiana Historical Bureau."
  Originally published: Indianapolis : Indiana Historical Press, 1957.
  Includes bibliographical references and index.
  ISBN 0-253-35989-9 (alk. paper). — ISBN 0-253-35988-0 (pbk. : alk. paper)
    1. Afro-Americans—Indiana—History—19th century.
  2. Indiana—History. I. Title.
E185.93.I4T48   1993   92-46430
977.2'00496073—dc20

1 2 3 4 5 97 96 95 94 93

To My Father

CONTENTS

PREFACE TO THE SECOND EDITION

The *Negro in Indiana before 1900* was first published in 1957. The title of the book dates it. In 1957 "Negro" with a capital *N* was the word by which most Americans of African descent wished to be called. The adjective "colored" was also widely used and was not considered offensive. During the sixties, however, militants began to use the word "black" in such phrases as "Black is Beautiful" and "Black Power," and the word "Negro" came to be considered derogatory. The term "Afro-American" also had some advocates. For example, the organization founded by Carter G. Woodson, the Association for the Study of Negro Life and History, changed its name to the Association for the Study of Afro-American Life and History. More recently the term "African American" (sometimes hyphenated) has gained wide popularity, although some persons continue to prefer "black."

The use of the word "Negro" in a collective sense was common in other historical works in the period when *The Negro in Indiana* was published. Two examples are Vernon L. Wharton's *The Negro in Mississippi, 1865–1890*, published in 1947, and Rayford Logan's *The Negro in American Life and Thought: The Nadir*, published in 1954. The use of the word "Negro" in this collective sense in the title and subtitle of my book suggests a sociological treatise rather than a historical work. However, any reader will recognize that I do not treat Negroes as a group of nameless people but rather as individuals. One of the most rewarding aspects of my research was the discovery of individuals who played a part in shaping black institutions and society. I consider the biographical sketches one of the most significant and interesting features of the book.

Since 1957, partly as the result of the civil rights movement, there has been an upsurge of interest in the history and culture of African Americans and an increased appreciation of the part they have played in our nation's history. This is reflected in the curricula of universities and public schools and in historical research and publication. Relatively little, however, has been published on African Americans in Indiana in the nineteenth century. The following include details not found in my book: Darrel E. Bigham, *We Ask Only a Fair Trial: A History of the Black Community of Evansville, Indiana* (Indiana University Press, 1987); Willard B. Gatewood, editor, *Slave and Freeman: The Autobiography of George L. Knox* (University Press of Kentucky, 1979); and Philip Foner, editor, *The Black State Conventions, 1840–1865* (Temple University Press, 1979). There have also been a few articles in the *Indiana Magazine of History* and in *Black History News and Notes* published by the Indiana Historical Society.

Interest in African American history has led libraries to search for and collect manuscripts and other source materials which were not available to me in the 1950s. The Indiana Historical Society Library has assembled and has continued to acquire an excellent collection. There are also manuscript collections in the Lilly Library at Indiana University, and smaller libraries and some county archives throughout the state have begun to recognize the value of such materials and to collect and preserve them. Some of these materials would have enriched details of my study, but I do not think that using them would have altered my book significantly. Nevertheless, these new materials should enable other scholars to add to popular understanding of African American history through articles and monographs on a variety of subjects.

EMMA LOU THORNBROUGH
March 1992

PREFACE TO THE FIRST EDITION

IN THIS VOLUME I have attempted to explore a field which has heretofore been little touched by historians—the story of the Negro minority in a Northern state, Indiana, and the relationship of that minority to the dominant white element in the period before 1900. (I use the word "Negro" in the sense in which it is commonly used in the United States, to designate a person with any discernible amount of Negro blood.) Although the proportion of this group relative to the white population was extremely small until the twentieth century, the question of the status of this minority was a perennial political issue and one which loomed large in popular thinking. Throughout the period covered, a large element of the white population manifested racial attitudes usually thought to be characteristic only of a certain class of Southern whites. That the colored population was inherently inferior was a doctrine which the majority accepted without question, and in line with this belief racial barriers, both legal and social, were tightly drawn. But all the while the Negroes themselves were demonstrating the fallacy of the popular belief by the progress they were making in spite of the obstacles thrown in their way. It is a record which I think speaks for itself, and I have tried to present it without sentimentality and with a minimum of interpretation.

During the territorial period, in spite of the well-known words of the Northwest Ordinance, nearly all of the Negro population was held in slavery or under a system of long-term indentures which differed little from outright slavery. By the time of the framing of the first state Constitution in 1816 opponents of the extension of the slave system were in the ascendancy, but although they were antislavery in this sense, the opposition of most of them stemmed more from a desire to preserve the soil of Indiana for white men than from any humanitarian interest in black men.

In the period from the admission of Indiana into the Union until the Civil War, Negroes were regarded as aliens whom the white population sought to prevent from settling in the state. In addition to efforts at exclusion there were also efforts to expatriate those already resident by colonizing them in Liberia. Those who came in spite of these obstacles were denied the right to vote and subjected to various legal disabilities, while their children were barred from the public schools. But hostile legislation notwithstanding, Indiana was a "free" state to which thousands of Negroes, both free and escaped slaves, migrated before 1850. Many of those who found relative security on free soil in turn risked their own freedom in helping fugitive slaves who came into the state via the Underground Railroad. A minority of the white population, especially the members of the Society of Friends, did not share the prejudices of the dominant group but assisted Negro immigrants in a variety of ways and sought, though without success, to secure the repeal of the laws against them. One result was that much of the colored population of the pre-Civil War period was found near Quaker communities. Most of the Negroes, like their white contemporaries, made a living from the soil, although some of them settled in the towns. In the face of prejudice and with no resources except the labor of their own hands, a substantial number became successful independent farmers. With some assistance from the Friends they established churches and schools, and sought to improve their condition. Although regarded as aliens, they showed an attachment to the land of their birth which caused them to resist efforts to expatriate them.

During the decade of the fifties, in consequence of the Fugitive Slave Act of 1850, which caused an exodus of some Negroes to Canada, and the adoption of the exclusion article in the second Indiana Constitution, the total number of

Negroes in the state increased but slightly. But Civil War and Emancipation changed this, with the result that from 1860 to 1900 the colored population showed more than a fivefold increase, largely from the migration of former slaves from the states of the upper South. Most of the newcomers moved to the towns and the cities, so that by the end of the century the Negro population had become predominantly urban.

The years immediately after the Civil War were marked by substantial legal and political gains. Although these were partly incidental to the conferral by the Federal government of rights upon the freedmen of the South, some of the white leaders in Indiana in this period showed a genuine desire to correct the injustice of the past so far as their own state was concerned. Nearly all racial distinctions were removed from the state Constitution and laws. Negroes were recognized as citizens under equal protection of the laws and were given the right to vote and to hold office. At the same time legislation was adopted which resulted in public schools for colored children, although on a segregated basis in most parts of the state.

In spite of the fact that the period from 1865 to 1900 was one of real progress in some areas, much of the optimism as to the future of the race which had prevailed immediately after the Civil War was dissipated after a few years. In spite of constitutional guarantees and the adoption of a civil rights law by the state legislature, discrimination continued with little abatement. It often seemed that a double standard of justice prevailed—one for the white population, another for the colored. An ugly tradition of mob violence persisted, while lynchings of Negroes became increasingly frequent toward the end of the century. Moreover the enthusiasm which had followed the adoption of the Fifteenth Amendment gradually turned into disillusionment and frustration as Negroes came to realize that white leaders generally regarded them merely as pawns in the game of politics. While there was real progress in education, particularly in the eradication of illiteracy, colored schools were likely to be inferior to those for white children, while poverty prevented many colored children from taking advantage of the opportunities open to them. A small group succeeded in attaining a formal education only to find that their training had opened no new occupational opportunities. In the economic realm prejudice against colored workers created insurmountable obstacles to entry into the skilled trades. The result was that, although a small middle class of business and professional men, who furnished race leadership, developed, the mass of colored workers lived in poverty, able to find only the most menial and unattractive kinds of employment. Socially an impassable gulf remained between the two races, with colored persons barred by custom, although not by law, from the places of entertainment frequented by white persons. This caused Negroes to create a society of their own, which was in many respects a replica of white society. Through their churches, fraternal organizations, and newspapers they sought to better the condition of members of their race while protesting against the discrimination and indignities heaped upon them.

At the same time among the white population there appeared to develop almost complete indifference to the Negro and his problems. Leaders tended to condone rather than to condemn racial injustice, while there were evidences that bigotry was on the increase among the rank and file. By 1900 patterns of race relationships had evolved which were to remain largely unbroken for almost half a century. The condition of Negroes in Indiana remained far more favorable than that of members of their race in the states of the South where white supremacy was rampant, but the hopes of equality and opportunity which had been bright in the years following Emancipation had fallen far short of realization.

The account which I have written of the gradual and uneven progress of the Negro minority toward equality is admittedly spotty and incomplete in some respects because materials necessary for a more complete treatment are not available. Sources showing what the white population thought about the Negro and his position are abundant, but those which reveal the thoughts and activities of Negroes themselves are meager. Much of my research consisted of sifting masses of materials which only occasionally yielded bits of evidence. The footnotes show the variety of sources which I used. In writing the book I have relied almost entirely upon primary materials since few aspects of the subject have been covered by earlier writers. In view of the limited educational opportunities and the low economic status of most members of the race during the period covered by the book it is not surprising that manuscript materials such as letters and diaries are almost nonexistent, at least in public collections. Undoubtedly some papers have been destroyed because they were regarded as worthless, while others still in private hands are unknown to me. I hope that the publication of my research may have the effect of bringing to light hitherto unused materials and inspiring more intensive research in aspects of Negro life and thought with which I was unable to deal adequately.

The major part of the research for this volume was done at the Indiana State Library, where the entire staff gave me assistance above and beyond the call of duty. I should like to acknowledge especially the help of Mrs. Hazel Hopper of the Indiana Division, Mr. Harold Burton of the Archives Division, and also Miss Caroline Dunn of the Indiana Historical Society Library. My manuscript has benefited by the meticulous attention given it by the editors of the Indiana Historical Bureau. My interest in the field of Negro history, especially the legal and constitutional aspects of the subject, was first aroused when I was a student in the graduate seminar of Dwight L. Dumond at the University of Michigan. I shall always be indebted to him for his kindly advice and criticism. I am also grateful to Butler University for a Faculty Fellowship which relieved me of part of my teaching duties for one year and enabled me to carry on part of the research embodied in this book.

THE NEGRO IN INDIANA
BEFORE 1900

1

INVOLUNTARY SERVITUDE

THE DATE AND CIRCUMSTANCES surrounding the arrival of the first Negroes into the region which became Indiana are shrouded in obscurity, but it can be stated with certainty that there were Negro residents within a few years after the arrival of the first white settlers. As early as 1746 a report on the French settlements in Louisiana mentioned a post on the Wabash River (Vincennes) where there dwelt a group of forty white men and five Negroes. This little group, as well as other Negroes brought later to Vincennes and to the larger settlements of Kaskaskia and Cahokia in the Illinois country to the west, were slaves of the French settlers. During the early history of Vincennes Negroes were outnumbered by Indian slaves, but their numbers, while never large, increased steadily until they replaced the aborigines. Most of the Negroes were probably acquired as the result of trade with posts on the Lower Mississippi.[1] It is also possible that a few slaves from the island of Jamaica were brought to the post on the Wabash after the western country passed to the

[1] Jacob P. Dunn, *The Mission to the Ouabache* (*Indiana Historical Society Publications*, Vol. 3, No. 4, Indianapolis, 1902), 327. Bills of sale and receipts in the Lasselle Collection in the Indiana State Library throw light on the purchase of slaves. Maj. Francis Bosseron of Vincennes, whose papers are in the collection, included the buying and selling of slaves among his far-flung business activities. For example, a bill of sale dated September 19, 1766, shows that he bought a Negro at Pointe Coupée on the Mississippi River, while a note dated April 3, 1771, shows that Bosseron owed a Madame Drouete the sum of 2,200 livres "for a negress whom she sold to me and delivered at the post Vincennes."

British in 1763. It is known that enterprising British mer-
chants brought at least one cargo of Negroes from the island
to the French settlements.[2]

Trade with the Indians was another source of supply of
Negroes. The red men, who were themselves sometimes
enslaved by the French, had early adopted the practice of
carrying off Negroes when they raided white settlements.
Since they were salable, Negroes were seldom massacred
but were taken to distant white settlements and bartered.
Some of the slaves in Vincennes and a few who were held
at the post farther north, which became Fort Wayne, were
bought from Indians. Slaveholders in these frontier settlements also had to be constantly on the alert against attempts
of Indians to carry off their property. Some Negroes were
kidnaped and taken to other settlements and sold; others
were held for ransom.[3] In a few instances Indians them-

---

[2] Clarence W. Alvord and Clarence E. Carter (eds.), *Trade and Politics, 1767-1769 (Illinois Historical Collections,* Vol. 16, Springfield, 1921),
128, 135, 161-62, 181, 228, 232-33, 331. James Rumsey of a Philadelphia
firm purchased a group of more than thirty Negroes in Jamaica. They
were brought from the Atlantic Coast to Pittsburgh and floated down
the Ohio River and up the Mississippi to Kaskaskia. There Rumsey had
difficulty in disposing of them and in 1768 set out for Vincennes in the
hope of selling some of them to the residents there in exchange for cattle
and peltry.

[3] In a massacre by the Natchez Indians in Louisiana in 1730 only
three white men were spared, but a rescue party found that 106 Negroes,
including men, women, and children, were unharmed. Reuben G. Thwaites
(ed.), *The Jesuit Relations and Allied Documents . . . 1610-1791* (73 vols.
Cleveland, 1896-1901), 68:167, 189. In a journal which he kept on a
trip from Detroit to Fort Wayne in 1790, John Hay mentioned several
instances in which Negroes were taken in raids on Kentucky by members
of the Shawnee and Miami tribes. Milo M. Quaife (ed.), *Fort Wayne
in 1790 (Indiana Historical Society Publications,* Vol. 7, No. 7, Indianapolis, 1921), 309, 343, 358. An item in the Lasselle Collection shows that
on October 11, 1777, Louis Chavrard (or Chamard?) of Vincennes agreed
to pay Francis Bosseron for the expense of sending Bosseron's clerk to
ransom Chavrard's Negro from the Indians. In 1782, after George Rogers
Clark had captured Vincennes, Col. J. M. P. Legras, writing to Clark,
told him how the Indians had carried off a Negro belonging to Col.
William Pope and were trying to ransom him in exchange for liquor.

selves owned Negroes, and such ownership was apparently regarded as a mark of distinction. On the other hand, runaway slaves sometimes took refuge with the Indians and were adopted by them and intermarried with them.[4]

There are almost no documents which describe the life of the Negroes in the French settlements, but their lot certainly was not so burdensome as that of plantation slaves. All accounts, whether friendly or hostile, agree that the French settlers were a carefree people who disliked hard work. The rich soil of the Wabash Valley produced corn and tobacco with little effort, but the settlers at Vincennes brought only a small amount of land under cultivation. They raised a few cattle and tapped the trees for sugar, but they relied principally upon the sale of peltries for a livelihood. In this society a few Negroes worked in the fields, but since agriculture was relatively unimportant, most of them were household slaves. The Black Code promulgated by the French government to regulate the condition of the slaves was less harsh than some codes. It provided that slaves who were manumitted should enjoy the same rights and privileges as free persons, emphasized religious instruction, and required that slaves be baptized and marriages be performed by the Church.[5]

James A. James (ed.), *George Rogers Clark Papers, 1781-1784* (*Illinois Historical Collections*, Vol. 19, Springfield, *c* 1926), 85.

[4] For example, at a later date, when Governor William Henry Harrison was negotiating a settlement with the Miami chieftain, Little Turtle, he wrote to the Secretary of War: "In pursuance of the President's directions, I have promised the Turtle fifty dollars, per annum, in addition to his pension; and I have, also, directed Captain Wells to purchase a negro man for him, in Kentucky." Logan Esarey (ed.), *Governors Messages and Letters. Messages and Letters of William Henry Harrison, Vol. I, 1800-1811* (*Indiana Historical Collections*, Vol. 7, Indianapolis, 1922), 164. In 1806 Moravian missionaries mentioned that an old Negro man and his sister had moved into their village on White River. The Negro had an Indian son-in-law. Lawrence H. Gipson (ed.), *The Moravian Indian Mission on White River* (*Indiana Historical Collections*, Vol. 23, Indianapolis, 1938), 422, 445-46.

[5] Alcée Fortier, *A History of Louisiana* (4 vols. Paris and New York, 1904), 1:90-94.

The portions of the code relating to religion were not a dead letter in the western posts. There were four Jesuit missions in the Illinois district, including one at Vincennes. The priests themselves were slaveholders and interested in promoting the Christianization of Negroes as well as Indians. An account of their work at Kaskaskia spoke not only of the religious instruction of the white children but also of "the instruction of the negroes and the savages, slaves of the French, to prepare them for baptism and for the reception of the other sacraments. . . . On Sundays and feast days two instructions in the catechism were given, one for the French children and the other for the black slaves and the savages." In spite of the fact that the number of slaves at Vincennes was smaller than at Kaskaskia the records of St. Xavier Parish, which extend back to 1749, attest to the activities of the Jesuits among the Negroes along the Wabash. Indeed the first Negro residents of Indiana who can positively be identified by name were Alexandre and Dorothée, "negro slaves belonging to the Jesuit fathers and lawfully married," whose child, Agatha, was baptized on May 30, 1753. The parish records contain numerous entries showing the baptisms, marriages, and burials of Negro slaves. For example, Susanne, the slave of M. Crepau, was baptized on July 12, 1760, and on the same day was married to Joseph, another slave of Crepau. The master was a witness to the ceremony and signed the record with his X. In September, 1761, the priest entered the record of the baptism of the daughter of Susanne and Joseph, who was also named Susanne.[6]

6 Thwaites (ed.), *Jesuit Relations,* 70:233, 235; St. Francis Xavier Parish Records, 1749-1838 (6 vols. Photostatic copies in Indiana State Library, from originals in Burton Historical Collection, Detroit Public Library), 1:10, 32, 34, 49. All the baptismal records show that the children were given Christian names. The name of the mother of the child was recorded and that of the father if the parents were married. White persons acted as godparents.

For a period of twenty-two years after the members of the Jesuit order were banished from the French colonies and their property confiscated for the benefit of the King, there was no regular priest to administer the sacraments to the residents of Vincennes or to give religious instruction to the children and slaves. After Father Gibault took up permanent residence in Vincennes in 1785 the parish records once more showed numerous entries of baptisms of Negroes.

The transfer of the French colonies to the British in 1763 made little difference in the way of life of the French and in no way affected the status of the Negro slaves, but a new chapter began when Vincennes was captured by George Rogers Clark in 1779. As the result of his conquest the territory north of the Ohio came temporarily under the jurisdiction of the State of Virginia, which passed legislation confirming the personal and property rights of the French inhabitants. In 1783 Virginia in turn gave up her claims to the region to the United States in an act of cession which declared that the residents of the French settlements who had professed themselves citizens of Virginia should "have their possessions and titles confirmed to them, and be protected in the enjoyment of their rights and liberties." In 1787 the Continental Congress adopted the Northwest Ordinance for the government of the territory. As every textbook in American history points out, the Ordinance in Article VI provided: "There shall be neither slavery nor involuntary servitude in the said territory, otherwise than in punishment of crimes, whereof the party shall have been duly convicted." But in spite of these words both slavery and involuntary servitude persisted for many years in Indiana.[7]

[7] Francis N. Thorpe (ed.), *The Federal and State Constitutions, Colonial Charters, and Other Organic Laws of the United States* (7 vols. Washington, D. C., 1909), 2:956, 962. After Clark's conquest some slaves were brought from Virginia to Vincennes. A bill of sale dated

At first the French settlers in the Illinois towns and Vincennes thought that the intent of the Ordinance was to deprive them of their slaves, and some of them moved to the Spanish territory west of the Mississippi in order to keep their slaves. Several memorials were sent to the Continental Congress by the French seeking assurances that they would not lose their rights to their Negroes. A report of the committee of the Congress to which the memorials were referred declared that the purpose of the Ordinance had not been to deprive the French "of their right and property in Negro or other Slaves which they were possessed of at the time of passing the said Ordinance."[8] Apparently the whole Congress took no action on the report of the committee, but in practice the Ordinance was interpreted as if the framers had not intended that it be retroactive in effect.

The first governor of the Northwest Territory was Arthur St. Clair, who had been president of the Congress which had passed the Ordinance. St. Clair repeatedly asserted that the clause in Article VI did not free slaves of persons who had been residents of the territory before 1787 but that it was intended merely to prevent the introduction of more slaves after 1787. One of the judges of the Northwest Territory, George Turner, put a different construction on the clause. Two Negroes, a man and wife, held as slaves by Henry Vanderburgh, who was judge of the probate court and justice of the peace for Knox County, applied to Turner for a writ of habeas corpus to secure their freedom. Turner

March 25, 1784, in the Lasselle Collection shows that Esther and her child Betsy were sold by John Minor of Culpeper County to Francis Bosseron of Vincennes. See also the case of Harry and others *v.* Decker and Hopkins, below, 24.

8 Clarence E. Carter (ed.), *The Territorial Papers of the United States* (Vols. 2- , Washington, D. C., 1934-   ), 2:247, 332; Clarence W. Alvord (ed.), *Kaskaskia Records 1778-1790* (*Illinois Historical Collections*, Vol. 5, Springfield, 1909), 488, 493, 503, 509; *Journals of the Continental Congress, 1774-1789*, edited by Worthington C. Ford, *et al.* (34 vols. Washington, D. C., 1904-1937), 34:541.

was of the opinion that the Negroes were "free by the Constitution of the Territory," i.e., the Northwest Ordinance, but Vanderburgh thwarted the move to liberate them by having the couple carried off forcibly. Turner regarded this as a "violent outrage against the laws," and announced to the Governor his intention of impeaching Judge Vanderburgh before the territorial legislature, but he received no support from St. Clair. The Governor repeated that the prohibition against slavery applied only to slaves brought into the Territory after 1787. Turner subsequently resigned from the court and left the Territory.[9]

To the reader today St. Clair's interpretation of the Ordinance appears to be a distortion of the obvious meaning, but at the time no one successfully challenged it. There is no record of any decision by a court in Indiana Territory that the Ordinance affected pre-existing rights. On the other hand, there are records of numerous cases in which the judges clearly assumed the legality of slavery. The members of the legislature recognized the existence of slavery in numerous acts which they passed. Negroes who were in the Territory before 1787 and their children continued to be held as slaves until after Indiana became a state. Although the Ordinance was interpreted as prohibiting the bringing of slaves into the Territory, this was made virtually meaningless by laws permitting long-term indentures.

Following the organization of Indiana Territory in 1800 the population increased rapidly. Many of the new settlers came from the slave states of the South. Some of them came North to get away from the system of slavery, but others wished to be able to bring their slaves with them. In the early years proslavery men were in the ascendancy in territorial politics. They were powerful in Knox County, where Vincennes was located, and in the Illinois counties to the

9 William H. Smith (ed.), *The St. Clair Papers. The Life and Public Services of Arthur St. Clair* ... (2 vols. Cincinnati, 1882), 2:245, 318-19, 325, 332; Carter (ed.), *Territorial Papers*, 2:248.

west. Until the division of the Territory they controlled the legislature. William Henry Harrison, first governor of Indiana Territory, was closely identified with this group. However, in the newer settlements in the eastern part of Indiana antislavery men were in the majority.

The first efforts of the proslavery group were directed at trying to persuade Congress to amend the Ordinance of 1787 so as to permit slaves to be brought into the Territory for a limited number of years. A number of petitions to this effect were sent to Congress, but these efforts failed completely since Congress did not act favorably upon them.[10] However, the advocates of slavery, thwarted in these attempts, achieved their ends through a system of indentured servitude that differed little from slavery. At first this was apparently done without the sanction of any particular law.

In 1803 the Governor and Judges of Indiana Territory adopted an act from the Virginia Code which compelled Negroes and mulattoes who were brought into the Territory "under contract to serve another in any trade or occupation to perform such contract specifically during the term thereof."[11]

In 1805, after the attainment of the second stage of territorial government permitted the people to elect a legislature, that body enacted a more sweeping measure entitled "An Act concerning the Introduction of Negroes and Mulattoes into This Territory." Under this act any person owning or purchasing slaves outside the Territory might bring them

[10] The efforts to legalize slavery are discussed in detail by Jacob P. Dunn in *Indiana, A Redemption from Slavery (American Commonwealths Series,* revised ed., Boston, 1905), and most of the papers connected therewith are reproduced in Jacob P. Dunn (ed.), *Slavery Petitions and Papers (Indiana Historical Society Publications,* Vol. 2, No. 12, Indianapolis, 1894).

[11] Francis S. Philbrick (ed.), *The Laws of Indiana Territory, 1801-1809 (Illinois Historical Collections,* Vol. 21, Springfield, 1930. Reprinted with supplementary material by Indiana Historical Bureau, 1931), 42-43. The Ordinance of 1787 and the act creating Indiana Territory provided that during the earliest stage of territorial government the Governor and Judges should adopt laws from the codes of the original thirteen states.

into Indiana and bind them to service. If the slaves were over fifteen years of age, "the owner or possessor" could make a contract for service with them for any term of years. The indenture was to be recorded with the county clerk within thirty days after the arrival of the slave into the Territory, but if the slave refused the terms offered him, the master could have him taken out of the Territory within sixty days without losing his title. This meant, of course, that the master could hold a slave for sixty days in the Territory and then send him out of the Territory and sell him if he proved recalcitrant. Slaves who were under fifteen years of age were to be registered and required to serve until the age of thirty-five if they were males, thirty-two if females. Children born to the slaves after they were brought into the Territory were to serve the master of the parent until they reached the age of thirty for males, or twenty-eight for females.[12]

This act was clearly a brazen attempt to evade the prohibition against involuntary servitude in the Northwest Ordinance. As its opponents pointed out, it was absurd to speak of the agreement between the master and slave as a "contract," since slavery by its very nature made a person incapable of contracting. Negroes brought into Indiana under the terms of the law had a choice of binding themselves for a term of years fixed by the master (which might extend beyond their life expectancy), or of being sent out of Indiana to be sold for life. A report of a committee of the territorial legislature which asked repeal of the law in 1808 declared that it was "contrary both to the spirit and letter of the Ordinance," and added that, "the most flagitious abuse is made of that law; that negroes brought here are commonly forced to bind themselves for a number of years reaching or extending the natural term of their lives, so that the condition of those unfortunate persons is not only involuntary servitude but downright slavery."[13]

[12] *Ibid.,* 136-39.
[13] Dunn (ed.), *Slavery Petitions and Papers,* 523.

Under the act, which remained in effect until 1810, some masters coming into Indiana to settle brought slaves with them while other persons already resident in the Territory bought slaves and indentured them. Books kept by county clerks in which indentures were recorded in Knox and Clark counties survive. The Clark County volume covers the period from 1805 to 1810, but the Knox County record covers only the years 1805 through 1808. These books throw some light on the place of origin of the early Negro population of Indiana as well as upon the operation of the indenture law. Thirty-two indentures, involving a total of thirty-six persons, were recorded in Clark County; forty-six indentures for fifty persons in Knox County. They show that by far the largest number of Negroes, sixty in all, were brought from Kentucky. There were eleven from South Carolina, five from Tennessee, three from Virginia, and one each from North Carolina, Georgia, and Maryland. Most of the slaves were young—less than twenty-five years old. Only two over fifty years of age were recorded. Seventeen children of less than fifteen years were registered. In some cases they were children of slaves who were registered at the same time, but several children were registered in Clark County without their parents. The following entry, made in Knox County before the Clerk of Common Pleas in 1805, is typical:

"Be it remembered that . . . personally came Eli Hawkins of the said county and a negro lad of the age of sixteen years being a slave named Jacob belonging to the said Eli Hawkins and by him brought into this Territory from the state of South Carolina, which said Hawkins and the said Jacob . . . agreed among themselves . . . that said Jacob shall and will serve the said Eli Hawkins and his assigns for term of Ninety years from the day of the date hereof, he, the said Eli Hawkins and his assigns providing the said Jacob with necessary and sufficient provisions and clothing, washing and lodging, according to his degree and station.

From and after the expiration of said term the said Jacob shall be free to all intents and purposes."[14]

The foregoing indenture, calling for a term of ninety years, would mean that the slave would be one hundred and six years old when he became "free to all intents and purposes." Two indentures for ninety-nine years were recorded in Knox County and two for ninety years. Others for seventy, sixty, and fifty years were also found. The most common terms were for forty or twenty years. The shortest term recorded was ten years. Those who were bound to serve for forty or more years would, of course, have either died or reached old age before attaining their freedom.

Many of the wealthy and prominent men in the Territory held Negroes under the indenture law, among them Governor William Henry Harrison. A letter to Dr. Frederick Ridgely in Kentucky, which is among the Harrison papers in the Indiana Historical Society Library, shows the Governor in a dilemma over the status of a Negro girl whom he had acquired. He wrote: "I am totally at a loss what to do with Molly. Because I am yet uninformed whether she has been emancipated in Ky. & bound for 15 years or whether you have made a contract with her former master to have her set free in 15 years—If she has not been indentured it must be done in 30 days after her arrival in the vicinity or loose her service altogether—& if she refuses to indent herself I must remand her in 60 days or likewise loose her service. But in case of Refusal where am I to remand her? No person in Kenty. will buy an Indented Servant. Indeed I would send her back & sell her at any rate but for your contract to free her at the end of 15 years for reasons not sent at all—Do my Dr Sir inform me as soon as possible

[14] Knox County, Register of Negro Slaves, 1805-7 (microfilm, Indiana State Library) ; Clark County, Register of Negroes, 1805-10 (MS in Indiana State Library). The indenture quoted above and some of the other Knox County indentures are reproduced in Daniel Owen, "Circumvention of Article VI of the Ordinance of 1787," in *Indiana Magazine of History*, 36(1940) :110-16.

what is the nature of the bargain you made that I may know how to govern myself."[15]

Although a majority of the people in the Vincennes area probably continued to favor the system of indentures, opposition increased with the growth of population in eastern Indiana. Criticism was leveled at Governor Harrison and other territorial officers for their support of involuntary servitude.

Harrison's successor, Thomas Posey, appointed in 1813, was a former Virginian and a slaveholder. In a letter which he wrote at the time of his appointment he sought to allay opposition from the antislavery group in the Territory by asserting: "I am as much opposed to slavery as any man whatsoever; I have disposed of what few I had sometime since to my children and by emancipation. I am sure I shall never sanction a law for slavery . . ." However, in his will, which was made in 1816 and entered for probate in 1818, he left two slaves to each of his three children, and two of his indentured Negroes were sold in Vincennes after his death.[16]

Meanwhile, there had been a lively contest in the territorial legislature over the repeal of the indenture law. In the 1808 session General Washington Johnston of Vincennes, chairman of a committee to which had been referred several petitions on the subject of slavery, submitted a

[15] May 24, 1807, William Henry Harrison Papers, Miscellaneous Collection, in Indiana Historical Society Library. In the same collection there is a letter from Harrison to Col. James Henry of Somerset County, New Jersey, May 10, 1806, in which Harrison asked that Henry "make every exertion" to sell his, Harrison's, property in New Jersey and remarked: "I would freely take one or two negroes either male or female & get the favor of you to keep them til an oppurtunity of sending them occured—it would make no difference whether they are slaves for life or only serve a term of years."

[16] Letter of Posey to John Gibson, secretary of Indiana Territory, March 3, 1813, in William H. English Collection, Indiana Historical Society Library. Posey's will is printed in "Some Vincennes Documents," in *Indiana Magazine of History*, 4(1909) :9. The bill of sale for the two Negroes, dated April 4, 1818, is in the Lasselle Collection.

vigorous report denouncing the indenture law and the attempts to foist slavery upon the Territory as a "retrograde step into barbarism." The House of Representatives responded to the report by passing a bill to repeal the indenture law but the Legislative Council refused to concur. By the time of the meeting of the next session of the legislature the proslavery forces in Indiana had been reduced by the division of Indiana and Illinois territories. In 1810 the law authorizing the bringing in of slaves and holding them under indentures was repealed.[17]

Repeal did not, however, affect in any way indentures made before repeal. Neither did it bring to an end completely the practice of bringing Negroes into the Territory and binding them to long terms of service. After repeal persons who brought Negroes into the Territory sometimes went through the form of "emancipating" them, after which the "free" Negroes signed contracts for long terms of service. It is impossible to determine how widespread this practice was, but several instances of it have been found. For example, on July 4, 1814, in Gibson County, Indiana, Robert M. Evans emancipated John Born, who had formerly been a slave in Virginia. On July 5 an instrument was recorded under which Negro John became the indentured servant of Evans for a term of thirty years. The following December Evans sold John to Nathaniel Evans for $550.00. In 1814 Benjamin I. Harrison purchased a Negro woman slave in Kentucky. In January, 1815, he brought her to Vincennes where she was indentured to him for a term of thirty years. In November, 1815, Pickard, a man of color who had been emancipated by Toussaint Dubois, entered into an indenture with Dubois under which he agreed to serve him for twenty years. Dubois had purchased Pickard for the sum of five

17 Gayle Thornbrough and Dorothy Riker (eds.), *Journals of the General Assembly of Indiana Territory, 1805-1815 (Indiana Historical Collections,* Vol. 32, Indianapolis, 1950), 232-38, 257, 289, 301; Louis B. Ewbank and Dorothy Riker (eds.), *The Laws of Indiana Territory, 1809-1816 (Indiana Historical Collections,* Vol. 20, Indianapolis, 1934), 138-39.

hundred dollars and agreed in the indenture to pay the
Negro the sum of twenty dollars.[18]

Although there were really two classes of Negroes held
in bondage—slaves who had been in the Territory before
1787 and their descendants and persons held under indentures—in practice there was little difference in the condition
of the two. Throughout the territorial period Negroes in
both categories were bought and sold. Numerous examples
of such sales have been found but a few examples will suffice. A record of the sale of goods and chattels in connection
with the settlement of the estate of Mrs. Margaret Gamelin
of Vincennes in 1804 lists the sale of "an old Negroe
wench about 90 years of Age" for one dollar (the purchase
presumably being an act of charity) and of "a young mu-
lattoe Boy 14 years of age . . . born of a Negro woman
Slave" for $150.00. These were slaves of a French inhab-
itant, but not all of those sold belonged to French owners.
Knox County records show that in 1808 Robert Evans
purchased five slaves from A. H. H. Buck, presumably with
the intention of indenturing them. In 1813 it was recorded
in Gibson County that John Goodwin of that county sold
to Benjamin Seales for the sum of $371.00 "a certain Negro
woman Dinah, aged about seventeen years."[19]

In some instances it is impossible to determine whether
the Negro sold was a slave or an indentured servant.
Strictly speaking the term of service rather than the person
of the indentured servant was sold, but the documents do
not always make this distinction. The act of 1803 concerning
servants and the revised laws of 1807 expressly provided
for the transfer of the term of service. An act of 1806
provided that the time of service of servants might be sold

18 James T. Tartt & Co., *History of Gibson County, Indiana* (Edwards-
ville, Ill., 1884), 78; "Two Indentures of Negroes," in *Indiana Magazine
of History,* 7 (1911) :134-35; see below, 28.

19 Bill of sale, July 4, 1804, in Lasselle Collection; Knox County,
Minutes of Court of Common Pleas, 1807-10 (microfilm, Indiana State
Library), 137; Tartt, *Gibson County,* 77.

on execution in the same manner as personal estate. Such sales continued after the repeal of the indenture law. For example, a document in the library of the Indiana Historical Society shows that a Negro named Sam was transferred by sale to Toussaint Dubois in 1813 and from Dubois to Jacob Kuykendall in 1816. In another case the child of a Negro woman who had been indentured under the act of 1805 was sold three times. The first sale was to a resident of Indiana who in turn sold the girl to a resident of Kentucky. In Kentucky she was sold again as a slave for life. But the highest court of Kentucky set her free, asserting that she had ceased to be a slave when she was first brought to Indiana and that once free she could not be reduced to slavery again. However, the court did not rule on the legality of holding her under the indenture law.[20]

Negroes, both slaves and servants, were frequently mentioned as a part of the estate in wills found in Knox County and Clark County. The laws of the territory provided that at the death of a master the remainder of the term of service provided in an indenture should go to the heirs. The wills usually do not indicate whether the Negro in question was a slave or servant. However, the will of Henry Vanderburgh mentions two slaves and two indentured servants who were bequeathed to his wife. Some wills provided that one or more Negroes should be sold at the death of the master. The will of Toussaint Dubois expressed the hope that none of his Negroes should ever be sold out of the family unless they were guilty of misconduct. His will also promised that two of his Negroes should be given their freedom when his youngest child reached the age of twenty-one. Other wills promised Negroes their freedom within a term of years.[21]

20 Philbrick (ed.), *Laws of Indiana Territory, 1801-1809*, 42, 189, 463, 541; bills of sale, June 30, 1813, November 18, 1816 (after the adoption of the state Constitution), in William Prince Papers, Indiana Historical Society Library; Rankin v. Lydia, 2 Marshall (Ky.), 472 (1820).

21 Wills of Henry Vanderburgh, John McClure, Jacob Warrick, Toussaint Dubois, Jonathan Logan, William Embry, Hugh McGary, Peter

From the foregoing it is evident that for some purposes slaves and indentured servants had the status of property—to be bought and sold and bequeathed by will. The property status is further illustrated by suits in the territorial courts over claims to Negroes. For example, one suit arose over conflicting claims to three Negroes who were part of an estate, while another suit was brought to compel the payment of the balance of the purchase price of a mulatto girl. In a third case, which dragged on for years, Ma-son-ce-gah, the "Owl," a Miami chieftain who had settled near Vincennes and adopted the white man's way of life, sought to recover a mulatto girl to whom he claimed title.[22]

Special police regulations for slaves and servants were adopted in imitation of the codes of the states of the South. The indenture law of 1803 provided that lazy or disorderly servants might be punished by a whipping by a justice of the peace. It also provided that in the case of penal offenses in which free persons were subject to fines servants were to be punished by whipping. Under an act of 1806 servants or slaves who were found ten miles or more from the home of their master were subject to a public whipping. Similar penalties were provided for participation in "riots, routs, unlawful assemblies, trespasses, and seditious speeches." An act of 1807 prohibited the sale of liquor to slaves or servants, and in 1808 it was made unlawful for anyone to permit three or more slaves or servants to congregate on their property "for the purpose of dancing or revelling, either by night, or by day."[23]

Hambrough, in Knox County, Will Record A, 1806-1852 (microfilm, Indiana State Library), 3, 20, 46, 61, 64, 70, 71, 75; wills of William Smith and Joseph Bowman in Clark County, Will Record A, 1801-17 (microfilm, Indiana State Library), 9, 134. See also Earl E. McDonald, "Disposal of Negro Slaves by Will in Knox County, Indiana," in *Indiana Magazine of History*, 26(1930):143-46.

[22] Knox County, Minutes of Court of Common Pleas, 1796-99, pp. 66-68; 1807-10, p. 65; Knox County, Minutes of Circuit Court, 1816-18, pp. 41, 70, 72, 89, 93. All on microfilm in Indiana State Library.

[23] Philbrick (ed.), *Laws of Indiana Territory, 1801-1809*, 42-43, 203-4, 287, 657-58.

The act of 1803 and the revised laws of 1807 required masters to supply wholesome and sufficient food, clothing, and lodging to their servants and permitted the latter to retain any property or money which they might lawfully acquire. Servants were also given the right to appeal to the courts against their masters in cases of "undeserved or immoderate correction, insufficient allowance of food, raiment or lodging." However, only one instance has been found in which a servant appears to have succeeded in getting a court order to restrain a master.[24]

In spite of the fact that the territorial courts recognized the legality of the system of slavery and indentured servitude, they also entertained suits of Negroes who claimed that they were held unlawfully. Several unsuccessful freedom suits were brought in the General Court of the Territory, but in some of the other courts Negroes won their freedom. In 1811 a Negro who was held under an indenture brought suit in the Knox County Court of Common Pleas, claiming that his master had not discharged him from service when his indenture expired. The court found that he had served his time and declared him a free man. In Harrison County a woman who had been brought from Kentucky charged her master with assault and battery and false imprisonment. Although the master tried to prove that she had voluntarily agreed to serve him until she was fifty-two years old and produced an indenture, there was no evidence that this document had been recorded, and the jury gave a verdict in favor of the woman and awarded her damages of $14.00. In Clark County a Negro girl whose mother had been indentured in 1800 (before the adoption

[24] *Ibid.*, 42-44, 63-64, 139. In 1807 the Court of Common Pleas of Knox County heard a complaint on behalf of a mulatto girl and ordered that her master post bond as security that he would not "abuse or unreasonably chastise his said servant" during the time that she remained in his service. Knox County, Minutes of Court of Common Pleas, 1807-10, p. 64.

of the law legalizing indentures) was declared free by a court.[25]

In two cases in Jefferson County Negroes who had been slaves but who had gained their freedom successfully resisted efforts to re-enslave them. In the first case three young men, who had been promised their freedom in their master's will when they reached the age of twenty-one, had migrated to Indiana from Kentucky. The heirs of their deceased master tried to claim that they were still slaves, but the Jefferson County court ruled that the Negroes were free and issued an injunction restraining the heirs who had claimed them from disturbing them. The second case, which was much more complicated, involved a Negro named Benjamin who had been the slave of a Peter Wooley in Kentucky, but who had been taken to Illinois by Wooley's son and bound under an indenture to serve thirty years. While in Illinois he was permitted to buy his freedom, after which he came to Jefferson County, Indiana, just across the Ohio River from his old home in Kentucky. There the elder Wooley discovered him and tried to carry him off, claiming that he was still his slave—that the indenture signed in Illinois was invalid since Benjamin had not given his consent. Therefore he was still a slave, and a fugitive from Kentucky! After several attempts had been made to carry him off by force, Benjamin invoked the protection of the court against his former master. The judge ruled that the Negro was free and issued an injunction to prevent Wooley from interfering with him in the future.[26]

[25] Order Book of the General Court of Indiana Territory, 1801-10, pp. 90, 325, 328-29, in Archives Division, Indiana State Library; Knox County, Order Book of the Court of Common Pleas and Circuit Court, 1811-17 (microfilm, Indiana State Library), 22; Harrison County, Record of Circuit Court, 1814-17 (microfilm, Indiana State Library), 83-86; Clark County, Order Book of Court of Common Pleas, 1810-17 (microfilm, Indiana State Library), 245, 257, 328-30.

[26] Jefferson County, Minutes of Court of Common Pleas and Circuit Court, 1812-18 (microfilm, Indiana State Library), 214-17, 334-40; Jef-

In another case in Gibson County a group of Negroes who had come from Kentucky were less successful in claiming their freedom. Even the legal language of the court record cannot completely conceal the pathos of their story. Their former master, Alexander Carson, followed them to Indiana and swore that all of them—Harry, Amy, Joe, Bill, Lucy, Sam, Ben, and "little Amy"—were his slaves. Proceedings began in the Gibson County court in 1815 which were to drag on for five years. At three different trials different juries at first decided that Harry was free but that the rest of the group were still slaves, then that all the group were free, and finally that Bill, Ben, and "little Amy" were Carson's property. In the meantime, Amy and Joe had died before the jury could dispose of them, while Carson had sold Lucy and her child, Sam, to an Indiana resident. Before the three who were awarded to Carson could be carried out of the state an unknown donor paid $350.00 to buy the freedom of "little Amy," so that only Bill and Ben were taken back to Kentucky.[27]

There were other Negroes in the Territory who were neither slaves nor indentured servants but were entirely free.[28] Their numbers increased as the result of manumissions and the expiration of indentures. Persons who were born free or who were emancipated in other states or terri-

ferson County, Proceedings of Court of Common Pleas and Circuit Court, 1811-19 (microfilm, Indiana State Library), 251-58.

[27] Gibson County, Order Book of the Court of Common Pleas and Circuit Court, Vol. A, 1813-18 (microfilm, Indiana State Library), 97, 117, 160-61, 226, 263, 268; Gibson County, Complete Record of Common Pleas and Circuit Court, 1813-20 (microfilm, Indiana State Library), 52-54, 263-68, 270-71.

[28] Although there were probably some free Negroes in the French period, the earliest record that the author has found is a court order in 1803 that a guardian should be appointed for "the person and estate of Abraham a free Negro boy of age thirteen years." Knox County, Minutes of Orphans Court, 1796-1805 (microfilm, Indiana State Library), 50. In 1804 the parish records show the baptism of Pierre, the son of Marie, a free Negress. St. Francis Xavier Parish Records, 4:470.

tories also migrated to Indiana. In some instances masters from slave states appear to have brought groups of slaves into Indiana for the purpose of freeing them. These may have been attempts to evade the laws in force in some slave states requiring that a master who emancipated his slaves post bond that they would not become public charges. Other cases were due to the fact that the laws of some states required that emancipated slaves leave the state. A memorial to Governor Posey from a group of residents of Harrison County shows that a Kentucky master had brought forty-seven slaves into that county and freed them. The memorial also asserted that there were rumors that sixty or seventy more Negroes would be brought from Kentucky in the near future.[29] Fugitive slaves who crossed the Ohio River into Indiana in an attempt to gain their freedom also added to the free Negro population.

The migration of free Negroes into the Territory was regarded with disfavor by most of the whites. Many of the early settlers who were antislavery in their views were also anti-Negro. There were repeated attempts to secure measures excluding free Negroes from the Territory. A petition sent to Congress in 1813 on the subject of land said: "Your Petitioners also humbly pray that if your honourable boddy think propper to allow a donation of lands to actuel Setlers People of Colour and Slaveholders may be debared from the Priveladges of Setling on the Lands so apropiated."[30] The memorial from Harrison County mentioned above stated: "We are opposed to the introduction of slaves or free Negroes in any shape. . . . Our corn Houses, Kitchens, Smoke Houses . . . may no doubt be robbed and our wives, children and daughters may and no doubt will be insulted and abused by those Africans. We feel for our property, wives and daughters. We do not wish to be saddled with them in any way."

[29] The memorial, undated, is in the William H. English Collection in the Indiana Historical Society Library.

[30] Carter (ed.), *Territorial Papers*, 8:235. Spelling as in original.

None of the efforts at securing legislation barring free Negroes from the Territory was successful. In 1813 a bill to prohibit the immigration of Negroes, mulattoes, and slaves was passed by the legislature but was vetoed by the Governor. At the next session a petition from Gibson County asking for the exclusion of free people of color was reported upon unfavorably by the committee to which it was referred. The committee expressed the opinion that an exclusion law would be "contrary to the Laws of humanity, inasmuch as it would prevent the free sons of Africa from becoming citizens of our Territory and would also be contrary to the constitution of this our Territory." Nevertheless, the House of Representatives passed an exclusion measure which was rejected by the Legislative Council. At the next session the House appointed a committee to prepare a bill "to prevent persons owning slaves in any of the United States from bringing them into this Territory & liberating them in order to evade the Laws of their respective States." A bill passed the House, but the Legislative Council rejected it. In 1815 both houses passed separate measures on the subject of Negroes and slavery but were unable to agree on amendments, so that neither measure became a law.[31] In spite of the fact that the territorial legislature failed to pass a measure excluding Negroes, there remained strong sentiment in favor of such action. The question was to be pressed in later years, and drastic legislation was ultimately enacted.

Although immigration was not restricted, territorial laws contained various discriminatory features against free Negroes. The right of suffrage was limited to free white males, and only white men were subject to militia duty. In place of such service free colored men between the ages of twenty and fifty-five were subject to a special poll tax of

31 Thornbrough and Riker (eds.), *Journals of the General Assembly of Indiana Territory*, 544, 550, 592, 601, 606, 634, 711, 765, 809, 811, 886, 890-91.

three dollars a year. In 1803 a law was adopted which prohibited Negroes, mulattoes, and Indians from giving evidence in any case except indictments against Negroes, mulattoes, or Indians or in civil actions in which members of these races alone were parties. The act defined a mulatto as any person having one fourth or more Negro blood.[32] These disabilities imposed during the territorial period were continued after Indiana became a state and remained in effect until after the Civil War.

Throughout the territorial period Negroes constituted only a tiny fraction of the entire population. No accurate figures are available before the census of 1810, the first taken after the division of Indiana and Illinois. At that time there were only 630 Negroes and 23,890 white persons in Indiana. Of the Negroes 237 were listed as slaves and 393 as free, although many of the latter group were undoubtedly held under indentures. Most of the Negro population was concentrated in and around Vincennes in Knox County, but smaller numbers were found in all of the counties.[33]

As increasing population brought statehood closer there remained some proslavery feeling among the settlers. The slavery issue played a part, although not a significant one, in the contest over the election of delegates to the convention which drew up the state constitution. The formal petition adopted by the territorial legislature in December, 1815,

---

[32] Philbrick (ed.), *Laws of Indiana Territory, 1801-1809*, 40, 400; Ewbank and Riker (eds.), *Laws of Indiana Territory, 1809-1816*, 226, 485, 489.

[33] The distribution of Negroes by counties was as follows:

County	Slaves	Free Negroes
Dearborn	—	92
Clark	81	40
Harrison	21	12
Knox	135	249
	237	393

U. S. Bureau of the Census, *Aggregate Amount . . . of Persons within the United States . . . in the Year 1810* (Washington, D. C., 1811), 86.

asking Congress for statehood, expressed devotion to the principles of the Ordinance of 1787, "particularly as respects personal freedom and involuntary servitude." In spite of this assurance, letters in the Vincennes newspaper warned voters against the election of delegates who would favor slavery or the introduction of colored servants.[34]

The constitutional convention which met on June 10, 1816, completed its labors on June 29, and the finished Constitution went into effect at once without being submitted to the voters for ratification. The first mention of slavery in the convention came during debate on an article on amending the Constitution. As adopted the article provided that there should be an opportunity to revise the Constitution every twelve years, with the limitation: "But as the holding of any part of the human creation in slavery or involuntary servitude can only originate in usurpation and tyranny, no alteration of this Constitution shall ever take place so as to introduce slavery or involuntary servitude in this State otherwise than for the punishment of crimes whereof the party shall have been duly convicted." A motion was offered to strike out the words "or involuntary servitude," but it was rejected.

The Bill of Rights in the finished document declared: "There shall be neither slavery nor involuntary servitude in this State, otherwise than for the punishment of crimes, whereof the party shall have been duly convicted, nor shall any indenture of any negro or mulatto hereafter made and executed out of the bounds of this State be of any validity within the State."[35]

This clause spelled the final extinction of slavery and involuntary servitude in the state, although its effect was not immediate. Some masters, in anticipation of the effect

[34] Charles Kettleborough, *Constitution Making in Indiana* . . . (3 vols. *Indiana Historical Collections*, Vols. 1-2, 17, Indianapolis, 1916, 1930), 1:72; Vincennes *Western Sun*, February 3, March 2, March 30, 1816.

[35] Thorpe (ed.), *Constitutions*, 2:1068, 1070; *Journal of the* [Constitutional] *Convention of the Indiana Territory* . . . (Louisville, 1816), 38.

which the work of the constitutional convention might have on their slave property, hastened to sell their Negroes outside of Indiana. For example, an instrument recorded in Gibson County on March 18, 1816, shows that a Negro man named Mathew made an agreement with his master, James Lyon, whereby he "consented" to be removed from Gibson County to any other state or territory as a slave for life. In May, 1816, Jean Laplante of Vincennes sold to François Lasselle of Detroit, Michigan, for the sum of six hundred dollars a Negro boy, the offspring of a woman slave.[36]

In July, 1816, after the new Constitution was proclaimed to be in effect, three Negroes held as slaves by the Decker family in Vincennes were taken to Mississippi. There they instituted a suit for their freedom on the grounds that they were free by the Ordinance of 1787 and the Indiana Constitution. In the evidence presented to the court it, was shown that they had originally been held as slaves in Virginia but had been taken to the vicinity of Vincennes by John Decker in 1784 and held there until July, 1816. The Mississippi court decided in 1818 that they were free. It held that Decker was not entitled to any of the special benefits enjoyed by the French settlers before 1787 and that the Ordinance of 1787 had probably extinguished his title to the slaves. And regardless of the effect of the Ordinance it held that slavery had been completely extinguished by the adoption of the Indiana Constitution in June, 1816.[37]

Two years after the Mississippi decision the Indiana Supreme Court handed down a similar decision regarding the effect of the Indiana Constitution, but until 1820 the new Constitution does not appear to have brought any change in the status of most of the persons held as slaves

36 Tartt, *Gibson County,* 78; bill of sale in Lasselle Collection, May 7, 1816.

37 Harry and others *v.* Decker and Hopkins, 1 Walker (Miss.) 36-43 (1818).

before its adoption. Although a few masters tried to dispose of their slaves outside the state, others believed that the Constitution was not retroactive and did not interfere with pre-existing rights in slaves and servants. In view of the fact that the Ordinance of 1787, which employed almost exactly the same words as the Constitution, had been so interpreted this view is not surprising. The United States census of 1820 listed 190 slaves in Indiana, 118 of them in Knox County, 30 in Gibson County.[38]

After the adoption of the Constitution a number of freedom suits were instituted in the Knox County court. At the terms of the circuit court which began in October, 1817, and April, 1818, at least seven suits, involving the freedom of fifteen persons, were begun. From the record it is not always clear whether the persons were slaves or indentured servants. In spite of the Constitution, in all of the cases except one the Knox County court ruled in favor of the master.[39]

Early in 1820 another suit was begun which was to lead to a decision by the Supreme Court. Most of the credit for prosecuting this case, which finally extinguished slavery in the state, goes to a young Vermont-born lawyer, Amory Kinney. After studying law in New York state Kinney had opened a law office in Vincennes in 1819. Like some other immigrants from the East he was shocked to find that persons were still held in slavery in Indiana in spite of the Northwest Ordinance and the Constitution of the state. Through his efforts a test case was instituted in behalf of a Negro girl named Polly, who was held as a slave by Hyacinthe Lasselle, member of one of the leading families in Vincennes and a descendant of one of the early French

---

[38] U. S. Bureau of the Census, *Census for 1820* . . . (Washington, D. C., 1821), 190.

[39] Knox County, Minutes of Circuit Court, 1816-18 (microfilm, Indiana State Library), 170, 178, 181, 217; Knox County, Order Book of the Circuit Court, 1817-20 (microfilm, Indiana State Library), 104, 159, 179, 217, 269, 371, 396.

settlers. A writ of habeas corpus was sued out in the Knox County court by Polly. To this Lasselle replied that Polly was the daughter of a colored woman who had been purchased as a slave from the Indians prior to the Ordinance of 1787. Lasselle's counsel argued that since the woman had been enslaved before 1787 the Ordinance had not affected her master's claim and that her child followed the condition of the mother. The Knox County court ruled in favor of Lasselle, holding that the Ordinance could not affect rights which existed before its passage. It made no mention of the Constitution of 1816 but ordered the girl restored to her master.[40]

The Supreme Court reversed this decision in June, 1820. It rejected the argument that the French settlers enjoyed vested rights which could not be destroyed by the state Constitution. It held that it was not necessary to go into the question of the effect of the Ordinance of 1787 on the rights of the French but rested its opinion on the Constitution, asserting that the convention chosen to write a state constitution had been given the right to prohibit slavery if it chose and that it had exercised that right. Indeed, the court declared, "We can conceive of no form of words in which that intention could have been more clearly expressed." It concluded that "under our present form of government, slavery can have no existence in the State of Indiana."[41]

[40] Knox County, Order Book of the Circuit Court, 1817-20 (microfilm, Indiana State Library), 396; transcript of proceedings in case of Polly v. Hyacinthe Lasselle in Knox County Circuit Court, in Supreme Court Papers, Archives Division, Indiana State Library, May term, 1820; Dunn (ed.), Slavery Petitions and Papers, 528-29.

[41] State v. Lasselle, 1 Blackford (Ind.) 61-62. Polly not only won her freedom, she also sued her former master for damages and was awarded the sum of $25.16 2/3. Knox County, Order Book of the Circuit Court, 1821-25 (microfilm, Indiana State Library), 33, 42-44, 85, 129. In another case involving the same question the Supreme Court reversed the Knox County court, ordering Francis Jackson, a man of color, discharged from the service of François Tisdale. Ibid., 112-13.

Although the Lasselle case clearly established that slavery had been abolished by the adoption of the state Constitution, it did not deal with the effect of the Constitution upon indentures. It will be recalled that the repeal of the territorial law for the introduction of Negro servants had not affected indentures already made and that even after the repeal free Negroes had continued to sign contracts for long terms of service. The Constitution declared invalid indentures made outside the state after its adoption but was silent on the subject of indentures made in the state either before or after its adoption. The prevailing opinion was that the constitutional prohibition against involuntary servitude did not affect indentures.

After Indiana became a state indentured servants continued to be bought and sold. For example, in connection with the settlement of the estate of Judge Henry Vanderburgh, his administrators placed the following newspaper advertisement:

> Will on Friday the 28th of Feb. 1817 at the door of Peter Jones in Vincennes, sell to the highest bidder, a
> NEGRO WOMAN AND CHILD
> belonging to the said estate.—She was brought into the Territory of Indiana & registered in the clerk's office under the act of the Territorial Legislature . . . For the health and qualities of the Woman, enquire of the Adms.

In 1818 Hyacinthe Lasselle purchased for seven hundred dollars two indentured Negroes who had been a part of the estate of Governor Thomas Posey. In 1819 Thomas Dubois advertised in the *Western Sun* that he would like to sell A LIKELY NEGRO WOMAN.[42]

42 Vincennes *Western Sun,* February 8, 1817; October 9, 16, 1819; bill of sale dated April 4, 1818, in Lasselle Collection and also printed in *Indiana Magazine of History,* 5(1909) :27. A letter from Daniel Jenckes

It was not until 1821 that the Indiana Supreme Court handed down an opinion regarding the position of indentured servants under the state Constitution. Until the higher court ruled on the matter the Knox County court continued to hold that such servants were required to fulfill the terms of their contracts. In 1821 in four cases it dismissed writs of habeas corpus brought by colored servants against their masters.[43] In a fifth case, when the court ordered a servant remanded to her master, an appeal was taken to the Supreme Court. The servant in the case was Mary Clark, who had been held as a slave in Kentucky until January, 1815, when she was brought to Vincennes by Benjamin I. Harrison. In Vincennes she entered into an indenture under which she was to serve Harrison for thirty years. In October, 1816, Harrison manumitted her, and on the same day she signed another indenture which stated that Harrison freed her at her request and that "of her own free will and accord and for a valuable consideration" she bound herself as a servant to General Washington Johnston for a term of twenty years. In 1821 Mary sought release from her indenture in the Knox County Circuit Court. Her attorney was the same Amory Kinney who had acted in behalf of Polly against Hyacinthe Lasselle, and it is probable that the case was begun more at the initiative of Kinney than of Mary. The Knox County court denied her appeal and ordered her remanded to Johnston.[44]

of Vigo County written in 1819 spoke of his decision to buy a Negro boy for a term of twelve years and added: "At any rate if I do not want him he can be disposed of . . . on the same terms." C. C. Oakey, *Greater Terre Haute and Vigo County* . . . (2 vols. Chicago, 1908), 1 :52.

[43] Knox County, Order Book of the Circuit Court, 1821-25 (microfilm, Indiana State Library), pp. 73, 89, 93, 120.

[44] Transcript of proceedings in case of Mary Clark, a woman of Colour (complainant) *v.* G. W. Johnston in Knox County Circuit Court, in Supreme Court Papers, Archives Division, Indiana State Library, November Term, 1821; Knox County, Order Book of the Circuit Court, 1821-25, p. 84. One of the puzzling features of this case is that as a member of the territorial legislature Johnston had led the fight for the repeal of the indenture law. See above, 12-13.

The Supreme Court reversed the decision of the lower court. Judge Jesse L. Holman held that the mere fact that she applied for release from her indenture was evidence that the service she rendered had become involuntary even though she had signed the contract of her own volition. The court distinguished between this case and the cases of apprentices in which the latter were not considered as performing contracts of their own but only contracts made by their parents or guardians and enforceable on the grounds of parental authority. In the present case the woman was "of legal age to regulate her own conduct; she has a right to the exercise of volition; and having declared her will in respect to the present service, the law has no intendment that can contradict that declaration. We must take the fact as it appears, and declare the law accordingly. The fact then is, that the appellant is in a state of involuntary servitude; and we are bound by the constitution, the supreme law of the land, to discharge her therefrom."[45]

The indenture in this case had been made after the Constitution had gone into effect, but the reasoning of the court seems to have been broad enough to cover indentures made prior to the adoption of the Constitution. In the opinion the court made no reference to the date when the indenture had been made but stated that the mere fact that application was made for release was evidence that the service was involuntary and hence prohibited by the Constitution. This would seem to mean that any adult held under an indenture might gain release by applying to a court.

In the months following the decision several more Negroes were discharged from service in suits in Knox County. In one case Charles Vulkin was ordered discharged from the service of Hyacinthe Lasselle. Lasselle in turn tried to sue Charles for broken contract but lost his case. In three other cases brought in the same court in 1822 Negroes were discharged from service. In one case a mother was discharged

---

[45] Mary, a woman of Colour, 1 Blackford (Ind.) 125-26.

but her three children were remanded to the master. This seems to indicate that the children were regarded as apprentices and required to serve until they were of legal age.[46]

In spite of the decisions of the Supreme Court vestiges of slavery and involuntary servitude lingered on for some years. Some Negroes no doubt continued to be held in bondage because they were unaware that they were entitled to freedom. Others, while legally free, continued to stay with their old masters because they knew or wanted no other way of life. An instrument recorded in Gibson County in 1828 shows that Bill, a man of color, who had been indentured under the law of the Territory "and set free by the constitution of the same though not feeling disposed to take advantage of the constitution and law of said state," agreed to serve Montgomery Warrick for a term of years. A local census taken by order of the Board of Trustees of the town showed thirty-two slaves in Vincennes in 1830, although the United States census for the same year showed but three.[47]

[46] Knox County, Order Book of the Circuit Court, 1821-25, pp. 73, 89, 93, 120, 174, 185, 252, 272, 311, 316, 324.

[47] Gibson County, Deed Record D, 1824-33 (microfilm, Indiana State Library), 217. In 1828 Warrick recorded that Bill had completed his term of service to his full satisfaction and was entitled to his freedom and that "no other person whatever has any claim or claims to service from him." *Ibid.*; Henry S. Cauthorn, *A Brief Sketch of the Past, Present and Prospects of Vincennes* (Vincennes, 1884), 23; U. S. Bureau of the Census, *Negro Population in the United States, 1790-1915* (Washington, D. C., 1918), 57.

2

POPULATION MOVEMENT 1816-1860

THE YEARS FROM ADMISSION into the Union in 1816 until the Civil War saw Indiana transformed from a pioneer wilderness into a flourishing agricultural state. Whereas in 1816 population had been confined to a narrow fringe of settlements along the Wabash and Ohio rivers, and in the Whitewater Valley, by 1860 settlements had been made as far north as the shores of Lake Michigan, and the population of the state had grown to more than 1,350,000. The same period saw a marked increase and diffusion of the Negro population, although the rate of increase was not so rapid for Negroes as for whites. This was partly due to the hostility of the latter group. After 1831 Negroes seeking to settle in the state were required by law to register with county authorities and to give bond as a guarantee of good behavior and against their becoming public charges. Under the state Constitution adopted in 1851 they were absolutely prohibited from coming into the state to settle. In addition to these exclusion measures, state laws barred Negroes from voting, from serving in the militia, from testifying in court in cases in which a white person was a party, and deprived Negro children of the right to attend public schools. Moreover, there was a movement, financed in part from state funds, to persuade Negro residents to leave the state and go to Liberia.

In spite of legal barriers and discrimination, to Negroes in slave states Indiana was a land of freedom, and thousands of them migrated to the state, some of them risking their lives to reach free soil. The census of 1860 showed a total of 11,428 Negroes as compared with only 1,420 in 1820,

an increase of more than 800 per cent. Most of the new
arrivals came from the states of the Upper South. The
census of 1850, the first to indicate the place of birth, shows
that the largest group, 1,426, came from North Carolina.
Virginia was second with 1,172, Kentucky third, with 1,116,
while Tennessee sent 600. Ohio, which 826 claimed as their
birthplace, was the only free state to send a substantial number. A total of 329 had been born in the states of the Lower
South—South Carolina, Georgia, Mississippi, Alabama, and
Louisiana. Eight were reported as having been born in
Africa, 6 in Canada, and 3 in the British West Indies.[1]

Negroes who moved into Indiana in the ante-bellum period
fall into three general groups. The first of these were free
persons in the states in which they resided before coming
to Indiana. The second group consisted of recently emancipated slaves. Their coming was due in part to the fact that
laws of the Southern states put increasing restrictions upon
the rights of masters to emancipate their slaves, many of
them requiring that upon emancipation they be removed to
another state. The third group of Negro immigrants were
fugitive slaves. Their position was always precarious, and
in later years, after the passage of the Fugitive Slave Act
of 1850, they tended to move on to Canada rather than
remain in Indiana.

Information regarding free Negroes who moved northward is meager. The states of the South with the largest
population of free colored persons were Virginia, Maryland,
and North Carolina. Since the Negro population of Indiana
was drawn largely from North Carolina and Virginia, it
is reasonable to suppose that a considerable number of free
Negroes came from those states. A few authenticated examples, such as the settlement of the Roberts family in

[1] Lois McDougald, "Negro Migration into Indiana, 1800-1860" (unpublished M.A. thesis, Indiana University, 1945), 33-34. It is probable
that some of those born in Virginia, North Carolina, and other older
states were taken first to Kentucky as their masters moved westward and
from there came to Indiana.

Hamilton County, can be found. The fact that many Negro families in Indiana had the same names as free Negro families in North Carolina is suggestive. Such names as Chavis [Chavers], Bass, Revels, Steward, Valentine, Hawkins, Weaver, Artis, Mitchell, and Mitchum are frequent in the census lists of free Negroes in North Carolina and also appeared frequently in Negro settlements in Indiana.[2]

A substantial number of Negroes came in company with white Quakers and settled near them. Quakers in both North Carolina and Indiana also assisted others who came later to find homes. Members of the Society of Friends in North Carolina were hindered by state law in emancipating their slaves. Like most states North Carolina required that masters who freed their slaves must give bond that they would not become public charges, but in 1830 this was amended to require that manumitted slaves must leave the state within ninety days. In consequence a system was devised under which a committee of Friends acted as trustees for masters who wished to free their slaves. Masters turned their slaves over to the committee, which in turn sought to find a means of transporting them to free states. The 1808 Yearly Meeting of North Carolina first authorized such a committee. By 1814 it was reported that more than three hundred and fifty Negroes had been transferred to Quaker agents. In 1824 the committee had five hundred charges under its care; in 1826 it reported six hundred.[3]

Some of these Negroes were removed to Liberia, particularly in the years from 1825 to 1830, but most of them

[2] Carter G. Woodson, *The Free Negro Heads of Families in the United States in 1830* . . . (Washington, D. C., 1925), 110-13; John Hope Franklin, *The Free Negro in North Carolina 1790-1860* (Chapel Hill, 1943), *passim;* Richard R. Wright, Jr., "Negro Rural Communities in the North," in *The Southern Workman* (Hampton, Va.), 37(1908) :163-64.

[3] Franklin, *Free Negro in North Carolina,* 23-37; Stephen B. Weeks, *Southern Quakers and Slavery. A Study in Institutional History* (Johns Hopkins University *Studies in Historical and Political Science,* Extra Volume 15, 1896), 224, 227-28.

preferred to go to the free states of the Northwest, where many Southern white persons were also moving. In 1822 the Deep River Quarterly Meeting of North Carolina appointed a committee to examine the laws of the free states to find where Negroes might settle. The committee reported that the laws of Ohio, Indiana, and Illinois contained nothing to prevent the introduction of free Negroes. The Yearly Meeting then instructed its agents to remove the slaves in their charge as rapidly as they were willing to go. The records show that by 1830 the committee had assisted 652 Negroes in reaching the free states.[4]

At the first meeting of the Indiana Yearly Meeting of Friends in 1821 a committee on the concerns of People of Color was appointed. The committee was reorganized several times but remained active until the Civil War. All Quarterly Meetings also had continuing committees on the subject. The minutes of the Yearly Meeting of 1824 show that Friends in the New Garden Meeting (Wayne County) had been aiding Negroes who arrived from North Carolina, having "given them such advice as they apprehended might be useful, provided places, and procured wages for a part of them." The 1826 minutes reported a communication from the North Carolina Yearly Meeting which described "the difficult and perilous situation of persons of color under the care of Friends," and asked assistance in caring for those who might come to Indiana. The report of the Indiana committee on People of Color shows that some Indiana Quakers were reluctant to encourage the migration of a large number of Negroes, but they reported, "after solidly deliberating on the subject, and having our minds clothed with feelings which breathe 'good will to men' " that they had decided to extend such assistance as they could.

4 Weeks, *Southern Quakers and Slavery,* 228. In 1822 both Ohio and Illinois had laws requiring that Negroes coming into the state must post bond. Indiana adopted a similar law in 1831. None of the laws seem to have been enforced.

They added: "Although it is desirable to avoid an access [*sic*] of this class . . . as neighbors, we are concerned to impress it on the minds of all, that our prejudices should yield when the interest and happiness of our fellow beings are at stake; and, that we exert no influence that would deprive them of the rights of free agents, in removing to any part of the world congenial to them, and that Friends everywhere, render them such assistance, in procuring them employment, and promoting a correct deportment among them, as occasion may require." In 1827 Quarterly Meetings in Indiana were directed to make an appeal for subscriptions to assist Friends of North Carolina in removing colored persons to free soil.[5]

The North Carolina records give an account of a removal of a band of one hundred thirty-five Negroes to the northwest in 1835 which throws light on the manner in which these exoduses were carried out. The Quakers bore the greater part of the traveling expenses. Thirteen wagons and carts were furnished, and warm clothing was purchased for the travelers since winter was approaching. The total cost was $2,490. A group of young men of the Quaker faith accompanied the Negroes and were given the power of attorney to manumit and settle their charges or to bind them out to service. The entire band was divided into three companies. One of these consisted of thirty-eight slaves held in trust by Friends. Four of these were women whose husbands were still in slavery. The women had planned to leave their husbands so that they might take their children to free soil, but as the time for their departure approached, they grew more and more reluctant to leave their mates, even though remaining meant being reduced again to slavery. At the last moment the masters of the husbands were

<hr>

[5] Minutes of the Committee of Indiana Yearly Meeting of Friends on the Concerns of People of Color (MS, Earlham College Library), *passim; Minutes of Indiana Yearly Meeting of Friends,* 1824, p. 10; 1826, pp. 13-14; 1827, pp. 13-14.

persuaded to sell them so that they might accompany their families. Five other members of the party were slaves belonging to an individual Quaker who was sending them out of the state at his own expense. Six were the wife and children of a free colored man who had purchased his wife out of slavery years before and was now seeking to take his family to a free state. The party of Negroes was accompanied by a young Quaker, David White, who disposed of four of them in Chillicothe, Ohio, and twenty-three others at Leesburg, Ohio. The remaining twenty-six were taken to the vicinity of Newport in Wayne County, Indiana. White reported that he met no opposition on the journey and, in fact, was received more cordially in Ohio and Indiana than he had expected to be. He had no difficulty in making arrangements to have his colored charges hired out to clear and cultivate the land of white farmers.[6]

In later years, as the non-Quaker population of Wayne County increased, groups of Negroes who tried to settle there encountered more hostility. A group sent to Indiana in 1837 found conditions so unfavorable that they turned back east. Nevertheless, groups of colored settlers continued to arrive and the Quakers continued to help them. The enactment of the Black Law of 1831, which required Negroes to give bond, does not appear to have had any perceptible effect upon this immigration. An article in a Richmond newspaper in 1842 reported the arrival of six wagonloads of North Carolina Negroes who had been brought into the state by a white Friend. The writer of the article protested: "This town is one of the great headquarters for these blacks, that the semi-abolitionists of the South, who are horror struck by the idea of colonization, are continually throwing off their own hands and sending here to steal their living from the hospitable citizens of our place. . . . It is a disgrace to our town, and a dead weight

6 Wright; "Negro Rural Communities," in *Southern Workman,* 37:162-63.

to its improvement, that these things are permitted to remain here. We are a by-word abroad."[7]

Although the work of the North Carolina Quakers in behalf of Negro immigrants declined in the forties, Indiana Quakers continued their assistance to colored settlers. Records of the Anti-Slavery Friends show that in 1851 money was raised by voluntary subscription to bring a group of fourteen Tennessee Negroes to Indiana. The Negroes had been freed by will, but under Tennessee law were liable to be re-enslaved unless they were taken out of the state. Many Negroes who were not assisted directly by Friends flocked to the vicinity of Quaker settlements. The fame of these communities, where Negroes were well treated, spread to the slave states, and they became havens of refuge for fugitive slaves as well as free Negroes.[8]

Emancipated slaves were brought into Indiana by persons other than Quakers, but information about them is scant. In some instances large groups of former slaves appear to have been settled on Indiana soil. In November, 1816, M. E. Sumner of Williamson County, Tennessee, wrote to the Indiana House of Representatives stating his desire to bring his slaves, about forty in number, to Indiana to emancipate them. All the slaves had been reared by Sumner and his father. The eldest was about forty-six years old. The writer expressed the opinion that after a man had the use of slaves or their parents for twenty or thirty years, it was inhumane to set them free without providing for their security. Hence he hoped to buy land and animals and equipment so that the freedmen could set themselves up

[7] Richmond *Jeffersonian* reprinted in *Free Labor Advocate* (Newport, Ind.), January 8, 1842.

[8] Minutes of Anti-Slavery Friends (MS, Earlham College Library), 288-89. For a further discussion of the Anti-Slavery Friends, see Chapter III. The Vincennes *Western Sun & General Advertiser,* July 4, 1829, contains an advertisement for a slave who had run away from Kentucky and who was thought to be fleeing to "the Quaker settlement in Indiana."

as independent farmers. He added that he planned to come to Indiana himself, explaining, "I am also very desirous to leave the slave states, and spend my few remaining days in that state where involuntary servitude is not admissible."[9]

Sumner wrote to the House of Representatives because he wished to learn whether there was anything in Indiana law prohibiting his bringing the Negroes into the state and emancipating them. The committee to which the question was referred drew up a report in which they stressed the prejudice against Negroes among the white population of Indiana and sought to dissuade Sumner from carrying out his plan. The report said: "While we rejoice that the Ruler of the Universe has bestowed on you a benevolent heart, we regret that sound policy forbids us to encourage your intentions further than already given by our constitution and laws." The House rejected the report, and no reply was made to Sumner's inquiry.[10]

All masters did not show the same feeling of responsibility for the welfare of their emancipated slaves which Sumner's letter revealed. The white population frequently expressed alarm lest Indiana become a dumping ground for aged and destitute slaves. Many charges were made that masters sought to avoid the burden of caring for aged slaves by bringing them to Indiana, although authenticated instances are hard to find. E. S. Abdy, an Englishman with a marked sympathy for Negroes, who visited Madison, Indiana, in the early thirties, reported that it was a common practice for Kentucky slaveholders to free slaves who were too old

9 Indiana *House Journal,* 1816-17, pp. 33-34.

10 *Ibid.,* 1816-17, pp. 43, 49. Sumner did not carry out the plan to bring his slaves to Indiana. He remained in Tennessee, where he died in 1819. In his will he left his Negroes in trust to the Pennsylvania Society for Promoting the Abolition of Slavery, with the provision that the society should use $5,000 from his estate to buy land and settle them in a free state. Information and copy of Sumner's will furnished by Ernest K. Lindley, Washington, D. C., whose ancestor, Jonathan Lindley, was a member of the Indiana General Assembly when Sumner submitted his inquiry.

or feeble to work and send them across the Ohio River, where they became the charges of the people of Madison and had to be cared for at public expense. In his message to the legislature in 1829, Governor James B. Ray spoke of the need to check the immigration of a "non-productive, and in many instances, a super-annuated population," which he described as "pouring in." The fact that the Negro population increased by only 1,212 in the years from 1820 to 1830, while the white increased by 193,641 in the same period, would suggest that the Governor gave an exaggerated picture. However, the fact that these Negroes were congregated in a few counties along the Ohio River undoubtedly tended to arouse alarm in those counties.[11]

The colored population was also swelled by fugitive slaves. Unlike the other groups already mentioned, these had not been emancipated but had escaped from bondage illegally. Even though they settled in a free state, they were still slaves in the eyes of the law and subject to recapture and return to slavery. Closely related to the story of the migration of this group is the story of the organized efforts to help slaves escape to free soil known as the "Underground Railroad." Because these activities were illegal and clandestine there are few contemporary accounts of them; and because of their secret and hazardous nature a great deal of folklore developed about them. There were undoubtedly many heroic escapes and cunning ruses used to thwart slave hunters. But the written accounts, nearly all of which belong to the period after the Civil War, contain embellishments which make it difficult for the historian to separate fact from fiction.

[11] Edward S. Abdy, *Journal of a Residence and Tour in United States of North America from April, 1833, to October, 1834* (3 vols. London, 1835), 2:379; Indiana *House Journal,* 1829-30, p. 35. Appeal to the fear of the effects of unrestricted immigration of such Negroes became a perennial issue in Indiana politics and was responsible for the exclusion article of the state Constitution of 1851 discussed in the next chapter. In the Constitutional Convention of 1850-51 it was reported that 150 cast-off slaves had been settled in Floyd County in one year. *Report of the*

Because Indiana was bounded along her southern border by a slave state, it was natural that many runaway slaves should try to reach her soil. Wilbur H. Siebert, who made the pioneer study on the subject of the Underground Railroad, points out that the migration of fugitives into the free states of the Old Northwest was much greater than into the states farther east. Because they bordered on slave states, "with a length of frontier greatly increased by the sinuosities of the rivers, the states of Ohio, Indiana and Illinois were the most favorably situated of all the Northern states to receive fugitive slaves. Not only the bounding rivers themselves, but also their numerous tributaries, became channels of escape into free territory."[12]

Many of the fugitives who escaped via the Underground Railroad merely passed across Indiana on their way to Michigan or Canada, hence their story is outside the scope of this work. Others remained in Indiana permanently, while some settled there temporarily but moved on farther north after the passage of the Fugitive Slave Law of 1850 made their position precarious. Professor Siebert distinguished three main routes along which fugitives traveled across Indiana. The first of these was a continuation of routes from Cincinnati and Lawrenceburg which converged in Wayne County. Thence a main line ran north through Winchester, Portland, Decatur, Fort Wayne, and Auburn into Michigan. The second main line originated from three branches which crossed the Ohio River at Madison, New Albany, and the vicinity of Leavenworth. These converged near Columbus and passed north through Indianapolis, Westfield, Logansport, Plymouth, and South Bend. The third main route crossed the Ohio at Evansville and followed the Wabash River through Terre Haute and then

Debates and Proceedings of the Convention for the Revision of the Constitution of the State of Indiana (2 vols. Indianapolis, 1850), 1 :446.

[12] Wilbur H. Siebert, *The Underground Railroad from Slavery to Freedom* (New York, 1898), 134.

up to Lafayette.[13] In addition to these main routes there were, of course, numerous cross routes and variations on the main routes. Continued use of the same route or stations might become dangerous if they became known to persons hostile to the activities of the underground, and different routes would then become necessary.

Both white and Negro residents gave the fugitives shelter and guided them across the state. Especially in the settlements along the Indiana side of the Ohio River Negroes were active in helping them across the river and giving them shelter before sending them northward. Sometimes there were confederates in Kentucky with whom signals were exchanged to indicate when it was safe to cross the river. Bonfires lighted on the hilltops might be used as signals. When the way was clear the fugitives were ferried across the river in skiffs.

The best known Negro members of the underground were those in Jefferson County around Madison. The leader among them was Chapman Harris, a preacher, who was born in Virginia of a free mother and who came to Indiana in 1839. With his wife and four sons he lived in a cabin at the mouth of Eagle Hollow three miles above Madison, a point at which many fugitives crossed the Ohio. He and his sons were all large and powerfully built and utterly fearless in helping slaves escape. Closely associated with Harris was Elijah Anderson, who came from Lynchburg, Virginia, in 1837 and settled in Eagle Hollow. His cabin, like that of Harris, was a stopping place on the underground. Anderson repeatedly went to Kentucky to help escapees. Two other intrepid Madison Negroes who aided runaways were Henry Thornton and Griffith Booth. On one occasion the latter was attacked by a proslavery mob in Madison because of his activities. On another occasion he was thrown into the Ohio River and almost drowned in an effort to force him to divulge the hiding place of some slaves. His

13 *Ibid.*, 138.

underground activities finally made it too dangerous for him to remain in Madison, and in 1848 he moved to Michigan. Another agent was George Baptiste, a Virginia-born Negro who came to Madison about 1838. Baptiste was a barber by trade but also engaged in a variety of business enterprises. Because his underground activities made him unwelcome in Madison he moved to Detroit in the fifties.[14]

While men of this sort were risking their lives to help slaves, there were a few Negroes who were willing to betray fugitives in the hope of collecting rewards. On one occasion a group of twenty-five or thirty Negroes nearly whipped to death a member of their own race who had revealed the whereabouts of a slave. After the episode Chapman Harris and Elijah Anderson were charged with being parties to the flogging. At their trial it was almost impossible to get evidence since none of the colored people who knew the facts in the case would testify against them. The jury was sufficiently convinced of Harris' guilt that it levied a fine on him. However, Harris was never prosecuted for his underground activities. Anderson, on the other hand, was finally apprehended on one of his trips to Kentucky. He was convicted and sentenced to a term in the state penitentiary at Frankfort, where he died. It was rumored that he had been betrayed to the authorities by another Negro.[15]

Slaves also crossed the river at New Albany and Jeffersonville, which were opposite Louisville, Kentucky. In Portland, on the outskirts of Louisville, was a colored Masonic lodge, where many plans for aiding the escapees were hatched. After being carried across the Ohio in skiffs, the

[14] "Negroes in and around Jefferson County" (typed copy in Jefferson County Historical Society), 7-9. In Detroit Baptiste became an important Negro leader. Booth moved to Kalamazoo, where he became a well-known Republican. Henry Thornton was a drummer in the Union Army during the Civil War. He died in Madison in 1892. *Ibid.*; Indianapolis *Journal*, February 11, 1890; Indianapolis *World*, August 13, 1892.

[15] "Negroes in and around Jefferson County," 8, 20.

slaves took refuge with Negro families on the Indiana side. When they headed northward, some of them went next to a tiny settlement of Negroes near Hanover, known as Greenbrier. Here the home of George Evans was a station on the underground, and Evans helped them on their way to stations in Jennings or Decatur counties. Farther down the Ohio River at the little town of Rockport the principal agent of the underground was a Negro named Ben Swain. At Corydon, in Harrison County, lived Oswald Wright, who helped several slaves escape from Kentucky. He was arrested and sent to the Frankfort penitentiary for five years, but after serving his term returned to Corydon.[16]

In the counties farther north, although most of the Underground Railroad work was done by white persons, runaways frequently headed for colored settlements, and the names of several colored agents are known. At Clarksburg in Decatur County lived Miles Meadows who conducted fugitives to the vicinity of Rushville or Carthage in Rush County. At Rushville the principal agent was a colored man named Burns, while among those active in the underground in the Carthage area was Jim Hunt. In Wayne, Randolph, and Henry counties were several Quaker settlements which were noted as centers of antislavery activity. Most of the agents of the underground in these counties were white men. Best known was Levi Coffin of Newport in Wayne County whose activities on behalf of runaway slaves became legendary. But Negroes frequently assisted Coffin. Among those at Newport whose names are known were William Bush, William Davidson, Douglas White, James Benson, and Cal Thomas.

16 Folder marked "Racial, Floyd County," in papers of Indiana Writers' Project, Work Projects Administration (Indiana State Teachers College Library, Terre Haute); Emery O. Muncie, "A History of Jefferson County, Indiana" (unpublished M.A. thesis, Indiana University, 1932), 3; William M. Cockrum, *History of the Underground Railroad as It Was Conducted by the Anti-Slavery League* (Oakland City, Ind., 1915), 98; Charles H. Money, "The Fugitive Slave Law of 1850 in Indiana," in *Indiana Magazine of History*, 17(1921):289, 290, 297.

Elsewhere in the state, with one or two exceptions, Negroes who worked in the underground are anonymous. In the western part of the state in Parke County in the fifties there was a station at the home of Reuben Lawhorn, a freeborn Negro, who had come from North Carolina. At Bloomington in Monroe County a colored woman named "Aunty Myears" frequently gave shelter to runaways.

An examination of the Negro settlements in Indiana shows that in nearly every case they were located on one of the routes of the Underground Railroad. This suggests two things—that runaways tended to seek out members of their own race and that many of them remained in Indiana instead of pushing on northward.[17]

The figures in the decennial censuses give additional information on the pattern of Negro migration. In 1820 there were 1,420 Negroes in the state; in 1860, there were 11,428, an increase of about eight hundred per cent. In the same period white population increased more rapidly— from 146,758 to 1,338,710, an increase of more than nine hundred per cent. In 1820 Negroes represented 1 per cent of the total population; in 1860 only 9/10 of 1 per cent.[18] In 1820 the colored population, like the white, was concentrated in the river counties along the border. Knox County had the largest colored population, Clark County second, Jefferson third. In 1830 Knox was still first, but

[17] N. T. Rogers, "Decatur County's Part in the Historic Underground Railway of Slavery Days" (typed copy, Indiana State Library), 11-13, 21-22; O. N. Huff, "Unnamed Anti-Slavery Heroes of Old Newport," in *Indiana Magazine of History*, 3(1907):135; Henry L. Smith, "The Underground Railroad in Monroe County," in *Indiana Magazine of History*, 13(1917):293, 295.

[18] The totals of Negro population by decades were as follows:

1820	1,420
1830	3,632
1840	7,168
1850	11,262
1860	11,428

U. S. Bureau of the Census, *Negro Population, 1790-1915*, 44-45.

Wayne County in the east had almost as many Negroes. The 1840 census showed some marked changes. Both white and Negro population had moved north. By this time Wayne County stood first in colored population, a position it was to retain until after the Civil War. After Wayne, which had a total of 626 Negroes, came Knox, but Randolph County and Rush County had become third and fourth. Then followed Jefferson, Vigo (in the extreme west), Floyd, and Clark counties. Marion County, where the new state capital, Indianapolis, was located, stood in ninth place. By 1850 Wayne remained first, but Vigo had the second largest colored population, Randolph third, Marion fourth, Clark fifth, Floyd sixth, Jefferson seventh, Knox eighth, and Rush ninth. The rapid growth of Negro population in Wayne, Randolph, and Rush counties, which were all centers of Quaker settlements, reflects the efforts of the Friends mentioned earlier in the chapter.

During the decade of the fifties the total number of Negroes in the state remained almost unchanged. The census of 1850 showed 11,262 Negroes, that of 1860 showed 11,428 or a net increase of only 166 persons in ten years. A closer examination of the records shows that in several counties there was a decline in these years. By 1860 although Negroes had spread to all but six of the ninety-two counties of the state, more than half the total number were concentrated in the following counties: Wayne, Marion, Randolph, Floyd, Vigo, Clark, Jefferson, Knox, Rush, Grant.[19]

[19] The table below shows the Negro population of these counties by decades. These figures and the other statistical data in the chapter, unless otherwise identified, are from the U. S. Bureau of the Census, *Census for 1820*, p. 39; *Fifth Census* (1830), 144-45; *Sixth Census* (1840), 346-68; *Seventh Census* (1850), 755-79; *Eighth Census* (1860), 112-28.

COUNTY	1820	1830	1840	1850	1860
Clark	138	243	388	582	520
Floyd	69	265	402	574	757
Grant	---	---	---	147	384
Jefferson	112	240	429	568	512
Knox	284	446	561	530	449

A somewhat different picture emerges when the percentages of Negroes relative to the entire population are considered. From this standpoint Randolph County, where Negroes constituted 4.3 per cent of the whole, ranked first in 1860. Floyd County with 3.7 was second; Vigo third with 3.1; Wayne fourth with 2.8; Knox fifth with 2.7; Rush sixth with 2.5; Clark seventh with 2.5; Grant eighth with 2.4; Marion ninth with 2.07; and Jefferson tenth with 2.04. In all of these except Grant there had been a slight relative decline in the percentage of Negroes between 1850 and 1860.

The census figures showed that a large part of the Negro population remained concentrated along the southern border of the state—especially in Jefferson, Floyd, and Clark counties. In 1860 Negroes constituted almost 5 per cent of the population of New Albany, the principal town in Floyd County (627 out of a total of 12,647). In Clark County, Jeffersonville showed about 5 per cent (209 out of 4,020); while Charlestown had 6 per cent (198 out of 3,161). In Madison in Jefferson County, Negroes constituted only about 3 per cent of the total (247 out of 8,130). In all three counties there was also a sizable colored population in the hills back of the towns.[20] There were smaller numbers of Negroes in Dearborn County, in and near Lawrenceburg; in Harrison County, especially in Corydon; and in Vanderburgh and Posey counties. But it is remarkable that there were almost no Negroes in some of the Ohio River counties. For example, Crawford County reported only one Negro in 1850 and none in 1860. In Perry County there

COUNTY	1820	1830	1840	1850	1860
Marion	---	---	255	650	825
Randolph	5	123	544	662	825
Rush	---	107	481	427	419
Vigo	26	123	425	748	706
Wayne	66	417	626	1,036	870

20 *Eighth Census* (1860), 115, 117, 119.

were only three in 1860, while Spencer reported only two, and Warrick only nineteen.

In Knox County, where most of the colored population had been found during the territorial period, a large element remained, especially in Vincennes, where in 1850 Negroes constituted more than 10 per cent of the total (221 out of 2,070). In Gibson County to the south of Knox, where there had been a few Negroes in the territorial period, there was a fairly large community known as the Lyles settlement in Patoka Township, about five miles from Princeton. It took its name from the leading family, who had come from North Carolina and acquired 1,200 acres of land.[21]

In some of the other southern counties most of the first Negroes came in the company of white Quakers. Members of the Friends denomination began to move into Washington County as early as 1808, and the Blue River Meeting was established in 1815. By 1850 there were 252 Negroes in the county, mostly in Posey and Washington townships, but the number declined thereafter. In Jackson Township of Jackson County was one of the earliest Friends churches in Indiana, and in that township and the neighboring Redding Township there were numerous Negroes, most of whom came from North Carolina. In Orange County Quakers settled around Orleans and Chambersburg, and near them were several colored families. There were also several Negroes in Paoli Township.[22]

In some of the counties in the southeast rural communities developed which appear to have been made up largely of fugitive slaves. One of the largest was in Jennings County in Vernon Township. A large family named Kersey moved

21 *Seventh Census* (1850), 767; *Eighth Census* (1860), 117; Wright, "Negro Rural Communities," in *Southern Workman*, 37 :165.

22 Warder W. Stevens, *Centennial History of Washington County, Indiana* . . . (Indianapolis, 1916), 282, 362-64; Lillie D. Trueblood, "Story of John Williams, Colored," in *Indiana Magazine of History*, 30(1934) :147.

here from Georgia sometime before 1830. During the forties the settlement grew so rapidly that part of the county came to be called "Africa." The fact that some of the white families in the vicinity were strongly antislavery and were active in the Underground Railroad undoubtedly accounts in part for the presence of the Negroes.[23] In the older settlements along the Whitewater in Franklin County there had been a few Negroes since the territorial period, but in later years most Negroes moved into the hilly region in the northwest. The largest influx occurred in the forties. In 1850 there were 122 Negroes in Salt Creek Township, and 209 in the entire county. A little to the west in Fugit Township in Decatur County there was a settlement of Negroes near a community of whites who were noted for their antislavery activities. The census of 1850 showed 149 Negroes in this township out of 156 for the whole county. Many of the settlers in both Franklin and Decatur counties appear to have been fugitives who moved on to Canada in the fifties.[24]

One of the most striking features of the pattern of settlement by Negroes in some of the eastern and central counties was their tendency to settle near communities of Quakers. In 1850 Wayne County, which had the largest number of Negroes in the state, also had the largest number of Friends churches. Henry County had the second largest number of such churches, while Grant, Marion, Rush, Randolph, and Morgan counties followed in that order. All these counties except Morgan had large numbers of Negroes.

23 In 1850 there were 323 Negroes in the county, 211 of them in Vernon Township. Woodson, *Free Negro Heads of Families*, 25; Luke Thomas, "The Thomas Family," in *Indiana Magazine of History*, 19 (1923) :352; folder marked "Racial, Jennings County" in Indiana Writers' Project, Work Projects Administration; Siebert *(Underground Railroad, 408)* lists thirteen persons in Jennings County as agents of the underground.

24 August J. Reifel, *History of Franklin County, Indiana* . . . (B. F. Bowen & Company, Indianapolis, 1915), 535; Rogers, "Decatur County's Part in the Underground Railway," *passim*.

The largest number of Quakers were in the Whitewater and New Garden Quarterly Meetings, which embraced principally Wayne, Randolph, and Henry counties.[25]

The first Negroes in Wayne County were found in Wayne Township, along the Whitewater River, but in later years they were scattered throughout the county. Some of the Negroes who settled in nearby Randolph County, which had the largest percentage of Negroes of any county in the state in 1860, came from Wayne. Most of the Randolph County Negroes were originally from North Carolina. They were settled in a number of rural communities. The earliest appears to have been the Greenville settlement, northeast of Spartanburg, adjoining a larger colored settlement in Ohio. The first Negro to settle on the Indiana side appears to have been Thornton Alexander who came from Warren County, Ohio, in 1822 and entered three hundred acres of land in Greensfork Township. Another colored farming community, known as Cabin Creek, included parts of West River, Nettle Creek, and Stoney Creek townships. The earliest settlers, who came about 1825, were from North Carolina and Virginia. The first appears to have been John Demary from North Carolina. About 1838 another settlement known as Snow Hill was begun between Winchester and Lynn in Washington Township.[26]

In Henry County, which borders on Wayne and Randolph, there was a large Quaker element from North Carolina and Negroes scattered throughout the county. The largest group of the latter were in Greensboro Township. In Rush County Quakers from North Carolina and Virginia settled principally in Ripley Township near Carthage. Nearby was a sizable settlement of Negro farmers known as the Beech settlement. Vinchen Roberts, who came from North Carolina about 1829 with the Binfords, a white Quaker family, was probably the first colored settler. Other colored

---

[25] *Seventh Census* (1850), 800-801.

[26] Ebenezer Tucker, *History of Randolph County, Indiana* . . . (Chicago, 1882), 133-34, 171.

families who settled there by 1830 included Harmons, Scotts, Lancasters, Williams, and McCowens. Most of them became landowners and successful farmers.[27]

The fact that Quakers were numerous in Hamilton County no doubt accounts in part for the fact that Negroes settled there. The largest group of Negroes was in Jackson Township in the northern part of the county in the "Roberts settlement." In 1837 a group of free colored families came from North Carolina. These included Hansel, Dolphin, Elias, Elijah, Jonathan, and Stephen Roberts, and Micajah Walden, Guilford Brooks, Bryant Walden, Harry Winbern, and James White. They purchased land and cleared it and became prosperous farmers. In time other families moved away or died out until the settlement became in truth almost exclusively persons named Roberts. The census of 1850 listed fifty persons of that name in the township. It is one of the few pre-Civil War Negro farming communities of which some trace remains today.

In Liberty Township in Grant County was a settlement of Quakers and nearby a Negro community. A white man named Aaron Botts brought the first Negroes to the neighborhood and helped them in entering land. Some of those who settled there were free Negroes and fugitive slaves from the South; others came from older communities in Ohio and Indiana, particularly Wayne County. The settlement came to be known as Weaver from the name of the leading family.[28]

27 *History of Henry County, Indiana* . . . (Inter-State Publishing Co., Chicago, 1884), 61, 640-43; Thomas T. Newby, *Reminiscences* (Carthage, Ind., 1916) ; "History of Carthage Friends Church" (typed copy, Indiana State Library), 5; Nathan Hill, "The Beech Settlement," in Indiana Negro History Society Bulletin (mimeographed, Indiana State Library), May, 1943, p. 2; Woodson, *Free Negro Heads of Families*, 26. The census of 1860 shows 283 Negroes in Henry County, 353 in Ripley Township of Rush County.

28 Wright, "Negro Rural Communities," in *Southern Workman*, 37: 164; John F. Haines, *History of Hamilton County, Indiana* (Indianapolis, 1915), 173, 238; Rolland Whitson (ed.), *Centennial History of Grant*

In Howard County near the Poplar Grove Friends meeting were two small settlements of Negro farmers in Ervin and Clay townships. One was known as the Bassett settlement from the name of the leading member of the community, who was also the minister of the little Baptist church. The other, the Rush settlement, clustered around the Methodist church and also took its name from the minister. Both communities were entirely rural, and in the post Civil War period most of the residents moved away to Kokomo or Logansport.[29]

In the western part of the state the largest groups of Negroes were found in Vigo County. Although there were a number of Quakers in this county, they do not appear to have played as important a part in encouraging Negro immigration as did Friends in other parts of the state. The first Negroes, some of whom were free, some emancipated slaves, came from North Carolina. One of the first was Armistead Stewart, who came to Vigo in 1815 in the company of his master, Daniel Durham, a North Carolina Quaker. Durham later returned to North Carolina and brought back other Negroes. About 1830 colored settlers began to arrive in large numbers. Most of them settled in Lost Creek Township, where they cleared the land and became successful farmers. Others settled in Nevins and Otter Creek townships. By the time of the Civil War a sizable group had also settled in the town of Terre Haute.

County, Indiana 1812-1912 (2 vols. Chicago, 1914). The 1860 census shows 284 Negroes in Liberty Township.

29 Wright, "Negro Rural Communities," in Southern Workman, 37: 164-65; Charles Blanchard (ed.), Counties of Howard and Tipton, Indiana (Chicago, 1883), 300; Indiana Historical Society, Committee on Pioneer Cemeteries and Churches, Report on Howard County (typed copy, Indiana State Library). Among the first Negroes in this area was a group of emancipated slaves from Tennessee, whose master had freed them in his will but who had been kept ignorant of the fact that they were free. A group of Quakers learned of the will and secured their freedom and sent them to Howard County. Henry C. Cadbury, "Negro Membership in the Society of Friends," in Journal of Negro History, 21 (1936):207.

In nearby Parke and Montgomery counties, where there were also Quaker communities and one of the main routes of the Underground Railroad, by 1860 there were also a few Negroes. In Fountain County there was a Quaker settlement in the Bethel neighborhood, about five miles east of Attica. This was a station on the underground, and nearby was a small settlement of fugitive slaves. A little farther north in Lafayette, which was also a station on the underground, there was a small colored community.[30]

In the center of the state Indianapolis, the state capital, had one of the largest Negro communities in the state by 1860, and there were also Negroes in the rural parts of Marion County. Although there were Quakers in the county, the presence of the Negroes was probably due more to the fact that Indianapolis was a growing city which offered opportunities for employment than to active assistance from Friends. A few Negroes lived in the state capital from the time of its founding. Gen. John Tipton is supposed to have brought a colored boy with him when he was helping select the capital site. Alexander Ralston, one of the founders of the city, brought with him a colored housekeeper, Chiney Lively, to whom he left some property in his will. Chiney later married John Britton, one of the outstanding Negroes in the history of the city. A census of the infant city in 1827 showed a total of 58 Negroes. By 1860 this number had increased to 498, but the rate of growth of the colored population was slower than that of the white. In 1850 Negroes had constituted 5 per cent of the total, but by 1860 only about 2½ per cent.[31]

[30] Wright, "Negro Rural Communities," in *Southern Workman, 37*: 165; John Lyda, "History of Terre Haute, Indiana," in Indiana Negro History Society Bulletin (mimeographed, Indiana State Library), January, 1944; Hiram W. Beckwith, *History of Vigo and Parke Counties, together with Historical Notes on the Wabash Valley* (Chicago, 1880), 389, 393-94; folder marked "Racial, Fountain County" in Indiana Writers' Project, Work Projects Administration. In 1860 there were 215 Negroes in Terre Haute, 133 in Lafayette.

[31] Jacob P. Dunn, *Greater Indianapolis: The History, the Industries,*

In the counties in the extreme north there were few Negroes before the Civil War. In 1860 there were 63 in Allen County, site of Fort Wayne (although there had been 102 in 1850), 88 in St. Joseph County, site of South Bend, and 135 in La Porte County. In the other northern counties the numbers were so small as to be almost negligible.

During the fifties the total colored population was almost stationary, census records showing a net increase of only 160 persons for the entire decade. An examination of the population of individual counties shows that in some there was a marked decline in the number of Negroes during these years. The principal reason appears to have been the alarm aroused by the Fugitive Slave Act of 1850. After the adoption of this legislation, Negroes who had been living in relative security in the northern states left their homes and pushed on towards Canada. In Indiana increasing hostility on the part of the white population was an added incentive for the exodus, and it likewise probably discouraged others from coming into the state. Although the exclusion article of the 1851 Constitution, which is discussed in the next chapter, was largely unenforceable, its adoption served warning to Negroes that they were not welcome in the state and no doubt deterred some from settling there.[32]

Throughout the state in communities where fugitives were numerous there was a decline in Negro population. Even in the friendly atmosphere of the Quaker communities in Wayne County some runaways felt insecure. Levi Coffin told of the case of Ralph Burrell, a slave who had escaped from Tennessee. Through Coffin's efforts his freeborn wife and children were brought to Newport, where they lived

and the People of a City of Homes (2 vols. Chicago, 1910), 1:239; Indianapolis Indiana Journal, December 11, 1827. The Negro population of Indianapolis by decades was: 122 out of a total of 2,662 in 1840; 405 out of 8,091 in 1850; 498 out of 18,611 in 1860.

32 Siebert, Underground Railroad, 246-50; Fred Landon, "Negro Migration to Canada after 1850," in Journal of Negro History, 5(1920):22-36. The exclusion article in the 1851 Constitution and the operation of the Fugitive Slave Law are dealt with in Chapters 3 and 4.

happily for several years, but after 1850 Burrell became apprehensive and moved on to Canada. But more striking evidence of the effect of the law is found in the counties farther south. In Washington County, alarm growing out of the capture of a slave who had been dwelling as a free woman for years, plus the increasing hostility of the white population, was reflected in a decline in the Negro population from 252 persons in 1850 to 187 in 1860. In Posey Township, where there had been ninety Negroes in 1850, not one remained in 1860. In Jennings County, where there was a large settlement of fugitives near Vernon, the number declined from 323 to 151 in the same period. In Fugit Township in Decatur County, another haven for escaped slaves, the colored population dropped from 175 in 1850 to a mere nine in 1860. In neighboring Franklin County there was a decline of from 209 to 103. Altogether in thirty-four counties, most of them in the southern part of the state, there was a decrease in Negro population during the ten-year period.[33] In *The Voice of the Fugitive,* a newspaper which he published from his sanctuary behind the Canadian border, Henry Bibb mentioned the increased migration after 1850, including the exodus from Indiana. In 1852 he reported: "22 from Indiana passed through to Amherstburg, with four fine covered waggons and eight horses. A few weeks ago six or eight such teams came from the same state into Canada. The Fugitive Slave Law is driving out brains and money."[34]

[33] Levi Coffin, *Reminiscences of Levi Coffin, the Reputed President of the Underground Railroad* . . . (Cincinnati, 1876), 144-47. Other counties which showed marked declines were: Bartholomew from 82 to 7; Jackson from 214 to 179; Knox from 530 to 449; Owen from 156 to 85; Vanderburgh from 227 to 127.

[34] Quoted in Landon, "Negro Migration to Canada after 1850," in *Journal of Negro History,* 5:28.

3
EXCLUSION AND COLONIZATION MOVEMENTS

IN THE DECADES before the Civil War the assertion that the United States, especially the state of Indiana, was a "white man's country" became a well-worn cliché in the mouths of a certain brand of politicians. The Declaration of Independence and the Constitution of the United States, these men insisted, had been framed "by white men, for white men." To support their racial theories they also invoked divine authority. The fact that God had made one group of men of darker hue than others was evidence that He intended the darker group to be inferior to and separate from those of fairer skins. Divine Providence had ordained that Africa should be the continent of the black man and North America of the white. Arguments of this sort were repeated endlessly in support of state laws which limited or prohibited the immigration of Negroes and to justify the colonization movement which sought to remove Negroes from the United States to Africa.

In Indiana proposals both for preventing Negroes from settling in the state and for persuading or compelling those already resident there to go to Liberia found a receptive audience. They resulted first in a law adopted in 1831 which limited the right of settlement and later in an article in the second state Constitution which completely prohibited Negroes from seeking residence in the state. The white population showed considerable interest in the colonization movement, which received a blessing in the Constitution of 1851 and which was given some financial support by the state.

In enacting measures to discourage Negroes from settling within her borders Indiana was following the example of her neighbor states. Ohio laws adopted in 1804 and 1807 and the Black Law of Illinois adopted in 1819 attempted to restrict immigration. Indiana was also influenced by the acts of the slave states on the subject of free Negroes and emancipated slaves. Nearly all of the slave states had laws prohibiting free Negroes from settling within their borders or limiting their right of settlement, while laws requiring that emancipated slaves leave the state or be re-enslaved became more and more common.[1]

As shown in an earlier chapter there had been several unsuccessful attempts to pass laws on the subject of Negro immigration during the territorial period. After Indiana's admission as a state the General Assembly considered some such proposal at almost every session, although no legislation was actually adopted until 1831. Most of the measures merely sought to prevent fugitive slaves from coming into the state by requiring that Negroes show proof of their freedom, but others were more sweeping.[2] In the 1829

[1] Salmon P. Chase (ed.), *Statutes of Ohio and of the Northwest Territory, 1788-1833* (3 vols. Cincinnati, 1833), 1:55-56, 393; *Laws of Illinois, 1819*, pp. 354-55. A Kentucky law adopted in 1808 had as its preamble: "Whereas it is represented to the present assembly, that a very serious evil is likely to be produced by the emigration of emancipated slaves from different parts of the Union to this state, and that many states have passed laws compelling slaves when emancipated by citizens of their respective states to remove out of such within a given time;" therefore it was provided that any free Negro coming into the state was to be arrested and confined in jail until he gave bond to leave the state within twenty days. If unable to give the security, he was to be sold for one year. *Kentucky Digest of 1834*, 2:1220-21. A Virginia law of 1806 provided that if an emancipated slave remained in the state for more than a year, he was to lose his freedom. *Virginia Revised Code, 1819*, 1:436. A Tennessee law of 1831 provided that slaves might be emancipated only on the express condition that they would be removed from the state immediately. *Tennessee Compilation of Laws 1836*, 279.

[2] At the first session in 1816 a bill for "establishing the mode of admitting free persons of color into this state" was taken under consideration. An amendment provided that any Negro who could not prove

session Governor James B. Ray devoted a portion of his message to the General Assembly to the subject. He asserted that the laws of some of the slave states made it mandatory that Indiana take steps to protect itself from an influx of superannuated and indigent Negroes, saying: "Whilst our laws and institutions proclaim the State an asylum for the good, virtuous, and useful of all nations and colors, it is due to ourselves and to the rights of posterity, that we should not tamely submit to any imposition, which is the direct effect of foreign legislation. Though it may savour somewhat of injustice to interfere with any [Negroes] that are already here, it will still become your province as it is your right, to regulate for the future, by prompt correctives, the emigration into the State, and the continuance of *known paupers,* thrown upon us from any quarter. Such, if they cannot afford, by sureties, indemnity to our citizens in a reasonable time, should be thrown back into the State or country from whence they came." A letter from a resident of Posey County which was published about the same time in an Indianapolis newspaper reflected the popular attitude. It warned that the people of Indiana would be "recreant to their best interests and greatest duties to posterity, if they supinely continue to permit the migration of free negroes to the state. The dregs of offscourings of the slave states are most likely to change residence, and they are too incurably affected with that horrible gangrene

his right to freedom should be expelled from the state. Both amendment and bill failed to pass, but at the next session a bill regulating Negro immigration passed the House but was lost in the Senate. In 1820 a House bill requiring Negroes coming into the state to produce a freedom certificate was tabled. Another bill regulating immigration was introduced in 1821, and in 1822 the judiciary committee of the House was instructed to inquire into the expediency of such a law, but none of the proposed measures were adopted. Indiana *House Journal,* 1816-17, pp. 54-55; *ibid.,* 1817-18, p. 38; Indiana *Senate Journal,* 1817-18, pp. 75, 111; Indiana *House Journal,* 1820-21, pp. 125, 207; *ibid.,* 1821-22, p. 81; *ibid.,* 1822-23, p. 127.

of morals which slavery engenders, to be welcomed among
a virtuous and intelligent people."[3]

In 1831 the General Assembly enacted legislation which
embodied Governor Ray's suggestions. As originally passed
by the House the bill declared that any Negro who came
into the state without a certificate of freedom should be
considered a fugitive slave and turned over to the sheriff
to be advertised as a runaway, but this section was later
dropped. As finally adopted the law did not prohibit Negroes
from settling in the state, as some of the more zealous
Negrophobes urged, nor did it require proof of freedom
It required colored persons who came into the state to post
bond of five hundred dollars as a guarantee against becoming
a public charge and as a pledge of good behavior. Conviction of a crime or misdemeanor meant forfeiture of the
bond. If the bond was not paid, the overseers of the poor
could either remove the Negro from the state or hire him
out at the best price that they could get for a period of
six months. Any person who knowingly hired or harbored
a Negro who came into the state without complying with
the law was subject to a fine.[4]

The law satisfied for the time the demands of the portion
of the population most strongly opposed to Negroes, but
it was attacked by Quakers and others as being inhumane
and unconstitutional. In the General Assembly there were
repeated proposals for repeal or modification, usually by
representatives from counties where Quakers were influential. A report of the House Judiciary Committee at the
1834-35 session expressed the opinion that portions of the
law were unconstitutional and branded it as "oppressive"
and "unjust." But the House voted to table the bill which
the committee recommended. Efforts at repeal in later

---

[3] Indiana *House Journal*, 1829-30, pp. 35-36; Indianapolis *Indiana
Journal*, March 3, 1830.

[4] Indiana *House Journal*, 1830-31, pp. 247-48; *Revised Laws of Indiana*,
1831, pp. 375-76.

sessions were also defeated, as was also an attempt made in the 1850-51 session to strengthen it.[5]

Although questions as to the wisdom and justice of the law continued to be raised, doubts as to its constitutionality were set aside by the Indiana Supreme Court, which upheld the law on three different occasions. The first of these cases involved a free Negro, Edward Cooper, who had settled in Vigo County following the adoption of the law and had failed to post the required bond. A justice of the peace ordered him to be hired out for six months, but Cooper appealed to the circuit court on the grounds that the law was unconstitutional. The judge of the circuit court who heard the case was Amory Kinney, the same man who years before had acted as attorney for Polly against Hyacinthe Lasselle in the case which resulted in the final extinction of slavery from Indiana. Kinney was of the opinion that the law of 1831 violated rights that were guaranteed by both the Constitutions of the United States and Indiana and ordered Cooper released. An appeal was then taken to the state Supreme Court on the issue of constitutionality. In the higher court Kinney's ruling was reversed and the law upheld in an opinion which declared: "In questions of this kind, it is our duty to decide in favour of the validity of the statute, unless its unconstitutionality is so obvious as to admit of no doubt. . . . We have examined the statute in question, and are of the opinion that the objection made to it cannot be sustained."[6]

[5] *Minutes of Indiana Yearly Meeting of Friends,* 1831, p. 14; Indiana *House Journal,* 1834-35, pp. 584-85; *ibid.,* 1848-49, pp. 84, 100; *ibid.,* 1849-50, pp. 34, 55, 97, 117-18; *ibid.,* 1850-51, pp. 516, 623. At the 1834-35 session the Senate also rejected a bill to amend the 1831 law. Indiana *Senate Journal,* 1834-35, pp. 448-49.

[6] Transcript of proceedings in case of State *v.* Cooper in Vigo County Circuit Court in Supreme Court Papers, in Archives Division, Indiana State Library, November term, 1839; State *v.* Cooper, 5 Blackford (Ind.) 258-59. The question of the constitutionality of such laws hinged principally upon the interpretation of the clause of the U. S. Constitution (Art. IV, Sec. 2) which declares: "The citizens of each state shall

In another case decided by the Supreme Court a few
weeks later the principal figure was the Madison Negro,
George Baptiste, mentioned in an earlier chapter as an
agent of the Underground Railroad. Baptiste, who had
lived in the state for several years without paying the bond
which the 1831 law required, was taken before a justice
of the peace who ordered him to comply with the requirement. The circuit court at Madison affirmed the ruling and
ordered that a warrant be issued for the removal of Baptiste
from the soil of Indiana "to the state where he last legally
resided." Baptiste, who was probably being prosecuted because of his suspected activities in behalf of runaway slaves,
was saved from expulsion and possible enslavement by the
assistance of Stephen C. Stevens. Stevens, a former member
of the Indiana Supreme Court and one of the most successful lawyers in the state, was almost unique among his
colleagues at this time in being an ardent antislavery man.
The brief which he filed in the Supreme Court in behalf
of Baptiste was a fiery denunciation of the 1831 law and
the proslavery group whom he accused of instigating it. He
pointed out that the laws of several slave states provided
that free Negroes who came into their borders should be
sold into slavery. Hence the effect of the Indiana law might
be to condemn a man who was sent to one of those states
to slavery. Stevens also assailed the law as "contrary to
the Universal principles of Jurisprudence acknowledged by
all Christiandom and contrary to morality and religion"
because it would have the effect of separating Baptiste from
his wife and children since he had married after coming into
the state. He attacked the order expelling Baptiste because
it did not show the state from which the Negro had come
nor specify where he was to be sent. He charged: "I can
tell you where they will carry him. They will carry him
to a distant slave state and sell him for money,—pocket

be entitled to all privileges and immunities of citizens in the several
states." Opponents of the laws argued that free Negroes were citizens
and that the laws violated their constitutional rights.

the money and return and say they have left him where he last came from, and none will ever know the contrary." Therefore he urged: "I then say beware how you enforce such a Statute as this. It deserves no countenance. Its principles originate in the deep and bitter enmities of persons, who are friends of absolute slavery. Persons who cannot bear with any degree of patience, to see a coloured person free. Persons whose hearts would leap for joy, if they could extend slavery into our State. Persons who warmly enter into the interests, desires & sympathies of the slave holder,—but who have no bowels of mercy for the coloured person, be them free or be them slaves."

The Supreme Court was unmoved by the argument that the law was unconstitutional but agreed that the order for Baptiste's expulsion was defective. It held that if a Negro were to be removed from the state, the overseers of the poor must determine his last place of residence and send him there, not merely expel him from Indiana.[7]

Stevens took another case, testing another part of the 1831 law, to the Supreme Court a few years later. In this case a white man, Thomas Hickland, a member of a Jennings County family that was known for its antislavery views, was charged with knowingly hiring a Negro who had come into the state since 1831 and had not posted bond. A jury in Vernon found Hickland guilty of violating the law and fined him. The case was appealed, and Stevens filed a brief with the Supreme Court attacking the constitutionality of the portion of the law involved in this case. Once more the court upheld the validity of the statute and sustained the action of the lower court.[8]

[7] Stevens' brief, signed "Pro the coloured man and the wrongfully oppressed African," in the Supreme Court Papers, November term, 1839, Box 74, No. 322; Baptiste v. the State, 5 Blackford (Ind.) 283-88. In spite of this reprieve Baptiste found the atmosphere of Madison so hostile that he moved to Detroit.

[8] Hickland v. the State, 8 Blackford (Ind.) 365-66. In the forties Stevens emerged as an antislavery leader, running for governor on the Liberty party ticket.

These cases indicate that in some counties there were at least sporadic efforts to enforce the 1831 law, but it appears that generally it was a dead letter. As opponents of the act observed, it was more of a symbol of racial prejudice than anything else. An editorial in a Richmond newspaper in 1842 inveighed against the fact that numbers of Negroes continued to settle in Wayne County in spite of the law and made a plea for its enforcement: "We presume there is not a nigger in this town that has given his bond, and any white man that employs them is daily exposing himself to an indictment and heavy fine. By enforcing this law, we should rid ourselves of a worse than useless population, drive away a gang of pilferers, make an opening for white laborers to fill the places of the blacks, and relieve our town of the odium now resting on it."[9]

An antislavery paper published in the same county denounced the editorial as an appeal to race prejudice and asserted that it had been written merely to "excite the jealousies of the vulgar, to stimulate the unprincipled to insult and abuse the colored people." As for the law of 1831—"We hardly suppose our neighbor is so ignorant as to know that this law cannot be executed, and that all the use that can be made of it is to encourage and foster that wicked policy that shall prepare the rabble to wreak its vengeance upon an inoffensive people, in acts of unrestrained licentiousness."[10]

Further evidence of the futility of the law is the fact that Cambridge City, another Wayne County community,

[9] Richmond *Jeffersonian* reprinted in *Free Labor Advocate* (Newport, Ind.), January 8, 1842.

[10] *Ibid.* Levi Coffin of Newport, Wayne County, whose activities in behalf of colored people were well known, was once summoned before a grand jury which was investigating reports that he had harbored fugitive slaves and had hired Negroes who had not given bond. Coffin admitted that he had probably violated the law, but added that he knew of no one in the county who had attempted to obey the law of 1831, which was a dead letter in that part of the state. Coffin, *Reminiscences,* 193.

passed an ordinance in 1845 requiring colored residents to appear within thirty days to give bond for good behavior and as a guarantee that they would not become public charges.[11] In 1850 in the same community a mass meeting of citizens was called for the purpose of devising the "best means, to rid our city of the very great portion of Negro citizens that now inhabit it." About the same time there appears to have been a concerted effort to compel the Negroes living in Clark County to give bond as security for their good behavior. Some of the Negroes, unable to raise the money, fled from the county. There was alarm in neighboring Floyd County lest they settle there, and the New Albany *Ledger* urged that the example of the Clark County officers be followed: "Would it not be well for our own officers to enforce the same provisions against this class? If not, we shall soon be overrun with all the worthless, idle, and dissolute Negroes in the surrounding counties."[12]

These developments occurred on the eve of the meeting of the convention to revise Indiana's Constitution. They reflected the increase in racial prejudice which led that convention to adopt an article completely excluding Negroes from settling in the state. The growing antipathy to Negroes was due in part to the tension over the slavery question which gripped the country in the years after the Mexican War. Although there were some militant opponents of slavery in Indiana, the opposition was generally milder there

11 A committee of the Cambridge City Anti-Slavery Society protested against the ordinance, asserting that the colored population of the town consisted of only three or four families, "most of whom for moral worth, and habits of temperance and industry, will compare very advantageously with citizens of the more favored complexion," and adding that the framers of the ordinance were motivated simply by prejudice. "Had they erected some standard of morality, or decency to which, all of every complexion should be answerable, it would . . . be less objectionable. But not so. The color of the skin is the offense." *Free Labor Advocate,* April 26, 1845.

12 Centreville *Indiana True Democrat*, September 17, October 4, 1850; New Albany *Daily Ledger,* August 10, 1850.

than in most Northern states. There was a widespread desire to prevent agitation on an issue which threatened to disrupt friendly relations with the states of the South.[13] At the same time there was a fear that any weakening of the slave system might result in an influx of Negroes into Indiana. Although the people of Indiana wished to maintain harmonious relations with the slave states, they also wanted to prevent immigration of Negroes from those states. The fact that Southern states were passing more and more stringent legislation on the subject of free Negroes and emancipated slaves gave an impetus to the demand for stronger measures against Negroes in the Northern states. In 1847 a constitutional convention in Illinois made it mandatory that the state legislature pass a law prohibiting Negroes from coming into the state. It was generally believed that an Ohio convention would adopt a similar article.[14]

Under these circumstances it is not surprising that the question of Negro immigration played a large part in the constitutional convention which assembled in Indianapolis in October, 1850. The following editorial from the *Indiana State Sentinel* is representative of much of the editorial comment on the subject in linking the demand for colonization with the movement for exclusion of Negroes:

[13] An editorial in the Terre Haute *Journal* reflected the popular attitude: "The negro fanaticism which prevails to such an alarming extent in many of the Northern States, has but few devotees in Indiana; and those who are tinctured with the abolition malady are in a great measure prevented from carrying their opinions into practice by the immense preponderance of the public sentiment in favor of sustaining the compromises of the constitution, the laws of the land, and the rights of our southern brethren." Reprinted in Indianapolis *Indiana State Sentinel* (semiweekly), November 21, 1850.

[14] Thorpe (ed.), *Constitutions*, 2:1009. The Ohio convention failed to adopt the Negro exclusion article although the question was debated at length. The action of Kentucky was especially influential in Indiana. The Kentucky Constitution of 1850 and legislation implementing it provided that any free Negro coming into the state or any emancipated slave who did not leave the state would be deemed guilty of a felony and subject to five years in the penitentiary. *Ibid.*, 3:1310; *Revised Statutes of Kentucky 1852*, 647.

"The slave states by common consent will adopt such stringent measures as will rid themselves of this most worthless and degraded population. In this event what is the duty of the free States? Their course is plain. Illinois and California have led the way. The emigration of colored persons is prohibited by organic law. Indiana and Ohio being border States will have to adopt similar measures for their own protection. It may be urged that such provisions are cruel and inhuman, but this is no argument when the absolute necessity of such a law arises. . . . We honestly believe that it will be to the interest of the descendants of those unfortunate beings [Negroes] now among us, to hold out every inducement and grant every facility for their removal to the land of their forefathers. This can never be done so long as a quiet home is given them in the free States. . . .

"A proposition is before the Convention, now in session, to prevent their further emigration into this State, and to prohibit their acquiring or holding real estate in future. This is the sentiment of our people, and we trust that some such measure will be inserted in our Constitution, and we shall be pleased to see a separate vote of the people for this provision. Let those tender-footed negro-loving philanthropists vote against it, and we shall see in what a hopeless minority they will stand."[15]

The strongest expressions of sentiment in favor of exclusion of Negroes came from some of the counties in the southern part of the state. In the convention, delegates from Floyd and Clark counties said that they had canvassed their districts on the issue and found their constituents

[15] Indianapolis *Indiana State Sentinel* (semiweekly), November 28, 1850. An editorial in the same paper a few weeks earlier in commenting on a meeting of Negroes in Ohio in protest over the Fugitive Slave Act of 1850 declared of the resolutions adopted by the Negroes: "They speak in trumpet tones to the orderly, law abiding people of the country. They tell the danger of encouraging a distinct and inferior race to abide in the same community with us. They are aliens and enemies, and some mode should be adopted to rid the country of their presence, or at least of preventing their further emigration." *Ibid.*, November 2, 1850.

almost unanimous in demanding that immigration be stopped. A delegate from Monroe County asserted that nineteen twentieths of the people of his county were opposed to Negro immigration and added: "We cannot be charged with inhumanity in preventing our State from being overrun with these vermin—for I say they are vermin, and I know it." On the other hand petitions were received from Randolph, Grant, and Union counties urging that colored settlers not be barred.[16]

The speeches of the advocates of exclusion ran the gamut of the arguments in defense of white supremacy. One man asserted that the white race must act in the interest of self-preservation: "However much we may pity these men [Negroes], we know that we and they cannot live together in peace. We know that when we are overrun with them—as we most assuredly will be unless we adopt some stringent measures to prevent it—there will be commenced a war which will end only in extermination of one race or the other." Another delegate declared that the races could not live together peaceably because the Negro race was "under the ban of Heaven—a curse that was pronounced upon them by Almighty God. . . . The race was cursed, and it was declared that they should be the servants. That curse has never been removed."

Another speaker, after warning that the continued influx of Negroes would create bitterness and tension, blandly suggested: "I would say—and I say it in all sincerity, and without any hard feelings toward them—that it would be better to kill them off at once, if there is no other way to get rid of them. We have not come to that point yet with the blacks, but we know how the Puritans did with the

[16] *Debates and Proceedings,* 1:445, 446, 451, 557, 989; 2:1608; *Journal of the Convention of the People of the State of Indiana to Amend the Constitution, Assembled at Indianapolis, October, 1850* (Indianapolis, 1851. Reprinted by offset by the Indiana Historical Bureau, 1936), 257, 264, 281, 285, 359, 664.

Indians, who were infinitely more magnanimous and less impudent than this colored race. . . ."[17]

A few delegates bitterly denounced the proposal for exclusion. One declared that the "proposition . . . to prohibit the immigration of any portion of God's rational human beings, born on American soil, and under the protection of the stars and stripes" was "an outrage upon all the principles of our boasted institutions. . . ." Others pointed out that any measure which endangered the basic rights of any group was a potential threat to the liberties of all. A delegate from Henry County declared that if the state had the right to exclude colored citizens of other states it might also exclude Dutchmen, Quakers, Methodists, or any other group.[18]

One of the most powerful speeches against racial discrimination was made by Daniel Crumpacker, delegate from Lake and Porter counties. He pointed to the progress that Negroes had made even while in slavery as evidence of their capacity for improvement and declared, "If we legislate for them as brutes, we shall make brutes of them. If we legislate for them as men, we shall make men of them." He also assailed the inconsistency of boasting that the United States was an asylum for the oppressed of all nations and then, "when these individuals, who have been born in the United States, but who have been so fortunate as to rise above the injustice and oppression which, at first, bound them down to slavery, present themselves at the door of our State, we reject them with scorn; we will have nothing to do with them. Because they are clothed with a dark skin, we will tread them down to earth."[19]

Arguments of this sort were unavailing, and the convention adopted an article barring Negroes from the state by a vote of 93 to 40. The vote did not follow party lines, the op-

[17] *Debates and Proceedings,* 1:446, 451, 574.
[18] *Ibid.,* 1:237, 585.
[19] *Ibid.,* 1:563.

ponents of the article being equally divided between the two parties represented in the convention. Twenty Democrats and twenty Whigs (including one Free Soil Whig) voted against the proposal. The only delegate from the extreme south to vote against the article was William McKee Dunn of Jefferson County. Most of the opponents were delegates from the Quaker counties in the east plus a small group from the counties in the extreme north.[20]

Article XIII, as incorporated into the finished Constitution, provided: "No negro or mulatto shall come into, or settle in the State, after the adoption of this Constitution." Furthermore it provided that all contracts made with a person coming into the state in violation of the article were void, while persons who employed such Negroes or encouraged them to stay in the state were subject to fines ranging up to five hundred dollars. A third section provided that money from such fines should be used to colonize Negroes already in the state. The article was submitted to the voters separately from the rest of the Constitution and was ratified by a larger vote than that given the main body of the document. In only four counties did a majority of the voters cast their ballots against Article XIII. One of these was Randolph, which had a higher ratio of Negro residents than any other county. The others were Elkhart, LaGrange, and Steuben, all of them sparsely populated counties in the far north, where there were almost no Negroes. On the other hand in Clark County the vote in favor of the article was 2,197 to 95; in Floyd County 1,711 to 143; in Knox County 1,461 to 89; in Marion County 2,505 to 308; and in Vigo County 1,974 to 107.[21]

At the first session of the General Assembly after the adoption of the new Constitution legislation was passed to

[20] *Debates and Proceedings,* 2:1817; Kettleborough, *Constitution Making,* 1:221-22: Appendix XV, 639-42. The convention was predominantly Democratic, with a total of 95 members of that party and 55 Whigs.

[21] Kettleborough, *Constitution Making,* 2:Appendix VII, 617-18; Thorpe (ed.), *Constitutions,* 2:1089-90.

enforce Article XIII. Under it Negroes were prohibited from coming into the state in the future, while those who were residents before November, 1851, were required to register with the county clerk. Those who produced witnesses to prove their right to reside in the state and who convinced the clerk that their residence was legal were to receive certificates attesting to the fact. Contracts made with Negroes who came into the state thereafter were declared void. Persons who employed Negroes in violation of the act were subject to fines of as much as five hundred dollars, while Negroes who violated the act were subject to the same penalties.[22]

Although the provisions of Article XIII and the above law appear to have met with the approbation of most of the white residents, a minority continued to denounce them and to urge their repeal. An antislavery meeting in Jefferson County adopted resolutions which declared that the article was "contrary to the Constitution of the United States, in palpable violation of the laws of God," and added: "We will suffer the penalties of an unrighteous law sooner than violate the law of a righteous God, and we will not cease our opposition until its repeal." In 1855 there was a move in the House of Representatives to introduce a constitutional amendment striking out Article XIII, but it was decisively defeated. In 1857 and 1859 there were efforts to strike out parts of the law of 1852 which imposed penalties on Negroes coming into the state, but they failed to pass.[23]

In spite of the overwhelming endorsement given to Article XIII by the voters the legislation implementing it was not systematically enforced. Like the law of 1831 it was significant primarily as an expression of racial prejudice, and

[22] *Revised Laws of Indiana,* 1852, vol. 1:376; Indiana *House Journal,* 1851-52, pp. 240, 267, 636, 1246, 1252, 1499, 1504, 1576, 1980, 2287.

[23] Indianapolis *Indiana Daily State Sentinel,* May 17, 1852; Kettleborough *Constitution Making,* 1:cxxxiii; Indiana *House Journal,* 1855, p. 785; *ibid.,* 1859, p. 198; Indiana *Senate Journal,* 1857, pp. 290, 352.

as such it probably deterred Negroes from coming into the state. The provisions of the law requiring Negro residents to register appear to have been largely ignored. Although registers were begun in most counties, the names of only a very small fraction of the Negro residents were recorded in them. Even in Clark County, where demand for an exclusion law had been loudest before the constitutional convention, only 74 Negroes were registered in the period from July, 1853, to October, 1864, although the census of 1850 showed a total of 582 in the county. In Marion County, which had one of the largest Negro populations in the state, only 25 names were recorded in the same period. In Randolph County, where Article XIII was unpopular with a majority of the people, only 12 Negroes were ever registered.[24]

Thousands of Negroes continued to live in the state without complying with the registration requirements, and only occasionally was an effort made to prosecute a person who had come into the state in violation of the law. From the records which have been found it appears that prosecutions were likely to be attempts to settle personal grudges. An example was a case which arose in Fort Wayne in 1860. A complaint was lodged against a Negro named Logan who had been an occasional resident of the city for a year or more. He was brought before the mayor and fined ten dollars for coming into the state in violation of the law. The newspaper account admitted that the affidavit against

[24] The original register for Clark County, now in the Archives Division of the Indiana State Library, contains columns for the name of the registrant, age, physical description, place of birth, residence, and names of witnesses. In the column headed "physical description" are such details as "no white blood," "teeth defective," and "slightly marked by smallpox." The register for Marion County was found in the courthouse in 1887 and its contents described in an article in the Indianapolis *Journal*, May 22, 1887. See also Tucker, *Randolph County*, 198. When a survey of county archives was undertaken in the 1930's under the Works Progress Administration, Negro registers were found in many of the courthouses of the state.

him was "undoubtedly made from personal malice." Occasionally a white resident was prosecuted for giving employment to a Negro who had come into the state contrary to the law. In Jefferson County a man named Curzy was charged with employing a Negro and furnishing him a home, although he had entered the state after the adoption of Article XIII. The lower court dismissed the case, but on an appeal to the Supreme Court the ruling was reversed.[25]

A defect of the law, from the standpoint of those who hoped that it would help rid the state of Negroes, was the fact that it made no provision for removing a person who settled in the state illegally. This was illustrated in the case of Mason Hatwood, a mulatto who had come to Daviess County about 1856 and who was tried and convicted for violating the exclusion law but continued to live in the county. In 1861 he was prosecuted again for the same offense. At his trial it was argued that he could not legally be tried twice for the same offense. His case was appealed to the Indiana Supreme Court on the grounds that the second trial was in violation of the constitutional guarantee against being put twice in jeopardy for the same offense. The Supreme Court found it unnecessary to go into the question of double jeopardy in rendering its decision but found that the action against Hatwood was barred by the statute of limitations since he had come into the state six years before the second prosecution. The court held that the exclusion law was constitutional but remarked: "It seems to be defective in failing to provide for the removal of them [Negroes violating the act] upon conviction; and, also, in making the offense a continuing one, so that they may be punished for continuing their settlement in the State after having been convicted of making it."[26]

The law, although seldom invoked, violated basic prin-

25 Fort Wayne *Times* quoted in Indianapolis *Daily Sentinel,* August 22, 1860; State *v.* Curzy, 19 Ind. 430 (1862).
26 Hatwood *v.* the State, 18 Ind. 492-93 (1862).

ciples of humanity. In 1851 a committee of Anti-Slavery
Friends pointed out that under it the colored people of the
state would be "liable to heavy fines if they but afford the
duties of common hospitality to their fathers, mothers,
brothers and sisters, or sons and daughters who might come
to visit them from other states."[27] The provisions of the
law regarding contracts, if literally applied, even had the
effect of penalizing a resident of Indiana who married the
resident of another state. The law was actually so applied
in the case of Arthur Barkshire, a Negro who had lived
in the town of Rising Sun near the Ohio border for several
years prior to the adoption of the exclusion law. In 1854
he went to Ohio and brought back Elizabeth Keith. They
were then married in a ceremony performed on Indiana soil.
After the wedding Barkshire was charged with bringing a
Negro into the state and harboring her in violation of the
law and was fined $10. When the case was appealed to the
Supreme Court the conviction was upheld. The court declared that Barkshire could claim no exemption from the
operation of the law from "the supposed relation of husband
and wife" and could be regarded "only as any other person
who had encouraged the Negro woman Elizabeth to remain
in the state." It was added that Elizabeth was also liable
to prosecution under the law. The court declared: "The
policy of the state . . . is clearly involved. It is to exclude
any further ingress of negroes, and to remove those among
us as speedily as possible. The 13th article of the Constitution . . . was . . . submitted to a vote of the people. . . .
It is a matter of history how emphatically it was approved
by the popular voice. . . .

"Marriage . . . is but a civil contract. . . . it is clearly
embraced in the constitutional provision, . . . which declares all contracts made with negroes and mulattoes coming
. . . contrary to the provisions of the 13th article, void. . . .

[27] Minutes of Anti-Slavery Friends (MS, Earlham College Library),
289.

A constitutional policy . . . so clearly conducive to the separation and ultimate good of both races should be rigidly enforced."[28]

The measures to prevent the migration of Negroes to Indiana constituted only one part of the efforts to preserve the soil of Indiana for white men. As the Indiana Supreme Court had observed in the Barkshire case it was also the policy of the state to remove those Negroes already resident in the state. The latter part of the policy involved the "colonization" movement, which took the form of persuading and assisting free Negroes to leave the United States and settle in the Negro republic of Liberia on the west coast of Africa.

The colonization idea had strong and lasting appeal not only in Indiana but throughout many parts of the United States. The American Colonization Society was formed in 1817 with the active support of many distinguished men of the day, including Bushrod Washington, Henry Clay, John Randolph, and Francis Scott Key. The constitution of the society declared that its sole object was "to promote and execute a plan for colonizing (with their consent) the Free People of Colour residing in our country, in Africa, or such other place as Congress shall deem most expedient. And the society shall act to effect this object, in cooperation with the General Government, and such of the States as may adopt regulations upon the subject."[29]

A memorial presented to Congress throws more light on the objects of the society. It called attention to the fact that some of the slaveholding states had enacted laws restricting emancipation out of fear of the growth of a free Negro population. The memorial pictured free Negroes as constituting a separate class, dangerous to the peace and

28 Barkshire v. the State, 7 Ind. 389-91 (1856).

29 Quoted in Early Lee Fox, *The American Colonization Society 1817-1840* (Johns Hopkins University *Studies in Historical and Political Science,* Series 37, No. 3), 47.

safety of the country. Colonization was urged as a means of removing this class of people from the United States and also as a means of elevating their condition, since it was argued that Negroes could never attain the full development of their capacities in the United States. Furthermore, colonization was presented as an instrument for missionary activity and for spreading civilization to Africa.[30]

Although the hoped-for financial aid from Congress was not forthcoming, funds were raised from various other sources, including receipts from auxiliary societies, bequests, appropriations from state legislatures, and gifts from church groups. Title to a strip of land on the west coast of Africa was acquired by the society. This was the origin of the republic of Liberia, to which a few thousand free Negroes and emancipated slaves were sent from the United States.[31]

At first the colonization movement received support in nearly all parts of the country, North and South, among men who hoped for the ultimate extinction of slavery. Its aims and efforts were endorsed by most Protestant churches, and resolutions of numerous state legislatures put their stamp of approval on the movement.[32] In the 1830's there was a split between the "immediate" abolitionists and the colonizationists. Such men as James G. Birney and Gerrit Smith, who had been colonizationists, broke away and denounced colonization as a scheme to strengthen the hold of slavery by removing all free Negroes. Colonization was also condemned as being founded on racial prejudice and as a means of strengthening prejudice. The immediatists among the antislavery men took the position that free Negroes and emancipated slaves must remain and be permitted to develop their capacities in the United States, the land of their birth.

Colonization appealed strongly to the people of Indiana,

[30] Fox, *American Colonization Society,* 51-52.

[31] Fox says that by 1867 the number of emancipated slaves actually sent to Liberia was six thousand. *Ibid.,* 211.

[32] *Ibid.,* 78-79.

not only as a possible means for bringing about the extinction of slavery, but even more as a means of ridding Indiana of its Negro population. A report drawn up by a committee of the first session of the state legislature expressed the hope that Congress would undertake a scheme to promote the colonization of the free black population of the United States as a measure conducive to the happiness of both the white and black races. In 1825 the General Assembly concurred in a joint resolution proposed by the Ohio legislature which asked Congress for aid in promoting emancipation and foreign colonization. In 1829 another resolution was passed in favor of Federal aid to the American Colonization Society.[33]

In November, 1829, the Indiana Colonization Society was organized in Indianapolis as an auxiliary to the American Colonization Society. That interest in colonization was related to the desire to prevent Negroes from migrating to Indiana was shown in the statement of purpose of the society, which mentioned the laws of the slave states requiring the removal of emancipated slaves and declared: "The existence of these laws, and the increasing desire to be rid of the evil of slavery, is continually pouring upon the free states a flood of suspected and unwelcome population." Colonization was declared to be the solution of this problem, and it was added optimistically that there would be far greater inducement to colored people to go from the United States to Africa than there had been for Europeans to come to America. All that would be necessary to effect the exodus of the black population would be to supply the means of transportation.[34]

At the second annual meeting of the society it was reported that auxiliary societies had been formed at Richmond, Connersville, Brookville, Aurora, and Madison. Resolutions were adopted at this meeting condemning slavery as a

[33] Indiana *House Journal*, 1816-17, p. 43; *Laws of Indiana,* 1825, pp. 105-6; *ibid.,* 1828-29, pp. 153-54.

[34] Indianapolis *Indiana Journal,* November 12, 1829.

"national evil," which was "incompatible with the genius of our republican institutions." The yearly report of the society stated: "Our black population adds nothing to the strength, and little to the wealth of the nation. Let them be removed and their places supplied with intelligent free-men, and we venture to say that a saving equal to the cost of their removal would be gained in the expense of courts of justice and poor houses." The same general theme was repeated in an address at the third meeting. The object of the society was declared to be "the removal of a class of people, who though they may arise to honour and usefulness in their native country, as long as they exist *here*, must be dangerous to some, suspected by others, injurious to all, and pernicious to themselves." Another note was added, which was to be played upon constantly in later years, that the free colored population caused poor white men to suffer by competing with them for employment.[35]

The colonization societies received the support of various church groups, but as militant antislavery doctrines gained strength in the 1830's members of some denominations stopped their contributions because they felt that the evils of slavery could be remedied only by immediate emancipa-tion and elevating the condition of Negroes within the United States. For example, an antislavery society organ-ized at Hanover College, a Presbyterian school, in 1836, while not denouncing colonization by name, included in its constitution an article upholding the right of slaves to be free and to enjoy their freedom in America.[36]

[35] Terre Haute *Western Register,* February 5, 1831; *Indiana Journal,* January 5, 1833.

[36] *Preamble and Constitution of the Anti-Slavery Society of Hanover College and Indiana Theological Seminary* (Hanover, Ind., 1836). The treasurer's report of the Indiana Colonization Society showed contribu-tions from Methodist and Presbyterian churches. It was customary in some churches to take up a collection for colonization on the Sunday nearest to the Fourth of July. Indianapolis *Indiana Journal,* January 12, June 22, 1833; Methodist Episcopal Church, *Minutes . . . of the South-Eastern Conference,* 1852 (Cincinnati, 1852), 37; Methodist Episcopal

The colonization question contributed to creating a schism in the Indiana Yearly Meeting of Friends which grew out of differences of opinion as to how best to deal with the slavery problem. At first the more militant opponents of slavery appeared to be in the ascendancy, and in 1836 an epistle from the committee on the concerns of the people of color urged Friends to take no part in associations on the subject of slavery which had "a tendency to promote the unrighteous work of expatriation." In 1838 the committee cautioned members against "too much countenancing the policy of the day, which denies to that class of our fellow-beings [colored people] the capacity of enjoying the natural rights of man, only on terms of expatriation, or some tedious plan of preparation." The report of the committee in 1839 expressed succinctly the conviction shared by militant antislavery men everywhere that colonization doctrines strengthened race prejudice. It expressed disapproval of a policy "by which it is proposed to remove the colored population from our country; thereby contributing to the support of that unchristian prejudice which denies to the colored man privileges that we claim for ourselves; professing much opposition to slavery, and at the same time attaching burdensome conditions to their plan of emancipation."[37]

In spite of the adoption of these resolutions Indiana Friends became increasingly divided over the question of whether members should be active in antislavery societies outside the Society of Friends. In 1841 in an effort to quiet the turmoil, the Yearly Meeting closed meetinghouses to antislavery lectures. In spite of this action the more extreme antislavery Quakers, who were most numerous in the vicinity of Newport in Wayne County, continued their activity in antislavery societies. In 1842 an open break occurred when

Church, *Minutes of the Indiana Annual Conference,* 1862-63 (Cincinnati, 1863), 15.

[37] *Minutes of the Indiana Yearly Meeting of Friends,* 1836, p. 16; 1838, p. 19; 1839, p. 24.

the conservatives, who controlled the Indiana Yearly Meeting, "disqualified for usefulness" on important committees eight of the leading antislavery Quakers. The radicals responded by organizing the Indiana Yearly Meeting of Anti-Slavery Friends, a group to which perhaps two thousand members out of the twenty-five thousand Friends in Indiana adhered. The members of the schismatic group continued to oppose colonization vigorously.[38]

An even more formidable obstacle to the success of the colonization movement than the opposition of the abolitionists was the lack of enthusiasm displayed by the colored population. From the beginning Negroes were suspicious of the motives of the colonizationists and ready to resist efforts to expatriate them. Only a few weeks after the organization of the American Colonization Society resolutions against African colonization were adopted by a meeting of free colored residents of Richmond, Virginia. They declared: "We prefer being colonized in the most remote corner of the land of our nativity, to being exiled to a foreign country."[39]

Efforts to persuade them to leave the land of their birth stimulated a feeling of national consciousness and played an important part in uniting Negroes in all parts of the North. Opposition to colonization was a powerful reason for the development of the Negro convention movement. At the first National Negro Convention, which met in Philadelphia in September, 1830, an "Address to the Free People of Color of these United States," was issued which said in part: "We who have been born and nurtured on this soil, we,

[38] A brief account of the schism is given in Thomas E. Drake, *Quakers and Slavery in America* (New Haven, 1950), 162-65. Walter Edgerton, *A History of the Separation in Indiana Yearly Meeting of Friends . . .* (Cincinnati, 1856), is a detailed account written by one of the leading members of the Anti-Slavery Friends.

[39] Quoted in Bella Gross, *Clarion Call: History and Development of the Negro People's Convention Movement in the United States from 1817 to 1840* (New York, 1947), 5.

whose habits, manners and customs are the same in common with other Americans, can never consent to take our lives in our hands, and be the bearers of the redress offered by that Colonization Society to that much afflicted country. . . .

"Tell it not to the barbarians, lest they refuse to be civilized and eject our christian missionaries from among them, that in the nineteenth century of the christian era, laws have been enacted in some of the states of this great republic, to compel an unprotected and harmless portion of our brethren, to leave their homes and seek an asylum in foreign climes."[40]

Efforts to persuade Indiana Negroes to go to Africa generally encountered the same spirit of resistance, although a small group were favorably impressed by the arguments of the colonizationists. E. S. Abdy, an English traveler who visited the Negro settlers near Madison in the early thirties, spoke of their reactions to efforts of their white neighbors to persuade them to go to Liberia. The Negroes resented the attempts especially since they were made in the guise of appeals to religion. "These importunate solicitations, too, were doubly galling, as they came chiefly from the teachers of a Sunday school, which had been established by some whites, who thus took advantage of the opportunities they had, while instructing the children, to urge upon the parents the necessity of emigrating to the promised land." The parents, according to Abdy, were unmoved by the appeals and regarded colonization merely as a scheme with "nothing to recommend it but the hope that it held out [to the whites] of lessening their [the Negroes'] numbers, and perpetuating their degradation."[41]

Opposition to colonization was the principal factor in the movement for the calling of the first state convention of Indiana Negroes of which any record has been found. During the winter of 1841-42 a meeting in Madison adopted res-

40 Quoted in *ibid.*, 11.
41 Abdy, *Journal of a Residence,* 2:365-66.

olutions to the effect that: "No well informed colonizationist is a devoted friend to the moral elevation of the people of color." At the same time the group called upon Negroes in other parts of the state to hold meetings. In January at a meeting in the African M. E. church in Indianapolis the question of a state convention was discussed and resolutions were adopted endorsing the Madison resolution. A committee was appointed to correspond with colored people throughout the state in preparation for a convention in Terre Haute. After these preliminaries a convention of some sort appears to have been held in Terre Haute although no record of it appeared in the newspapers. The delegates expressed opposition to African colonization but showed an interest in the possibility of migrating to the Oregon country.[42]

Meanwhile, the Indiana Colonization Society had languished and become inactive in 1838, but it was revived in 1845. At that time the Reverend B. T. Kavanaugh was appointed as an agent of the American Colonization Society for Indiana and Wisconsin.[43] In an effort to overcome the prejudice of the Negroes against Africa the society voted to send a colored man in whom the colored people of the state would have confidence to Liberia as an agent to investigate and report upon conditions there. William B. Revels, an itinerant preacher of the African M. E. church, who was recommended by a white Methodist minister of Terre Haute, was selected for the assignment. Meetings of colored people

<hr />

[42] Indianapolis *Indiana State Sentinel,* March 1, 1842; *Free Labor Advocate* (Newport, Ind.), December 21, 1842. The movement for a convention appears to have been inspired in part by an appeal of Philadelphia Friends for a national convention of colored people in Philadelphia, but the author has found no evidence that any Indiana Negroes attended such a national convention.

[43] *The African Repository and Colonial Journal* (Washington, D. C.), 22 (1846) :176. Concerning the revival of the society, an antislavery newspaper remarked: "Seventeen citizens of the city of Indianapolis have agreed to exhume the society for manufacturing *prejudice against color."* *Indiana Freeman* quoted in *Indiana State Sentinel* (semiweekly), April 2, 1846. By 1846 there were auxiliary societies in fifteen counties as well as in several towns.

at Terre Haute and Lafayette were reported to have endorsed the plan, and other meetings throughout the state were planned to arouse interest. However, Revels suddenly resigned after he was bombarded with letters protesting his proposed trip and his association with the colonization movement. The letters were said to hold out the threat that he could never again hope to be received as a regular minister of the African M. E. church if he accepted the post. He refused to go ahead with the proposed visit, and the colonizationists were left in an embarrassing position.[44]

In spite of the unco-operative spirit manifested by the Negroes, or perhaps because of it, Indiana politicians gave increasing support to the colonization movement. A joint resolution adopted by the General Assembly in February, 1848, praised the efforts of the American Colonization Society and declared that, "while we should rejoice in the universal emancipation of the slave, we can never consent that Indiana shall be made the receptacle of manumitted negroes of other states, as their color and character would forbid political and social equality, and their migration here could but be injurious to us and detrimental to them." The following session passed a similar resolution and called for the recognition of the independence and sovereignty of Liberia "to make it as attractive as possible."[45] A House committee report of the 1849 session predicted that internecine warfare would result if the white and colored races were not separated through colonization.[46]

[44] Indianapolis *Indiana State Sentinel* (weekly), April 30, 1846. It is possible that "William" Revels mentioned in the newspaper account was the Willis Revels who later served as pastor of the Bethel Church in Indianapolis during the Civil War.

[45] *Laws of Indiana*, 1847-48, pp. 111-12; *ibid.*, 1848-49, p. 156.

[46] Indiana *House Journal*, 1849-50, pp. 598-602. At this session a memorial was presented from the Covington Colonization Society asking financial assistance for certain colored persons who wished to go to Liberia but were prevented from going because of lack of funds. The select committee to which the memorial was referred expressed sympathy for the plight of the Negroes but it did not recommend an appropriation in view of the "embarrassed condition" of the treasury. *Ibid.*, 599.

In his message to the General Assembly in 1850 Governor
Joseph A. Wright asked that state funds be appropriated
for putting a colonization agent in the field and for establishing Indiana's own settlement in Liberia. He called attention to the fact that "our southern brethren are making rapid
movements toward abridging the privileges of this class
[free Negroes] even to banishment," while the Northern
states "are adopting extraordinary means for removing
them, by prohibiting them from holding property, excluding
them from the protection of the laws, and denying them any
rights whatever." The answer to this deplorable situation
he insisted was colonization in Liberia, and he called upon
Indiana to take her stand in "this great struggle for the
separation of the black man from the white."[47]

In the constitutional convention of 1850-51 the two ideas
of exclusion and colonization were inseparably linked.
Speakers who urged measures to prevent the migration of
Negroes nearly always coupled them with proposals for
removing the colored residents of the state to Liberia. The
more extreme members of the convention sought to make
conditions so unattractive for those Negroes already residing
in Indiana that they would have no alternative but to leave
the country. At the same time these gentlemen invariably
expressed an abhorrence of slavery and professed an interest
in the welfare of the colored race. The following remarks
of one delegate are typical and revealing: "The negro race
and the white race cannot live together; and it behooves us,
under these circumstances, not only to furnish no encouragement to the colored race to enter our borders, but effectually
to protect ourselves against their entrance. Nay, more; we
must not afford encouragement to those who are already
here to remain here. We have a colony on the coast of
Africa of his own race, but there the negro will not go if
he can help it. No, no; he wishes to be fed and fostered here,
with the hope of being put upon an equality with the white

47 Indiana *House Journal,* 1850-51, p. 39.

man. So long as he has friends among the whites, so long as he may hold property and transmit it, so long as he can find friends in the State, you can never induce him to leave the country and go to Africa, although I believe the scheme of African colonization is one of the most benevolent that ever was attempted."[48]

Another delegate declared that the best thing that could be done for the Negroes of Indiana was to send them to Liberia. He added: "And to have the proper effect upon the colored population, they should be told from this chamber, by the voices of people assembled, in the persons of their delegates, that they must emigrate to Liberia, and that they need hope for no extension of political privileges, and no amelioration of their present condition in Indiana. But, sir, so long as delusive hopes are cherished of their being favored, so long as efforts are made by a certain class in their behalf, so long will the negroes look upon this as their home, and clamor for protection and political privileges."[49]

One of the means used to persuade the Negroes that the only prospect of bettering their condition lay in going to Africa was a proposal to prevent them from acquiring property in Indiana. A delegate from Washington County, speaking in favor of this inducement to colonization, declared that Africa was the land of the Negro and that he should return there. "I shall favor that proposition which tends to increase their disabilities, with the confident hope that the results will be most advantageous to themselves. When they discover that they can never be elevated to the rank of citizens amongst us, then, and not until then, will they feel that their own welfare, as well as the redemption of their race, are involved in accepting the proffered bounty of their friends."[50]

Expressions of this sort of "humanitarian" interest in the black race finally moved a delegate to exclaim: "Sir,

48 *Debates and Proceedings*, 1 :448-49.
49 *Ibid.*, 1 :248-49.
50 *Ibid.*, 1 :604.

with your permission and the permission of the Christian world generally, I unhesitatingly say, d—n such humanity. If such sentiments and conduct constitute him a man of humanity, I would ask what would constitute him a barbarian? . . . I do object to the use of the word humanity, in connection with sentiments and conduct that would make a decent devil blush."[51]

A more moderate point of view was represented by Robert Dale Owen, who expressed the opinion that in view of the popular prejudice against Negroes the only solution of the problem lay in separation of the races through colonization. "To those whom we are not willing to treat here as men ought to be treated, let us afford the chance of seeking a free home elsewhere." He proposed using the revenue from the swamp lands of Indiana for a colonization fund.[52]

This latter proposal met with no support, and in the end the convention also rejected the proposal to deny the right of acquiring property. However, a section was incorporated into Article XIII which provided that all fines collected for any violation of the article or the violation of any exclusion law which might be passed should be set aside for the colonization of Negroes already resident in Indiana.[53]

In his first message to the legislature after the adoption of the new Constitution Governor Wright called attention to the fact that Article XIII had been adopted with near unanimity and urged legislation to carry it into effect.

51 *Debates and Proceedings*, 2:1932-33.

52 *Ibid.*, 2:1792-93, 1817.

53 *Ibid.*, 2:1819. The idea of denying Negroes the right to acquire and hold property was not killed in the convention. In 1853 a representative from Vigo County introduced in the General Assembly "A bill to encourage a spirit of colonization by preventing negroes and mulattoes from acquiring real estate." The committee to which the bill was referred reported an additional section which would have made it a misdemeanor for a white person to give, sell, or convey real estate to a Negro. At this point one representative proposed another amendment offering a bounty for the taking of Negro scalps. None of the proposals were adopted. Indiana *House Journal*, 1853, pp. 272, 386-87.

Again he called for state aid for colonization "to restore the black man to the land of his fathers, benefit his condition, and remove from us this great source of evil."[54] At this session legislation was passed creating a state fund for colonizing Negroes who had been resident of the state before the adoption of the new Constitution. The fund was to consist of five thousand dollars appropriated by the state for the year 1852 plus any fines collected for violation of Article XIII and voluntary contributions. Three thousand dollars were to be used to buy land in Africa for an Indiana colony. This was to be allotted in grants of one hundred acres to Negroes who would emigrate. In addition the State Board of Colonization was authorized to grant fifty dollars to each Negro emigrant.[55]

In spite of prolonged correspondence and negotiations land for a separate Indiana colony was not acquired, but in 1853 the General Assembly authorized a paid agent to promote colonization under the State Board of Colonization. James Mitchell, a Negro Methodist minister, who had been acting as agent for the Indiana Colonization Society, urged that the position should be filled "by a man of color devoted to the separation of the races." He asserted that this step would do more than anything else to help the cause of colonization among Indiana Negroes. By carrying forward a state-supported program of colonization he assured the legislators Indiana would become a bright example to her sister states. "Humanity, as well as the reputation of your State, demand benevolent measures in regard to your colored inhabitants; and undoubtedly Indiana will be infinitely the gainer by such, for with her well digested *separation policy* firmly based on the rights of races, . . . she will present alike a brazen and unbroken front on her northeast border, to that crude and thoughtless benevolence which would Africanise a continent, given by Providence to the white

54 *Ibid.*, 1851-52, p. 23.
55 *Revised Laws of Indiana*, 1852, vol. 1 :222-23.

races, and the equally unjust aggressions of the South whereby she would throw off, and force upon a homogeneous, peaceful and democratic people, an incompatible and servile race, to disturb the republican institutions of your commonwealth."[56]

John McKay, another colored minister, was appointed as agent of the State Board of Colonization, while Mitchell was employed as secretary. It was planned that McKay should travel to Liberia to negotiate for the purchase of land and that on his return he should travel over the state promoting interest in colonization among the colored population. McKay made the trip to Africa, Mitchell continued to file optimistic reports, the legislature continued to appropriate money to aid colonization, but few Negroes were transported to Africa.

At the 1855 session of the legislature, a select committee headed by Thomas Stanton of Wayne County presented an indictment of the colonization scheme, declaring that it "originated in the basest motives and from the most mercenary considerations. It is one of the offspring of slavery . . . intended to remove the free blacks from the country in order to increase the value and security . . . of slaves." The committee recommended that "instead of making large appropriations for their expatriation, such sum be appropriated for the education and elevation of this class in our midst; and thus make virtuous and intelligent citizens out of those whom our policy has hitherto kept in ignorance and degradation." But the views expressed were those of a hopeless minority. The report was tabled without a roll call, and instead of following its recommendations the legislature authorized an increase in the amount of money which the state was giving to assist emigration.[57]

[56] Indiana *House Journal,* 1853, pp. 566-67; *Laws of Indiana,* 1853, p. 23. For a resumé of the negotiations with Liberia, see *House Journal,* 1857, pp. 485-96.

[57] Indiana *House Journal,* 1855, pp. 885-89; *Laws of Indiana,* 1855, p. 88.

But although James Mitchell reported that, "Africa, as the home of the free colored man, where he may move in the true dignity of his nature, is becoming increasingly inviting," none of the inducements which were held out persuaded Negroes to leave. Except for the salary of the secretary most of the money appropriated by the legislature went unspent because Negroes showed a stubborn attachment to the land of their birth. Even increasing evidences of racial intolerance in Indiana during the fifties did not make Africa any more attractive.

Various efforts were made to counteract the antipathy to expatriation. One method was to publish letters from colored men urging members of their race to emigrate. For example, the report of the Indiana Colonization Society contained a letter from William Findlay of Covington explaining the reasons for his desire to go to Liberia. Since he could not find freedom in the United States, he intended to seek it in Liberia and urged others to go with him "to that land of liberty, where we may likewise aid in the elevation of our whole race." He expressed the opinion that Providence would ultimately bring about the extinction of slavery in the United States but doubted whether it was the will of Providence that the colored race should enjoy social equality with the white race.[58] After his emigration Findlay wrote to James Mitchell that he had become "a true Liberian in feeling." He urged other Negroes to come to Africa, asserting that more emigrants were needed in order that the Negroes from America might be able to protect themselves against the native tribes, who apparently did not welcome the newcomers.[59]

Another emigrant, S. B. Webster, who had been a barber in Lafayette, wrote an enthusiastic account of Liberia, which was published in Indiana newspapers. In describing the

[58] *Report of Rev. John McKay, Colored Agent of the State Board of Colonization. On Liberia* (Indianapolis, 1854), 36-38.

[59] Indianapolis *Indiana Daily State Sentinel,* August 9, 1852.

beauties of the valley of the St. Paul River he declared, "There are no parts of the Wabash, from its mouth to its head that can in any way compare with it in beauty and fertility. I positively saw with my own eyes, large fields of sugar cane and drank the syrup made of it; and as fine specimens of coffee as the world produces. I also saw rice, cotton, cassada, yams, chickens in abundance, cats, dogs, &c. as fine, if not finer hogs, than you see running around the streets of Lafayette, and plenty of them." In describing Monrovia, the capital, he said that the houses were much better than those occupied by colored people in the United States. Of the other Negroes who had gone from Indiana to Liberia, he asserted: "They all say that they have no desire to return to America."[60]

Despite accounts such as this, few Indiana Negroes chose to leave. Three from the northern part of the state apparently went to Liberia in 1849, sailing from New York. The aforementioned Findlay and his party probably went the same year by way of New Orleans. In 1852 James Mitchell reported that he had letters of application which showed that at least seventy-five people in Indiana wished to go to Liberia, but there is no evidence that any such number actually went. The largest group appears to have gone in 1853 with John McKay. He sailed from Baltimore in November, 1853, with a party of twenty-five. A total of thirty-three persons went from Indiana that year. Mitchell reported that a much larger number had sent in applications but that "owing to the labored efforts of those unfriendly to Liberian emigration, many were hindered" from going.[61]

[60] Lafayette *Journal* reprinted in Indianapolis *Daily State Sentinel,* April 2, 1853.

[61] Indianapolis *Indiana State Journal,* December 24, 1849; *Answer of the Agent of the Indiana Colonization Society to the Resolution of Inquiry on the Subject of African Colonization. . .* (Indianapolis, 1852), 15; *Report of the Secretary of the State Board of Colonization of the State of Indiana to the Governor for 1853* (Indianapolis, 1853), 9. The state of Indiana appears to have paid $3,000 to the American Colonization Society for the purpose of transporting Negroes to Liberia. Most of the Negroes

In 1854 fourteen persons embarked for Africa—a family from Putnam County and one from the town of Montezuma.[62]

Although state aid to emigrants was increased in 1855, not a single Negro from Indiana went to Liberia that year. Over fifty had been prevailed upon to agree to emigrate, but in the words of the secretary of the Colonization Board: "Owing to unexpected adverse influences which the board could not foresee, counteract, nor control, when the time for departure for the port of embarkation came, the acting Agent suddenly resigned, and the emigrants refused to go, except one family, and they were in such a condition of destitution and sickness that it was deemed inadvisable to send them at that time."[63] After this fiasco not a single application for transportation was received, and colonization efforts were at a standstill.[64]

As a means of reducing the Negro population of Indiana, colonization was a total failure, but politicians continued to profess devotion to the movement. Even after the outbreak of the Civil War some leaders continued to insist that the solution of the race problem lay in removing Negroes from the soil of the United States. Former Governor Wright, now a member of the United States Senate, was a typical

who went contributed nothing to the cost of their own transportation. State grants were sometimes supplemented by private donations. *Ibid.*, 14-15.

[62] *African Repository*, 3(1854) :381.

[63] Indiana *House Journal*, 1857, p. 125; *Report of the Secretary of the State Board of Colonization to the General Assembly* (Indianapolis, 1857), [333].

[64] The report of the secretary of the State Colonization Board to the legislature in 1859 showed that to the end of 1858, out of a total appropriation of $15,000, only $6,499 had been spent, of which $3,025 had been for the salary of the secretary. Although not a single application from Negroes desiring to emigrate was received after 1856, the legislation on colonization remained on the statute books until 1865. Apparently the secretary continued to draw a salary throughout the entire period. In 1865 the legislature repealed that part of the law which provided state funds for salaries of the secretary and agent. Indiana *House Journal*, 1859, pp. 278-82, 420, 760; *Laws of Indiana*, 1865, p. 63.

example. He continued to praise Indiana's exclusion policy and to insist that any program of emancipation which might result from the war must be coupled with colonization. In a speech in the Senate in April, 1862, he warned: "We intend to have in our State, as far as possible, a white population, and we do not intend to have our jails and penitentiaries filled with free blacks."[65]

President Lincoln favored colonization in principle, and several measures adopted by Congress during the early part of the war contained support for colonization. The Reverend James Mitchell, who had served as secretary of the Indiana Colonization Board, was appointed by Lincoln as Agent of Emigration under the Secretary of the Interior, Caleb B. Smith of Indiana, a conservative Republican opposed to abolition. Presumably it was hoped that the appointment of Mitchell would win the confidence and support of northern Negroes for colonization schemes. In his new position Mitchell published at government expense a plea entitled, *Letter on the Relation of the White and African Races in the United States Showing the Necessity of Colonizing the Latter*. The letter, which was addressed to the President of the United States, contained all of the stereotyped arguments in favor of separation of the races, including a warning of race warfare and amalgamation of the races if colonization was not carried out.[66]

Even after the Emancipation Proclamation, which made colonization schemes more unrealistic than ever, some groups continued to urge Negro emigration. The secretary of the Indiana Board of Colonization continued to make reports, although no Negroes had left Indiana for Africa since 1855.

[65] *Congressional Globe,* 37 Congress, 2 session, 1468; Indianapolis *Daily Journal,* April 9, 1862. The occasion for Wright's speech was the debate over emancipation in the District of Columbia.

[66] *Report on Colonization and Emigration Made to the Secretary of the Interior* (Washington, D. C., 1862), *passim; Letter on the Relation of the White and African Races in the United States, Showing the Necessity of the Colonization of the Latter* (Washington, D. C., 1862); Benjamin Quarles, *The Negro in the Civil War* (Boston, 1953), 146.

In the last report, which covered the year 1863, there was an admission that colonization had been a failure so far as Indiana Negroes were concerned. The writer predicted however that after the war returning white soldiers might take jobs away from Negroes and that this might lead to a clamor among Negroes to go to Africa. But he warned that the outcome of the war might also mean greater equality for the Negro, and if this should be the case, he prophesied with more accuracy than elegance that all colonization efforts would be "a stink in the African nostril."[67]

[67] *Report on Colonization for 1863 to the State Board* (Indianapolis, 1864), 493-95.

4

PERSONAL LIBERTY

So long as color was *prima facie* evidence of slavery in half of the states of the Union, even in a "free" state like Indiana black persons were less secure in the enjoyment of personal liberty than were white. Negroes who were legally free lived in danger of being kidnaped and reduced to slavery, while escaped slaves were in peril of being returned to bondage.

Dangers to the liberty of free Negroes grew in part out of the abuse of the provisions of the Constitution and laws of the United States regarding the return of runaway slaves. The Constitution, in the same section which provided for the rendition of persons accused of crime (Article IV, section 2), declared that slaves who escaped from one state to another should not be free but should be returned to the person to whom they owed service. In 1793 Congress passed "An act respecting fugitives from justice and persons escaping from the service of their masters."[1] The second part of the measure provided that when a slave escaped, the master or his agent might pursue him into any state or territory and seize him and take him before any Federal judge or local magistrate. In order to prove his claim the master or agent was to submit oral testimony or an affidavit. After he had proved his right to the satisfaction of the magistrate hearing the case, the latter was required to give a certificate to the claimant authorizing him to remove the slave to the state from which he had fled. The law also imposed penalties upon persons who obstructed the capture of a fugitive or who concealed such a person.

[1] U. S. *Statutes at Large,* 1 :302-5.

There was no provision for the alleged fugitive to testify or submit evidence in his own behalf or any guarantee of the right to legal counsel. In practice Indiana magistrates seem to have granted these rights in some cases although the law did not mention them, but under the Federal law a jury trial was impossible. The case depended entirely upon the arbitrary decision of the magistrate.[2] Theoretically, if he were held illegally, the fugitive could institute a freedom suit after he was returned to the slave state, but in practice the hearing determined his fate, and the proceedings were subject to flagrant abuse. The most conspicuous deficiency of the Federal law was the failure to provide any protection to free Negroes against being seized illegally and enslaved.

As a result of this situation the governments of free states were faced with a dilemma. On the one hand was the obligation to protect their free colored inhabitants from being kidnaped; on the other was the obligation under the Constitution and law of the United States to return persons who were actually fugitive slaves. Even in the territorial period Indiana legislators had been aware of the danger to free Negroes and had provided stiff penalties for kidnaping. In 1810 the legislature declared that a person who attempted to remove a Negro from the Territory without proving before one of the judges of the Court of Common Pleas that he was "legally entitled to do so according to the laws of the United States and of this territory," and without receiving a certificate authorizing the removal, was liable to a fine of one thousand dollars. The act also permitted the Negro to sue for damages.[3]

[2] It has been shown that the summary nature of the proceedings was due to the fact that the framers of the law did not regard the hearing before the magistrate as a trial but intended it to be more in the nature of an extradition proceeding. For a discussion of this point and other constitutional questions, see Allan Johnson, "The Constitutionality of the Fugitive Slave Acts," in *Yale Law Journal*, 31 (1921) :161-82.

[3] Ewbank and Riker (eds.), *Laws of Indiana Territory, 1809-1816*, 138-39. In Jefferson County in 1815 Samuel Higby was indicted for at-

In his message to the first session of the legislature after Indiana had become a state Governor Jonathan Jennings called attention to the problem of kidnaping. He urged the enactment of legislation which would prevent unlawful seizures of free Negroes and which would at the same time protect the right of masters from other states to retake runaway slaves. The legislature responded with "An Act to Prevent Manstealing," which declared that any person who forcibly seized another with the intention of carrying him out of the state without first establishing his claim according to the law of the state or of the United States, was guilty of manstealing and subject to a fine of from five hundred to one thousand dollars for each offense. The law also required that a person seeking to arrest a fugitive slave must secure a warrant from a justice of the peace or a judge of a circuit court. After the arrest a hearing was to be held before a justice of the peace at which both claimant and alleged fugitive were allowed to submit testimony. If the claim appeared to be well founded, a trial was set for the next session of the circuit court. At the trial the person claimed as a fugitive was to "have a fair and impartial trial by jury." If the jury decided in favor of the claimant, the latter was to be granted a certificate authorizing him to carry the Negro out of the state. The law also provided penalties for forging a certificate of emancipation and for harboring or employing fugitive slaves. In 1819 it was amended to provide that a person found guilty of manstealing should receive from ten to one hundred stripes on his bare back in addition to being fined. Thus the Indiana law differed from the Federal law in two important respects— in requiring a warrant for the arrest of the alleged fugitive and in guaranteeing a trial by jury.[4]

tempting to remove a Negro from the Territory without authority, but a jury found him not guilty. Jesse Gray was indicted for the same offense, but the indictment was quashed. Jefferson County, Minutes of Court of Common Pleas and Circuit Court, 1812-18 (microfilm, Indiana State Library), 163, 167, 170, 178.

[4] Indiana *House Journal,* 1816-17, p. 11; *Laws of Indiana,* 1816-17, pp.

The adoption of these measures showed a commendable desire on the part of the lawmakers to deal with a nefarious practice, but the legislation does not appear to have been effective in stamping out the crime. Records from Clark County, which was located opposite the town of Louisville on the Ohio River, suggest that the kidnaping of Negroes was not uncommon. Several cases arose under the manstealing law, but in no case does a person appear to have paid the penalty which the law imposed. In November, 1818, two persons were indicted for kidnaping, but the case was dismissed. Counsel for the accused claimed first, that the manstealing act was unconstitutional, and second, that the indictment was too vague and uncertain to be valid. The court sustained the second argument without going into the question of the constitutionality of the law.

At the same session two other men were charged with the same offense. In April, 1819, a jury found them guilty, but a new trial was granted. At the second trial the same verdict was returned, and a fine of five hundred dollars was assessed. However, the operation of the judgment was suspended until the next session of the court, and eventually the fine was remitted. In November, 1819, another indictment was returned against a group of eight men, including Jacob Brookhart, a justice of the peace in Jefferson Township. Brookhart was accused of having issued orders for the arrest of a Negro man, Isaac Crosby, and of having carried him forcibly out of the state "without first establishing any claim to said Isaac under the laws of the state of Indiana, or under the laws of the United States, and without the consent of said Isaac, against the form of the statute of the state, entitled, 'an act to prevent manstealing.' " The

150-52; *ibid.*, 1818-19, p. 64. Laws of this sort, known as "personal liberty laws," obviously raised the question as to whether they contravened the Federal law of 1793 on fugitive slaves. For a more detailed discussion of the constitutional question, see William R. Leslie, "The Constitutional Significance of Indiana's Statute of 1824 on Fugitives from Labor," in *Journal of Southern History,* 13 (1947) :338-53.

House of Representatives of the General Assembly instituted impeachment proceedings against Brookhart, and the Senate made preparations to try the case, but the proceedings were dropped when the accused man resigned his office. The case also appears to have been dropped from the docket of the Clark County court, and the fate of Isaac Crosby is unknown.[5]

Some of the persons indicted in Clark County were Kentuckians who came across into Indiana to carry off Negroes purported to be runaway slaves,[6] and in neighboring Harrison County a notorious case arose out of the attempts of a Kentucky resident to carry off a Negro woman whom he claimed as his slave. The woman, Susan, had been held as a slave by a master who lived near the boundary between Virginia and Pennsylvania and operated a ferry on the Monongahela River. She was later sold to Richard Stephens of Bardstown, Kentucky, but ran away from him and came to Indiana in 1816 or 1817. In Indiana she brought suit for her freedom in the Harrison County court, claiming that she had lived in Pennsylvania, a free state, and hence was free. The jury which heard the case decided that she was the property of Stephens and ordered her returned to him, but Susan's attorney persuaded the court to order a new trial. The case was continued for several terms of the court. The elder Stephens, impatient at this delay, sent his son Robert to bring Susan home. Accordingly, young Stephens and two accomplices carried her off from the home where she was staying while awaiting a new trial. For this abduction Robert Stephens was indicted for manstealing by a Harrison County grand jury. However, efforts to secure his extradition from Kentucky were unavailing. The

[5] Clark County, Order Book of Circuit Court, 1817-19 (microfilm of transcript, Indiana State Library), 454-57, 572, 575, 581, 661-63, 790; Dorothy Riker (ed.), *Executive Proceedings of the State of Indiana 1816-1836* (*Indiana Historical Collections*, Vol. 29, Indianapolis, 1947), 120; Indiana *House Journal*, 1820-21, pp. 93, 118, 120, 131, 153, 155.

[6] See Riker (ed.), *Executive Proceedings, 1816-1836*, 74.

Governor of Kentucky refused repeated requests sent by the Governor of Indiana for the surrender of Stephens, and the case against him was finally dropped. A lengthy wrangle developed between Indiana and Kentucky over their mutual obligations regarding the extradition of persons accused of crime and the return of fugitive slaves. The correspondence of the Governor of Kentucky suggested that the law under which Stephens was indicted was unconstitutional because in conflict with the Federal law of 1793. A report of a committee of the Indiana House of Representatives denied that Congress alone had the right to regulate the manner of reclaiming fugitive slaves and insisted that Indiana had an obligation to legislate on the subject, since Congress had made no provision for punishing abuse of the law of 1793.[7]

From the time of its adoption opponents of the Indiana law insisted that it was unconstitutional because it conflicted with the Federal law. The Indiana legislators had foreseen this problem and had sought to forestall it by providing that fugitive slaves should be retaken according to either the law of Indiana or the law of the United States, thus making the legislation permissive rather than mandatory. The constitutionality of the law was argued for the first time in a Federal court in a case which came before Judge Benjamin Parke in the United States District Court for Indiana in 1818. The case involved the freedom of another Negro woman named Susan, whom a Kentuckian, John L. Chasteen, claimed as his slave. Susan was arrested under the Indiana law, and the case was certified to the Jefferson County court for trial. However, Chasteen signified his intention of taking the case to the Federal court instead and asked that the case in the state court be dismissed. Thereupon, Susan's lawyers sought an injunction in the Jefferson County court to prevent Chasteen from carrying

[7] The controversy between Indiana and Kentucky and its constitutional implications are treated at length in "Indiana and Fugitive Slave Legislation," by Emma Lou Thornbrough, in *Indiana Magazine of History*, 50 (1954):207-14.

her out of the state until she had a trial under the Indiana
law. The Jefferson County court decided that the case should
be tried under the state law and ordered the claimant to
post bond as security that Susan should not be removed
before the trial.[8]

Chasteen ignored this order and sought a warrant from
the Federal court. In this court Susan's lawyers moved for
a dismissal of the case on two grounds: first, that the fugitive slave clause of the United States Constitution imposed
an obligation upon the states but did not give Congress
power to legislate on the subject; and second, that even if
the constitutionality of the Federal law of 1793 were admitted, the states had concurrent power to legislate on the subject. These arguments were rejected by Judge Parke in
an opinion which was probably the first one handed down
by a Federal court concerning the constitutionality of the
law of 1793. He held that the act of Congress was valid
and superseded state laws on the subject. He admitted that
a concurrent power might be exerted by the state on the
same subject "for different purposes, but not for the attainment of the same end." He pointed out that the methods
prescribed by Federal law and the Indiana law were incompatible and that since appeal had been made to the
Federal law, that procedure must be used in this case. "It
is unnecessary to inquire whether one or the other [state
or Federal law] is best calculated to promote the ends of
justice. It is sufficient that congress have prescribed the
mode." Therefore the motion of Susan's lawyers to dismiss
the case was overruled.[9]

Although Parke did not declare the Indiana law unconstitutional, it is obvious that his opinion would have the
effect of limiting the use of the state law.

In 1824 the Indiana legislature modified its law on the
retaking of fugitives. The revision of the laws which was

8 Jefferson County, Minutes of Court of Common Pleas and Circuit
Court, 1812-18 (microfilm, Indiana State Library), 496-98, 532-33.

9 *In re Susan,* 23 *Federal Cases* 444-45.

made that year was under the general supervision of Judge
Parke, and the new law on runaway slaves was no doubt
influenced by his views and also by the repeated protests
of Kentucky officials over the older law. The new law made
concessions to slaveholders and was less favorable to the
Negro who was claimed as a fugitive. Under it the claimant
was allowed to secure a warrant from any county clerk
and to make the arrest himself, whereas the earlier law
had required that the arrest be made by a sheriff or a constable. After arrest the alleged fugitive was to be taken
before a justice of the peace or a circuit court judge for
a trial, at which it was the duty of the presiding magistrate
"to hear and determine the case in a summary way." If
the case was decided in favor of the claimant, he received
a certificate authorizing him to carry the Negro out of the
state. Either party might appeal the decision, but the appellant was required to pay the cost of the first trial and to
give security for the cost of the appeal, requirements which
would probably make it impossible for the Negro to appeal.
The Negro was also required to give security for his appearance at the new trial or be jailed in the interim. At the
second trial a jury heard the case.[10]

The revised laws also contained penalties of fine and
imprisonment for persons who forcibly took or arrested
any man, woman, or child "without establishing a claim
according to the laws of this state, or of the United States."
Subsequent revisions retained the same penalties.[11]

In spite of these measures of the Indiana lawmakers
Negroes continued to be seized and carried off into slavery
without an opportunity to prove their right to freedom.
Some cases were simply forcible abductions; in others Negroes were carried off under the guise of the Federal law
of 1793. The procedure prescribed by the Indiana law for

10 *Revised Laws of Indiana*, 1824, pp. 221-22.
11 *Ibid.*, 142-43; *ibid.*, 1831, pp. 168, 183, 276-78; *ibid.*, 1843, pp. 962,
984, 1032-34.

recovering fugitives was used less frequently because it was more cumbersome and less advantageous to the claimant. Some of the Negroes who were seized were legally free; others were escaped slaves who had in some instances lived for years as free persons.

Kidnapings were most frequent in the counties near the southern border but were not confined to that area. William Forster, a minister of the English Society of Friends who visited Vincennes in 1821, was alarmed for the security of Negroes in that vicinity. In describing their plight he said: "We hear sad stories of kidnaping. I wish some active benevolent people could induce every person of colour to remove away from the river, as it gives wicked, unprincipled wretches the opportunity to get them into a boat, and carry them off to Orleans [sic] or Missouri, where they still fetch a high price. I have been pleading hard with a black man and his wife to get off for some settlement of Friends, with their five children; and I hope they will go." The gentle Quaker added: "I hardly know anything that would make me more desperate than to be in the way of this abominable system of kidnaping; I cannot say, when once set on to rescue a poor creature where I would stop." Forster said that one Negro in the vicinity told him that he never went to bed without having his arms in readiness for defense against attempts to abduct him.[12]

There is no record of how many unknown and friendless Negroes were carried off, but in some cases, where it was known that a Negro had been illegally enslaved, efforts were made to secure his release. Members of the Society of Friends in particular interested themselves in such cases. The reports of the Committees on People of Color in the Indiana Yearly Meeting are one index of the number of kidnapings. Nearly every year the reports showed one or

[12] "Memoirs of William Forster," in Harlow Lindley (ed.), *Indiana as Seen by Early Travelers* (*Indiana Historical Collections*, Vol. 3, Indianapolis, 1916), 257-58.

more cases in which Friends had furnished legal counsel or made other efforts to secure the freedom of persons illegally enslaved. For example, in 1825 it was reported that the Whitewater Quarterly Meeting had procured the liberty of a black boy who was illegally arrested in Kentucky, while members of the Blue River meeting had freed a black man who was held in Louisville. In 1832 the Whitewater Branch was reported as having been engaged in rescuing a colored boy about eleven years old who had been kidnaped in Richmond, Indiana, and taken to St. Louis and sold. Abner Haines, an attorney at Centerville, and Abel Gore, of Richmond, who were employed to rescue the boy, followed him to St. Louis, where they learned that he had been sold to the captain of a steamboat which operated between St. Louis and Louisville. They continued their pursuit to Louisville, where they found the boy and succeeded "after much fatigue and expense, in obtaining and returning him to his distressed parents, relations and friends, to their great joy and consolation."[13]

In 1835 and 1836 it was reported that Friends of White Lick were endeavoring to secure the freedom of a colored girl who had been seized in Hendricks County and taken to Kentucky and sold. Court records show that a man named M'Roberts was indicted in Hendricks County for forcibly carrying off a colored woman, Susanna, without legally establishing claim to her services. This was probably the same person whom the Quakers were trying to free. The Hendricks County court quashed the indictment against M'Roberts, but on appeal the Indiana Supreme Court found the indictment good and remanded the case to the county court. The record does not show the final settlement, nor does it reveal the fate of Susanna. The minutes of the 1837 Yearly Meeting showed that one person had been restored to freedom, and that several other cases were

13 *Minutes of Indiana Yearly Meeting of Friends,* 1825, p. 12; 1833, p. 17.

pending. In 1838 it was reported that one meeting had succeeded in "reclaiming two of our fellow beings from illegal bondage," and that their labors appeared likely to "secure the permanent freedom of a third individual." In 1841 it was reported that John Benbow of Richmond had been arrested and imprisoned as a slave in Kentucky, but that he had been released through the efforts of Friends of the Whitewater Meeting. In 1844 Friends sent a deputation to St. Louis to procure deeds of emancipation for fourteen colored persons and obtained the liberation of a man who had been arrested and imprisoned in a slave state because of his color. In 1845 a free Negro named Graham who disappeared in Cincinnati while on his way from North Carolina to Indiana was found in jail in Louisville, where he was being held as a slave. Through the efforts of the Quakers he was freed.[14]

In 1849 Indiana Friends spent more than six hundred dollars and much time and effort in rescuing Eli Terry, a free Negro who had been enslaved. Terry, who had been living in Hamilton County, Indiana, was employed by a white man named James Carter in 1841 and taken by Carter on a business trip to St. Louis. From that city he was carried off to Texas and sold as a slave. Eight years later his whereabouts was discovered, and a group of Quakers set out to rescue him. After an arduous boat trip from Cincinnati to New Orleans and an overland trek from there to the Red River country they found Terry. They secured a writ of habeas corpus and brought the Negro before a judge. The evidence which they presented convinced the judge that Terry was held illegally, and he ordered him released.[15]

14 Minutes of Indiana Yearly Meeting of Friends, 1835, p. 13; 1836, p. 15; 1837, p. 20; 1838, p. 18; 1844, p. 24; 1845, p. 23; State v. M'Roberts, 4 Blackford (Ind.) 178-79; Free Labor Advocate (Newport, Ind.), August 31, 1844.

15 Minutes of Indiana Yearly Meeting of Friends, 1850, p. 32; Haines, Hamilton County, 477-80.

These cases indicate that in any part of the state free Negroes were in peril of being kidnaped and a free Negro traveling in strange territory was in especial danger. In an effort to protect themselves some free Negroes who came into the state to live had certificates attesting to their freedom recorded in county courts, even though there was no provision in Indiana law requiring them to do so. Many Negroes carried freedom certificates with them when traveling.[16] In some parts of the free state of Indiana every unknown Negro was suspected as a runaway slave. It is related that in Jackson County every Negro who came into a country store to buy food was seized and tied up and held until it could be ascertained whether or not a reward was offered for him among the notices of runaway slaves displayed at the local post office.[17] Negroes were sometimes arrested and jailed on the suspicion that they were fugitives even though no one had advertised for them. The following notice is an example:[18]

[16] Examples are found in Clark County, Order Book of the Circuit Court, 1817-19 (microfilm of transcript, Indiana State Library), 445, 586; Gibson County, Deed Record D, 1824-33 (microfilm, Indiana State Library), 330, 360.

[17] John C. Lazenby, "Jackson County prior to 1850," in *Indiana Magazine of History,* 10 (1914) :273.

[18] Vincennes *Western Sun & General Advertiser,* June 27, 1818. In 1820, John Tipton, sheriff of Harrison County, sent a letter to the postmaster at Nashville, Tennessee, asking him to publish in the local newspaper a notice that a Negro named Lemuel, who admitted to being the slave of Joseph Shaw of Jackson County, Tennessee, had been captured and was confined in the Harrison County jail. Tipton also wrote to Shaw to inform him that he would keep the Negro in jail for a month and then free him if no one claimed him. A reply from Shaw shows that the slave was returned to him and that Tipton was compensated for his efforts. Nellie A. Robertson and Dorothy Riker (eds.), *The John Tipton Papers* (3 vols. *Indiana Historical Collections,* Vols. 24-26, Indianapolis, 1943), 1 :227.

NOTICE

There has lately been committed to the Goal
[sic] of Posey County, State of Indiana, a
Negro by the name of

ARCHIBALD MURPHEY

of dark complexion, 5 feet 8 or 9 inches high,
subject to the rheumatic pains, and can write
sufficiently well to forge his pass. He says his
master lives in East-Tennessee near Mary-
ville. The owner is requested to come forward, pay charges, and take him away.

JAMES ROBB, Sff. P.C.

June 22, 1818.

In another case a private citizen of Bowling Green, Indiana, published an advertisement stating that he had apprehended a Negro man, supposing him to be a slave. The
man had a pass signed by the clerk of Highland County,
Ohio, but admitted that it was a forgery.[19]

There is evidence that some public officials as well as
private citizens connived at the illegal enslavement of free
persons. For example, during the summer of 1842 two
colored men who were traveling northward were seized
near Washington, Indiana, by two men who had no war-
rants. One of the Negroes escaped, but the other was
thrown into jail. A white resident of Washington, learning
of his plight, sought a writ of habeas corpus. When the
Negro was brought before the local judge the latter held
that there was no authority for arresting and holding him
since there was no evidence that he was a slave and ordered
his release. However, no officer of the law made any attempt to protect the Negro from a hostile crowd which
gathered outside the courtroom. The Negro lingered in the
office of the county clerk until the sheriff ordered him to
leave. After he left the office he was seized by a group of
three men, one of whom was reported to be the sheriff himself, and carried off toward Kentucky.[20]

19 Terre Haute *Wabash Courier*, January 11, 1838.
20 *Free Labor Advocate*, February 8, 1843.

Accounts of other kidnapings in the vicinity of Washington indicate the complicity of local residents. In one case there was an attempt to seize two Negroes who had been working on the Wabash and Erie Canal. The kidnapers produced handbills describing the Negroes as fugitives from Tennessee—but the handbills had been printed in Washington, Indiana, after the plot to seize the two men had been hatched. In another instance there was an attempt to kidnap a Negro barber who had recently opened a shop in Petersburg. Again the kidnapers had a confederate in Washington who gave them a description of the Negro and had handbills printed which described him as a runaway from Tennessee. This time the abductors were thwarted. A friend of the Negro delayed proceedings until a runner was dispatched to Vincennes, who brought back a sworn statement from Robert Laplant of that city that the barber had been born on his father's farm near Vincennes and that his parents had been employed by Laplant's parents. The Negro was freed, but the would-be kidnapers were not arrested.[21]

In 1843 two constables in Lawrenceburg arrested two free Negroes and carried them across the Ohio to Kentucky. They signed affidavits that the Negroes had been taken up as fugitive slaves, in anticipation of collecting the reward which Kentucky law provided for the capture of fugitives. It was reported that the people of Lawrenceburg were so aroused over the abduction that they offered a reward for the capture of the constables, who had meanwhile disappeared.[22]

Shortly before this another Negro, who claimed to be a freeborn resident of Cincinnati, was returning overland from New Albany to Cincinnati. In Jefferson County he

---

[21] Cockrum, *Underground Railroad,* 152-62, 250-51. Cockrum's work contains many accounts of kidnapings and attempts to foil them. The book was written many years after these events and no doubt contains inaccuracies and elaborations, but the picture which it gives of the dangers under which free Negroes lived is essentially accurate.

[22] *Free Labor Advocate,* July 11, 1843.

was decoyed into a private dwelling by an offer of shelter
and food and then seized by kidnapers and carried to Kentucky. In that state he was jailed, and his abductors collected a reward. Under the Kentucky law the Negro would
be kept in jail for one year and then sold for one year if
no one claimed him. If unclaimed at the end of the second
year the law provided that he should be sold for life. In
this case a friend traced the captive to the jail and proved
that he was a free man and saved him from permanent
enslavement.[23]

Although some officers of the law connived at illegal seizure others showed a real interest in protecting Negroes.
In 1821 in New Albany a judge decided that a Negro boy
who was claimed as an escaped slave from Kentucky was
legally free. The claimant, in anticipation of such a decision, had brought a group of about forty fellow Kentuckians
with him to the trial with the intention of taking the boy
by force. However, the Indiana authorities were prepared.
When an attempt was made to seize the boy, the sheriff and
a group of militia intervened. A free-for-all fight, in which
the judge himself was knocked flat on the ground, followed,
but the Negro was saved from abduction.[24]

Another attempt at forcible seizure was foiled in Lawrenceburg in 1845. In this case a Negro man who had been
living in the neighborhood for about seven years was seized
without a warrant. While his captors were preparing to
take him before a justice of the peace to get a certificate to
take him out of the state, a local merchant came to his aid.
Legal counsel was secured for the Negro, and he was given
thirty days in which to gather evidence, although in the
meantime he was confined in jail in irons. At the trial the
men who had seized him produced evidence to show that
he was a slave who had escaped from New Orleans seven

[23] *Free Labor Advocate*, March 11, May 6, 1843.

[24] New Albany *Chronicle* reprinted in Vincennes *Western Sun &
General Advertiser*, March 24, 1821.

years earlier. In handing down his decision the judge held that in a free state every person, regardless of color, was presumed to be free. In order to prove that the Negro was a slave the claimants must prove not only that he had once been a slave but also that he had not been freed by some subsequent act. He ruled that it had not been proved that the Negro was actually a slave in Louisiana—that the fact that he was held as a slave was not proof since he might have been kidnaped and illegally enslaved. Hence he ordered the man freed.[25]

Most of the Negroes mentioned in the cases above were legally free but were victims of attempts at illegal enslavement. Even more precarious was the condition of persons who were legally slaves but who had escaped to free soil. These lived in constant peril of being returned to slavery. Sometimes after living as free persons for years they were apprehended. Two notorious cases of this sort occurred in southern Indiana in 1851. In the first case a Negro named Mitchum, who had lived near Vernon in Jennings County for years with his wife and child, was seized by a group of men from Kentucky who claimed that he was a slave who had run away nineteen years before. He was taken before a justice of the peace and given the benefit of legal counsel. The lawyer who represented him argued that since the adoption of the Fugitive Slave Law of 1850 the justice of the peace had no jurisdiction to hear the case, but this was rejected and the trial proceeded. The only evidence that the claimant was able to produce was the testimony of a fellow Kentuckian, who swore that Mitchum was the escaped slave whom they were seeking, although Mitchum bore no distinguishing physical marks and the witness admitted that he had not seen him for nineteen years. Nevertheless, on this flimsy evidence, the justice awarded the Negro to the claimant, and he was carried

[25] *Indiana Freeman* reprinted in *Free Labor Advocate,* October 11, 1845.

off to Kentucky. The local newspaper commented: "We are happy to state that no excitement tending towards mob law existed, and we think our Kentucky neighbors leave our town satisfied that how great soever [*sic*] our abhorrence to the institution of slavery may be, we still are a law abiding people."[26]

An even more brutal seizure occurred in Washington County the same year. It involved a Negro woman, Martha, the wife of Charley Rouse, who lived on a rented farm in Franklin Township. From subsequent testimony it appears that Martha was a slave who had escaped to New Albany from Kentucky about ten years earlier. She had been married to Charles without disclosing to him that she was a slave. After their marriage the couple had moved to Washington County and lived quietly for several years. One evening when Charles was away from home a band of armed men entered their home and carried off Martha, claiming that she was a runaway slave who belonged to a man living in Louisville. The entire neighborhood was aroused over the abduction, and a group of white neighbors pursued the kidnapers to Jeffersonville, where they tried to buy Martha's freedom. The leader of the band agreed to sell her for $600, but insisted that the contract must be signed in Kentucky since the sale would be illegal in Indiana. The offer was merely a ruse, and once the woman was in Kentucky the men refused to sell her at any price. She was not heard of again.[27]

Regardless of whether or not Martha was legally a slave, the manner in which she was taken was in flagrant violation of both state and Federal law. In commenting on the tragedy, the Salem *News* admitted that Martha and Charley "were highly respected by their neighbors for their honesty and peaceable dispositions, and all appear to regret the

26 Vernon *Times* reprinted in Indianapolis *Indiana State Sentinel*, February 26, 1851.

27 Money, "Fugitive Slave Law," in *Indiana Magazine of History*, 17:272-73.

event which has separated them." Nevertheless it counseled: "We are not in possession of all the facts in the case, but if what we have heard be true, it appears to us that it would be wisdom on the part of our citizens in that neighborhood not to interfere in the matter. We already have difficulties and dangers enough to encounter upon the subject without getting into more of the same kind."[28]

Attitudes on the subject of the rendition of runaway slaves varied in different parts of the state. As the newspaper comments quoted above indicate, in the southern counties, while there might be sympathy for individual Negroes, public opinion generally supported the right of masters to reclaim their human property, and there was a desire to avoid anything that might offend the neighboring slave states. The same attitude prevailed in the state capital. In 1850 a group of slaveholders from LaGrange, Kentucky, came to Indianapolis to take a fugitive slave. They came expecting hostile treatment from the residents of a Northern city but were pleasantly surprised at the fair treatment which they received. They encountered no disposition on the part of the people of the city to interfere with them in any way. The slave was arrested in accordance with the Indiana law, his identity proved, and he was carried off without any excitement. The Kentuckians were so pleased with their reception that they published an advertisement in an Indianapolis newspaper expressing their gratification.[29]

On the other hand, in communities where antislavery feeling was strong slave hunters encountered hostility and were likely to be thwarted in their efforts. An illustration is a case arising in Hamilton County, where there were many Quakers who regarded human slavery as a greater sin than the breaking of a manmade law. The Negroes in the case were a man, Sam, his wife, and child, who had once been the slaves of a Kentucky master who had moved

28 Quoted in *ibid.*, 273.
29 Indianapolis *Indiana State Sentinel* (semiweekly), July 6, 1850.

to Illinois taking his slaves with him. In Illinois he became alarmed lest he lose title to them and took them to Missouri and sold them to a man who knew nothing of their sojourn in Illinois. Sometime later they escaped from their new master, whose name was Vaughan, and with the aid of members of the Underground Railway they reached Hamilton County, where they acquired a small farm and lived unmolested under the names of John and Louan Rhodes.

In 1844 Vaughan learned of their whereabouts and came to Indiana to claim them. Armed with a warrant he went to their cabin. He found the cabin barricaded, for Sam (or John), like most fugitives, lived in constant fear of being retaken. While Vaughan was battering down the door, neighbors arrived to aid the Negroes. When their former master prepared to take the family before a judge to prove his claim, he found himself accompanied by a large throng which kept growing as they proceeded along the road. When they came to a fork in the road, an argument arose between Vaughan and some of his uninvited escort as to which way he should go. During the delay the driver of the wagon in which the Negroes were riding whipped up his horses and dashed off. Before he was overtaken the Negroes had disappeared into a swamp and could not be found. Vaughan later brought suit in a Federal court against the ringleader of the group who had aided in the escape but lost the case, the jury believing that the Negroes were free as the result of residence in Illinois. Under the name of Rhodes the family continued to live in Hamilton County for the rest of their lives.[30]

In Wayne and Randolph counties, the hotbed of the anti-slavery movement in Indiana, the chances of a slave hunter retaking a fugitive were slight. In one case a master from Tennessee pursued two girls who had run away to the residence of their grandparents in the Cabin Creek settlement

---

[30] Vaughan v. Williams, 28 *Federal Cases* 1115-18 (1845); Haines, *Hamilton County*, 494-501.

in Randolph County. He obtained a writ for their arrest and hired a band of men from Richmond and Winchester to accompany him to Cabin Creek. The colored people lived in readiness for such an emergency, and when it was learned that the slave hunters were in the neighborhood a signal was sent out. Soon most of the colored persons in the neighborhood and some of the whites appeared. They succeeded in diverting the posse until the girls had escaped from the cabin. The slave hunters scoured the neighborhood for miles around but finally gave up. Before returning to Tennessee the disgruntled master started to institute a damage suit against the Negroes who had foiled the capture of the girls. The case never came to trial, probably because the plaintiff was convinced of the futility of bringing suit in that community.[31]

A similar incident occurred near Newport in Wayne County, where there was a settlement of runaway slaves who were ready to fight and even to kill to preserve their freedom. When a group of Kentuckians came to the neighborhood in pursuit of a runaway, they were warned that "not one would leave that town alive if they fired a pistol, struck a blow, or attempted to seize anyone." The slave hunters appealed to the white men of the neighborhood who were present to help them, but they were deaf to their pleas. The Kentuckians "looked about them and saw themselves surrounded by determined men, with arms ready for the work of death." They gave up their hunt and fled.[32]

Persons who tried to carry off fugitives in the counties in the north near the Michigan border found that they were in hostile territory. Two notorious cases occurred in Elkhart and St. Joseph counties in which state officials aided in preventing the recovery of persons claimed as slaves.

In Elkhart County a man named Joseph Graves at-

---

[31] Coffin, *Reminiscences*, 170-77 ; Tucker, *Randolph County*, 197-98.

[32] Salem (Ohio) *Anti Slavery Bugle* reprinted in Indianapolis *Indiana State Sentinel* (semiweekly), January 4, 1851.

tempted to capture a Negro under the authority of a warrant obtained from a justice of the peace. A riot resulted when a crowd came to the defense of the Negro and tried to prevent the capture, and Graves was indicted for inciting the disorder. At the trial the judge of the circuit court instructed the jury that the warrant issued by the justice of the peace was void, that Graves should have obtained a warrant from the county clerk, as the Indiana law provided. He also declared that the Indiana law on the retaking of fugitives was not in contravention of either the Constitution or laws of the United States. The case was appealed to the Indiana Supreme Court, which overruled the lower court and held the judge's instructions had been in error. The higher court ruled that the Indiana law on fugitive slaves was void in view of the decision of the United States Supreme Court in Prigg v. Pennsylvania, in which it had been decided that Congress alone had the right to legislate on the subject of fugitive slaves and that state laws on the subject were unconstitutional, regardless of whether they attempted to check or to facilitate the return of fugitives.[33]

Shortly after the Graves case, in the neighboring county of St. Joseph, there occurred what was probably the most sensational attempt to thwart a slave catcher in the history of Indiana. The Negroes in the case, a family of five, had run away from the farm of John Norris in Boone County, Kentucky, and had reached the settlement in Cass County,

---

[33] Graves *et al. v.* the State, 1 Ind. 368-73 (1849) ; Prigg *v.* Pennsylvania, 16 *Peters* 539. The opinion in the Prigg case, which concerned a Pennsylvania statute on kidnaping, was extremely nationalistic and a blow at states' rights. Another famous rescue occurred in Fugit Township in Decatur County, where a slave woman and her children, who were fleeing from Kentucky, were rescued by a group of Negroes and a white man, Luther Donnell, and sent on their way to Canada. Donnell was indicted under the Indiana law of 1824 for aiding in the escape of the slaves and was convicted in Decatur County. The Indiana Supreme Court reversed the decision, holding that the Indiana law was null and void in the light of the decision in the Prigg case. N. T. Rogers, "Decatur County's Part in the Underground Railway" (typed manuscript, Indiana State Library), 20-30; Donnell *v.* the State, 3 Ind. 480 (1852).

Michigan, one of the largest Negro communities in the Middle West. Norris traced the slaves to their new home, and with a band of fellow Kentuckians forcibly entered the cabin where they were living. He seized the mother and three sons during the absence of the father, bundled them into a wagon, and started south. After they crossed the Indiana border they were stopped by a group of several persons, including the sheriff of St. Joseph County, who had a writ of habeas corpus. Norris was ordered to go to South Bend to prove whether or not he had a legal claim to the Negroes.

Word of the capture spread quickly, and by the time of the hearing, which was held a few hours later, the courthouse at South Bend was crowded with spectators, many of them armed with clubs. Norris replied to the writ of habeas corpus that the Negroes were his slaves who had run away and had been retaken by him. The judge ruled that under the Federal law of 1793 Norris was required to secure a certificate showing his right to the slaves before he took them out of Michigan. Anticipating this ruling Norris, on the advice of his lawyer, applied for a warrant to arrest the slaves under the Indiana law. The lawyer who was representing the Negroes objected on the grounds that the Indiana law was unconstitutional, but despite this the warrant was issued. During the hearing tension in the courtroom had mounted. Some of the spectators were urging that the Negroes be freed by force, while the Kentuckians, realizing the hostility of the crowd, began to draw knives and revolvers. The Negroes were lodged in jail for safekeeping until a trial could be held under the new writ.

The next day, as the result of the disorders in the courtroom, members of the Kentucky party were arrested on charges of assault and battery and riot. A civil suit in behalf of the Negroes was also filed. Although the grand jury which met two days later returned no indictments on any of the charges, the arrests convinced the Kentuckians that their cause was hopeless. The fact that the streets of the village of South Bend were thronged with Negroes from Cass County no doubt strengthened their conviction. When the circuit court met, the judge ordered Norris and the erstwhile slaves into court for another hearing. But Norris, convinced that he would never be allowed to retake the Negroes in this hostile community, failed to appear and the judge discharged the Negroes. They started happily back to Michigan in the company of their colored friends. The only recourse left to Norris was to sue for the recovery of the value of his human property under the terms of the Federal law of 1793. He brought suit against the lawyer who had represented the Negroes and some of the persons who had assisted him and was awarded $2,850 in damages by the United States Circuit Court.[34]

The procedure for the retaking of runaway slaves was modified by the Fugitive Slave Act of 1850, an amendment to the law of 1793 adopted in response to the demands of the representatives of the slave states. The principal change was that the 1850 measure relied for enforcement upon Federal rather than state officers. Federal commissioners, appointed by Federal judges, had concurrent jurisdiction with these judges in hearing fugitive slave cases. Testimony of the persons claimed as slaves was expressly prohibited from being admitted as evidence at these hearings. If the commissioner decided in favor of the claimant, he issued a certificate for the removal of the fugitive out of the state, and if the claimant had reason to fear that there would be an attempt to rescue the slave by force, it was the duty of the commissioner to give him protection in escorting the slave out of the state, the cost being borne by the United States government. The commissioner also had the power to deputize any private citizen to assist in the capture of a fugitive.[35]

---

[34] *The South Bend Fugitive Slave Case, involving the Right to a Writ of Habeas Corpus* (New York, 1851); Norris v. Newton *et al.,* 18 *Federal Cases* 322-27 (1850); Indianapolis *Indiana State Sentinel* (semi-weekly), October 10 and 17, 1849.

[35] U. S. *Statutes at Large,* 9:462-65.

This act, which was one of the series of measures known as the Compromise of 1850, was supported by a majority of the Indiana delegation in Congress as necessary for quelling the sectional bitterness which threatened to disrupt the Union. In most parts of the state the measure did not evoke the immediate and universal condemnation which it brought forth in some Northern states. Abolitionist groups branded the "blood hound fugitive slave bill" as unconstitutional and pledged themselves to prevent its enforcement, but Governor Joseph A. Wright told the General Assembly that it must be carried out in good faith.[36] Although Wright and most Indianans hoped for the "finality" of the Compromise of 1850 and the end of agitation on the slavery question, the operation of the new fugitive law had the effect of converting men who had heretofore been moderates into outspoken opponents of the slave system.

A notorious case in Indianapolis in 1853 caused a wave of revulsion against the system of slave catching. The central figure was John Freeman, a Negro who claimed to have come to Indianapolis from Georgia about 1844, and who through hard work and thrift had acquired some real estate, including a house and garden and a restaurant. In 1853 a Missourian by the name of Pleasant Ellington, who professed to being a Methodist minister, appeared in Indianapolis and filed a claim with the United States commissioner that Freeman was his slave, Sam, who had escaped in 1836 when Ellington was residing in Kentucky. Freeman was arrested, but before a hearing could be held friends learned of his plight and the commissioner was persuaded to allow him to have legal counsel. One of the ablest lawyers in the city, John L. Ketcham, came to Freeman's aid, and the commissioner, much to the disgust of Ellington, agreed to a delay. The case soon attracted wide attention in the newspapers, and public opinion apparently compelled the commissioner to see that Freeman was given a chance to prove

36 Indiana *House Journal,* 1850-51, pp. 40-41.

his right to freedom. A postponement of nine weeks was granted for the securing of evidence. Efforts to secure the release of Freeman on bail were unavailing, although some of the most prominent men in Indianapolis helped raise the bond. The commissioner decided that bail was not permissible, and the Negro was kept in jail for nine weeks, and as an added injury was compelled to pay the cost of a special guard that was hired to see that he did not escape.

Two other lawyers, John Coburn and Lucian Barbour, joined Ketcham in the case, and the three worked tirelessly and brilliantly to secure evidence. Correspondence with persons in Georgia corroborated Freeman's claim that he had resided there and was free, while witnesses from Georgia were brought to Indianapolis to identify him. Meanwhile, the real Sam, who had escaped from Ellington, was traced to Canada. He freely confessed his identity, and witnesses who had known him in Kentucky went to Canada to identify him and brought depositions to Indianapolis. This sworn testimony showed that the physical characteristics of Sam and Freeman were quite different as to both height and color; nevertheless Ellington and three witnesses whom he had brought with him had not hesitated to swear that Freeman was Sam after compelling him to submit to a physical examination.

To clinch the case for Freeman his old guardian arrived from Georgia to identify him, and six other witnesses from Georgia arrived on the day set for the final hearing of the case. Their testimony was not called for because Ellington had given up and left the city. The commissioner dismissed the case, and Freeman was released. He was free, but the cost of proving his freedom in the face of a wanton and unscrupulous attempt to enslave him had cost him everything that he had saved from a life of hard work. The only redress which the law afforded for the financial loss and the indignities which he had suffered was a damage suit. He won an award of two thousand dollars in a suit against Ellington, but this was a hollow victory. The award was never paid since Ellington sold his property and left St. Louis to escape payment. Freeman also brought suit in the Marion County Circuit Court against the United States marshal who had imprisoned him. The case was taken to the Indiana Supreme Court which upheld the right to sue the United States official since the acts with which he was charged—assault, forcing the prisoner to strip naked, and extorting money from him for the pay of the guard— were not part of his official duties and were unlawful. But again this was only a technical victory since the court ruled that the suit should have been brought in Rush County, the residence of the marshal. In the end Freeman was able to save his home and a garden plot through the help of many persons in both Indiana and Georgia who had become interested in his case. Nevertheless, he left Indianapolis and moved to Canada at the outbreak of the Civil War, apparently because he feared a southern victory.[37]

Freeman's case was watched with intense interest throughout the state, and there was widespread relief and satisfaction when his freedom was assured. The case showed more forcibly than all the speeches of antislavery orators the woeful inadequacy of the Federal law to protect the rights of free Negroes. As a Fort Wayne newspaper observed: "A more flagrant case of injustice, we have never seen. It appears to us in such cases, that if the person swearing to the identity of the accused and seeking to consign a free man to slavery, were tried and punished for perjury, a wholesome lesson would be given which might prevent injustice to free persons of color. The fugitive slave law evidently needs some amendment, to give greater protection to free persons of color. As it now stands, almost any of them might be dragged into slavery. If Freeman had not

---

[37] A detailed account of the Freeman case is given in Money, "Fugitive Slave Law of 1850 in Indiana," in *Indiana Magazine of History,* 17 :180-97. See also Dunn, *Greater Indianapolis,* 1 :248-50; Oliver H. Smith, *Early Indiana Trials and Sketches* . . . (Cincinnati, 1858), 278-79; Freeman *v.* Robinson, 7 Ind. 321-24 (1855).

had money and friends he must inevitably have been taken off into bondage. Any poor man, without friends, would have been given up at once and taken away, and it was only by the most strenuous exertions that Freeman was rescued. A law under which such injustice can be perpetrated, and which holds out such inducements to perjury, is imperfect and must be amended or repealed. The American people have an innate sense of justice which will no longer allow such a law to disgrace our statute books."[38]

Cases such as this, which were widely publicized, hastened the final extinction of slavery. But in the meantime, as the editorial observed, in spite of his ordeal, Freeman was more fortunate than many members of his race. No one will ever know how many anonymous Negroes were carried off into slavery without the benefit of counsel or a fair hearing simply because they were without friends or money.

[38] Fort Wayne *Sentinel*, September 8, 1853, quoted in Money, "Fugitive Slave Law of 1850 in Indiana," in *Indiana Magazine of History*, 17:193.

5

LEGAL, ECONOMIC, SOCIAL PATTERNS

"DENIED THE PRIVILEGE of voice in the government, they are yet compelled to submit to the laws; debarred from bearing legal testimony in a case where whites are interested, they still may be convicted by the unsupported oath of a single white person; and yet the testimony of a score of men of sable brown, though of unsullied reputation may not bring the decrees of justice upon the head of any single white villain, who may choose to distress them. Deprived of the means of an education, so far as common schools are concerned, and left to their own unassisted individual enterprise, they have in the face of all these discouragements, made considerable improvement, by toiling on in meekness and patience, in a good degree consonant with the precepts of the Christian religion."[1]

The quotation above, part of an address which the Anti-Slavery Friends prepared for the people of Indiana in 1854, epitomizes rather accurately the conditions of Negroes in that period. In an earlier chapter it was seen that efforts were made to prevent Negroes from coming into the state and to remove those who did settle there. The exclusion and colonization movements were merely one evidence of the hostility of the white population toward the colored. Negroes who settled in the state in spite of these restrictions found themselves subject to various forms of discrimination, legal and otherwise. In the eyes of the law Negroes did not enjoy full citizenship; economically their position

[1] Minutes of Anti-Slavery Friends (MS, Earlham College Library), 337-38.

(119)

was weak and their opportunities for progress limited; socially they were a people apart.

The laws of the territorial period had imposed various disabilities upon free Negroes which were copied from the laws of the slave states. After the attainment of statehood these legal disabilities were retained, and in some cases increased. Although the men who framed the Constitution of 1816 were resolute in their determination to rid Indiana of slavery, they showed no further interest in the rights of colored people. The finished Constitution limited the right to vote to white male citizens and excluded Negroes, mulattoes, and Indians from the militia.[2] Both of these provisions had been in force during the territorial period, and neither excited much discussion before the Civil War, although the question of Negro suffrage was raised in the constitutional convention which met in 1850. A number of petitions were received, principally from groups of Baptists and Anti-Slavery Friends asking that the right to vote be extended to Negroes, but all were tabled. Indeed, the bias of the convention was so strong that a debate developed over the question of receiving the petitions. In one case a delegate expressed the opinion that petitions should "eminate from respectable men," but the petition under consideration was finally sent to a committee when it was ascertained that no Negroes had signed it. When a petition from a colored group was presented, it was suggested that petitions on behalf of such persons violated the Constitution of the United States.

Nevertheless, Schuyler Colfax, delegate from St. Joseph County, had the temerity to offer a resolution that the Committee on the Elective Franchise be instructed to consider the question of submitting an article on Negro suffrage to the voters separately from the rest of the Constitution. Colfax was quick to explain that he personally opposed

2 Article VI, section 1; Article VII, section 1.

extending the franchise but was merely making the proposal to gratify certain groups in the state. Even this was too much for one delegate, who offered an amendment to Colfax's proposal that "all persons voting for negro suffrage shall themselves be disfranchised," in case a majority of votes were cast against the proposal. He exclaimed : "Whenever you being to talk about making Negroes equal with white men, I begin to think about leaving the country. . . . I am satisfied that perhaps three-fourths of the State would rather leave, if the Negroes were allowed to come here and exercise the right of franchise." The proposal to give the voters of the state an opportunity to vote separately on the question was lost by a vote of 62 to 60. Only one member of the convention, Edward May, delegate from DeKalb and Steuben counties, where there were almost no Negroes, admitted that he favored giving the right to vote to Negroes. When he proposed incorporating a provision for Negro suffrage into the main body of the Constitution, it was rejected by a vote of 122 to one.

The Constitution as finally adopted not only restricted the franchise to white citizens but added for good measure : "No negro or mulatto shall have the right of suffrage."[3]

Negroes themselves rarely asked for the privilege of voting, nor did even their more aggressive friends in the white race urge it for them. Instead efforts were concentrated on securing the removal of some of the more burdensome features in the legal code. Of these the provisions limiting the right of Negroes to give evidence in courts of justice were probably the most notorious.

In 1818 the state legislature had adopted a law, similar to a territorial measure, which declared that no Negro or mulatto should be a competent witness except in pleas of

[3] *Debates and Proceedings,* 1 :77-80, 101, 207, 228-29, 232, 242-44, 246, 253-54; *Journal of the Convention,* 112-13; Constitution of 1851, Article II, sections 2 and 5. Article XII, section 1, limited the militia to white persons.

the state against Negroes and mulattoes or in civil cases in which Negroes or mulattoes alone were parties. A mulatto was defined as a person with one fourth or more of Negro blood. The injustice of the measure is obvious, but it was not until the rise of militant antislavery societies in the forties that serious efforts were made to change it.[4]

At the 1846 session of the General Assembly numerous petitions asking for the repeal of disabilities upon Negroes were received. The report of the select committee to which they were referred urged the repeal of the law on testimony, which it denounced as having the effect of obstructing justice. It was pointed out that the law might work to the disadvantage of white men as well as colored. The report further declared: "Evidence in a court of justice, is that which demonstrates and brings to light. Everything which tends to this end should be used to ferret out the complicated and mysterious deeds of man. The track of the foot, the nail of the shoe, the bark of the dog, or the bray of the donkey, may be given in evidence to ferret out villainies; but the negro, unless in the course of *modern civilization,* more than three fourths of his blood is merged in that of the white man, though acquainted with the villain, and cognizant to the villainy, for no reason than because he is a negro, is not even permitted to develope corroborating circumstances." The report was laid on the table, however,

---

[4] *Laws of Indiana,* 1817-18 (general), pp. 39, 40. Among Northern states only Indiana, Ohio, Illinois, and Iowa had laws excluding the testimony of Negroes. In 1836 a bill to amend the law on testimony reached a second reading in the Indiana House of Representatives but was then tabled. Indiana *House Journal,* 1835-36, pp. 335, 453. Antislavery groups consistently denounced the law. For example, "An Address of the Henry County Anti-Slavery Association to the People of Indiana" in 1841 pronounced the law evidence of the evil influence of slavery upon the institutions of Indiana. *Free Labor Advocate* (Newport), July 8, 1841. The Indiana Yearly Meeting of Anti-Slavery Friends each year prepared a petition to the legislature asking repeal of the law on testimony as well as the other parts of Indiana's Black Laws. See Minutes of Anti-Slavery Friends, 96-97, 154, 200, 269, 333.

and a motion to reconsider was lost.[5] In 1849 another proposal to repeal the limitation on testimony was voted down
by the House. A report of the Judiciary Committee of the
Senate at the same session admitted that the existing laws
"in some cases operate harshly and unjustly on the white
man, as well as the black," and stated that a "revision and
amelioration" of the laws should be made, but advised postponement of such action until after the constitutional convention which was soon to meet.[6]

The constitutional convention did nothing about "amelio-
rating" the condition of the Negro but considered numerous
proposals to add to his disabilities. Among them was a proposal for a constitutional provision forbidding the use of
the testimony of Negroes in cases involving white persons.
The convention did not adopt the article, but in 1853 the
legislature adopted an even more extreme measure than the
earlier one. Whereas the old law had prohibited testimony
by a person with one fourth or more of Negro blood, the
new law declared: "No Indian, or person having one-eighth
or more of Negro blood, shall be permitted to testify as a
witness in any cause in which any white person is a party
in interest."[7]

The ban on Negro testimony was not removed until after
the Civil War, but the use of the law was limited somewhat
by judicial interpretation. One example occurred in Indianapolis in the thirties when a Negro sought a peace warrant

5 Indiana *House Journal*, 1846-47, pp. 612-15.
6 *Ibid.*, 1849-50, pp. 34, 443-45; Indiana *Senate Journal*, 1849-50, p. 151.
7 *Journal of the Convention*, 139, 142, 164; *Laws of Indiana*, 1853, p.
60. At the next session measures to repeal the 1853 law were introduced
into both houses but failed to pass. In 1859 a committee of the House,
which was controlled by the new Republican party, recommended repeal,
but the proposal was rejected 65 to 20. In 1861, with Republicans in control of both houses, the law on testimony was modified slightly by the
proviso that: "where a negro, Indian, or person excluded on account of
mixed blood is a party to a cause, his opponent shall also be excluded."
Indiana *House Journal*, 1855, pp. 106, 512, 660; *ibid.*, 1859, pp. 355-56;
Indiana *Senate Journal*, 1855, pp. 64, 83-84; *Laws of Indiana*, 1861, p. 52.

against a member of a gang of white ruffians who entertained themselves by annoying Negroes. The judge to whom
the appeal was made placed the white man under bond.
The latter objected on the grounds that the Negro was not
a competent witness. The judge ruled that the law against
Negro testimony did not prevent the man from taking legal
steps for his own protection and that the affidavit which
he had sworn to was not being used as evidence in a trial
—hence he was not a witness within the meaning of the law.[8]

A more significant case was taken to the Indiana Supreme
Court in 1855. It involved an Indianapolis Negro named
Jordan Woodward who was found guilty of making a mur-
derous assault with a club upon a white man. During the
trial John L. Ketcham, Woodward's lawyer, tried to introduce testimony by another Negro to prove that his client
had acted in self-defense, but the testimony was rejected
because of the color of the witness. Ketcham appealed the
case on the grounds that this testimony should not have
been barred. In his brief he argued: "Woodward is a
negro—but the State is not 'a white person'—but is rather
a lady of changeable complexion—graciously taking the
hue she finds in her adversary—

"If the defendant may not call a Negro as witness, neither
could the State. The act . . . forbids their testifying in
cases where one party is white—

"Now if a negro murder a white man, in the presence of
a crowd of Negroes, but unseen by any white man, can it
be pretended that he shall escape punishment for want of
evidence to convict? . . .

"It has ever been the practice, where deft. [defendant]
is a Negro, in criminal cases, to swear Negroes as witnesses,
both for the state and the defendant."

The Supreme Court accepted Ketcham's argument and
ordered that the testimony of the colored witness be admit-

8 Dunn, *Greater Indianapolis,* 1:116, 240.

ted, remarking: "We do not think that the State was contemplated as a person of any particular color by the statute."[9]

In another case in which white officers had levied an execution upon the horse of a Negro resident of Morgan County the latter brought suit to recover his horse and won his case in the lower court. In the trial the white defendants tried to introduce the testimony of two mulattoes, but the judge refused to permit this since white men were parties to the case. The defendants appealed the case, insisting: "that in a suit wherein one party is white, and the other colored, the white party may introduce a colored witness against the other party, but the colored party cannot introduce the same or other witnesses of like color against the white party." This interpretation was rejected by the Supreme Court which held that neither side could use colored witnesses.[10]

Except for the school laws, which are dealt with in another chapter, the only other important racial distinction in Indiana law was found in the laws on marriage. A law prohibiting mixed marriages was passed by the legislature in 1818, but it did not appear in the Revised Laws of 1824, nor was there any prohibition against intermarriage in the revisions of 1831 and 1838.[11] The lawmakers did not appear to take any particular interest in the matter until 1840, but that winter, while the legislature was in session, a marriage occurred in Indianapolis which created an uproar in the infant city. The principals in the case were a white girl and a young man who, although white in appearance, was known to have Negro blood. He had been a servant of the family of his bride and had become almost their sole means of support when they fell on evil days after the death

---

9 Woodward v. the State, Supreme Court Papers, No. 879, Box 242, in Archives Division, Indiana State Library; Woodward v. the State, 6 Ind. 492 (1855).

10 Graham v. Crockett, 18 Ind. 119-20 (1862).

11 *Laws of Indiana,* 1817-18 (general), p. 94; *Revised Laws of Indiana,* 1824, pp. 262-64.

of the head of the family. In spite of the fact that the girl's mother gave her consent to their marriage, on their wedding night a mob of Indianapolis residents surrounded the house where they were staying and dragged them outside. The bride was ridden on a rail, and the groom was driven out of town and warned not to return.[12]

It was during this period of excitement that the legislature passed a drastic law on the subject of intermarriage. Various extreme proposals were made during the debates on the measure, including a provision to disfranchise for life any minister who performed a marriage between persons of different colors. It was also proposed that a section be included "disfranchising persons who shall sanction or countenance amalgamation." These were rejected, but the bill "to prohibit the amalgamation of whites and blacks" which finally passed not only prohibited marriages between white persons and persons having one eighth or more of Negro blood but imposed fines ranging from one to five thousand dollars and prison terms of from ten to twenty years for persons who married in violation of it. Clerks who issued marriage licenses contrary to the law were subject to a fine of five hundred dollars, while ministers who performed marriage ceremonies for persons who were prohibited from marrying were subject to fines of from one to ten thousand dollars. At the next session of the legislature the sections of the law imposing penalties were repealed, although the marriages remained unlawful. At the 1842 ses-

---

[12] Coffin, *Reminiscences*, 155-60; Dunn, *Greater Indianapolis*, 1:240. The girl's family was en route from Missouri to Massachusetts when they became stranded in Indianapolis. The young man was accompanying them in accordance with a promise he had made to the girl's father before his death. During their stay in Indianapolis the girl and her sister were accepted in respectable society and sang in the choir of one of the leading churches. After he was driven out of Indianapolis, the young man fled to eastern Indiana and was befriended by Levi Coffin. According to Coffin, he was eventually reunited with his bride and her mother in Cincinnati. There are some discrepancies between the accounts of Coffin and Dunn. The account given above follows Coffin.

sion penalties almost as severe as those in the 1840 law were again enacted and remained in force in the revision of the laws made in 1852.[13]

There is no record that the extreme penalties were ever invoked, nor is there any evidence that there was any tendency toward miscegenation in Indiana. As antislavery advocates frequently pointed out, miscegenation was an inevitable result of the system of slavery in the South, and the way to stop it was to put an end to slavery. Antislavery groups charged that the real motive for the laws on the subject of marriage was the desire of Indiana's politicians to play upon the racial prejudices of their constituents. An editorial published in the *Free Labor Advocate* at the time of the adoption of the 1842 law declared: "We are far from *advocating* an amalgamation of the whites and blacks, but when the legislature of an enlightened republic, so far forget their dignity as to spend their time, and the money of their constituents in prescribing the precise color of the skin of those who may be allowed to marry together . . . we think it high time they were invited by the voice of an insulted constituency to return home. . . . Such legislation is not only pitiably contemptible, but it is wicked and tyrannical; tending directly to increase that abominable prejudice which is crushing to the earth the free people of color in the professedly free states."[14]

None of the discriminatory legislation was repealed before the Civil War. During the forties and fifties two opposing

13 Indiana *House Journal*, 1839-40, pp. 196-98; *Laws of Indiana*, 1839-40 (general), pp. 32-33; *ibid.*, 1840-41 (general), p. 128; *ibid.*, 1841-42 (general), p. 142; *Revised Laws of Indiana*, 1852, vol. 2, p. 422.

14 *Free Labor Advocate*, February 16, 1842. A resolution adopted at an antislavery meeting at Newport, Wayne County, declared: "Resolved; That we are opposed to the amalgamation, of the white and black inhabitants of our country, and that we have ocular demonstration, that the only means by which it can be prevented, is to abolish slavery, so that colored females, may be instructed in their moral and religious duties, and be placed under the protection of righteous laws." *The Protectionist* (Newport, Ind.), April 1, 1841 (vol. 1 :no. 7 :107).

forces were at work. On the one hand were the antislavery groups, who sought the removal of disabilities based on color; on the other were the Negrophobes, who sought to bar further immigration and to impose further restriction upon the colored population. The latter group was in the ascendancy. During the period when sectional tensions were increasing as the result of the excitement over the slavery issue in national politics, intolerance of Negroes seemed to be increasing in Indiana. This feeling was evident in the state legislature and especially in the Constitutional Convention of 1850, in which delegates seemed to vie with each other in heaping abuse upon the despised race. So marked was this that one delegate remarked that there appeared to exist in the convention "a very decided disposition" not only "to crush every expression of sympathy for the negro race," but also a disposition to "crush to the ground every man who ventured to give utterance to such sympathy."[15] It was in this atmosphere that Article XIII of the new Constitution, which is discussed elsewhere in this book, was framed. That this article on Negroes was ratified by an even larger vote than that cast in favor of the main body of the Constitution is evidence that the delegates to the convention gauged accurately public opinion on this question.

Prejudice took not only the form of restrictive constitutional and legislative proscription but sometimes erupted into acts of violence. When Frederick Douglass, the most famous Negro in the United States in this period and one of the leaders in the antislavery movement, spoke in Indiana in 1843, the presence of a colored speaker before a white audience led to violence. The *Wayne County Record* reported that among the speakers at an abolition meeting in Richmond "was a negro man [Douglass]" who made an address in which he "abused, in the most bitter terms, all those whose views did not comport with his own. His slang so incensed the people, that at night, when the meeting was

15 *Debates and Proceedings,* 1 :246.

still going on, he, and probably some of the other lecturers present, was egged, and the house of one Abolitionist in Town was stoned." The paper expressed the view that the Negro was "impudent," although it asserted that mob violence was not the way to deal with such a person.[16]

A week later when Douglass spoke at Pendleton in Madison County another mob assailed the meeting. Several persons were wounded, and "a colored lecturer," presumably Douglass, barely escaped with his life. It was reported that the violence had been encouraged by some of the leading Baptists and Methodists of the community, among them a man who was a member of the state legislature. One member of the mob was apprehended and brought to trial in Anderson, the county seat, and sentenced to twenty days in jail. Thereupon a crowd of about two hundred persons, including some "respectable men" (among them the aforementioned legislator), descended upon the jail, threatening to free the prisoner by force. Further violence was averted by the timely arrival of an order from the Governor pardoning the prisoner.[17]

In Indianapolis in 1845, John Tucker, one of the Negro pioneers in the city, was murdered on a downtown street in an unprovoked attack by a group of white ruffians, who fell upon him with cries of, "Kill the damned nigger!" Two of the men involved in the affray were arrested, and one

[16] Quoted in *Free Labor Advocate,* October 6, 1843, which reported that Douglass had spoken principally on ecclesiastical subjects and the relation of the churches to slavery. It denounced the account given above as an "exhibition of spleen and prejudice against colored people and the anti-slavery cause . . . . 'Among the Lecturers is a Negro man.' What monstrous outrage upon the good taste of the citizens of Richmond! For a negro to presume to tell the horrors of slavery . . . is in the judgment of our neighbor of the Recorder a piece of impudence. . . . IMPUDENT!! Why was he impudent? Simply because he was a Negro. No man in his senses would call a white man *impudent* for talking just as Douglass did, under precisely similar circumstances." *Ibid.*

[17] *Ibid.,* October 13, 20, November 1, 1843. An antislavery meeting at Goshen in Wayne County condemned Governor Samuel Bigger for extending pardon to "mobocrats." *Ibid.,* December 15, 1843.

of them was convicted of manslaughter and sentenced to three years at hard labor in the state penitentiary. Some surprise was expressed at a verdict which punished a white man for an attack upon a Negro, but a motion for a new trial was denied, and Governor James Whitcomb refused to intervene in behalf of the convicted man. However, the actual murderer escaped and was never brought to trial.[18]

The attack upon Tucker terrorized the other Negroes in Indianapolis. Many of them went about thereafter armed with clubs. A local newspaper sought to convince them that this was a mistake, that their actions would tend to provoke rather than allay ill feeling against them. It assured them that they were "as safe from harm, and as much under the protection of the laws, as any member of the community." At the same time the paper warned the Negroes against "doing anything having a tendency to arouse latent prejudice and hatred in the breast of those who entertain them."[19]

Throughout the late forties and the fifties racial intolerance mounted, and there were increasing instances of mob violence against Negroes. One example occurred in Jeffersonville in 1850, when two Negro men, who were accused of consorting with white women, were tied to posts and whipped in the presence of a large crowd.[20]

The most notorious outbreak of mob violence occurred in 1857 in the vicinity of Evansville, where trouble had been brewing for a long time between a group of Negroes who had settled on the river bottom below the town and their white neighbors. One of the Negroes was accused of beating a white family. He was arrested, but the fact that he was released on bond aroused the ire of some of the whites and

18 Indianapolis *Indiana State Sentinel,* July 10, August 14, 21, 1845; Smith, *Early Indiana Trials and Sketches,* 337-38.

19 Indianapolis *Indiana State Sentinel,* August 28, 1845.

20 New Albany *Daily Ledger,* August 3, 1850. This incident was followed by the attempt to enforce the 1831 Black Law described in Chapter III and gave an impetus to the demand for an exclusion article in the state constitution.

fired them with the determination to get rid of the entire colored community. Accordingly, a group, estimated at between fifty and seventy-five persons, charged the house of the Negro and battered down the door with a fence rail. The Negro and his friends had been expecting the attack and were prepared to resist it. Shots were fired by both sides, although there were conflicting stories as to which side fired first. Hand-to-hand fighting followed, in which bowie knives, clubs, and cleavers were used. One white man was killed, a second critically wounded, while several members of both races suffered less serious wounds. The whites withdrew, but threatened to come again and wipe out the community. In order to forestall further violence the sheriff of the county went to the Negroes' cabins and persuaded them to place themselves in his custody. They were taken to Evansville, where some of the men were lodged in the jail for protection. Most of the group was removed to Gibson County to prevent further trouble. Apparently the officers of the law did not attempt to deal with the whites who had made the attack.[21]

In 1860 a group of Negroes who had settled in New Albany contrary to the state exclusion law were compelled by "public sentiment" to leave and find homes elsewhere. Some of them sought to settle in the neighboring town of Jeffersonville, but it was reported that the citizens of that place, "unwilling to maintain such an obnoxious class of population at public expense, have taken measures to drive them away. They held a meeting last night and committees were appointed to carry out the object."[22]

Some of the press adopted a benevolent attitude toward the white perpetrators of violence, and in some cases seemed almost to encourage resort to mob law. For example, as the result of publicity in the Fort Wayne *Times* about an

21 Evansville *Journal* reprinted in Indianapolis *Daily Journal*, July 27, 29, 31, 1857; New Albany *Daily Ledger*, July 29, 1857.

22 Louisville *Courier* quoted in Indianapolis *Daily Sentinel*, August 14, 1860.

alleged Negro house of prostitution the house was attacked by a mob. In reporting the event the same newspaper commented: "The Negroes are becoming intolerable . . . and it is full time they were drummed out of town." When an Indianapolis mob demolished two houses said to be used for the same purpose, the Indianapolis *Sentinel* remarked: "If ever mob law is justifiable, it was in this instance." In reporting the arrest of a Negro for making an assault on a German, the same paper referred to the former as a "malicious nigger," and added: "Mr. Tom [the Negro] is aching for the penitentiary or for lynching, and another act and it is not unlikely his aspirations will be realized."[23]

Incidents of violence and comments of this sort could be multiplied. Racial prejudice certainly did not diminish, but on the contrary seemed to increase, in the period just before the Civil War. In 1858 a series of resolutions was offered in the state legislature endorsing the majority opinion on the Dred Scott case, which had recently been decided by the United States Supreme Court. They asserted in part:

"That we affirm the original and essential inferiority of the negro."

"That we deny that the negro was intended to be embraced within the abstractions of the Declaration of Independence, and assert that the right of freedom and equality was predicated only for the dominant race of white men."

"That we deny that negroes are citizens of the United States."[24]

The resolutions were not adopted, but the mere fact that they were considered is evidence of the drastic change in

[23] Quoted in Indianapolis *Daily Sentinel*, April 25, 1860; *ibid.*, March 13, July 20, 1860.

[24] Indiana *Senate Journal*, 1858 (special session) pp. 12-13. One of the most controversial parts of Chief Justice Taney's opinion in the case of Scott *v.* Sandford (19 Howard 393) was the passage in which he stated that Negroes were "not included, and were not intended to be included, under the word 'citizens' in the Constitution," but were at the time of the framing of the Constitution "considered as a subordinate and inferior class of beings."

attitude which would have to occur before Indiana would accord Negroes legal and political equality.

In the economic realm, as in others, Negroes were in a disadvantageous position. Their resources were small and prejudice against them strong. Nevertheless, a sizable number were able to establish themselves as independent farmers. Prior to the Civil War the colored population, like the white, was largely rural. The census of 1850 showed that of 2,150 Negroes who were listed as following an occupation, 976 were farmers. Of the remainder, 720 who were listed as "laborers" were in many cases farm laborers. In clearing the forest and transforming the state from a wilderness into a prosperous agricultural society these Negroes played a part.

Early settlers acquired land in two ways—by purchase from the government or from private owners. Most Negroes who owned land acquired it in the second way, but thousands of acres were acquired directly from the United States government. The earliest example of entry of government land by a Negro which the present writer has discovered is the record of an entry on July 15, 1813, of a quarter section of land in Wayne County by Spencer, a free man of color. On October 19, 1815, the same man entered another quarter section.[25]

In nearby Randolph County between 1832 and 1845 about two thousand acres of land were entered by Negroes. Among those acquiring government land was Thornton Alexander. He, together with Thornton Alexander, Jr., and Gabriel and John Alexander entered four hundred acres of land between 1832 and 1836, most of it in tracts of eighty acres. William Benson entered eighty acres in 1832

---

[25] Margaret R. Waters (comp.), Indiana Land Entries, Volume I, Cincinnati District (mimeographed copy in Genealogy Division, Indiana State Library), 111-12. It is impossible in most cases to determine when government land was purchased by Negroes because the tract books and the records of the land office usually do not indicate the color of the purchaser. The case of Spencer is exceptional.

and an additional 120 acres with Michael Benson in 1836, while Benjamin Tann entered a quarter section in 1837. Other Negroes entered smaller tracts, usually of forty acres.[26]

In Jackson Township in Hamilton County the Roberts family entered 960 acres between 1835 and 1838. In Grant County the Weaver family acquired two hundred acres in the same way, while in Gibson County between 1847 and 1853 Daniel and Thomas Lyles entered 360 acres and Elias Roberts eighty acres. There were also entries by Negroes in Vigo County. Here Dixon Stewart acquired eighty acres of government land, while Jeremiah and Abel Anderson acquired 240 acres and the Roberts family 280 acres. In the counties mentioned Negroes owned more than 2,500 acres purchased from the government, all of it virgin land which had to be cleared by felling trees and removing brush before it could be farmed.[27]

Colored laborers cleared other land in addition to this. Usually Negroes were too poor to buy any but the least desirable land, so they frequently bought small uncleared tracts from white neighbors. Sometimes they were employed to clear the land of white settlers and earned money in this way to buy some of their own. For example, William Trail, a former slave, came to Brookville from Maryland in 1814 and was thereafter employed at clearing land in Union County. From his savings he was able to buy twenty-five acres in Fayette County on which he built a cabin. In 1832 he sold this land and moved to Henry County, where he entered 160 acres of land in Greensboro Township.[28]

In the early thirties when E. S. Abdy, the English traveler, visited the vicinity of Madison he found about eleven colored families, the first of which had arrived in Indiana some

26 Waters, op. cit., 125-26, 183-84; Tucker, Randolph County, 136-37.

27Wright, "Negro Rural Communities," in Southern Workman, 37: 165-66.

28 William Trail, "The Story of a Slave in Indiana," in The Indianian, 3(1899) :257-62.

time before 1820. They had cleared land and become successful farmers, growing wheat, rye, hemp, and a little tobacco. Abdy's host, a colored farmer named Crosby, had come from Kentucky thirteen years before and had since acquired two small farms, totaling 137 acres. He had cleared about one fourth of the land and was the owner of six cows, four horses, and other farm animals. A neighbor was Fountain Thurman, a man of unusual intellect and skill, who had mastered several trades, including those of mason, well digger, and rock blaster while yet a slave. He had been able to persuade his master to let him buy his freedom by earning money at his various trades. The master agreed, on the terms that Thurman should pay him one hundred dollars a year for seven years. In the seven years the slave was able to earn not only the money to purchase his own freedom but enough besides to redeem his wife and children from slavery. He came to Jefferson County, where he bought an eighty-acre farm at three dollars an acre. As the result of the improvements he made on it, he was later offered seven hundred dollars for the land.[29]

The story of the farmers whom Abdy found in Jefferson County could be duplicated in other parts of the state. Even more successful was Thornton Alexander of Randolph County, who was mentioned above. He had been born a slave in Virginia about 1780 but was set free in 1816 and taken by his master to Ohio. In 1822 he moved to Randolph County where he later acquired 320 acres of land. In 1850 he was reported as owning property valued at four thousand dollars. William Shoemake, a free Negro from South Carolina, came to Randolph County in 1855 after living for a time in Wayne, and acquired five hundred acres of land. Collier Simpson from North Carolina owned land in the same county valued at $3,500. These men were exceptional. There were many other landowners among the Negroes in the county, but they usually held tracts of forty acres or so,

[29] Abdy, *Journal of a Residence*, 2:367-69, 378.

worth only three or four hundred dollars. Other Negroes, who did not own land, worked as tenant farmers. The land on which the Negroes lived in this county was not as fertile as that found in some parts of Indiana, but these farmers appear to have made a more successful adjustment than almost any other group in the state. A Quaker visiting the Cabin Creek settlement in 1842 observed with satisfaction the progress of the farmers, many of whom had formerly been slaves. He remarked: "It seems to me that no reasonable person could visit this settlement, become acquainted with the situation and character of the inhabitants and witness the improvements many of them are making and not be an abolitionist! At any rate he would be satisfied that they are capable of taking care of themselves if they have any thing like a fair chance."[30]

Many of the Randolph County farmers had come there from Wayne County, probably because it was easier to acquire land in the former county. Although the Negro population in Wayne was larger than in any other county, the number of independent farmers was small, probably because the county had been settled early and land was not so easily acquired. The census of 1850 showed one Negro farmer, named Seth Thomas, as owning property worth four thousand dollars in Clay Township, and one named Douglas White in Franklin Township who owned a farm worth six thousand dollars.

In Rush County there were a number of prosperous colored farmers. Among them were Turner Newsom and his family, who had only 37½ cents when they reached Indiana. Newsom went to work, accepting any kind of a job that was offered him. When he died, he owned a 160-acre farm, a two-story house, a barn, and a two-horse carriage. Another successful farmer in the same community,

---

[30] Census of 1850, Randolph County, Original Returns (microfilm, Indiana State Library); Tucker, *Randolph County,* 133-40; *Free Labor Advocate,* April 30, October 15, 1842.

who also came from North Carolina, was Emsley Lassiter. A report of the Committee on the Concerns of People of Color of the Spiceland Quarterly Meeting of Friends, which embraced this area, said that in 1857 there were eighty-one families of colored people, most of them farmers, within their limits. Forty-six of the families owned land, totaling more than three thousand acres, valued at from thirty to thirty-five dollars an acre, "nearly all of which has been acquired and the improvements made thereon by their own industry." The farmers were able not only to make a comfortable living for themselves but also to market their surpluses. Most of the children of these families attended schools, and all but seven families paid their own tuition.[31]

In the western part of the state the largest number of Negro farmers was found in Lost Creek Township in Vigo County, with smaller numbers in Nevins and Otter Creek townships. In addition to acquiring government land they purchased from private owners. Most of the land was entirely unimproved. The Negro settlers cleared it, drained it, built houses and barns, and became generally successful. Among the most prosperous was Dixon Stewart, who acquired a total of nine hundred acres, most of which he divided among his children before his death—one hundred acres to each of his four sons, seventy-five acres to each of four daughters. Jeremiah Anderson, who came from North Carolina about the same time as Stewart, eventually increased his holdings to 730 acres, which he divided among his children in his old age. Hezekiah Roberts, also from North Carolina, and his son, Reden, each acquired a farm of three hundred acres, while Kinchen Roberts from Virginia became the owner of 280 acres.[32]

31 Report of Spiceland Quarterly Meeting of Friends, 12th mo. 9, 1857, quoted in Herbert L. Heller, "Negro Education in Indiana from 1816 to 1869" (unpublished doctoral thesis, Indiana University School of Education, 1951), 166-67.

32 Beckwith, *Vigo and Parke Counties,* 393-94; Wright, "Negro Rural

In most of the southern counties of the state independent farmers were fewer. An exception to this is found in John Williams who came to the Blue River settlement in Washington County with the family of William Lindley, a Quaker, at an early date. Williams was able to buy 160 acres of land, which he cleared and on which he built a cabin and raised grain to feed his cattle and hogs. At his death in 1864 his property was worth more than six thousand dollars.[33]

In newly settled communities, so long as there was a need for laborers to clear the land, colored workers were welcome, but as population grew and land values increased Negroes found it increasingly difficult to acquire land. E. S. Abdy found that this situation had developed in Jefferson County by the early thirties. He remarked that after the Negro settlers had brought the land under cultivation and were rising in the world, "the avarice of the white man's pride was offended at the prosperous appearance of the negro's sons and daughters." He related that a Negro who had recently come from Kentucky with expectations of buying land in the community found that such hostility against Negroes had developed that it was doubtful whether he could buy land. Abdy's colored host told him that at first he had been well treated by his white neighbors but that recently he and his family had been plagued almost beyond endurance by the efforts of the whites to persuade him to sell his land to them and to go to Liberia.[34]

By 1850 prejudice had reached such a point that several proposals were made in the state constitutional convention to limit the rights of Negroes to acquire and hold real estate. Some of the extremists in the convention urged that

Communities," in *Southern Workman*, 37:167. The census returns for Vigo County substantiate these accounts.

[33] Trueblood, "Story of John Williams," in *Indiana Magazine of History*, 30:149-52. For the tragic circumstances of Williams' death, see Chapter VIII.

[34] Abdy, *Journal of a Residence*, 2:367.

one means of "persuading" the colored population to go to Liberia was to deny them property rights. One delegate proposed that one year after the adoption of the Constitution no Negro would be allowed to acquire real estate and that property already owned by Negroes would escheat to the state at the death of the owner, with the proviso that heirs should be compensated by a cash payment by the state. Most members of the convention were opposed to the proposal to prevent an owner from leaving his property to his heirs, but there was considerable sentiment in favor of limiting rights to acquire property in the future. Another delegate wanted to make it impossible for a Negro to sell real estate to another Negro, which, he said, would have "this good effect, that whenever the holders among the colored race are disposed to sell, they must of necessity sell to a white man." In defense of his proposal he argued: "The time is not far distant when every foot of soil in Indiana will have an owner. Let us, then, keep steadily in view the fact that every negro freeholder necessarily excludes from the same land, some one of our own race." A special committee to which the question of rights of Negroes was referred recommended: "After the year 1860, no negro or mulatto shall acquire real estate, or any interest therein, otherwise than by descent." The article was tabled, and no legal limitations were imposed upon the right of Negroes to own real estate.[35]

No accurate figures on the amount of land acquired by Negroes are available, but the value of their holdings is given in the 1850 census, which shows that at that date 671 Negroes owned real estate with a total value of $421,755. This included town property as well as farms and is therefore not an accurate index of the number of independently owned farms, but most of the real estate reported was farm property. The figures show that of the more than eleven thousand Negroes less than 6 per cent

[35] *Debates and Proceedings,* 1:444-59, 591; 2:1796, 1798.

owned land. The eleven thousand figure, of course, represents the number of individuals in the state, and a different picture emerges if this is taken into account. If the size of the average family were five (and many of them were much larger), the proportion of families owning real estate would be more than one in four. The value of the individual holdings ranged from $40 to $7,700, the average being $628. These holdings were distributed throughout all of the counties of the state except twenty-four, although in several counties there were only one or two Negro owners. Of the persons owning real estate, more than half lived in nine counties. These nine counties, as one would expect, were those in which the Negro population was largest. However, Randolph County, which stood third in the total number of Negro residents, ranked first in the number of property owners and had a substantially larger number than any other county.[36]

These figures show that there was a sizable group of independent farmers, a few of whom had acquired farms as large as those of their more prosperous white neighbors. In addition to those who owned their land there were numerous tenant farmers and farm hands who hoped to acquire their own land. It seems safe to conclude that these

[36] Heller, "Negro Education," Appendix, 303-5. The following table shows these nine counties together with the number of Negro owners and the value of their holdings.

COUNTY	NUMBER OF NEGRO OWNERS	VALUE
Clark	24	$ 10,240
Floyd	46	29,500
Jefferson	46	35,480
Knox	27	9,150
Marion	36	32,700
Randolph	75	50,930
Rush	30	34,600
Vigo	41	37,850
Wayne	47	22,345
Total	372	$262,795

men who made a livelihood from the land were usually the most prosperous and contented part of the colored population. Although there were instances of prejudice against them, they were more independent than the Negroes in the towns and hence suffered less from intolerance. A report of the Committee on the Concerns of the People of Color of the Indiana Yearly Meeting of Friends supports this. It stated: "Whenever they [colored people] are found in *country* situations, they much more frequently become useful and moral citizens, than when employed in our cities and villages, as servants about hotels, &c a subject which we think ought to claim the attention of all who desire to elevate the character and condition of the colored man in the free States."[37]

In the nonrural communities the largest numbers of colored people were found in the following towns in 1860: New Albany, Indianapolis, Richmond, Madison, Terre Haute, Jeffersonville, Charlestown, and Vincennes. New Albany, with 627 colored residents, or 7½ per cent, out of a total of 8,181, ranked first both in total number and percentage. On the other hand in Indianapolis, which was second with a total of 498, Negroes constituted only 2.6 per cent of the population of 18,611.[38]

---

[37] Minutes of Committee of Indiana Yearly Meeting of Friends on the Concerns of People of Color (MS, Earlham College Library), 15. Another report urged: "We would encourage Friends in the different neighborhoods to use their influence so far as may appear necessary to dissuade them from settling in towns and vilages [*sic*] and to encourage them to engage in agriculture which appears to be more condusive [*sic*] to their general advancement as a people." *Ibid.*, 29. A Negro at the celebration of West Indian emancipation in Indianapolis in 1849 urged his people to leave the cities and towns, where they were compelled to be the servants of white men, and go to the country and secure a right in the soil. Indianapolis *Indiana State Journal,* August 13, 1849.

[38] *Eighth Census* (1860), 112-28. The other towns ranked by percentage of Negro population were as follows: Charlestown, 6 per cent; Jeffersonville, 5 per cent; Vincennes, 4.9 per cent; Richmond, 4 per cent; Madison, 3 per cent; Terre Haute, 2.4 per cent.

The largest concentration of Negro townspeople was found in the Ohio River towns—New Albany, Jeffersonville, Charlestown, and Madison—where many of them earned a living working on the river boats. In all of the towns in the state Negroes usually made a living from any kind of physical labor that was available and followed no particular trade. As noted elsewhere, of 2,500 Negroes listed in the 1850 census, 720 were classified simply as "laborers." Of the remainder there were 454 persons engaged in approximately sixty different occupations representing a variety of skills.

Of the trades the one listed most frequently was that of barber. In every community in which there were colored people at least one, and frequently several, followed this trade. A few of them prospered enough to acquire a little property. The wealthiest Negro barber in the state in 1850 was apparently Augustus Turner of Indianapolis, who owned property valued at five thousand dollars. A number of Negroes were blacksmiths, while others were found in the building trades. These included carpenters, plasterers, brickmasons, and white washers, of whom carpenters were most numerous. Other trades followed by fairly large groups were those of shoemaker and cooper. The work of wagoner or teamster was one that was open to Negroes, and a few who owned their own horses and wagons were quite prosperous. Many other Negroes earned a living either in domestic service or as cooks, waiters, stewards, etc., in hotels or restaurants. These were the occupations which the general public regarded as most characteristic of the race.[39]

"As to the free negro, I must confess, no one can covet his condition; as a free negro in Indiana is very little better

[39] Heller, "Negro Education," Appendix, 299. Few Negro townspeople acquired real estate, but as early as 1835 the assessment lists for Indianapolis showed that of 81 Negroes listed as residents of the city, 11 were assessed for real estate taxes. Eliza B. Browning (ed.), *Lock-*

off than a slave in Kentucky. In fact it were better to be the slave of a good and humane master in Kentucky, than to be a nominally free Negro in Indianapolis, with no political or social rights, and to be looked down upon as inferior by every person he meets on the streets."[40] This description of the condition of the Negro population by a white Protestant clergyman reflected the attitude of most of the white population. The fact that they were cut off from social intercourse with the whites and regarded as an alien people tended to foster a feeling of race consciousness and solidarity among the colored population. Moreover, the fact that they were oppressed and discriminated against by the dominant white group created the conviction among Negroes that if their condition was to be improved, it would have to be through their own efforts. But, although they were excluded from the white man's society, they patterned most of their social organizations after those of the whites.

One manifestation of race consciousness was the celebration of a holiday peculiar to Negroes, the anniversary of the emancipation of the slaves in the West Indies. As one Indianapolis newspaper expressed it, "The First of August is *their* Fourth of July—or Independence Day." The occasion was marked by parades, picnics, and speechmaking. At these affairs speakers exhorted their people to improve their condition through education and industry. Some of them urged their audiences to try to elevate themselves in this country; others rejected this as hopeless and suggested migration to an all Negro state somewhere in the western hemisphere.[41]

erbie's Assessment List of Indianapolis, 1835 (Indiana Historical Society Publications, vol. 4, no. 7, Indianapolis, 1909), 406-31. The census returns for Marion County in 1850 show that the wealthiest Negro in Indianapolis was John Freeman, mentioned in the last chapter as the victim in a notorious fugitive slave case, who owned property valued at $7,000.

40 *Eleventh Annual Report of the Indiana Colonization Society* . . . (Indianapolis, 1846), 27.

41 Indianapolis *Indiana State Journal*, August 13, 1849; *ibid.*, August 6, 1847; Indianapolis *Daily Journal*, August 1, 1857; Indianapolis *Daily*

Although the earliest state conventions of Negroes were not held in August it became a frequent practice for delegates from all parts of the state to meet at the time of the emancipation celebrations. These conventions, which were one of the most significant expressions of racial consciousness and solidarity, were modeled on conventions held in the older states. The first colored convention appears to have been held in Philadelphia in 1830, with Bishop Richard Allen of the African M.E. Church as the leading spirit, although white antislavery leaders also sponsored the movement. Various groups of free Negroes, representing churches, schools, and benevolent societies, were present and voted to form a Society of Free Persons of Color and to promote the organization of auxiliary societies and the calling of local and state conventions. Thereafter annual conventions attended by delegates from many of the older states in the East were held.[42]

It is impossible to determine how close the ties were between the Indiana conventions and the national movement or whether delegates from Indiana attended the national conventions. However, the earliest Indiana convention of which any record has been found was called partly through

Sentinel, August 2, 1860. The celebrations sometimes exceeded what the more strait-laced regarded as the bounds of propriety. In 1854 the annual conference of the African M. E. Church adopted the following: ". . . Whereas some of our ministers and people have participated with ungodly persons in those celebrations, in a manner which we believe to be contrary to the Gospel of Christ; Therefore,

"*Resolved,* That it be the duty of each Minister to hold divine service in his circuit or station, in the free States, during the first week of August, 1855, by delivering a lecture, or a sermon, in reference to the West India Emancipation, and the importance of Education." *Journal of Proceedings of the Fifteenth Annual Conference of the African Methodist Episcopal Church for the District of Indiana . . .* (Indianapolis, 1854), 24.

42 Gross, *Clarion Call,* 10-11 *passim.* The convention movement was supported by such white antislavery leaders as William Lloyd Garrison and Arthur and Lewis Tappan and groups of Friends. Some of the early conventions were mixed groups, but the later ones were attended by Negro delegates only.

the instigation of Friends in Philadelphia. The movement
for a statewide meeting, begun in Madison, led to a meeting
in the African M.E. church in Indianapolis in January,
1842, where plans were laid for a convention. The convention appears to have been held in Terre Haute the following
May. Among the men identified with the beginning of the
movement were John G. Britton, Turner Roberts, James
Overall, A. E. Graham, V. Morgan, and John Crowder, all
of Indianapolis. Britton was apparently the most active,
serving as corresponding secretary to arouse interest
throughout the state.[43] Whether conventions met regularly
thereafter is not clear, but there were meetings in 1847 and
1851 and probably others. The men most active in the
meetings appear to have been drawn from the clergy of the
African M.E. and Baptist churches and the colored Masons.
In Indiana, as in other states, opposition to African colonization gave an impetus to the convention movement. The
delegates with great unanimity opposed emigration to Liberia and were anxious to improve their status in the United
States, although interest was sometimes expressed in emigration to some other spot in the New World. The 1847
convention was concerned primarily with the question of
promoting opportunities for education.

In August, 1851, while adoption of the new state Constitution, with its notorious Article XIII, was pending, a
convention met in Indianapolis. Delegates were present
from the following counties: Marion, Vigo, Washington,
Madison, Floyd, Bartholomew, Ripley, Jefferson, Vanderburgh, and Ohio. John G. Britton was chosen president of
the group. In his presidential address Britton predicted the
adoption of the exclusion article in the Constitution, which
he said would "seal the destiny of the Colored Americans
in this State." In the face of this crisis he urged the convention to consider the following articles:

[43] Indianapolis *Indiana State Sentinel,* March 1, 1842.

1. "As Americans we are entitled to all the rights, privileges, and immunities of citizenship as other citizens, according to the letter and spirit of the Constitution of the United States."

2. "We are deprived of these inherent rights, set forth in the Declaration of Independence, and confirmed by the Constitution of the United States; they are taken from us and conferred upon foreigners that come to this country."

3. "Industry, Education, and Temperance should claim the undivided attention of each delegate to this Convention."[44]

Although Britton insisted that "as Americans" Negroes were entitled to the rights of citizens, he also urged the convention to consider the possibility of emigration to Jamaica and called attention to "the kind and friendly manner" in which Negroes were received in Canada. For African colonization he showed no enthusiasm, but he suggested, with a hint of irony, out of deference to the white newspapers which had been advertising the convention as a colonization meeting: "The African Colonization scheme, I do hope, will claim the special attention of this Convention, as it has been going the rounds of the public papers, that the colored people of Indiana had called a convention for the purpose of emigrating to Liberia."

In subsequent years other conventions were held, usually in the African M. E. Church in Indianapolis on the eve of the meetings of the state legislature, for the purpose of framing petitions for the removal of constitutional and legal disabilities. In January, 1857, fifty to sixty colored men from various parts of the state met to consider means of appealing for the removal of the restrictions upon the right of Negroes to give testimony in court.[45]

44 Indianapolis *Indiana State Journal,* August 6, 1851. For some unknown reason no delegates were listed from the large Negro communities in Wayne, Randolph, and Rush counties.

45 Indianapolis *Daily Sentinel,* January 7, 1857.

In the convention movement and other activities colored Masons were frequently leaders. The first Negro lodge in Indiana was organized in 1848 but there were colored members of the order in the state much earlier. There had been Negro Masons in other parts of the United States since the days of the American Revolution, when their first lodge was organized by Prince Hall in Massachusetts.[46] The first one in Indiana was formed in Indianapolis and known as Union Lodge Number One, later as Center Lodge. In 1849, Gleaves Lodge, number two, was organized in the same city and King Solomon Lodge, number three, in Madison, and Darnes Lodge, number four, in Terre Haute. These earliest lodges were under the jurisdiction of the Ohio Grand Lodge, until 1856, when a Grand Lodge of Masons for the State of Indiana was organized in Indianapolis. Representatives from the four lodges already mentioned were present, as well as members of the order who lived in other parts of the state. After 1850 lodges were organized in Spiceland, Connersville, Randolph County, Carthage, Noblesville, Newport, Thorntown, New London, New Albany, and Vincennes. Many of these became defunct in the period after the Civil War as the result of the movement of Negroes from rural areas.

The most important personalities in the early history of Negro Masonry in the state were John G. Britton and James S. Hinton. Britton came to Indianapolis from Ohio in 1835 and became a leader in the Baptist church, the

[46] Prince Hall, who was born in the West Indies, came to Boston in 1765, where he became a preacher. In 1775 he, with a group of fourteen Negroes, obtained the degree of Freemasonry in a lodge attached to one of the British regiments encamped near Boston. In 1784 this group petitioned for and was granted a charter from the Grand Lodge of England, made out to African Lodge, number 459. This became a regular Masonic Lodge with the right to confer degrees, but its relations with the Grand Lodge of England were somewhat anomalous. Other Negro lodges outside of white Masonry grew up as offshoots from this lodge. Harold U. B. Voorhis, "Negro Masonry in the United States," in *Gould's History of Freemasonry throughout the World* (6 vols. New York, 1936), 4:364-6⁷.

Masons, and the convention movement. Hinton, born in North Carolina, came first to Terre Haute and later to Indianapolis, where he was one of the outstanding Negro political leaders in the period after the Civil War. Britton served as the first Grand Master, from 1856 to 1859. Hinton succeeded him, serving from 1859 to 1864. The earliest Grand Secretaries were William T. Evans, 1856 to 1858; A. McIntosh, 1858 to 1861; and W. S. Lankford, 1861-62.[47]

The Masonic order played an important part in Negro society, especially in developing leadership, but the influence of the Negro churches was far more widespread. The history of the churches and their part in education are dealt with elsewhere, but the churches also played an important part in shaping social life. Numerous societies of a benevolent or self-improvement nature were organized in connection with them. There was, for example, a missionary movement in the African M.E. church, the Paul Quinn Missionary Society, which met in connection with the annual conference, and numerous temperance societies sponsored by the same church. At the annual conference in 1854 it was reported that societies had been organized in the towns of New Albany, Charlestown, and Terre Haute, as well as three societies in the rural communities in the Richmond circuit and one in the Blue River circuit. Nevertheless, the Temperance Committee reported: "The cause of temperance has not progressed among us to the extent that it should have done," and added that intemperance was "the besetting sin of our people."[48]

In all of their organizations Negroes manifested a desire for self-improvement and a spirit of self-criticism which were in marked contrast to the repeated refrains of the white-supremacy advocates on their degraded condition and

[47] William H. Grimshaw, *Official History of Freemasonry among the Colored People in North America* . . . (New York, 1903), 214-15; Indianapolis *Journal*, January 6, 1880.

[48] *Journal of Fifteenth Annual Conference of the African Methodist Episcopal Church of Indiana*, 15-16, 19, 21, 28.

lack of capacity for improvement. A touching example is found in a proposal by a Negro mother for organizing a Mothers Association in which the mothers should present talks relating to their "experience, observations or opinions, touching the government and training of children, physically, intellectually, and morally." She asserted: "If one half the time which has been spent in blaming and denouncing our oppressors had been employed in working out the results of such an institution, much, very much would have been accomplished to demonstrate our title to the respect and consideration of mankind."[49]

A somewhat more militant spirit was manifested by Samuel Smothers, who, as head of the Union Literary Institute, started a little periodical called the *Students' Repository*. One object of the publication, he said, was "to cultivate the moral, intellectual, and religious character of the colored people and to afford scope for their rapidly rising talents and aspirations." He added, "If we, as a race, ever become educated, elevated, and respected, we have got to do the work ourselves. No one else can do it for us. We must prove to the white man that we are as susceptible of improvement as he is." In the articles which he published Smothers sought to refute the arguments of the white supremacists. The following excerpts are an illustration:

"Our enemies say that the black race is naturally inferior to the white man. . . . And in keeping with this theory, they have resorted to every means in their power to degrade the colored race. They have struck down our liberties; they have sought to blot out our manhood; they have bought and sold us like beasts in the market; they have deprived us of the means of education, and left us to grovel in mental and moral darkness. And, then, after having inflicted such monstrous and inhuman outrages upon us, they tell us, tauntingly, that we are an inferior race!

"There are also many of our professed friends who regard us as an inferior race. They admit that it is wrong to enslave the black man. They claim for him equal political rights; but still they are unwilling to acknowledge that the black man is their equal, intellectually . . .; and I regret to say that there are some of our own people who believe that we are really inferior to the white race. They have so long been accustomed to seeing the white man filling all the offices and positions of honor and profit in this country, while they have been compelled to do his drudgery in the capacity of servants and waiters, that they think the present state of things is all right, and they do not aspire to any thing higher.

"Now, I claim that we are not an inferior race, but are the equals of the white race in all the elements of true manhood."[50]

[50] *The Students' Repository* (Spartanburg, Ind., 1863-64; microfilm, Indiana State Library from original in Duke University Library), 1:no.1:1; no. 3:66-67. For an account of the Union Literary Institute, see Chapter VI.

6

CHURCHES AND SCHOOLS

IN CHURCHES AS IN OTHER FORMS of social organization the color line was sharply drawn. In the slave states separate Negro churches were viewed with suspicion, and slaves, although relegated to the loft, attended the same church as their master. But in Indiana, as in the other free states, separate churches developed in the denominations in which Negroes were numerous. Most important of these was the African Methodist Episcopal Church, which was a potent force not only in the religious life but also in education and in the development of race pride and unity. To Negroes barred from an opportunity to rise in the white man's world this church became a symbol of the ability of members of their race to elevate themselves through their own efforts. This point of view, which was shared throughout the North, was thus expressed by a Negro, writing in 1858:

"If there never had been an A.M.E. Church in this country, there would have been no place where we could have exercised to any extent the talent which God has given us. . . . The African M.E. Church has done more for the elevation of the colored people than all the other denominations in this country." The writer pointed out that in the regular M.E. Church no colored man could hope to have a voice in the discipline and government of the church, but in the A.M.E. Church every local preacher who had passed a satisfactory examination might have a share. He declared, "No man of color can ever be a man in the M.E. Church." On the other hand he added proudly: "All the religious liberty that the colored people enjoy in this country is attributable to the organization of the A.M.E.

Church. . . . Some of the best educated minds that have
been found among our people were reared up in the A.M.E.
Church."[1]

Among Negroes moving into Indiana, as among white
persons, Methodists were most numerous. In the earliest
years some of them belonged to the same churches as the
whites, as they had done in the South. Journals of the Ohio
Conference, of which Indiana churches were at first members, show colored members in Lawrenceburg and the
Whitewater circuit as early as 1812. Nine colored members
were listed in Lawrenceburg and four in the Whitewater.
In 1820 the Madison church showed six colored members,
and three years later eleven.[2] As new churches were established throughout the state colored persons continued to
join them, but this membership was always small. It
reached its peak in 1839 when the records of the Indiana
Conference showed a total of 442 colored members. Thereafter the number declined until in 1851 there were only 138.[3]

Walnut Street Methodist Church in Madison was unique
among Methodist churches in Indiana in having a membership made up entirely of Negroes but remaining a part
of the regular Methodist organization. By 1850 the Negro
membership in the district had reached 108, but by the
following year had declined to seventy. This appears to
have been due to the withdrawal of part of the membership
of the Walnut Street Church, including the pastor, William

[1] A. W. Wayman, "On the Rise and Progress of the African Methodist Episcopal Church in the United States of America," in *Repository
of Religion and Literature and of Science and Art* (Indianapolis and
Philadelphia), 1 (1858) :52-57.

[2] William W. Sweet, *Circuit-Rider Days along the Ohio, Being the
Journals of the Ohio Conference from its Organization in 1812 to 1826*
(New York, 1923), 110, 118, 137, 148, 159, 169, 182, 195, 212, 238, 258.

[3] Heller, "Negro Education in Indiana," 130-31; Methodist Episcopal
Church, *Minutes of the Indiana Annual Conference*, 1851, p. 34. The
only example which has been found of a Negro being elected to office
in the regular Methodist church in Indiana was the case of Peter Boothe,
who was elected an elder by the Southeastern Indiana Conference.
Minutes of the South-Eastern Indiana Conference, 1852, p. 8.

Anderson, who then formed a branch of the African M.E. Church. Thereafter the Walnut Street Church declined rapidly and was without a regularly assigned minister.[4]

The decrease in the number of colored members in the regular Methodist churches throughout the state was the result of the establishment of branches of the A.M.E. Church. By 1860 such churches were found in nearly all of the Negro communities, and colored members were usually found in the regular churches only where there were too few Negroes to establish a separate church.

The African Methodist Episcopal Church had its origin in Philadelphia in the years following the American Revolution, a period when many Northern masters were manumitting their slaves. The founder of the church was Richard Allen, who was born a slave but allowed to purchase his freedom after his conversion to Christianity. He showed such unusual talent that Bishop Asbury of the Methodist Episcopal Church frequently gave him assignments to preach. In 1786 he came to Philadelphia to preach at the St. George Methodist Church. When there was a proposal to segregate the Negroes in the congregation, he led most of the colored members in a general withdrawal and the establishment of the Bethel Church, which was dedicated in 1794. Negroes in other cities followed this example, and in 1816 a conference of the African Methodist Episcopal Church was organized in Philadelphia, the beginning of the national organization of the church. At this meeting Allen was elected the first bishop, and a book of discipline was adopted which followed the general principles in practice among Methodists.[5]

[4] Heller, "Negro Education in Indiana," 130; William J. Anderson, *Life and Narrative of William J. Anderson, Twenty-four Years a Slave* (Chicago, 1857), 36-42.

[5] Carter G. Woodson, *History of the Negro Church* (2d ed. Washington, D. C., 1945), 62-66. Another organization of colored Methodists, the African Methodist Episcopal Zion Church, was formed in New York about 1800 independently of the A.M.E. Church. In 1821 a national body

By 1858 there were seven annual conferences in the United States. The Indiana Conference, embracing Indiana, Illinois, Wisconsin Territory, and Iowa Territory, was organized in 1840. The most important figure in its early history was Bishop William Paul Quinn, one of the greatest missionaries in the West. Some of the facts of Quinn's life are obscure, but his birthplace appears to have been Calcutta, India, and his father to have been a mahogany merchant and a Hindu. Young Quinn was repelled by some of the Hindu practices and became interested in the doctrines of the Quakers who had come to India from England. He was banished by his father because of his heretical beliefs and eventually came to the United States, where he was befriended by Elias Hicks, leader of the sect known as the Hicksite Friends.

In spite of his early Quaker associations Quinn became a convert to the Methodist Episcopal Church. When his dark skin proved a deterrent to his advancement in the regular church he affiliated with the African M.E. Church. He began his work as a circuit preacher and missionary in western Pennsylvania, Ohio, Indiana, and Illinois in 1832. By 1844 he had established forty-seven churches with a membership of two thousand. In addition he had organized fifty Sunday schools and forty temperance societies and had held seventeen camp meetings. As the result of this record he was elected a bishop of the A.M.E. Church in 1844—the first person to be elevated directly from the mission field to the episcopacy. He continued to serve in the West for many years and was particularly interested in the area around Richmond, Indiana, because of the friendly relations between white and colored persons there. He spent his last years in Richmond, dying there in 1873 and being buried in the cemetery of Earlham College.[6]

of the A.M.E. Zion Church was organized, but there were no churches of this denomination in Indiana before the Civil War.

[6] Wayman, "On the Rise and Progress of the African Methodist Episcopal Church," in *Repository of Religion and Literature and of Science*

In 1836 Quinn organized a church in Richmond. He also probably played a part in the establishment of churches at Greenville, Snow Hill, and Cabin Creek in Randolph County and the Mount Pleasant Church in Rush County. Some of these churches, like many others which he organized, disappeared in the period after the Civil War as the result of the Negro migration from rural areas.

In 1836 Quinn assisted in the organization of a Methodist society in Indianapolis which became the Bethel A.M.E. Chapel. Little is known of the early ministers of this church, but in the fifties an outstanding personality, Elisha Weaver, was appointed to the post. He did a great deal to increase the membership of the church and to improve the educational opportunities for Indianapolis Negroes.[7]

The Allen Chapel in Terre Haute was organized by Quinn in 1839. Among the early ministers was Hiram Revels, who later went South during Reconstruction and became a United States Senator from Mississippi and head of Alcorn University. In 1840 a church was formed in Lost Creek Township. In 1841 the Bethel A.M.E. Chapel, the first colored church in Posey County, was organized on a farm west of Mount Vernon. Its first pastor was the aforementioned Elisha Weaver. In 1849 the Hills Chapel A.M.E. Church was built near the Weaver settlement in Grant County. As already noted an African M.E. church was formed in Madison about 1850. A camp meeting at Vernon was also conducted by the Madison district.[8]

and Art, 1:53-56; Lewellyn L. Berry, *A Century of Missions of the African Methodist Episcopal Church 1840-1940* (New York, 1942), 52-55.

[7] Berry, *A Century of Missions,* 52; *History of Wayne County, Indiana* . . . (2 vols. Inter-State Publishing Company, Chicago, 1884), 2:133; Tucker, *Randolph County,* 135; *History of Rush County, Indiana* . . . (Brant & Fuller, Chicago, 1888), 806; Indianapolis *Daily Sentinel,* January 19, 1858; Indianapolis *Daily Journal,* September 20, 1858; Indianapolis *Recorder,* February 18, 1933.

[8] Beckwith, *Vigo and Parke Counties,* 119, 389; Mildred A. Clift, "A History of the Negro in Vanderburgh, Gibson, and Posey Counties in Indiana" (unpublished M.A. thesis, Indiana University, 1941), 14;

By 1854 the African M.E. Church had a total membership of 1,387 in Indiana, which meant that more than one
fifth of the Negroes in the state were members. By 1860
the Richmond church, with 270 members, was the largest
in the state, while the one in Indianapolis was second with
202 members. The importance of the church cannot be
measured merely in terms of church membership. It was a
significant force in educational, cultural, and social, as well
as moral progress.[9]

Next to the African M.E. Church the Baptist Church
claimed the largest number of Indiana Negroes. Because of
the decentralized type of government of this denomination
reliable data as to membership are not available. It appears
that in most cases Negroes were admitted to membership
in the same churches with whites before the Civil War.
Regarding the colored members of these mixed churches no
figures are available. However, in a number of communities
with a large colored population separate churches were
organized before 1860. As early as 1831 there is mention
of a colored Baptist meetinghouse in Ripley Township in
Rush County. The first colored church in Evansville was
a Baptist one, organized in 1842. The following year the
Regular Union Baptist Church was founded in Nettle Creek
Township in Randolph County. About 1846 a colored Baptist church was organized in New Albany and about the same

Whitson (ed.), *Grant County*, 1:350-51; Anderson, *Life and Narrative*,
40-42. Hiram Revels was born in North Carolina in 1822 and came to
Indiana in 1844, where he attended a Friends school at Liberty. He later
attended school in Ohio and Knox College in Galesburg, Illinois. After
being ordained a minister of the A.M.E. Church he preached in several
states including Indiana. In 1870 he was elected to the United States
Senate from Mississippi, the first Negro to attain that distinction. His
brother, Willis Revels, served as pastor of the Bethel Church in Indianapolis during the Civil War. *Dictionary of American Biography* (20
vols. and Index. New York, 1928-36), 15:513.

[9] *Journal of Proceedings of the Fifteenth Annual Conference of the
African Methodist Episcopal Church, for the District of Indiana,* 8; Indianapolis *Daily Journal,* October 7, 1859.

time one in the Weaver settlement in Grant County. There was also a Baptist church in the Bassett settlement in Howard County.[10]

There was no separate church for colored Baptists in Indianapolis until 1846. About that time Elder Charles Shachel came from Cincinnati as a missionary and "commenced preaching and hunting up the scattered Baptists," some of whom had joined the Methodists, and organized a few members into a church. This was the beginning of the Second Baptist Church. The church grew slowly. It was weakened by internal dissensions, and in 1851 the building was burned, probably as an act of malice. Since there was no insurance, part of the land owned by the church had to be sold to raise money to start another building.

In 1857 the church entered upon a new and more successful era when Moses Broyles, one of the most remarkable of Indiana Negroes, became its pastor. Broyles wrote a history of the church, which also contains much autobiographical material. He tells us that he was born a slave in Maryland and was sold at the age of four and taken to Tennessee. He was later sold to a Kentucky master named Broyles, who became fond of the boy and gave him many privileges. Most important of all he allowed him to be taught to read and allowed him to attend debates held by the white pupils in the local schoolhouse. While yet a slave Moses had read the New Testament five times and the entire Bible twice. He had also read the Constitution of the United States, Benedict's History of the Bible, and some of the writings of Alexander Campbell. When he was fourteen years old Moses' master promised him that he would free him in 1854. The boy remained in service until 1851, when he proposed to his master that he be allowed

10 Joseph P. Elliott, *A History of Evansville and Vanderburgh County, Indiana* (Evansville, 1897), 266; Tucker, *Randolph County*, 135; *History of Rush County* (1888), 805; Whitson (ed.), *Grant County*, 1:351; Indiana Historical Society, Committee on Pioneer Cemeteries and Churches, Report on Howard County (typed document, Indiana State Library).

to buy his freedom out of his own earnings. This was agreed upon, and by 1854 he had earned enough to buy his freedom and had saved three hundred dollars in addition. With these funds he came to Indiana and enrolled in the Eleutherian Institute, where he studied for three years.[11]

Although in his boyhood Broyles studied the writings of Alexander Campbell, founder of the Disciples of Christ Church, and for a time belonged to a Disciples church, he later withdrew and joined the Baptists, spending the remainder of his life in the service of that denomination. When he became pastor of the Second Baptist Church, its membership had declined to forty and it was heavily in debt, but under his leadership the church grew and prospered. Broyles was also the prime mover in the organization of the Indiana Association of Negro Baptist Churches in 1858. When the association was founded, it consisted of only three churches with a total membership of 83 persons. Apparently most of the rural churches were too poor and small to join. By 1864 there were eight member churches and a total membership of 306 persons. Besides the Indianapolis church the largest ones were at Charlestown, Cicero, New Albany, and Madison. Besides Broyles the principal Negro Baptist preachers in this period were Richard Bassett, Jesse Young, L. Artis, and Allen Brown.[12]

There were probably several other colored Baptist churches of which there is no record today, but there were comparatively few of them before the Civil War. However, as the result of the migration of Southern Negroes into Indiana in the postwar years, Baptists came to be the most numerous denomination.

Although the Presbyterian Church exercised a significant influence in early Indiana history, there is no evidence that

[11] Moses Broyles, *The History of the Second Baptist Church of Indianapolis* . . . (Indianapolis, 1876), *passim;* William T. Stott, *Indiana Baptist History 1798-1908* (Franklin, Ind., 1908), 265-67.

[12] Stott, *Indiana Baptist History,* 263; Broyles, *Second Baptist Church,* 34, 39.

there was any missionary work among Negroes, and very few Negroes adhered to that denomination. However, there does not appear to have been any discrimination as to color where membership was concerned. As early as 1827 a colored woman, Chiney Lively, was baptized and admitted to membership in the First Presbyterian Church in Indianapolis. Church records show that she cast her vote on a question of church government. In 1830 Milly Magill was admitted to membership in the Presbyterian Church in Franklin in Johnson County, and in 1838 two more colored women were admitted. There is also evidence of a Negro member in the Hanover church. No doubt an examination of the membership lists of other churches would reveal other examples. Probably the Negroes were the servants of members of the congregation. On the whole Presbyterians made little appeal and exerted little influence on Negroes.[13]

Quakers, on the other hand, showed much interest in promoting the religious instruction of Negroes although very few Negroes ever joined Friends churches. One of the activities of the Committees on People of Color of the various meetings was distribution of the Holy Scriptures to colored families and the promotion of the reading of the scriptures in the colored schools which were sponsored by Friends. A similar committee of the Anti-Slavery Friends was charged not only with distributing Bibles but with teaching illiterate Negroes to read the scriptures. Few Negroes were admitted to membership in the Friends churches in Indiana or elsewhere. The question of membership of Negroes had been settled officially by the Philadelphia Yearly Meeting in 1797, when a report was accepted which stated: "We are united in believing that our Discipline already established relative to receiving persons into membership is not limited with respect to nation or colour."

13 *Centennial Memorial First Presbyterian Church Indianapolis, Ind.* (Greenfield, Ind., 1925), 318-19, 345; Herriott C. Palmer, *The First Presbyterian Church of Franklin, Indiana . . . 1824-1944* (Franklin, Ind., 1946), 373, 376; Heller, "Negro Education in Indiana," 128.

However, few Negroes became members. Quakers helped sponsor the Free African Society in Philadelphia, which was a forerunner of the African Methodist Church and other colored churches, but no separate church of colored Quakers developed. The absence of colored members was perhaps due in part, as some writers have maintained, to the fact that Quaker worship, with its emphasis upon abstractness and quietness, did not appeal to Negroes. Another reason undoubtedly was that Quakers did not engage in prose-lytism to the same extent as the more evangelical sects. There was also some prejudice in Friends churches in spite of the official position against discrimination.[14]

Among Negroes who were brought to Indiana by Quakers or who migrated to Quaker communities, examples of membership in the Society of Friends are exceedingly rare. One colored man, Edmund Cary, who came to Rush County from Virginia, probably with the Binford family, was a member who sometimes spoke in meeting. There are also records of a colored member in the New Garden Meeting.[15] It is probable that some colored persons were members of the Anti-Slavery Friends since differences over the importance of the race question contributed to that schism. However, instead of joining Friends churches, most colored settlers in Quaker communities formed their own Methodist or Baptist meetings.

The first Constitution of Indiana (Article IX, Section 2) declared it to be the duty of the General Assembly "as soon as circumstances will permit, to provide by law for a general system of education, ascending in a regular gradation from

14 Minutes of the Committee of Indiana Yearly Meeting of Friends on the Concerns of People of Color, *passim;* Minutes of Anti-Slavery Friends, 149-51, 188; Cadbury, "Negro Membership in the Society of Friends," in *Journal of Negro History,* 21(1936):152-55, 174-84; Woodson (*Negro Church,* 21) asserts, as many other writers have, that the Friends' worship did not have enough emotional appeal to satisfy Negroes.
15 Newby, *Reminiscences;* Cadbury, *op. cit.,* 186.

township schools to a State University, wherein tuition shall be gratis, and equally open to all." Little progress was made in carrying out this admirable objective during the pioneer period. Before the Civil War Indiana was one of the most backward states in making provision for public schools. The educational opportunities afforded white children were limited and inadequate, but colored children were denied any public educational facilities whatsoever.

In spite of the fact that a school law was adopted by the first session of the state legislature and several supplementary measures were passed, progress in implementing the laws was slow. Sparse population, inadequate financial resources, opposition to public schools, and especially the feeling of many pioneers that other needs were more urgent than education contributed to the lag. The earliest school laws provided for the incorporation of townships for school purposes whenever a certain number of freeholders requested it. The local voters then elected trustees to administer the school and school funds. The system was haphazard and extremely decentralized. Some townships chose to open schools; others did not. None of the schools were public in the sense of being free since all charged tuition to pay part of the costs. In many places the only schools were private, usually church supported. Some of these received public school funds.

A law providing for a statewide public school system, supported in part by state taxes, was adopted in 1852. Under this, as in earlier laws, townships remained the unit for school administration although cities and towns were allowed to incorporate for school purposes. During the fifties some progress was made, but some communities remained without public schools, and the schools in many instances were supported by gifts and donations rather than local taxes. Illiteracy was higher in Indiana than in any other northern state in 1850 but declined somewhat during the next decade. It was not until after the Civil War that the state developed a school system comparable to the systems of the more advanced states.[16]

Inadequate as were the public schools in 1860, they were exclusively for white children. At that date about 65 per cent of white children were enrolled in some sort of a school, either public or private, while less than one fourth of the colored children were attending school. This discrepancy was due chiefly to the failure of the state to make any provision whatsoever for the education of colored children.[17]

The first school laws made no mention of color, and it is possible that a few Negro children attended the early township schools, but in 1832 in the state Senate the question was raised as to whether colored persons who were freeholders were eligible to participate in school elections. A report of the judiciary committee asserted that every inhabitant who was a freeholder or householder, without regard to color, had a right to participate in the school fund and have a voice in the ways and means of supporting the schools.[18] It is probable, however, that the failure to exclude Negroes from participation in the early schools was an oversight, and the 1837 law expressly stated that "the white inhabitants of each congressional township" were to constitute a body politic and corporate for carrying out the provisions of the act. An act of 1841, which permitted householders of a district to levy a special tax for school purposes, contained the proviso that the property of Negroes and mulattoes not be assessed for school purposes. Neither act expressly barred Negro children from the schools but

16 John D. Barnhart and Donald F. Carmony, *Indiana: From Frontier to Industrial Commonwealth* (4 vols. New York, 1954), 1: Chap. 16; 2: Chap. 6.

17 *Eighth Census* (1860): *Mortality and Miscellaneous Statistics,* 507-8.

18 *Revised Laws of Indiana,* 1824, pp. 379-85; *Revised Laws,* 1831, pp. 463-80; Indiana *Senate Journal,* 1831-32, pp. 186, 239-40.

the implication was that schools were for the white population.[19]

In 1842 a petition was presented to the state Senate asking a law "to prevent Negro and mulatto children from being forced into the district schools contrary to the will of the people concerned," which is evidence that Negroes were in attendance in some of the schools. The question was referred to the Committee on Education, which made a report stressing the inferiority of the Negro race and the necessity of excluding them from the schools for white children. The report stated that Negroes "are here, unfortunately for us and them, and we have duties to perform in reference to their well-being. It is our duty to elevate them and happify [sic] their condition so far as we can; but it is not our duty to do so by adopting any means calculated in its nature to degrade our own race. God in his wisdom has caused us to differ; this difference, too, consists in more than the color of the skin. . . .

"But the committee will not extend these remarks, nor enter into any elaborate discussion to show how far their admission into our public schools would ultimately tend to bring about that feeling which favour their amalgamation with our own people. That the *blacks* should be educated by some means, your committee do not doubt; but at this time they are not called upon to indicate the means. The opposition of the large majority of our people to any thing like a close intimacy with the African, is too well known to need comment. The only question for the committee is, whether it is expedient to have our public schools disquieted, and in many instances broken up, by having the negro thrust into them, contrary to the wishes of those concerned. In reference to this matter your committee are clear in the opinion that this should not be the case." The committee proposed a bill "to regulate the admission of negro

19 *Laws of Indiana,* 1836-37 (general), p. 15; *ibid.,* 1840-41 (general), p. 82.

and mulatto children into the public district schools," which passed the Senate but not the House.[20] In spite of the failure of this particular measure, the school section of the Revised Laws of 1843 incorporated a provision that public schools were open to the *white* children of the state between the ages of five and twenty-one.[21]

The legislative committee report quoted above, which coupled emphasis upon the alleged inferiority of Negroes with the somewhat inconsistent expression of alarm over the dangers of racial amalgamation, was a typical expression of the arguments of the advocates of white supremacy. These views were attacked by a small but vigorous group of antislavery men. A resolution of the Liberty party of Indiana adopted in 1844 declared that since virtue and intelligence were bulwarks of the republic, "education should therefore be diffused through all classes of the community, without regard to condition or color."[22]

Some of the colored residents also made efforts in their own behalf. A group of Jefferson County Negroes petitioned the House of Representatives for a share in the school funds, but the committee to which the petition was referred made an adverse report. In 1847 a convention of Negroes met in Indianapolis to petition the legislature for public school funds for members of their race. They adopted a resolution which declared: "That the white people of this State ought not to reproach us with being ignorant, degraded and poor, while they tax our property to support their own poor, and their own blind, deaf, and insane, and to educate their own children, while denying to ours the benefits and blessings conferred by this taxation."[23]

[20] *Senate Journal*, 1842-43, pp. 521-22, 615; Indiana *House Journal*, 1842-43, p. 788.

[21] *Revised Laws of Indiana*, 1843, p. 320.

[22] *Free Labor Advocate* (Newport, Ind.), June 14, 1844.

[23] "The Coloured People of Indiana," in *The Non-Slaveholder* (Philadelphia), 3(1848):88, quoted in Heller, "Negro Education in Indiana," 63; Indianapolis *Indiana State Journal*, August 6, 1847.

However, instead of conferring educational opportunities, the state legislature removed the one provision in Indiana law which had provided some training for colored children. An act of 1843 required that children who were apprentices be given some training in reading, writing, and arithmetic. In 1850 an amendment gave the masters of colored children the option of ignoring this requirement since colored children were barred from the public schools.[24]

In spite of the fact that the laws stated that public schools were for white children only, colored children were occasionally admitted to district schools in neighborhoods where the trustees and the public did not share the prevailing prejudices. For example, in 1846 the citizens of a school district in Wayne County decided without a dissenting vote to admit colored children. During the winters of 1846, 1847, and 1848 colored children attended the district school, paying special tuition since the law barred them from the benefit of the public school funds. James Lewis, one of the white householders whose children attended the school, objected to the presence of the Negroes and tried unsuccessfully to persuade the trustees to remove them. When they refused, he applied for a mandamus to compel the removal of the children, but the Wayne County court ruled against him. Lewis then appealed to the Indiana Supreme Court, which upheld him. The court decided that the law limited attendance at public schools to white children and that colored children might not attend even though they paid their own tuition. The court explained that Negroes were excluded by the legislature not "because they did not need education, nor because their wealth was such as to render aid undesirable, but because black children were deemed unfit associates of white, as school companions." This reason operated with equal force, whether the children paid their own tuition or were educated at public expense. The court suggested

[24] *Laws of Indiana,* 1849-50 (general), p. 141.

that separate schools for colored children (private, of course) might be organized.[25]

There were other isolated examples of Negroes attending district schools, and in some few places the practice appears to have persisted in spite of the Supreme Court ruling. One of the duties of the Committee on People of Color of the Anti-Slavery Friends was to attempt to secure admission of colored children to the common schools. Reports of the committee for 1844 showed that in some instances Negro children were "permitted to enjoy their distributive portion of the public school funds, through the mediation of Friends, and others friendly to their cause." As late as 1855 in the Cabin Creek settlement in Randolph County some colored children attended the district schools and participated in the common school fund.[26]

The school law of 1852 under which some state tax support for public schools was first provided and which permitted cities and towns to incorporate in order to set up their own school systems, contained provisions barring colored children from the benefits of the law. A law of 1855 further provided that Negro and mulatto children should not be counted in the enumeration for school purposes and that taxes for school purposes should not be collected from Negroes and mulattoes.[27]

In consequence of this legislative policy the only opportunities open to Negroes before 1869 were those afforded

[25] Transcript of proceedings in case of James Lewis *v.* John Henley, John Boren, Nathan Thomas, Trustees, in Supreme Court Papers, No. 547, Box 193, Archives Division, Indiana State Library; Lewis *v.* Henley *et al.,* 2 Ind. 332-35 (1850). In another case in which a group of white patrons had tried to compel a trustee to remove colored children who were attending a private school with white children in Henry County, the Supreme Court ruled that a trustee had no right to interfere in a private school. Polke and another *v.* Harper, 5 Ind. 241-42 (1854).

[26] Minutes of Anti-Slavery Friends, 65, 114-15, 343.

[27] Richard G. Boone, *History of Education in Indiana* (New York, 1892), 161; *Laws of Indiana,* 1855, p. 161. Heretofore, although colored children had been barred from the schools, the property of colored persons was taxed for school purposes.

by private schools and teachers. Most of these educational efforts were carried on by religious groups, in some instances by Negroes themselves, in others with the assistance of white persons. In education, as in other matters, Quakers showed more interest in the welfare of Negroes than did any other group. One of the principal functions of the Committees on People of Color of the various meetings was to promote education. The assistance which Quakers gave took several forms. In some cases Negroes attended the schools which were established for Quaker children, although this was unusual. There were frequently Negro children in attendance at a Friends subscription school near Carthage, and in 1853 twelve colored children were reported attending a Friends school in the Union Quarterly Meeting, which embraced the Hamilton County area. In 1852 a total of eighty-two colored children were reported in attendance at Friends Schools within the limits of the Indiana Yearly Meeting.[28]

Friends also conducted First Day schools for the instruction of adults. In 1840 four such schools with a total enrollment of ninety were reported. In 1852 nine schools were reported, one of which was attended regularly by almost one hundred persons. Much more important was the assistance given by Friends in the establishment of weekday schools for children. The Committees on Persons of Color helped to raise funds and to recruit teachers and frequently furnished books as well as exercising a general supervision over colored schools within the limits of the meeting. However, Quakers were usually not solely responsible for the schools. Colored people themselves played an important part in starting and maintaining the schools, and the costs were borne principally from tuition paid by the pupils. Some-

28 Newby, *Reminiscences;* Minutes of Union Quarterly Meeting Held at Westfield, Hamilton County, Indiana, 1849-61 (MS in Archives of Friends Church, Plainfield), 11th month 5, 1853; Minutes of the Committee of Indiana Yearly Meeting of Friends on the Concerns of People of Color, 9.

times teachers were white Quakers; more often they were colored persons of other faiths. In 1840, 309 colored children were reported as being taught through the assistance of Indiana Friends; by 1852 there were 632 pupils; and by 1860 the number exceeded seven hundred. In 1845 thirteen day schools sponsored by Friends were in operation; in 1851 twenty-one; and by 1855 between thirty and forty.[29]

The Western Yearly Meeting, embracing central and western Indiana, which was organized in the fifties carried on similar activities. In 1858 it was reported that the Blue River Meeting had raised funds to assist in rebuilding a colored school and meetinghouse which had been burned by "some malicious persons." The following year fifteen day schools, with terms varying from six weeks to nine months, were reported as being conducted under Quaker sponsorship. Twelve of these were taught by colored teachers. By 1861 it was reported that of 882 colored persons of school age resident within the limits of the yearly meeting, 318 were attending school. At this time there were eleven schools, all taught by colored teachers. In addition there were twelve First Day schools, which were attended by 346 persons.[30]

Among the Anti-Slavery Friends who split away from the parent body in the forties the cause of Negro education was especially significant. A report of the Committee on People of Color in 1845 pointed out the plight in which most Negroes found themselves. Most of the adults could not read or write because they had "toiled out the prime of their lives [in] abject and involuntary servitude to the whites, and wasted in fields of toil unremunerated, that portion of their days which is usually and appropriately devoted to the

[29] The material above is summarized from Minutes of the Committee of Indiana Yearly Meeting of Friends on the Concerns of People of Color, 9, 11, 14, 17, 22, and Minutes of the Indiana Yearly Meeting, 1840, p. 21; 1841, p. 19; 1842, p. 18; 1843, p. 23; 1845, p. 23; 1847, p. 25; 1848, p. 28; 1849, p. 31; 1850, pp. 30-31; 1851, pp. 37-38; 1852, p. 41; 1853, p. 31; 1854, p. 29; 1855, p. 27; 1857, p. 37; 1860, p. 42.

[30] Minutes of the Western Yearly Meeting of Friends, 1858, p. 31; 1859, p. 20; 1861, pp. 23-24.

cultivation of the mind." Because the parents were illiterate and unable to teach their own children and because the children were excluded from the public schools, white persons had a peculiar responsibility. "We would call the attention of our young Friends to this fact," the report continued, "and ask them, if upon calm reflection, they can feel satisfied, without devoting at least three months of their lives to the promotion of education amongst this people."[31]

The efforts of the Anti-Slavery Friends to secure the admission of colored children to the district schools have already been mentioned. In addition, the various meetings sponsored schools for both children and adults in Randolph, Wayne, and Henry counties.

Few documents have been preserved to show how the Negroes felt toward their Quaker benefactors, but the following letter, written just after the Civil War by a Negro boy who had attended a Quaker school in Henry County for a few months, probably expressed the feeling of other members of his race:

"To Teachers and Classmates:

"When I think of the eight happy months I have spent with you in the pleasant school-room at Rich Square, where I was received and much cared for by our truly distinguished and well-known teachers, I shall ever feel myself under many obligations to Mollie A. Wickersham and Debie Starr for the kindness and respect they showed to me. I shall forever remember them as ladies in my prayers. They did not say is your face white or is it black; but come in and we will aid you all we can; and we are disposed to act under the golden rule and be governed by it.

"My friends, that is religion according to the divine instruction. . . ."[32]

[31] Minutes of Anti-Slavery Friends, 152.

[32] New Castle *Courier*, August 2, 1866, quoted in Heller, "Negro Education in Indiana," 164-65.

The schools sponsored by Friends were frequently assisted also by colored Methodists or Baptists and were often held in the meetinghouses of these denominations. Colored ministers frequently were the teachers. A report of the annual conference of the Indiana district of the African M.E. Church in 1854 showed that eighteen day schools and twenty-two Sabbath schools were being conducted under the auspices of that organization. There were two day schools in Indianapolis, three of each in the Richmond and Vincennes circuits, two of each in the Salem, Blue River, and Cabin Creek circuits, and one of each in the town of New Albany, and the Charlestown, Bloomington, and Terre Haute circuits. Some of these schools were undoubtedly the same as some of those listed by the Quakers as being sponsored by them.[33]

Nearly all of the colored schools were of the most primitive sort. Some of them were conducted in log meetinghouses or in private homes. Occasionally there was a regular schoolhouse. In some instances Negro farmers donated land as a site for a school, and a log building was put up through the efforts of the colored population in the community. The school terms were extremely irregular, many of the schools being taught for only two or three months

[33] *Journal of Proceedings of the Fifteenth Annual Conference of the African Methodist Episcopal Church, for the District of Indiana,* 19. The regular Methodist organization showed little interest in assisting the educational efforts of the colored branch, although the question was discussed at some conferences. In 1853 the Southeastern Conference recommended that a school fund be provided by the legislature for the education of colored children. The question was considered at the meeting of the Northern Indiana Conference the following year, after which a committee made the following report: "Resolved, that we most heartily sympathize with them [people of color] in their literary and education enterprises and interests.

"Resolved, that we regard it inexpedient to take any specific action at this time, but will second the efforts of our sister Conferences in this regard." *Minutes of the South-Eastern Indiana Conference,* 1853-54, pp. 29-30; *Minutes of the North Indiana Annual Conference of the Methodist Episcopal Church . . . 1854* (Indianapolis, 1854), 22.

a year. Most of them offered only the rudiments of spelling, reading, writing, and arithmetic, but a few also offered grammar and geography.

Few of these early schools can be identified with certainty. One of the earliest met in 1831 in the Beech settlement in Ripley Township in Rush County. Later a school was built by some of the colored people and their friends on a farm owned by a family named Young. Another school was taught in the African M.E. meetinghouse, which was later known as the Mount Pleasant Church. Some of the teachers were local Quakers; others were members of the colored families.[34]

This Rush County settlement was distinctive not only because of the early interest in schools but also for the earliest circulating library for Negroes in the state of which any record has been found. In 1842 the Mount Pleasant Library was organized in the A.M.E. meetinghouse by a group of colored and white residents of the neighborhood. Any person might join the library association by paying a membership fee of twenty-five cents, and about sixty persons were listed as members. The books in the library included textbooks on ancient and American history and works on theology and rhetoric. One of the provisions of the constitution was that: "No Novels, Romances, or writings favourable to infidelity shall be admitted into this library." The library society continued to meet regularly and the library to function until 1867 when most of the books were moved to the Mount Pleasant schoolhouse.[35]

Of the numerous colored schools in Wayne and Randolph counties almost nothing is known. Many of them were housed in temporary quarters and did not have a continuous existence. An exception was the school in Dublin in Wayne

[34] Newby, *Reminiscences; History of Rush County* (1888), 805-6.

[35] A book containing the constitution, the list of subscribers, and the minutes of the library society from August 13, 1842, to October 12, 1867, as well as some of the books from the library, have been given to the Indiana Historical Society.

County, which was opened in 1843 and continued in existence as a private school until 1873. During that period it was taught by ten white and seven colored teachers. More typical was the school which was conducted for a few years on the farm of William Trail in Greensboro Township in Henry County. Trail was a prosperous farmer, but the local schools were closed to his children. Consequently his older sons had to leave home in order to get an education. When they returned, they opened a little school for their younger brothers and sisters and the other colored children of the neighborhood.[36]

In Vigo County as early as 1835 colored residents built a combined school and meetinghouse on land in Lost Creek Township donated by Kinchen and Nancy Roberts. The first teachers were Abel Anderson and Aaron Smith. Another Negro pioneer donated land for a school in Otter Creek Township. In Terre Haute the first Negro school was held in the Allen Chapel.[37]

Information about early educational efforts in Indianapolis is meager. Joseph J. Fitzgerald, who served for a time as pastor of the Second Baptist Church, gave private lessons. Moses Broyles of the same church organized a school which was in operation in the fifties. The earliest record of a school conducted by the African M.E. Church is in the fifties also, although it is probable that there was one much earlier. In 1858 Elisha Weaver, pastor of the Bethel Church, was also principal of a school, assisted by Miss Lucy Jefferson. The course of study included not only the usual reading, writing, and arithmetic, but also grammar, geography, history, and physiology. Weaver was very active in trying to raise money for the school. He held exhibitions

[36] History of Wayne County (1884), 1:517; Trail, "Story of a Slave in Indiana," in Indianian, 3(1899):257-62. William Trail, Jr., attended Union Literary Institute.

[37] Merle B. Shepard, "A History of the Negro Schools in Vigo County" (unpublished M.A. thesis, Indiana State Teachers College, 1948), 22-23, 28, 36.

of the work of his pupils, including recitations and singing, to interest the people of the city in the cause. In 1859 the members of his church organized an educational society to raise money to enable him to keep the school open for six months a year. Colored people were asked to contribute monthly dues as well as tuition payments, and white persons were also solicited.[38]

A few fortunate Negroes obtained training beyond that offered in these elementary schools by attending academies. There were occasional instances of Negro students in the various academies maintained by the Quakers throughout the state, but only three schools provided expressly for the admission of colored students. They were the Union Literary Institute in Randolph County, the Eleutherian Institute in Jefferson County, and Liber College in Jay County.

Of these, Union Literary Institute provided the most significant and successful experiment in Negro education. It was founded through the efforts of a group of Anti-Slavery Friends, although members of other denominations served on its board of managers. Four members of the original board were Negroes, and Negroes continued to serve on the board during most of the years that the school was in operation. Plans for the school were laid in 1845, and in 1848 a charter was obtained from the state legislature. The constitution, which was drawn up in the Friends meetinghouse in Newport in 1846, declared that the institution was principally for the "benefit of that class of the population whom the laws of Indiana at present preclude from all participation in the benefits of our public school system and further for the purpose of placing the blessing of an education in the higher branches of science within the reach of all who have not the means and facilities for the acquisition of scientific knowledge, which are always at the command of the wealthy." Distinctions based on color were expressly repudiated, and complete religious freedom was guaranteed. Article VIII declared: "There never shall be tolerated or allowed in the Union Literary Institution, its government, discipline or privileges, any distinction on account of color, rank or wealth." Elsewhere it was stated: "In all matters relating to ecclesiastics, each person connected with the school, either as teacher or pupil, shall be left to his or her denominational preference: nor shall any teacher be employed, or other instrumentalities used to favor one church organization or sect more than another. . . . The incompatibility of war and slavery with the Christian religion shall be a leading principle in the Institution."[39]

The school was operated on the manual training plan, with pupils working to earn part of their expenses. About one hundred and eighty acres of land were donated, and the institution was supported from income from the land, most of which was brought under cultivation, and from donations, as well as tuition. Agents traveled throughout the United States soliciting assistance. For several years a frame building served as a schoolhouse, but in 1860 a new building of brick was completed. In addition to this classroom building there was a boardinghouse or dormitory, which accommodated the principal and superintendent and their families and about fifty students. Part of the students lived at the school; others were day students.

In 1849 it was reported that a total of 230 students had enrolled in the school since its opening. Of these 165 were Negroes, 32 of whom were from states other than Indiana. The enrollment for the year 1850 was 131, of whom 92 were boys, 39 girls. Of the total 97 were colored. During the fifties enrollment declined, and by 1863 the attendance was only fifty. In later years the entire student body was colored,

[39] Heller, "Negro Education in Indiana," 191; *The Students' Repository*, 1(1863) :18-19.

and the institution was advertised as being located in "a large and flourishing settlement of colored people, and is designed for the education of that class of our population."[40] Pupils usually enrolled at the age of twelve years or older, although there were some younger ones. Most of them began their studies with the A B C's since they had not had the opportunity of attending school previously. The usual elementary subjects were taught, and advanced students might also study English grammar, physiology, chemistry, and natural philosophy. The length of the terms varied from year to year as did tuition.[41]

In some respects student life was rigorous and austere. Persons fourteen years or older were expected to perform four hours of manual labor each day under the direction of the superintendent. A large part of the work on the farm, plus such tasks as digging ditches, chopping wood, and assisting in the erection of school buildings was done by students. The rising hour was five, and time from five-thirty until noon and from one to five-thirty was spent in study or manual labor. There were daily scripture readings, morning and evening in the assembly room, and school regulations stated that quiet should be observed on the first day of the week. Further restraints were placed on the ebullience of youth by the following rules: "The sexes shall refrain from spending time with each other—provided that the public sitting room shall be free for such as choose to occupy it on first day (Sunday) from one to three p.m. and from half past six to half past seven on Thursday evening. Males

40 *Students' Repository*, 1(1863) :19-20; John L. Smith and Lee L. Driver, *Past and Present of Randolph County, Indiana* (Indianapolis, 1914), 599-608; Heller, "Negro Education in Indiana," 199-201, 205.

41 *Students' Repository*, 1:no. 1(July 1863), advertisement on back cover; *Free Labor Advocate*, October 14, 1847. In 1847 tuition charges ranged from $2.67 to $5.00 a term, while board was $1.00 a week. Students were expected to furnish an axe, a spade, and part of the furnishings for their rooms. The requirement that they were to keep their rooms in order included a stipulation that they must "mop the floors at least once in three weeks."

and females may walk out in company only by permission of the principal or male or female superintendent. Students shall not spend time in the kitchen except when engaged in necessary labor."[42]

The two outstanding personalities in the history of the school are two men who served as principals. The first of these, a white man, was Ebenezer Tucker, a native of New York state, who had attended Oneida Institute and graduated from the theological school at Oberlin. From 1846 to 1855 he served as principal of the Union Literary Institute. In 1859 he became principal of the Liber College in Jay County, where he remained until 1868. During the period of Reconstruction following the Civil War he went South to work with the freedmen and taught successively at Straight University in New Orleans and Tougaloo in Mississippi. In 1873 he returned to Union Literary Institute, remaining there until 1879. Under his direction the school in Randolph County enjoyed its greatest success. His efforts in behalf of the students were untiring. He was accustomed to spend at least twelve hours a day in teaching. A typical day included one recitation in his home before breakfast, a class in algebra and geometry at seven A.M., followed by one recitation after another until noon. After the midday meal he again heard recitations from one until six, and then held classes in his home at night.[43]

Another remarkable man, who served as principal of the school in the early sixties, was a young Negro, Samuel Smothers. Little is known about him except that he was a member of a Randolph County family, that he left his duties at the school to join the Union Army, and became a minister of the African M.E. church after the war, achieving notable success as a revivalist. By his own admission his formal education had been limited to nine months in a country district school, but through his own efforts

42 Smith and Driver, *Randolph County*, 603-4.
43 *Ibid.*, 609.

he was able to overcome this handicap. As head of the academy he sought to give other young Negroes opportunities which had been denied him. He constantly reiterated that education and elevation of the colored race must come through its own efforts. One means which he took to spread his ideas and to promote literary efforts among other Negroes was the publication of a little periodical called *The Students' Repository.* In the articles which he wrote on methods of teaching one catches a glimpse of the man. He showed an insight into child psychology in advance of his times. He insisted: "The old system of teaching children one thing at a time is a pernicious one. Children can be taught to spell, read, write, and count together, faster than they can be taught one of these branches. A variety of exercises rests the minds of children, and keeps up their interest in study. Children soon get tired of one thing, and if the teacher don't devise some plan by which to interest them, they will interest themselves in mischief."[44]

During Smothers' tenure attendance declined as the result of the Civil War, and in the spring of 1864 the school was closed temporarily. In September of that year Smothers announced that he had volunteered for service in the Union Army, declaring: "I feel that the time has come when the cause of our distracted and bleeding country, and the interests of my race, require me to act rather than to talk or write."[45]

---

[44] *Students' Repository,* 1(1863) :33-34. In another article Smothers described how he used the blackboard as a medium for teaching children in groups rather than individually. In another he described how he taught geography with the aid of a map of the world which he constructed on a grassy plot out of doors. The entire map was about twenty feet in diameter. Land masses were shown by grassy spots, oceans by spaces dug out between. *Ibid.,* 1 :65 ; 2 :15.

[45] *Ibid.,* October 1864, Foreword. The school was reopened after the Civil War. In 1869 some of the land belonging to the school was sold to raise funds for its operation. Ebenezer Tucker returned as principal in 1873. In 1874 the school was leased to the township as a public school. In the late nineteenth century the colored population of Randolph County

Next to the Union Literary Institute the most important school for Negroes was Eleutherian Institute in Jefferson County, located about ten miles northwest of Madison near the village of Lancaster in a community noted for its antislavery sentiment. In 1839 some of the residents had organized the Neel's Creek Anti-Slavery Society with a constitution which declared that one of the objects of the society was "to elevate the character and condition of the people of color by encouraging their education, moral and religious improvement, and by removing public prejudice." The membership of the Lancaster Baptist Church was so notoriously antislavery that for some years it was not allowed to affiliate with the Madison Baptist Association.[46]

The idea of establishing a school for the education of Negroes seems to have originated with the Reverend Thomas Craven, one of the pioneer Baptist ministers in the West, who had preached earlier in Lancaster and who returned there in 1854 and remained until his death in 1860. He donated the land on which the school stood and contributed heavily to the funds for erecting the two buildings which housed the school, a dormitory and classroom building which were completed in 1850 and 1856, respectively. When the school opened in 1849 the Rev. John G. Craven, son of Thomas Craven, was the first teacher. John C. Thompson, son-in-law of the elder Craven, also taught there.[47]

Something of the purpose of the institution, as well as the difficulties confronting it, may be read from a note attached to the catalogue which stated: "In this Institution the God

declined, and by 1911 there were only eight colored children in the district. After 1914 the children in the district were transported to Spartanburg to school. In 1919 the Indiana General Assembly disposed of the property of the Union Literary Institute. Heller, "Negro Education in Indiana," 205-6; Smith and Driver, *Randolph County*, 607.

[46] Minute Book of the Neel's Creek Anti-Slavery Society, 1839-45 (MS in Indiana State Library); William C. Thompson, "Eleutherian Institute: A Sketch of a Unique Step in the Educational History of Indiana," in *Indiana Magazine of History*, 19(1923) :109-10.

[47] Thompson, *op. cit.*, 110-11.

of the Bible is practically recognized as the Father of the
Human Race, its advantages being open to all without
regard to sect, sex, or color, 'moral and mental worth only
distinguishing.' The establishment of a good institution
of learning, under the most favorable circumstances, requires
no little energy and perseverance: occupying the high moral
position we do—so far in advance of public sentiment,—
especially in this locality—upon the confines of Slavery,
where the colored man and his friends are looked upon
with so much contempt, and shown so little kindness—ours
has been a most unthankful and laborious task." But, in
spite of the difficulties, the undertaking was considered
necessary because of the fact that the colored population
of the state was excluded from the benefit of public schools
and "therefore doomed to hopeless ignorance, unless extraordinary efforts are put forth by themselves and their
friends."[48] A primary purpose of the school was to increase
the opportunities for an elementary education for more
colored children through the training of more teachers.

A catalogue for the year 1857 showed that the staff
consisted of a president, a steward, a matron, and five
teachers. Subjects taught included mental and moral science,
mathematics, natural science, English, and German. There
was also a primary department. The 1856 catalogue showed
an enrollment of 109 students, of whom 18 were colored.
Ten of these had been born slaves. In 1857 it was reported
that 15 colored students and 85 whites had qualified themselves for teaching since the opening of the school. Negroes
were always in a minority, and it is unlikely that more than
40 Negroes attended the school throughout its entire history. Many of these were from the slave states, some coming from places as distant as Mississippi and Louisiana.[49]

This effort at education of Negroes, limited as it was, encountered opposition from some of the whites in the neigh-

---

[48] Quoted in Heller, "Negro Education in Indiana," 183.
[49] *Ibid.*, 182-84; Thompson, *op. cit.*, 114, 126.

borhood. Two instances in which planters brought children who had been borne to them by slave mothers to Lancaster caused the greatest excitement. In one of these cases a Mississippi planter had married a woman who was only partly colored but who was a slave. Since under Mississippi law the marriage was invalid and the children slaves, the father brought the family to Indiana to free them and to enroll the children in the Eleutherian Institute. An Alabama planter also brought his children and their slave mother to the community for the same purpose. In 1850 the houses of both families, as well as another house occupied by Negroes, were burned.

There was also an attempt to prosecute some of the persons connected with the school for violating Article XIII of the state Constitution. Three people, John G. Craven, teacher at the school, James Nelson, an antislavery leader and one of the sponsors of the school, and his wife, who supervised the dormitory, were charged with encouraging Negroes to come into the state contrary to the Constitution and law of the state. The trio were indicted but were aided by Judge Stephen C. Stevens, the antislavery lawyer mentioned elsewhere in this book, who evidently persuaded the authorities to drop the case.[50]

Liber College in Jay County was also open to Negroes in theory, at least. The school was established in 1853, largely through the efforts of the Reverend Isaac N. Taylor, a Congregational minister, who had also established the first church in the county. The constitution of the school provided that its purpose was "to furnish to any person whomsoever the facilities of a common and collegiate education." During the first term there was an attempt to enroll a Negro boy who had been living with one of the white residents of the neighborhood. The stockholders of the school were divided over the question of his admission, but a majority were of the opinion that the constitution

---

[50] Thompson, *op. cit.*, 111-12, 126.

required them to admit him. The decision evidently caused some dissension, for in 1855 the stockholders voted to reimburse those persons who had bought stock but who were opposed to admitting Negroes. No other examples of Negro students have been found, but the fact that Ebenezer Tucker, who devoted most of the rest of his life to teaching Negroes, was principal from 1859 to 1868 makes it probable that colored students were in attendance.[51]

In 1860 census figures showed a total of 1,122 colored persons enrolled in some sort of school. This represented less than one fourth of those in the state between the ages of five and twenty.[52] Most of those who were enrolled were receiving only the barest rudiments of an education, while a majority of Negro children were receiving no schooling whatsoever. Of all the disabilities imposed upon them by the state of Indiana, none seems to have weighed so heavily upon the colored population as the fact that they were barred from the schools. Samuel Smothers writing in 1860 upon the Black Laws declared: "The worst and most deplorable feature of these proscriptive laws, is, that they shut us out from the public schools, and leave us (so far as the State is concerned) entirely without the means of education." The writer called upon the members of the Republican party who were fighting for the end of slavery in the South to remove the shackles which prevented the intellectual advancement of Indiana Negroes. "Republicans, how long! Oh! how long will this be the case? When you support, by your votes and by your influence, the other proscriptive laws of this State, you indeed commit a crime against God and humanity of great magnitude; but when you deprive us of the means of education, you commit an outrage upon the SOUL; *a war upon* THE IMMORTAL PART!

51 M. W. Montgomery, *History of Jay County, Indiana* (Chicago, [1864]), 194.
52 *Eighth Census* (1860) :*Mortality and Miscellaneous Statistics,* 507.

"The strong probabilities are, that most of the colored population of these United States will remain here for all time to come. Then the question arises, would you rather have us among you in an educated and enlightened condition, or would you rather have us in an ignorant and degraded condition?"[53]

[53] *Students' Repository,* 1(1863) :4-5.

7

CIVIL WAR YEARS

"THE WAR IS NOW IN PART *our war,* and the free colored men of the North must help fight it," declared a Negro student in 1864. The challenge which the conflict between the states presented to the Negro population of Indiana was well recognized by the more thoughtful members of the race. Samuel Smothers of the Union Literary Institute wrote: "The time has now come for intelligent, decisive and energetic action on our part. For thirty years we have been lecturing, talking and praying for the liberation of our enslaved brethren. God has answered our prayers, and our brethren are being liberated by the thousands. The wonderful changes which are now taking place in our condition, brings [*sic*] upon us new duties.

"The first and most important of these duties is to stand by and defend the government. Our liberties, our interests and our happiness, in common with other citizens, depends upon the fate of this government. If the government stands, our liberties are secure; if the government falls, we will be doomed to life-long bondage and chains. It is true that we do not enjoy in some of the States all the rights and privileges other citizens enjoy, but our condition is certainly far better than it would be under Jeff. Davis' rule. Again, to fight in defence of the government, will confer lasting honor upon us and our posterity, and secure for us the respect and admiration of our white fellow-citizens."[1]

There was an awareness on the part of both Negroes and whites that the war which started with the firing on

---

[1] *Students' Repository,* 1(1863-64) :24, 81.

Fort Sumter would determine not only the fate of the Union but the future of the colored population in both the North and South. The champions of white supremacy recognized and feared the effects of the war upon the race situation in Indiana and sought to resist any change. During the war two opposing trends were in operation: on the one hand, an increase in the Negro population of the state and a beginning of the disintegration of racial disabilities as the result of military exigencies; on the other, efforts of the Negrophobes to resist the consequences of the war and to maintain the *status quo*. The result was an increase in racial tension and violence.

From the beginning there was apprehension that the war would lead to the liberation of the slaves and an influx of the freedmen into the North. A letter to the Indianapolis *Sentinel* in April, 1862, reported that Indianapolis and the towns along the Ohio River were rapidly "filling up with strange Africans" and urged enforcement of the exclusion law. The New Albany *Ledger* warned that if Union armies adopted a policy of emancipation, the result would be a migration of Negroes which existing laws would be power-less to check.[2]

In the river towns along the Kentucky border there was the greatest excitement over Negro immigration. In this region, where proslavery and anti-Negro feeling was strong-est, the outbreak of the war did not end the efforts of Indiana citizens to capture runaway slaves. For example, in May, 1862, it was reported that a fugitive belonging to a Louisville resident had been taken near New Albany and that the captors had received $75.00 as reward. But in spite of the vigilance of the whites, slaves continued to cross the Ohio River and to take refuge with colored residents on the

2 Indianapolis *Daily Sentinel*, April 19, 1862; New Albany *Ledger*, quoted in *ibid.*, April 22, 1862. There were some efforts to enforce the exclusion law in Fort Wayne. The Fort Wayne *Sentinel* reported five cases in which Negroes were convicted for coming into the state in vio-lation of the Constitution. Quoted in *ibid.*, May 5, 1862.

Indiana side. This increased the existing prejudice against the Negro residents and contributed to creating an explosive situation. When it was reported that a resident of the colored section of New Albany made a practice of aiding runaways and hiding them in his home, the New Albany *Ledger* warned: "The keeper of the house should be taught a lesson which would make him more careful in the future how he violates the laws."[3]

In July, 1862, there occurred in New Albany the worst race riot of the war years. It was set off by an affray in which two white men were reported to have been shot by Negroes. One of the two was killed; the other badly wounded. Some reports said that the shootings were entirely unprovoked, others that they were the outgrowth of a fight. Four Negroes were arrested on charges of being concerned in or having knowledge of the murder, but they all protested complete innocence.[4] Immediately after the shooting indiscriminate acts of violence against Negroes broke out in various parts of the city. Two Negroes were shot, and one was reported mortally wounded. Wherever Negroes appeared on the street, they were likely to be beaten up. After these sporadic incidents a mob started toward the Negro section and there engaged in an orgy of beatings and vandalism. A group of young boys followed in the wake of the older mobsters, pelting Negroes with stones and shouting, "We'll kill the damned niggers." Afterwards part of the mob went to the jail and demanded the release of the Negro prisoners. When their demands were refused, they threatened to batter down the jail, but they failed to force an entrance and finally dispersed. By this time patrols of soldiers had been called in to police the streets, and the

3 New Albany *Daily Ledger,* May 31, June 6, 1862.

4 *Ibid.,* July 22, 1862. Several days after the murder the authorities came to the conclusion that the murderer was a Negro barber who had escaped from New Albany on a river boat. He was later arrested in Cairo, Illinois. *Ibid.,* July 29, 1862.

following day it was reported that order had been restored after thirty hours of rioting.[5]

The day after the disorders it was said that the authorities were determined that the guilty should be punished, but there is no record that any of the rioters were ever arrested. After a few days the righteous indignation which the New Albany *Ledger* had at first manifested toward the mob subsided, and it began to place the blame for the disorders on the Negroes and abolitionists. Although it asserted that the riots had been disgraceful, "no women or children had been molested," except in one or two instances, and, contrary to the first reports, no Negroes had actually been killed. It expressed the opinion: "If the colored residents of this community who are lawfully so, were to discourage the immigration of negroes unlawfully [*sic*], we believe they would get along peaceably and without trouble. It is the strangers, who have no lawful homes here, who create nearly all the trouble."[6]

A few days after the riot in New Albany a Negro from that city who went to Bedford to visit a friend was driven out of town by a crowd which overtook him and beat him. In Indianapolis the *Sentinel* expressed satisfaction that "as yet we have had no disturbance with our colored population, and we sincerely hope we shall not have." In the same issue it published a letter signed "A Union Man," which admonished Indianapolis Negroes against "impudence." It ended: "Let this be a warning . . . to avoid insulting respectable *white men*, or my word for it, the time is not far distant when Indianapolis and vicinity will be a hot place for them [Negroes]."[7]

---

[5] New Albany *Daily Register*, July 22-24, 1862. George W. Julian's Centerville *Indiana True Republican* of August 7, 1862, charged that the civil authorities had made no effort to check the rioters and insisted that the riots were the results of the efforts of pro-Southern Democrats to convince white laborers that an increase in the number of Negroes would be a threat to their jobs.

[6] New Albany *Daily Ledger*, July 25, 29, 1862.

[7] *Ibid.*, August 1, 1862; Indianapolis *Daily Sentinel*, August 4, 1862.

The riots created a state of panic among the Negroes in New Albany and led to an exodus from that place. Young men who worked on the river and had been living in New Albany were reported to have moved across the river to Louisville, Kentucky, which caused the New Albany *Ledger* to comment: "They fly to a slave State to enjoy that liberty and security which is denied them in a free State, and this is one of the legitimate, the inevitable results of the efforts of the abolitionists for an equality of the races." At the 1862 Western Yearly Meeting of Friends it was reported that as a result of the hostility towards them, some Negroes from the southern part of the state had moved to Canada and other points farther north "where they may enjoy more privileges in educating their children and avoid the prejudices that prevail against them here."[8]

Although some Negroes left the southern counties, many more continued to arrive. Some of them were fugitives from Kentucky who came on their own initiative; others were so-called "contrabands," slaves who fell into the hands of members of the Union Army and were sent by them to the free states. As early as July, 1861, it was reported that a private from Indianapolis had brought back to Indiana a little Negro boy whom he had found wandering about after the battle of Cheat River in Virginia. As the war progressed, the number of Negroes sent North by members of the army increased. In October, 1862, it was reported that army officers had brought ten or twelve Negroes to New Albany. The following month several more Kentucky slaves who had been freed by an Illinois regiment were instructed to go to Indiana.[9]

Following the issuing of the preliminary Emancipation Proclamation in September, 1862, the number of runaway

[8] New Albany *Daily Ledger*, August 4, 1862; *Minutes of the Western Yearly Meeting of Friends*, 1862, p. 24.
[9] Indianapolis *Daily Sentinel*, July 26, 1861; New Albany *Daily Ledger*, October 20, November 21, 1862. The soldiers acted without any legal

slaves who came to Indiana greatly increased. Most of them came from Kentucky, although Kentucky was a loyal state and therefore not subject to the provisions of the proclamation. However, this fact was not understood or was ignored by the slaves who started flocking to Indiana. In some cases they were furnished passes by Union Army officers, even though their masters were loyal to the Union cause. In the face of the exodus from Kentucky the authorities at New Albany, the point at which most of them tried to cross the Ohio River, sought to set up a guard at the ferry docks on either side of the river to stop Negroes who had no passes. As the result of this vigilance, many slaves who tried to reach Indiana via this route were arrested and returned to their masters. Among them were fifteen Kentucky slaves who had been freed by members of a Michigan regiment. They crossed the Ohio River, expecting to follow the Underground Railroad route north. At least six of them, and perhaps all, were arrested, causing the *Ledger* to remark: "This section of Indiana is anything else than a good place for runaway negroes to visit."[10]

Even more unfortunate than the runaway slaves who were captured and returned to their masters were the ones who sought refuge on free soil only to be kidnaped and carried back to the South and sold. In spite of the announcement of the Emancipation Proclamation this nefarious traffic continued. Early in 1863 it was reported that an "extensive business" was being done by persons in Indiana and Kentucky who kidnaped contrabands and free Negroes and carried them off to Kentucky, where they were sold. Among the victims there were reported to be two or three free

authority in freeing the slaves, and the *Ledger* protested in vain that to send them to Indiana was a violation of the state Constitution.

10 New Albany *Daily Ledger*, December 5, 12, 19, 1862; February 3, 5, 1863. Slave hunting on Indiana soil continued at least as late as February, 1864. At that time it was reported that a group of armed citizens of Crawford County had set off in pursuit of two slaves from Kentucky who had crossed the Ohio River. *Ibid.*, February 23, 1864.

Negro residents of New Albany, a fact which did not appear to arouse the authorities of that city to any effort to rescue them. However, in April, 1863, some of the persons engaged in the traffic were arrested through the combined efforts of civil and military authorities.[11]

Fear of an increase in Negro immigration as the result of the war and fear of the competition of Negro laborers played a part in determining the attitude of Indiana voters toward the Lincoln administration. Throughout 1862 Democrats sought to play on these fears. The following editorial from the Indianapolis *Sentinel* is typical: "The thousands and tens of thousands of negroes [obviously a gross exaggeration] that are coming into this State, unprovided as they are with any means of making a living except by the hardest and roughest labor, is [*sic*] having the effect of reducing the price of labor. We already hear of farmers engaging these runaways to labor at greatly reduced prices, and this will continue and increase, until our white fellow-citizens, who labor for the support of themselves and their families, are compelled to compete with the labor of negroes, and that, too, in a State whose Constitution prohibits them from settling here. This is one of the effects of this war the laboring class will soon feel, by having the price of labor reduced to that of runaway or emancipated negroes."[12]

On the eve of the elections in October, 1862, the same newspaper declared that the only hope of protecting white men from competition with Negroes was to defeat the Republicans at the polls. "If Abolitionism triumphs at the

11 *Ibid.*, March 16, April 11, 1863. Throughout the war years free Negro residents of Indiana who traveled in slave states were in danger of being arrested on the suspicion that they were fugitive slaves. In May, 1862, a Negro resident of Indianapolis was jailed in Nashville, Tennessee. As late as February, 1864, a colored boy from Henry County, who went to Kentucky as the servant of an officer in an Indiana regiment, was arrested and jailed under the Kentucky law which presumed every colored person to be a slave. *Ibid.*, May 6, 1862; Indianapolis *Daily Journal*, February 29, 1864.

12 Indianapolis *Daily Sentinel*, April 29, 1862.

polls to-morrow our State will be flooded with negroes, devouring our substance like the locusts of Egypt."[13]

The Democrats triumphed at the polls, and in the next session of the General Assembly introduced numerous resolutions condemning emancipation. They also sought to enact a more drastic exclusion law. The proposed measure would have required all Negroes residing in the state to prove their rights to do so under the state Constitution. Those unable to produce such proof were to be compelled to leave the state within ninety days. If they failed to leave, they were subject to a fine of from five to five hundred dollars for the first conviction. If they continued to refuse to leave, they were to be deemed guilty of a felony, subject to imprisonment in the state penitentiary for from two to ten years.[14]

The proposed law, which failed to pass, would, no doubt, have been as ineffectual as the earlier exclusion law in halting the increasing flow of Negroes. Nevertheless, Democrats continued to urge the enactment of a new law and to assail the Republicans for failure to enforce the old one. The Democratic state platform adopted in 1864 contained the following article: "That the people of Indiana, having inhibited, by the State Constitution and law, the entrance of free negroes and mulattoes into this State, and as the present disturbances on our border are likely to bring in an influx of that population, ask the public authorities of Indiana to see that the Constitution and laws are enforced on that subject. When the people of Indiana adopted that negro exclusion clause by a majority of ninety thousand votes, they meant the honest, laboring white man should have no competition in the black race; that the soil of Indiana should belong to the white man, and that he alone was suited to her free institutions, and we call upon our Legislature to pass a more stringent law upon the subject."[15]

13 Indianapolis *Daily Sentinel*, October 13, 1862.
14 Senate Bill 140, Original Senate Bills, 1863 session (manuscript copy, Archives Division, Indiana State Library).
15 Indianapolis *Daily Journal*, July 13, 1864.

As the war progressed, the number of contrabands coming into the state increased. They frequently came in groups and were usually destitute and dependent upon the charity of local residents, white and colored.[16] Although there was no repetition of the New Albany riots of 1862, the newcomers met with hostility in many quarters, and numerous isolated acts of violence occurred. When a judge in the vicinity of Indianapolis, Daniel R. Smith, employed a contraband as a farm laborer, some of his white neighbors protested and threatened to prosecute him for violating the exclusion law. A letter to the Indianapolis *Sentinel* declared that both Democrats and Republicans in the community were opposed to the presence of the Negro. The writer added: "I know of no one who wants the negro, only those who love the negro better than the white man, and I suppose Judge Smith likes him much better than he does the white man, for I have been informed that he has said he (the negro) was the best hand he ever employed."[17]

In Evansville there was a report that an inoffensive colored preacher had been stabbed on the street. In Indianapolis the African M.E. Church was nearly destroyed by a fire which was generally believed to have been started by a malicious incendiary because its pastor, Willis Revels, was one of the Negroes most active in aiding the refugees. Near Indianapolis a Negro man was shot and wounded by two men on horseback and left bleeding and crying for help all night long although he was within a few feet of the dwellings of three white families. The Indianapolis *Journal* pointed out that a group of contrabands living in the neighborhood had received "repeated warnings and threats from the *loyal* law-abiding citizens, and it is presumable that this is the first installment of the threatenings they have made."[18]

---

[16] See for examples Indianapolis *Daily Sentinel*, December 3, 1863; July 14, 1864.

[17] *Ibid.*, April 16, 1864.

[18] Evansville *Journal* reprinted in *ibid.*, January 7, 1864; Indianapolis *Daily Journal*, July 11, 19, August 11, 1864.

Outrages such as these were not enough to check forces which were operating to increase immigration into Indiana and to bring about changes in the status of the Negro population. Just as military necessity played an important part in the decision of Lincoln to announce a policy of emancipation, so military necessity led the administration, although reluctantly, to the employment of Negro troops to crush the rebellion. And partly as the result of the part which they played in saving the Union, Negroes were to receive new rights in the North as well as the South.

As soon as the war started there were efforts on the part of some Northern Negroes to enlist in the Union cause. Abolitionists also were urging the employment of Negro troops, but throughout 1861 Lincoln and the Secretary of War, Simon Cameron, opposed the policy and refused all petitions for such recruitments. In September, 1861, Cameron announced that all recruiting was being turned over to the states, thereby shifting the responsibility as to the decision to use colored troops to the governors of the states. In the meantime Negroes had begun organizing military companies and drilling at various places in the North, including New York City, Philadelphia, Cleveland, and Washington, but none of these groups were accepted by the military authorities. However, limited use of contrabands by Union armies in the South began in 1861 and 1862, and an act of Congress approved in July, 1862, gave the President complete discretion as to the employment of Negroes for any purpose. The Enrollment Act of March, 1863, included among those liable to be drafted all male citizens in the prescribed age groups. The War Department interpreted free Negroes as falling within this category and hence as being subject to the draft. Any confusion on this point was clarified by the act of February 24, 1864, which explicitly stated that all male colored persons between the ages of twenty and forty-five might be conscripted. In all a total of 186,017 Negroes served in the Union Army, but most of them were recruited in the states which were in rebellion. About 82,000 were from the loyal states, which, of course, included four slave states. Of these some were volunteers, while others were drafted. The total number of troops from the free states was small because of the small Negro population.[19]

In Indiana proposals to arm Negroes created a state of near hysteria among Democrats, and even Republicans showed reluctance to endorse such a step. In the political campaign of 1862 Democrats sought to make use of the issue of Negro troops. In a speech before the Democratic State Convention Thomas A. Hendricks condemned the suggestion that the North, with a population which outnumbered the South, should need to use Negroes, and added: "What General would go into battle trusting to black regiments for his strength? and what regiment, made up of the proud men of Indiana, would stand in a battle, where they must lean for support upon armed negroes?" An editorial in the Indianapolis *Sentinel* expressed the opinion that volunteers would refuse to serve in an army which included colored troops. "Is it possible that the people of the North, the descendants of a proud and imperious race, will permit the negro to be armed and placed by his [*sic*] side in maintaining a white man's government?"[20]

Caleb B. Smith, secretary of the interior and one of the Indianans most prominent in the Lincoln administration, condemned proposals to arm slaves. He predicted that such a step would cause public opinion in Europe to turn against the Union cause and that white soldiers from southern Indiana and most of the other loyal states would "before God,

[19] Fred Albert Shannon, *The Organization and Administration of the Union Army 1861-1865* (2 vols. Cleveland, 1928), 2:147-48, 158, 160, 164; Quarles, *Negro in the Civil War*, 26-29. A more recent study than that of Shannon states the War Department records show that a total of 178,895 Negro soldiers served in the Union Army. Dudley Taylor Cornish, *The Sable Arm: Negro Troops in the Union Army, 1861-1865* (New York, 1956), Foreword, x.

[20] Indianapolis *Daily Sentinel*, January 9, July 17, 1862.

protest being thus put on an equality with Negro soldiers in their ranks."[21]

The abolitionists in Smith's party did not, of course, share his views, and as the war progressed even the more conservative Republicans began to urge the use of Negro troops. Most of the discussion centered on the question of arming the Negroes in the slave states since the number in the free states was so small as to be of relatively little military significance. An editorial in the Logansport *Journal* expressed approval of the proposals to arm the colored population, declaring: "To quote a vulgar and much abused saying, 'Negroes are no better than white men,' and no satisfactory reason can be shown why the lives and limbs and health of our white fellow citizens—our fathers, brothers and sons —may be jeopardized in war and the negro held safe and sacred."[22]

Some of Indiana's Negroes were ready and eager to serve the Union cause, but even Governor Oliver P. Morton showed reluctance to use them. In August, 1863, Willis Revels, pastor of the African M.E. Church, and ninety-one other Negroes tendered their services as members of the Home Guard for the city of Indianapolis and the state of Indiana, but the Governor rejected them, asserting that the Home Guard was already larger than necessary and that "the constitution and laws of the State gave him no authority to accept colored troops."[23]

Some other Negroes who had been refused in Indiana earlier had already enlisted under the banner of Massachusetts. The first recruiting of Northern Negroes had been carried on largely through the efforts of Governor John Andrews of Massachusetts, who had received authority from the Secretary of War in January, 1863, to raise a regiment of colored volunteers. Because the Negro popu-

---

[21] Centerville *Indiana True Republican,* January 2, 1862.
[22] Logansport *Journal,* February 21, 1863.
[23] New Albany *Daily Ledger,* August 14, 1863.

lation of Massachusetts was too small to supply the entire number, recruiting agents were sent to other states. Eventually about one thousand troops were enrolled in the regiment, representing every state in the Union and also Canada. In the Massachusetts regiment, as in all the colored regiments subsequently raised, the commissioned officers were white men.[24]

The news that Governor Andrews had received authority to raise the regiment evoked from the Indianapolis *Sentinel* a typical editorial which declared that this was further evidence of the design of the Lincoln administration to raise the Negro to the level of the white man and that "this Administration regards a nigger with more favor than a white man." When a recruiting agent came to Indianapolis, the same paper reported that he raised about "sixty ebony recruits" for Andrews' regiment and commented: "This arrangement of the superlatively patriotic Andrew—not the Merry Andrew—is a pretty cute Yankee trick. Each of these darkies counts as a white man in making up the quota of Massachusetts, while it relieves us of a class of population that we are not at all anxious to retain." Recruiting was also carried on in counties in the southern part of the state, and from the records of the Adjutant General it appears that eighty-one colored men from Indiana enlisted in the Massachusetts regiment in April and May, 1863.[25]

From this time on as public opinion regarding the use of colored troops underwent a rapid change, the Republican press began to carry numerous stories testifying to the valor of Negro soldiers. A potent force in effecting the changed attitude was the fact that Indiana was having difficulty in filling the quota of troops assigned to her and was faced with the unpleasant possibility of a draft. An obvious solu-

24 Quarles, *Negro in the Civil War*, 8-9.

25 Indianapolis *Daily Sentinel*, January 29, May 8, 1863; New Albany *Daily Ledger*, May 13, June 11, 30, 1865; W. H. H. Terrell, *Report of the Adjutant General of the State of Indiana* (8 vols. Indianapolis, 1869), 7:692.

tion lay in enlisting colored men, and in November, 1863, Governor Morton applied to raise colored troops to fill Indiana's quota. An editorial in the Indianapolis *Journal* on the changed attitude as to the capacities of the Negro commented: "Now he [the Negro] is regarded as excellent material for the army, and indeed no white soldier can now be found who would not sooner see a negro with one arm off, than to have one off himself."[26] Another newspaper remarked: "Indiana is just beginning to wake up on the subject of colored recruits. If it had not been for the existence of an insane prejudice on the subject, we might have had credit for large numbers who now swell the ranks of regiments formed in some of the more wide awake sister States. But now the work goes rapidly on, and not even the Copperheads can withdraw their rapidly glazing eyes from the dreadful draft long enough to look an objection to this method of disposing of 'free Americans of African descent.' "[27]

During the political campaign of 1864 the Republicans praised the use of the Negro troops and took satisfaction in pointing out that Democrats were not adverse to hiring Negro substitutes in order to avoid the draft. At a Union rally in Indianapolis one speaker observed: "There was much complaint by Democrats about the arming of Negroes; yet when a draft was ordered, these same men became so anxious to get negroes to take their places, that they scoured the whole country with bounty money in hand and even tolled the negroes from Kentucky."[28]

Once the decision to use Negro troops had been made, vigorous efforts were put forth to recruit volunteers so that Indiana rather than some other state would receive credit

[26] Dunn, *Greater Indianapolis*, 1:251; Indianapolis *Daily Journal*, November 17, 1863.

[27] New Castle *Courier* reprinted in Indianapolis *Daily Journal*, January 22, 1864.

[28] *Ibid.*, June 13, 1864. See also the speech of John P. Usher, member of the Lincoln cabinet from Indiana, in *ibid.*, September 16, 1864.

for them. The following artfully worded appeal was issued through the Indianapolis newspapers.

"To The Colored Men of Indiana

"The State of Indiana calls upon you to bear a part in the glorious work of putting down the slaveholder's rebellion and saving the Union. Hitherto you have been compelled to remain at home or enlist under the banners of other States. Many of your brethren, unable to repress their patriotic ardor, have enlisted in the regiments of various States, while some were of the rank and file of the gallant 54th Massachusetts, which immortalized itself at Fort Wagner. Whenever the colored men of Indiana have fought in this war, they have shown that they partake of the same spirit of heroic valor that has animated Indiana's sons wherever they have met the foe in arms. The President of the United States, in his late message, has reaffirmed his proclamation of emancipation of your oppressed brothers; and he guarantees that you and the officer who commands you in the field shall, when in the enemy's hands, be recognized and treated as prisoners of war. Will you not march to the rescue of your suffering brethren, and give to them in fact the freedom which is now declared to be theirs of right? . . . It has been said of you that you do not possess the manly qualities that fit a people to enjoy and preserve their liberty. You can now show to your detractors and the world the falsehood of the assertion, and place yourself in such a position that you may ask and obtain from a grateful people a full recognition of your worth and rights as men. . . . Show yourselves worthy soldiers, and the petty prejudices that weak and wicked men have endeavored to excite against you will be forever swallowed up in the gratitude of a nation that will own and applaud your heroic deeds."[29]

Recruiting agents were soon reported in Indianapolis, Terre Haute, Lafayette, New Albany, and Evansville, and

[29] *Ibid.*, December 12, 1863.

everywhere Negroes responded with enthusiasm. Counties vied with each other in their efforts to enroll colored men to help fill their troop quotas. Charges were made that Negroes who should have been credited to other counties were brought to Indianapolis and credited to Marion County, thus enabling that county to evade its responsibilities under the draft. The real reason that so many Negroes were enrolled from that county was the fact that they received a county bounty. The Federal government did not provide bounties for colored troops until June 15, 1864, but a few counties, including Marion, did raise bounties for them through private subscription. In Floyd County, Negroes were urged to volunteer instead of waiting to be drafted so that they might be eligible to receive the bounty of fifty dollars which the county paid all volunteers and also an additional fifty dollars offered by the city of New Albany. Under an act passed by Congress in June, 1864, Negroes who were subject to the draft and who enlisted were made eligible for a bounty of three hundred dollars from the Federal government, the same amount which white volunteers received.[30] In addition to the Federal bounty, local governmental units continued to offer additional inducements. An advertisement in the Indianapolis *Daily Journal* for January 21, 1865, announced:

COLORED MEN, ATTENTION
$375 EACH
Will be paid for twenty good men to go as
Volunteers, to be credited to the city of
Indianapolis

After Indiana began to use her colored population to fill her quotas, recruiting officers from other states were forbidden to operate within her borders. However, this prohibition does not appear to have been successfully enforced.

---

[30] Indianapolis *Daily Sentinel,* December 12, 22, 31, 1863; January 12, 1864; New Albany *Daily Ledger,* December 18, 21, 1863; Terre Haute *Wabash Express,* December 2, 29, 1863; Indianapolis *Daily Journal,* January 7, 1864; Shannon, *Organization of the Union Army,* 2:167-68.

Moreover, as it became increasingly difficult to find volunteers, efforts were made to entice slaves from Kentucky to help fill the troop requirements of the free states. Many of the Negroes enrolled at New Albany were actually recruited from Henderson, Kentucky, by men who received bounties for enlisting them. The New Albany *Ledger* reported one boatload of three hundred colored recruits was raised between New Albany and Henderson.[31]

Slaves underwent risks and hardships in order to come to Indiana to enlist. In one instance eight slaves escaped from Owensboro, Kentucky, with the intention of enlisting. They were pursued, and one was captured in Vincennes, but the remaining seven made their way to Indianapolis and enlisted in the colored regiment being raised there. Their masters discovered their whereabouts and followed them in order to try to collect the bounty money which an act of Congress allowed to loyal masters, whose slaves enrolled in the Union army. When the masters appeared at the camp where the colored troops were stationed, their reception was anything but cordial. They found themselves surrounded by angry Negroes who threatened them with violence until they left. The white officers were unable to restrain the colored men, and according to the newspaper account, the Kentuckians "deemed it prudent to withdraw" without pressing their claims to the bounty.[32]

Most Indiana Negroes were enrolled in the Twenty-eighth Regiment, United States Colored Troops, which was organized in Indianapolis. Others served in the Eighth, Thirteenth, Fourteenth, Seventeenth, Twenty-third, and Sixty-fifth colored infantry regiments, and in the Fourth Heavy Artillery Regiment. Men from Indiana were also found in the First Michigan Regiment and the Fourteenth Rhode Island U.S. T.C., as well as in the Massachusetts Fifty-fourth.[33]

[31] Indianapolis *Daily Journal,* June 9, 1864; New Albany *Daily Ledger,* April 18-19, June 3, 1864.

[32] New Albany *Daily Ledger,* March 28, 1864.

[33] Terrell, *Report,* 7 :660-89; 8 :347. One or two Negroes from Indiana

The number of colored troops from Indiana cannot be accurately ascertained. One writer states that the total was 1,537, although only eight hundred were credited to Indiana's quota. On the other hand, some of those credited to Indiana were actually from Kentucky. Since the entire Negro population of the state was only about eleven thousand at the beginning of the war, it appears that a large percentage of the men of military age entered service. One evidence of this is the fact that the colored Masons of the state did not hold their usual annual meeting in 1864 because so many of their members were in the army. The Masonic chapter in Richmond disbanded entirely for a time because its membership was so depleted by the war.[34] Individual families sacrificed heavily for the Union cause. Five sons of William Sawyer, a Randolph County farmer, were in the army, while four of the seven sons of William Trail also enlisted. Three of Trail's sons died in service.[35]

At first Negroes did not receive the same pay as white soldiers but were given only the pay of laborers working for the army. Not until June 15, 1864, did Congress expressly provide that they should receive the same uniforms, arms, equipment, rations, and pay as white soldiers. The policy of equal pay was criticized in some quarters. An address of the Democratic members of Congress from Indiana issued in 1864 condemned the use of Negro troops and added: "It ought to be manifest to every reasonable man that negroes in service should be paid less than white troops. . . . The market value of their labor is known to be less than that of citizens, and it is equally clear that their services are much less valuable in the army." On the other

were also found in each of the following regiments: Thirty-first, Fifty-eighth, Seventy-second, One Hundred Ninth.

[34] Dunn, *Greater Indianapolis*, 1:51; conversation of the author with Andrew Ramsey of Indianapolis, who is compiling a history of Negro Masonry in Indiana.

[35] *Students' Repository*, 2 (1864):23; Joseph C. Carroll, "William Trail: An Indiana Pioneer," in *Journal of Negro History*, 23(1938):423.

hand, the Republican Indianapolis *Journal* voiced approval of equal pay, though not out of any desire to see justice done to the Negro. Rather it argued that the equal pay induced Negroes to enlist, thereby saving white men from the necessity of military service.[36]

The men of the Twenty-eighth Regiment assembled and received preliminary training at Camp Frémont southeast of Indianapolis between December, 1863, and April, 1864. On the eve of their departure from Indianapolis they paraded through the streets of the city. The Indianapolis *Journal,* after commenting favorably upon their appearance and discipline, remarked: "They walk erect, and bear themselves as men who have rights and dare to maintain them."[37]

From Indianapolis the men were sent to a camp near Alexandria, Virginia, for a short period of additional training. Next they were sent to White House, Virginia, where they took part in an engagement on June 21. After this they were sent with Sheridan's cavalry through the Chickahominy swamps, suffering heavy losses from frequent skirmishes with the enemy. When the Indiana units arrived at Prince George's Court House, they were assigned to a division in the Ninth Army Corps, and under this command they participated in the entire campaign before Petersburg.[38] The most deadly engagement in which they took part was the battle of "the Crater," in which nearly half of their number was killed or wounded. The troops of the Twenty-eighth and Twenty-ninth regiments were charged by the enemy and temporarily thrown into disorder by the intensity of the enemy's fire. Both white and colored troops poured back in a panic, but later some reformed and fought on.[39]

[36] Shannon, *Organization of the Union Army,* 2:166-67; Quarles, *Negro in the Civil War,* 202; Indianapolis *Daily Sentinel,* July 26, 1864; Indianapolis *Daily Journal,* July 27, 1864.

[37] Indianapolis *Daily Journal,* July 21, 1864.

[38] Terrell, *Report,* 3:382-83; Dunn, *Greater Indianapolis,* 1:251; Indianapolis *Daily Journal,* January 9, 1866.

[39] *The War of the Rebellion: A Compilation of the Official Records of*

An account by an eyewitness, published in the New York *Evening Post*, defended the bravery of the colored troops. Describing the experience of the Twenty-eighth he said: "I was never under such a terrific fire, and can hardly realize how any escaped alive. Our loss was heavy. In the twenty-eighth (colored), for instance, commanded by Lieut.-Col. Charles Russell (a Bostonian), he lost seven officers out of eleven, and ninety-one men out of two hundred and twenty-four; and the colonel himself was knocked over senseless, for a few minutes, by a slight wound in the head; both his color-sergeants and all his color-guard were killed."[40] For his part in the action Russell was promoted to colonel and later to brevet brigadier general. Major Thomas H. Logan was then put in command of the regiment.

After the heavy losses at the Crater new recruits were brought in to fill the ranks of the Twenty-eighth, and four more companies were organized. The rejuvenated regiment took part in an engagement at Hatchers Run and then was assigned for a time to the Quartermaster's Department at City Point. Thereafter it participated in the operations against Richmond, and members of the Twenty-eighth were among the first troops to enter that city.

After the close of hostilities the regiment was sent to Texas for a time. It was stationed at Corpus Christi until November 8, 1865, when its members were discharged by the War Department. On January 6, 1866, a parade and official welcome in their honor were held in Indianapolis.[41]

the Union and Confederate Armies (4 series. 70 vols. Washington, D. C., 1880-1901), 1 series, 40:pt.1:599.

[40] Quoted in William Wells Brown, *The Negro and the American Rebellion* . . . (Boston, 1867), 268.

[41] Terrell, *Report*, 3:383; Indianapolis *Daily Journal*, January 9, 1866. In 1890 members of the Twenty-eighth held a reunion in Indianapolis at the time of the Indiana State Fair. Twenty-one members who were present elected officers and voted to form a permanent organization. Indianapolis *World*, August 9, October 4, 1890.

After the Emancipation Proclamation and even more after the induction of colored troops into the Union Army, the colored population of Indiana followed the events of the war with intense interest. Civilians tried to support the war effort in a variety of ways. They worked in the hospitals, in the camps for colored soldiers, and collected money in their churches for the relief of soldiers and their families. Women of Indianapolis contributed delicacies for the sick soldiers at Camp Frémont.[42]

In spite of the part which Negroes were playing in winning a Union victory, all of the old legal discriminations against them remained in effect, but the injustice of such disabilities was increasingly recognized by white groups. At their state convention in 1864 Indiana Baptists adopted the following resolution: "That God having made of one blood, all nations that dwell upon the face of the earth, all laws depriving the colored man from settling in this State and sharing a portion of the School Fund, are unjust, and should be repealed." A memorial of the Western Yearly Meeting of Friends in 1865 called for the removal of the prohibition against Negro suffrage and repeal of the law on testimony and other laws which embarrassed Negroes in their efforts at education.[43]

In the session of the General Assembly which met in January, 1865, attempts were made to strike out the exclusion article in the state Constitution and to permit the admission of colored children to the public schools, but both efforts failed in spite of the fact that Republicans controlled the Assembly. An editorial in the New Albany *Ledger* commented on the attempts of "Boston Yankees" to "foist the abominable doctrines of negro equality" upon the state by legislation admitting colored and white children to the

[42] Indianapolis *Daily Journal*, January 25, November 26, 1864. Interest in the war gave an impetus to the desire to learn to read so as to be informed on national affairs, and caused many Negroes to start reading newspapers for the first time. *Students' Repository*, 2(1864) :16.

[43] Indianapolis *Daily Journal*, November 5, 1864; January 17, 26, 1865.

same schools. It remarked with satisfaction: "Our Indiana legislature, republican though it was, decided by an immense majority against putting negro children into the public schools, or giving them the benefit of the school fund, and this is the all but universal sentiment of the people of the west, without regard to party."[44]

Efforts of Governor Morton to persuade the lawmakers to modify the law with regard to Negro testimony in law courts also met with failure, although by 1865 Indiana was the only Northern state to retain this vestige of the codes of the slave states upon her statute books. Meanwhile, Congress had passed legislation making testimony of Negroes admissible in Federal courts. The first case in which the testimony of a colored witness was admitted in the United States Court in Indianapolis was reported in December, 1864.[45]

The only step regarding the status of Negroes taken at the 1865 legislative session had no direct effect upon the Negro population of Indiana. This was the ratification of the Thirteenth Amendment to the Constitution of the United States, which abolished slavery. Democratic members of the Indiana delegation in Congress had opposed the amendment, and Senator Thomas A. Hendricks was one of a handful of six Senators who had voted against it. In the debate over the amendment in the Indiana legislature opponents dragged out all the old arguments about "government made by white men for white men" and charged that emancipation would lead to "negro equality" and the much dreaded "amalgamation" of the races. In defense of their position they insisted that the Almighty had decreed that the Negro race should be inferior to the white.[46]

[44] Indiana *House Journal*, 1865, pp. 44, 124, 489, 758-59; New Albany *Daily Ledger* reprinted in Indianapolis *Daily Sentinel*, March 20, 1865.

[45] Indiana *House Journal*, 1865, pp. 29-30; Indianapolis *Daily Journal*, December 29, 1864; January 7, February 4, 1865. Illinois repealed her ban on Negro testimony in February, 1865.

[46] Indianapolis *Daily Sentinel*, February 10, 1865; Indianapolis *Daily*

These men fought emancipation because they feared that it was but the prelude to other rights for the colored race. An editorial in the Indianapolis *Sentinel* summed up the attitude of the champions of white supremacy when it declared: "Negro agitation has but commenced. To be sure it has brought us the death of over one million of brave and true white men, and has fastened upon us a debt of from two to four billions of dollars but the end is not yet. We wish we might see some little good resulting from a question so productive of evil."[47] Indiana Negroes agreed with their detractors that as the result of the war they stood upon the threshold of a new era, but they did not share their apprehensions. They rejoiced in the extinction of slavery, and as the result of the part which they had played in war, they looked forward optimistically to opportunities to assume new rights and responsibilities in the postwar period.

Journal, February 10, 1865. The inconsistency of the white supremacists was pointed out in an editorial in the *Journal*: "The question suggested itself to our mind that, if Omnipotence had thus decreed, is it necessary that white men should come to his aid by passing inhuman laws against a race doomed by a higher power to a position of perpetual inferiority. It did seem to us that the Almighty might be trusted to inforce [*sic*] his decrees without human assistance." *Ibid.*

[47] Indianapolis *Daily Sentinel*, December 9, 1864.

8
POPULATION CHANGES 1865-1900

HOPES WHICH THE WHITE POLITICIANS of the fifties had entertained of maintaining the soil of Indiana as a "white man's country" were dissipated by the immigration of Negroes from the South which followed emancipation. In the sixties the colored population of the state more than doubled, and it continued to increase at a more rapid rate than the white population in succeeding decades. The exclusion article of the state Constitution, which had already proved unenforceable, was declared null and void by the state Supreme Court in 1866. In some places the Negrophobes, deprived of a legal deterrent, resorted to intimidation to check the influx, and in a few scattered communities they were successful, but not in the state as a whole. Between 1860 and 1870 the colored population increased from 11,428 to 24,560. It had reached 39,228 by 1880; 45,215 by 1890; 57,505 by 1900. At the last date there were more than five times as many Negroes in Indiana as on the eve of the Civil War.[1] Unlike the Negro immigrants of an earlier period, who had settled for the most part in rural areas, most of the new arrivals flocked to the cities and towns. At the same time there was a movement from the old farming communities to the cities, so that by the end of the century the colored population was predominantly urban. In spite of the rapid rate of increase Negroes remained a tiny fraction of the total population. They constituted 1.5 per cent of the whole in 1870; 2 per cent in

[1] U. S. Bureau of the Census, *Negroes in the United States* (*Bulletin 8*, 1904), 102.

1880; 2.1 per cent in 1890; and 2.3 per cent in 1900. However, most of them were concentrated in a few counties where their ratio to the white population was much larger.[2] The flow of Negroes into southern Indiana which had begun during the Civil War increased in the postwar years. Nearly all of the newcomers were recently emancipated slaves to whom liberation meant the opportunity to move about freely for the first time in their lives. Most of them were farm laborers from Kentucky who flocked across the Ohio River to the towns of Indiana in the hope of earning wages and getting away from the drudgery of farm life. In May, 1865, three hundred Negroes arrived in New Albany in less than a week, and a few days later it was reported that two hundred passes were being issued daily by the office of the Provost Marshal at Louisville to Negroes coming to Indiana.[3]

They crowded into the Negro quarters of the river towns, where they lived in conditions of unspeakable filth and squalor. In Evansville at least seventeen families were found packed into one shanty. In New Albany, where the colored district came to be known as "Contraband Quarters," police found six families, an aggregate of twenty-three persons, living in one two-room house. This was described as typical of many of the dwellings in the neighborhood. Although many of the freedmen were industrious and were attempting to improve their condition, others were irresponsible vagabonds. In view of the fact that they had just been freed from the condition of slavery, in which the marriage contract was legally impossible, it is not surprising that the sexes were found living together in an indiscriminate

[2] Ibid., 109. The rate of increase among the Negro population was much greater during the entire period than among the whites. Between 1860 and 1870 the Negro population increased 114.9 per cent, the white 23.7; between 1870 and 1880 Negro increase was 59.7 per cent, white 17.1; between 1880 and 1890 Negro increase was 15.3 per cent, white 10.7; between 1890 and 1900 Negro increase was 27.2 per cent, white 14.5. Ibid., 104-5.

[3] New Albany Daily Ledger, May 24, June 7, 1865.

fashion, although white observers regarded this as evidence of moral depravity.[4]

Sometimes women and children were brought to the Indiana shore by their former masters and left to fend for themselves. In one instance a man from Meade County, Kentucky, brought thirty of these helpless creatures to New Albany and left them, telling them they were now free and must take care of themselves. He explained to bystanders that all his male slaves had enlisted in the Union Army and that he himself had been robbed and his lands devastated by guerrillas, so that he was unable to care for the women and children.[5]

The white population viewed the newcomers with hostility, as was to be expected in this section where race prejudice had always been notorious. The New Albany *Daily Ledger* warned that there were not enough jobs in Indiana and urged the Negroes to remain in Kentucky and not to come to Indiana, "where almost the entire population, without regard to political sentiment, entertain feelings of strong prejudice against them." In May, 1865, a meeting of citizens of Warrick County adopted the following resolution: "We the undersigned, citizens of Anderson township, Warrick County, Indiana, do hereby bind ourselves by this article, that we will pay, according to what we are severally worth, to some competent counsel, for the purpose of prosecuting any man who shall bring, harbor or employ any negro or mulatto in this township, contrary to the Constitution of the State of Indiana." In August it was reported that returning Union soldiers were leading a movement to expel Negro settlers from Warrick County and that all Negroes in Boonville, the county seat, had been notified to leave under penalty of being expelled by force. In spite of these efforts, however, census figures show that the Negro

[4] New Albany *Daily Ledger*, April 11, 1865; *ibid.*, reprinted in Indianapolis *Daily Herald*, November 22, 1867.

[5] New Albany *Daily Ledger*, April 25, 1865.

population of the county increased from 19 in 1860 to 487 in 1870.[6]

In a number of places hostility to Negro immigration led to outbreaks of mob violence. In Evansville, where there had been an earlier wave of violence in 1857, in early August, 1865, there occurred a lynching, followed by a general riot against all the Negroes in the city. The outbreak began when two Negroes were accused of robbing and assaulting a white woman. They were arrested and confessed and were jailed. Thereupon a mob of whites stormed the jail where the prisoners were held, dragged them from their cells, beat them, and then shot them to death. Their bodies were hung from lamp posts as a warning to others.

The alleged crime of the two hapless creatures also served as an excuse for the launching of a reign of terror against all the Negroes in Evansville, which the authorities claimed they were powerless to halt. As a result there began a general exodus of Negroes from the city. The purpose of the mobsters was admitted in a report in the New Albany *Daily Ledger* which said: "Nothing but the complete riddance of that city of Negroes will satisfy those engaged in the riotous demonstrations."[7]

The exodus from Evansville was temporary. More and more Negroes continued to pour into the city in spite of the antipathy manifested toward them. There were no more lynchings or large scale disorders but hostility was shown in other ways. In December, 1867, for example, notices were posted in the German section of the city notifying Negroes that they must leave that locality before New Year's Day, and a man who had rented a house to a colored family was warned that if the family did not move, the house

6 *Ibid.*, May 15, August 9, 1865; Boonville *Enquirer* reprinted in Indianapolis *Daily Sentinel*, January 28, 1865.

7 Evansville *Journal* reprinted in New Albany *Daily Ledger*, August 1, 3, 1865; *ibid.*, August 3, 1865.

would be burned down.[8] In spite of such threats the Negro population of Vanderburgh County leaped from a mere 127 in 1860 to 2,151 in 1870, while the city of Evansville alone had 1,427 Negroes by the latter date.

The lynching in Evansville in 1865 was followed a few days later by an affray in New Albany. After visiting a saloon a group of white men went to the African M. E. church during Sunday evening services and fired several shots at the building, wounding one Negro slightly. The New Albany *Ledger* deplored the incident but added: "It is no use to disguise the fact that a spirit of lawlessness to a certain extent is manifested in this community, and collisions between whites and negroes are not infrequent." It urged the whites to respect the rights of the Negro but warned the Negroes to avoid exciting prejudice among the whites.[9]

On Christmas day, Negro soldiers from the hospital near the neighboring city of Jeffersonville came into that city with the permission of their commanding officer. There they became involved in a fight with a party of young whites who were "ripe for a dispute," which resulted in the death of a German youth at the hands of a Negro soldier. In consequence of the incident feeling ran so high that white troops were sent to Jeffersonville to quell the disturbance and maintain order.[10]

There were also efforts in some of the counties farther north to prevent the settlement of Negroes. In August, 1865, a mass meeting at the courthouse in Sullivan County

8 Indianapolis *Daily Herald*, January 3, 1868. *Ninth Census* (1870): *Statistics of Population*, 26-27.

9 New Albany *Daily Ledger*, August 7, 1865. The following month a New Albany Negro was assaulted by a gang of whites at a circus. He was beaten and stabbed, though not fatally, but no arrests were made. *Ibid.* reprinted in Indianapolis *Daily Journal*, September 26, 1865.

10 Louisville *Journal* reprinted in Indianapolis *Daily Journal*, December 29, 1865. In spite of racial tension in Clark and Floyd counties Negro population continued to increase. In Floyd County it rose from 757 to 1,462 between 1860 and 1870, in Clark from 520 to 1,970. *Ninth Census* (1870): *Statistics of Population*, 26-27.

adopted resolutions calling for the enforcement of Article XIII of the state Constitution and proposing that a vigilance committee be appointed in each township to ferret out violations of the article and report them to the authorities.[11]

Many of the new arrivals flocked to Indianapolis although part of the population of that city was almost as hostile as that of the Ohio River communities. Between 1860 and 1870 the colored population of the city leaped from 498 to 2,931, that of Marion County from 825 to 3,938. Around Indianapolis fear of the effect of competition of Negro labor was strong among the white population, and efforts to intimidate Negro workers as well as a few acts of wanton violence were reported.[12] But there were also organized efforts, especially among the Quakers, to aid the arrivals, most of whom were destitute. Among other activities Quakers maintained a storeroom in downtown Indianapolis where they distributed clothing to colored refugees. In 1867 the Committee on the Concerns of People of Color of the Plainfield Quarterly Meeting noted the rapid increase of the colored population, and reported: "Although mostly destitute on arriving they manifest a commendable disposition to support themselves and to pay the tuition of their children. And many are accumulating property. And some have bought for themselves comfortable homes. Yet a large portion of them are in quite destitute circumstances."[13]

The influx of Negroes which more than doubled the colored population of the state in the years immediately after the war declined in the early seventies, although it did

[11] New Albany *Daily Ledger*, August 28, 1865. Although Article XIII was declared null and void in 1866, the residents of Sullivan County were successful in discouraging Negro settlement. There was actually a slight decline in the number of Negroes between 1860 and 1870.

[12] Indianapolis *Daily Journal*, August 9, 1865; February 9, March 26, 1866.

[13] Mira T. Cope, "A History of Plainfield Quarterly Meeting" (unpublished thesis, Earlham College, 1908), 31; Minutes of Plainfield Quarterly Meeting of Friends (MS in archives, Friends Church, Plainfield), 8th month 3, 1867.

not cease. But in 1879 there was a sharp increase in immigration as the result of a widespread exodus from the Southern states. In fact immigration from North Carolina to Indiana reached such proportions in the last months of 1879 that it became the subject of an investigation by a committee of the Senate of the United States. It remains the most highly publicized chapter in the history of Negro migration to the state.

The year 1879 was a year of ferment and unrest among Negroes, which led many of them to forsake their old homes in the South and move north and west. The motives underlying the migration were various and complex and differed somewhat from state to state, but the general conditions underlying the exodus were pictured by Frederick Douglass in a speech before the American Social Science Association in September, 1879. In describing the condition of Southern Negroes he said that theirs was: ". . . a sad story, disgraceful and scandalous to our age and country. . . . They tell us with great unanimity that they are badly treated at the South. The land owners, planters, and the old master-class generally, deal unfairly with them, having had their labor for nothing when they were slaves. These men, now they are free, endeavor by various devices to get it for next to nothing; work as hard, faithfully and constantly as they may, live as plainly and as sparingly as they may, they are no better off at the end of the year than at the beginning. They say that they are the dupes and victims of cunning and fraud in signing contracts which they cannot read and cannot fully understand; that they are compelled to trade at stores owned in whole or in part by their employers, and that they are paid with orders and not with money;. . . that landowners are in league to prevent land-buying by Negroes; . . . that outside the towns and cities no provision is made for education; . . . that they are not only the victims of fraud and cunning, but of violence and intimidation; that from their very poverty the temples of justice are not open to them; that the jury box is virtually closed; that the murder of a black man by a white man is followed by no conviction or punishment."[14] The exodus began in the states bordering the Mississippi River, where in the latter part of 1878 and early 1879 bands of laborers from the plantations began to move with no clearly defined objective except to reach one of the states of the new west. The movement was spontaneous and lacked organization, but by April excitement over migration had reached such a pitch that a meeting of colored people assembled in New Orleans to consider the question. The delegates were far from unanimous in advocating that Negroes leave the South. Ex-governor P. B. Pinchback of Louisiana urged against it, and a statement in opposition from Frederick Douglass was read. Nevertheless a resolution in favor of migration was adopted.

In May another convention, including delegates from Northern as well as Southern states, assembled in Nashville, Tennessee. The delegates, after discussing various obstacles to the advancement of their race since emancipation, finally adopted a resolution which declared: "It is the sense of this conference that the colored people should emigrate to those States and Territories where they can enjoy all the rights which are guaranteed by the laws and Constitution

14 Quoted in Rayford W. Logan, *The Negro in American Life and Thought. The Nadir 1877-1901* (New York, 1954), 125-26. Political conditions also played some part in the exodus. By 1879 conservative governments were firmly entrenched throughout the South, and in practice the Fifteenth Amendment was being nullified in many places. Undoubtedly Republican politicians in the North, who had about given up hope of continued Republican domination of the South, looked with favor upon Negro migration. Their party stood to reap a twofold gain. In the first place, if enough Negroes left the South before the 1880 census, the number of Southern members of the House of Representatives and the Electoral College might be reduced. In the second place, the movement of Negro voters to "doubtful" Northern states would swell the Republican vote in those states. In May, 1879, the New York *Times* reported that the Principia Club of Boston was issuing tracts and sending agents throughout the South urging Negroes to migrate before the census of 1880. Indianapolis *Daily Sentinel,* May 9, 1879.

of the United States, and enforced by the executive departments of such States and Territories; and we ask of the
United States an appropriation of $500,000, to aid in the
removal of our people from the South."[15]

Meanwhile, thousands of Negroes had left their homes
and started west, most of them bound for Kansas. Many
became stranded en route, particularly in St. Louis, but by
August over seven thousand had reached Kansas. As the
exodus grew, organizations were formed to assist Negroes
who wished to leave the South. A national Emigrant Aid
Society was set up in Washington, D. C., and later several
relief societies were organized in Northern cities to send
aid to destitute travelers.[16]

Although Kansas was the objective of most of the emigrants, some of them turned northward. During the earlier
part of the exodus, migration from Kentucky to Indiana
was on the increase. In May, 1879, it was reported in the
Indianapolis *Sentinel* that more than two thousand Negroes
had arrived in the state in less than a month, a statement
which appears to be greatly exaggerated.[17] It was in the
later stages of the migration that the greatest influx into
Indiana occurred. Toward the end of the year the exodus
fever reached North Carolina, causing a mass movement
from that state to Indiana.

Throughout 1879 there were rumors afloat in the Democratic press that there was a Republican conspiracy to bring
large numbers of Southern Negroes into the state to assure
a Republican victory in 1880. The report of the arrival
of the Kentucky group mentioned above said that the new

---

[15] "Exodus of Colored People," in *Appleton's Annual Cyclopaedia and
Register of Important Events*, 1879, pp. 354-58. P. W. H. Johnson was a
delegate from Indianapolis to the Nashville convention. Indianapolis
Daily Sentinel, May 16, 1879.

[16] In April Indianapolis Negroes organized a relief society to send aid
to Negroes stranded in St. Louis. Indianapolis *Daily Sentinel*, April 29,
1879.

[17] *Ibid.*, May 7, 1879.

arrivals were being cared for by local politicians who were trying to find employment for them. In June there was another story of a plan to bring several hundred more Negroes from Kentucky to southern Indiana.[18] Warnings of such plots appeared regularly in the Indianapolis *Sentinel* together with almost daily editorials on the evil consequences that would ensue from Negro migration. Finally in November and December the rumors appeared to be given some substance by the arrival of large groups of Negroes from North Carolina. Between the beginning of the influx in late 1879 and the first of February, 1880, it was estimated that 1,135 colored people from that state passed through Indianapolis. Some of them remained in that city, but most of them moved on to points farther west in the state.[19]

As more and more arrived, excitement increased and charges of a political plot became more insistent.[20] These charges were partly responsible for the appointment of a committee of the United States Senate to investigate the reasons for the Negro exodus. The majority of the committee members were Democrats, the chairman being Daniel Voorhees, a resident of that part of Indiana into which many of the North Carolina immigrants flocked.[21] Alto-

18 *Ibid.,* June 19, 1879. See also *ibid.,* March 31 and April 4, 1879.

19 Indianapolis *Journal,* February 12, 1880. The *Journal,* the leading Republican newspaper in the state, would have no reason to exaggerate the number.

20 The *Shelby Democrat* (Shelbyville), November 27, 1879, carried an article which declared that "a grand Corps D'Afrique is to be organized in the Southern States, to be known as 'The Army of the Ebo-Shin and Gizzard Foot.' It will be under the command of Field Marshal Elijah Barksdale Martindale, the famous warrior (on paper) of Indianapolis. This bloody soldier will be assisted by Lieutenant-General Benjamin Harrison and Major-General Postmaster George Jefferson Langsdale as division commander." Folder marked "Racial, Shelby County," papers of Indiana Writers' Project, Work Projects Administration (Indiana State Teachers College, Terre Haute). The role of Martindale, editor of the Indianapolis *Journal,* and Langsdale, editor of the Greencastle *Banner,* in the exodus is mentioned later in the chapter.

21 The other Democratic members were Zebulon B. Vance and George Pendleton. The Republicans were William Windom and Henry W. Blair.

gether the committee heard one hundred and fifty-three
witnesses, who were drawn from states of the South and
from Kansas, Missouri, and Indiana, the states to which
most of the Negroes went. They amassed several thousand
pages of testimony, but, as might have been expected, split
along party lines in interpreting the testimony. In spite
of the political overtones the committee report throws light
on the exodus from North Carolina and the reasons underlying the northward movement of Negroes.

The report of the Democratic majority of the committee
indicated that the movement from North Carolina to Indiana "was undoubtedly induced in a great degree by
Northern politicians, and by negro leaders in their employ,
and in the employ of railroad lines." On the other hand,
the minority blamed the migration on outrages which the
Negroes suffered at the hands of Southern Democrats.
Specifically they charged that the discontent which impelled
the Negroes to leave could be attributed to the following:
1) abridgment of their rights of self-government; 2) lack
of educational facilities; 3) discrimination against them in
courts of justice; 4) memories of Democratic outrages.[22]
There were elements of truth in both reports, but neither
paid adequate attention to the desire for economic better-
ment, which appears to have been a basic motive. From the
testimony of witnesses it appears that the system of share
cropping and payment in scrip rather than money and
exploitation by land owners were influential factors.

The decision to emigrate was due also in large part to
the activities of two enterprising North Carolina Negroes,
Samuel Perry and Peter Williams, especially the former.
The dream of moving west had been born long before 1879.
As early as 1872, Perry testified, he had received circulars
from Omaha, Nebraska, describing how railroad and gov-

---

[22] *Report and Testimony of the Select Committee of the United States
Senate to Investigate the Cause of the Removal of the Negroes from the
Southern States to the Northern States* (U. S. *Senate Reports,* 46th Con-
gress, 2 session, No. 693, in three parts), pt. 1 :iii, ix-x, xvi.

ernment lands could be acquired with little cash. He told the committee that he distributed such literature among his neighbors and that: "We held little meetings then; that is, we would meet and talk about it [moving west] Sunday evenings." The idea of a western colony was discussed intermittently but died down. In 1878 it was revived because of crop failures and dissatisfaction with the mortgage system. By this time Perry had been reading accounts of Kansas, and he began to promote the idea of moving to that state. He organized a secret emigration society among his neighbors, collecting twenty-five cents from each member. He also persuaded the group to send a petition to the National Emigrant Aid Society, asking financial assistance, and designating Perry and Peter Williams as agents. The petition, which was accompanied by 168 names, read in part as follows:

"We, the undersigned colored people of the second Congressional district of North Carolina, having labored hard for several years, under disadvantages over which we had no control, to elevate ourselves to a higher plane of Christian civilization; and whereas, our progress has been so retarded as to nearly nullify all our efforts, after dispassionate and calm consideration, our deliberate conviction is, that emigration is the only way in which we can elevate ourselves to a higher plane of true citizenship."[23]

Part of Perry's enthusiasm for emigration seems to have arisen from the promise of a commission of a dollar for each full-fare railroad ticket over the Baltimore and Ohio Railroad which was sold through his efforts.[24] Having collected fifty-four dollars in dues from their neighbors he

23 *Ibid.,* pt. 1:280-82.
24 *Ibid.,* pt. 1:75, 103, 133, 218, 296, 316. Perry insisted that the railroad reneged on its promise and that he was unable to collect. Competition among railroad lines to sell tickets to emigrants was keen, and it was customary to pay drawbacks of one dollar on tickets to agents. The colored ticket agent at Goldsboro, North Carolina, was active in recruiting emigrants. *Ibid.,* pt. 1:73-74.

and Williams set out with the intention of going to Kansas to investigate the possibilities of a colony. That they were diverted to Indiana seems to have been largely a matter of chance. In Washington, D. C., they met a former resident of Indiana, who appears to have urged them to consider the possibility of bringing the colonists to Ohio, Indiana, or Illinois rather than to Kansas, and who probably told them the names of persons in Indiana who might be interested in assisting them.

Partly on account of this encounter and partly because they had run out of funds, Perry and Williams stopped in Indianapolis instead of going on to Kansas. There they met some of the leading Negroes, who introduced them to Judge E. B. Martindale, editor of the Indianapolis *Journal,* and William R. Holloway, treasurer of the Republican State Central Committee.[25] From Indianapolis Perry went on to Greencastle in Putnam County, about forty miles to the west. There he met two men who were already engaged in promoting Negro immigration—George J. Langsdale, editor of the Republican *Banner,* which advertised Indiana as a better place than Kansas for Negro farm laborers who did not have money to buy land, and the Reverend John H. Clay of the African M. E. church, who had written a circular published in the *Banner* advertising Indiana as a place of settlement.[26] After gathering information about the attractions of Indiana, Perry returned to North Carolina, taking with him some of Clay's literature for distribution, and

[25] *Report of the Removal of the Negroes,* pt. 1:85-86, 282-83; pt. 2:28 ff.

[26] Reprints from the *Banner,* in *ibid.,* pt. 1:97-98, 167-68; Indianapolis *Daily Sentinel,* November 11, 1879. Among the attractions listed by Clay were numerous free schools for Negro children and opportunities for employment for thousands of farm hands and domestic servants. Furthermore, it was added: "In Indiana all stand equal before the law—the black man being protected in his contracts, property, and person the same as the white." Clay assured prospective immigrants that Negroes in Indiana were eager to assist them. Some of Clay's circulars had already been distributed in North Carolina, where Perry had seen them before coming to Indiana. *Report of the Removal of the Negroes,* pt. 1:166.

traveling on a railroad ticket paid for by a person high in the Republican party.[27]

In November a group of 51 Negroes, mostly men, left North Carolina for Indiana. The Emigrant Aid Society furnished funds to transport those without money from Washington, D. C., to Greencastle. This first group seems to have been well received and to have secured employment without difficulty. They wrote enthusiastic reports back home, which no doubt prompted others to follow. During December 460 immigrants from North Carolina arrived in Indianapolis, and on New Year's Eve two hundred more. By February a total of 1,135 had reached the city.[28] A large part of them were women and children, including many infants. Perhaps as few as one fourth were men. Although they arrived in the middle of winter, most of them wore only the thin clothing that had been suitable for the milder climate from which they came. Many of the women had on sunbonnets. Few carried any luggage.

As they arrived the colored people of Indianapolis attempted to care for them. At first they were given quarters in the African M.E. and the Second Baptist churches, where they were fed by women of the congregations. A Christian Emigration Aid Society was organized by members of the churches to solicit funds. Nearly all of the money collected

[27] *Ibid.,* pt. 1 :203, 283, 346-47 ; pt. 2 :14, 29-30.

[28] In December 165 more North Carolina Negroes appeared in Washington. Sixty-four of these paid their own fares to Indiana, the Emigrant Aid Society paying the fares of the rest. About a week later three hundred more arrived in Washington. Between November 20 and December 26 the Emigrant Aid Society expended more than two thousand dollars in transportation. After its funds were exhausted the resourceful Perry, who accompanied the last-mentioned group, sent a telegram to Indianapolis asking for $625 so that the emigrants could complete their journey. The money was sent, but where it came from remains a mystery. It was generally agreed that the colored people of the city could not have raised so large a sum in such a short time. The agent of the Baltimore and Ohio Railroad, who denied knowledge of where the money came from, testified: "I know the Negroes came to Indianapolis, and we don't haul people for nothing." *Ibid.,* pt. 1 :191-92, 290-92, 368.

for relief was contributed by Negroes. Although white politicians may have encouraged them to come, none of them made any substantial contribution toward caring for the immigrants after they arrived. The money which was collected was insufficient to pay for the necessary food, clothing, and fuel, and the society was soon in debt.[29]

Crowded together, without adequate clothing or fuel, many of the new arrivals became sick. Dr. Samuel A. Elbert, a colored physician who was active in caring for them and in raising funds, issued a public plea for help. Between twenty-five and thirty persons, all of them ill, were crowded together in one house. Most of them were sleeping on bare floors, since there was only one bedstead in the building. He warned that they would die if help was not forthcoming. An Indianapolis undertaker testified before the Senate investigating committee that during December and January he had given pauper burials to twenty-five or thirty of the immigrants—most of them children. Some of them died from pneumonia, contracted because of the severe weather, others from scarlet fever and diphtheria. The witness stated that all the Negroes arrived in a destitute condition and were unable to obtain decent shelter. Ten or fifteen people were frequently crowded together in two or three rooms. One family of nine slept on a pile of straw with only one comfort to cover them.[30]

Many of the Negroes stayed in Indianapolis for only a few days and then moved on to points farther west in the state. Those who remained in the capital city appear to have had difficulty in finding work. Indianapolis had been hard hit by the panic of 1873, and for several years unemployment and suffering had been widespread. Although the worst period had been the winter of 1875-76, there was still a labor surplus in 1879. Moreover the Negroes had

29 *Report of the Removal of the Negroes*, pt. 1:355-57; Indianapolis *Daily Sentinel*, December 5, 1879; Indianapolis *Journal*, February 21, 1880.

30 Indianapolis *Journal*, February 16, 1880; *Report of the Removal of the Negroes*, pt. 1:317-18.

arrived at the worst part of the year since many of the jobs ordinarily open to members of their race were seasonal.[31] A considerable number of immigrants went on to Greencastle, where George Langsdale and the Reverend Clay had been urging them to come. More of them seem to have settled in Putnam County and the neighboring counties of Montgomery, Clay, and Hendricks than in any other part of the state. The first group, which was made up largely of men, was followed by several other carloads. Among the later arrivals there was a higher percentage of women and children. Greencastle was in a farming area where the demand for labor was seasonal, and many of the later arrivals had difficulty finding work. Anti-Negro whites sought to discourage the employment of the colored immigrants. Two houses which were prepared for their occupancy were burned down as was also the barn of a man who had employed one of them. Even some of the older Negro residents of Greencastle expressed opposition to the arrival of large numbers of Southerners because they feared it would lead to a lowering of wages. In nearby Hendricks County hostility was intense. A farmer who hired an immigrant was threatened with violence. When he refused to heed the threat, his haystack was burned, his fences thrown down, and his cattle turned loose. Some of the newcomers, destitute and unable to find work, wrote to their former employers, begging them for their fare back home. Others in desperation started back to North Carolina on foot.[32]

During the winter between one hundred fifty and two hundred of the North Carolina Negroes came to Terre Haute, where J. H. Walker, a colored politician, had been advertising the need for colored workers. Some of the other

31 *Ibid.*, pt. 1:332-33.
32 *Ibid.*, pt. 1:176, 220-22; Indianapolis *Daily Sentinel*, November 24, December 3-4, 1879; Indianapolis *Journal*, March 1, 1880. In the testimony before the Senate committee it was stated that four Negroes, unable to make a living in Indiana, had set out on foot for North Carolina. *Report of the Removal of the Negroes*, pt. 1:351.

colored residents of Terre Haute as well as the farmers of the Lost Creek community expressed fears that the presence of the immigrants would lead to competition for jobs and lower wages. As they arrived, they were quartered in the African M.E. Church and the surrounding community. A relief board was organized to take care of them, and they were fed by charity. Many of them were unable to get work, and some took to begging for money on the street.[33] Eventually most of them appear to have found employment in the mines and on the farms of the vicinity as well as in Terre Haute itself.

Smaller groups from North Carolina arrived in other parts of the state. In December a forlorn and helpless group of twenty-six, including only seven men, arrived by rail in Shelbyville during a period of intense cold. They were met by one of the few colored residents of the town, a barber, who gave them shelter in his place of business. Their coming created great excitement. Shelbyville was a Democratic stronghold, and the local Republican newspaper had been carrying articles encouraging Negro immigration. A meeting of the common council called by the mayor voted to feed and care for the Negroes out of public funds since otherwise they faced starvation. At the same time a citizens' meeting passed resolutions asking the officials to take steps to find out who was responsible for bringing paupers into the county and to prosecute them. A few days later other Negroes arrived in Shelby County in wagons. Others came by train to Greensburg in Decatur County and thence to Shelbyville. There was strong opposition to the later arrivals and reports of mob action against them.[34]

[33] *Report of the Removal of the Negroes*, pt. 1:18, 20, 150-51, 158-60. J. H. Walker, a colored Republican, had been attempting to encourage Negro immigration and had written a letter to the Emigrant Aid Society in Washington advertising the Terre Haute area as a desirable place for settlement, where Negroes would find employment in the mines at from $2.50 to $4.00 a day. *Ibid.*, pt. 1:92.

[34] *Ibid.*, pt. 1:265-67; Indianapolis *Daily Sentinel*, December 13, 1879. A group of five families which came from North Carolina to Hancock

In several respects the 1879 exodus constitutes a pathetic chapter in the history of Negro migration. Clearly the migrants were the victims of overly enthusiastic propaganda, which pictured conditions in Indiana as more favorable than they actually were. Instead of the promised land they found cold, hunger, and sometimes disease and death. Some of them in their disillusionment started back to North Carolina, but most of them stayed and were ultimately perhaps better off than they had been in their native state. It is difficult to blame any particular individuals for the suffering which the immigrants endured. It is probable that even the enterprising Perry believed the promotion literature which he distributed and that he hoped to improve the condition of his neighbors while at the same time enriching himself.

The role of the white politicians remains obscure. They were not responsible for causing the exodus, but some of them tried to turn it to their advantage. Certainly Republican politicians and the party press looked with benevolence upon the arrival of the Negroes and contributed some of the money for their transportation, but in so far as there was a political plot it was farfetched and ineptly executed. The percentage of adult males among the immigrants was small, and at the most the new arrivals meant only a few hundred votes.

No other migration of Negroes in the nineteenth century attracted such widespread attention as the 1879 exodus. During the eighties the rate of immigration to Indiana de-

County found themselves unwelcome to most of the white population. Notices were posted at various places warning white residents not to harbor Negroes or employ them. When a Quaker farmer gave some of the Negroes quarters in his barn in spite of the warnings, the barn was burned. The throat of a horse belonging to one of the older colored residents of the county was cut after the man gave lodging to some of the immigrants. Indianapolis *Journal,* January 26, 1879. Small groups from North Carolina found homes in other counties. About fifty went to the vicinity of the Quaker settlement of Annapolis in Parke County. *Report of the Removal of the Negroes,* pt. 1:150-51.

clined, but rose again in the nineties. The increase was due partly to economic factors but the final triumph of white supremacy and the lynchings and mob violence of the nineties also impelled Negroes to leave the South.

Before 1900 nearly all of the immigration into Indiana was from the states of the Upper South, especially Kentucky. In spite of the publicity given to the exodus from North Carolina the number of Negroes coming from Kentucky was much larger in the seventies. By 1900 the number of Kentucky-born Negroes in the state was 19,379 or about one third of the total. No other state contributed a comparable number. The number from Tennessee in 1900 was 3,459 or about 6 per cent. The number born in North Carolina declined from 3,167 in 1880 to 1,817 in 1900, while the number born in Virginia dropped from 1,563 to 1,232 in the same period. By 1900 there were 1,856 persons born in Ohio, 942 born in Illinois, and 499 born in Michigan in the Indiana population. Few Negroes came from the Lower South in the nineteenth century. In 1900 there were 425 persons from Alabama, 421 from Georgia, 267 from Mississippi, 185 from South Carolina, and 111 from Louisiana. Meanwhile, the ratio of Indiana-born Negroes was increasing until by the end of the century they constituted 25,304 out of a total of 57,505, or about 44 per cent.[35]

In spite of the fact that the total Negro population of Indiana showed a fivefold increase between 1860 and 1900 some parts of the state showed little or no increase, while there was actually a decline in some places. In some instances this was due to a deliberate anti-Negro policy; in others it was due primarily to economic causes. Some communities gained a reputation for being so hostile that no Negro dared stay overnight in them. In no part of the state was race hatred more virulent in the postwar period

---

[35] *Tenth Census* (1880) :*Statistics of Population,* 488-91; *Twelfth Census* (1900) :*Population,* pt. 1 :702-5.

than in Washington County, where during the pioneer period a number of Negroes had come with Quakers from North Carolina. The non-Quaker elements became increasingly intolerant, especially during the Civil War years, when fears of an influx of Negroes as a result of emancipation were whipped up. The result was a campaign of intimidation, of which one of the most tragic victims was John Williams, a pioneer who had acquired a farm and an unusual amount of wealth for a Negro. In December, 1864, he was shot to death in his own dooryard, apparently the victim of an irresponsible Negro hater, since no other motive for the murder was discovered. In 1867 there was another murder, the victim being an inoffensive old man who had aroused the ire of some of his white neighbors by persisting in attending their church, even after he had been warned to stay away.[36]

There were other acts of intimidation which led to an exodus of nearly all of the colored residents. Between 1860 and 1870 the number in the county declined from 187 to 18. By 1880 there were only three, and the county had become proscribed territory for Negroes, who were not allowed to come in even as servants, a fact which occasioned surprise among visitors from the South and which was considered remarkable since most of the early settlers had come from slave states. A county history published in 1916 asserted: "Washington County has for several decades boasted that no colored man or woman lived within her borders."[37]

Crawford County, just across the Ohio River from Kentucky, also barred Negroes. In 1850 there was one Negro

[36] Trueblood, "Story of John Williams," in *Indiana Magazine of History*, 30:150; Indianapolis *Journal*, September 23, 1867.

[37] Stevens, *Washington County*, 282. When a horsebreeder from Kentucky, who had bought a farm on Blue River, brought a colored boy to care for his horses, there was so much excitement that the boy was sent away. A visitor from Louisville who brought a colored cook was compelled to send her away because of threats of violence. Indianapolis *Journal*, August 10, 1888; Indianapolis *World*, September 30, 1893.

in the county; by 1860 none; by 1870 three; by 1880 two; by 1890 fourteen; by 1900 only two. It was an established policy that no member of the race was allowed to come in, even temporarily. In 1881 a contractor for the Louisville, New Albany and St. Louis Railroad, who had hired a gang of colored construction workers, was warned that they would not be allowed to work. When he sought protection from the county officials, they confirmed that it was an unwritten law that Negroes were not permitted in the county. Leavenworth, the principal town, had a reputation for being one of the most anti-Negro towns on the Ohio River. River captains were said to discipline colored crew members by threatening to put them ashore there.[38]

In spite of the fact that there was a heavy concentration of Negroes in Clark County, none were allowed within the corporation limits of the little town of Utica, about ten miles up the Ohio River from Jeffersonville. An excursion boat which attempted to make a brief landing there was said to have been driven off because there were a few colored persons on board. A prominent visitor to the place had difficulty securing permission to bring his colored carriage driver into the town. Another Ohio River town where Negroes were barred was Aurora in Dearborn County. When a Cincinnati contractor brought four Negro workers to the place, a crowd attacked them and tried to drive them away, while a citizens' committee warned the employer to get rid of them. This he refused to do, and the Negroes finished the job for which they were employed, but under police protection.[39]

Negroes were not allowed in Scottsburg or Lexington in Scott County, and the census figures for 1890 and 1900 show only one colored person in the entire county. In the little town of Linton in Greene County all Negroes were

[38] Indianapolis *Leader*, July 30, 1881; Indianapolis *Press*, July 5, 1900.
[39] Indianapolis *Journal*, April 22, 1880; Indianapolis *World*, September 30, 1893.

barred after a coal company attempted to use Negro strike-breakers.[40] In several other southern counties there was a marked decline in colored population between the Civil War and the end of the century. In most cases this was probably due to economic conditions, but in some it was probably due to intimidation or ostracism.

Virulent race prejudice was not confined to the south. In Wells County in the northern part of the state no Negroes settled for twenty years after the Civil War. In 1880 three—two barbers and a cook—ventured to come to Bluffton. All received written notices that they must leave, and the proprietor of the hotel who employed the cook, as well as the sheriff of the county, received warnings to get rid of the Negroes. In 1890 and 1900 there were only three Negroes in the county. When the historical records surveys were being made under the Works Progress Administration in the 1930's the record of only one Negro ever having been born in the county was found—a child born on July 20, 1880. A gravestone marked simply "Nigger Jim" was the only evidence of a Negro being buried in the county.[41]

As late as 1900 there were twenty-nine counties in the state in which there were fewer than fifty Negroes, but race prejudice was probably not a deterrent to settlement in most of these. All but seven were in the northern half of the state. In the counties of the extreme north almost no Negroes settled before 1900. On the other hand, there were eleven counties in each of which there were more than one thousand Negroes by the end of the century. The combined colored population of these was 41,112 out of a total of 57,505, or more than 70 per cent of the whole. The number of Negroes in Marion County alone was 17,536, while Vanderburgh had 8,059. On the basis of the ratio of

[40] Indianapolis *World*, September 30, 1893; Indianapolis *Journal*, July 7, 13, 1903.

[41] Indianapolis *Journal*, August 30, 1880; folder marked "Racial, Wells County," Indiana Writers' Project, Work Projects Administration (Indiana State Teachers College, Terre Haute).

colored population to the whole, Vanderburgh County, where Negroes constituted 11.2 per cent of the whole, stood first. Next was Clark with 10 per cent; Marion with 8.9 per cent; and Floyd with 7 per cent. With the exception of those in Marion County the greatest concentration of Negroes remained in the extreme south.[42]

In the period before the Civil War the colored population had been predominantly rural, but in the postwar years the newcomers moved into the cities and towns. In the older settlements the younger generation also abandoned farming for city life, with the result that by 1900 most of the agricultural settlements had almost disappeared. The factors which influenced Negroes were similar to those which were taking the white population to the cities in the same period. During periods of prosperity, when credit was easily obtainable, some farmers went into debt. Later, as the result of crop failures or falling prices, they were unable to keep up their payments and lost their land. In other places the land which Negroes had acquired was of the poorest quality and was abandoned because of the difficulty of eking out a living on it. With the rise of industry tenant farmers and farm laborers left the isolation of the farm in the hope of regular wages and an easier life in the city, although most of them were doomed to disappointment. The superior opportunities for education, recreation, and social life also attracted Negroes to the cities.

In Randolph County which had had the highest ratio of Negroes in the state before the Civil War the total had declined to a mere 396 in 1900. Some of them went to Marion in Grant County, others to Indianapolis and Richmond. In Grant County the agricultural community of Weaver en-

42 *Twelfth Census* (1900) :*Population,* pt. 1 :536-37; U. S. Bureau of the Census, *Negroes in the United States* (*Bulletin 8,* 1904), 281. The number of Negroes in the eleven counties with the largest Negro population in 1900 was as follows: Clark, 3,182; Floyd, 2,107; Gibson, 1,481; Grant, 1,366; Madison, 1,179; Marion, 17,536; Posey, 1,226; Spencer, 1,321; Vanderburgh, 8,059; Vigo, 2,253; Wayne, 1,402. *Ibid.*

joyed a period of prosperity in the seventies, but declined thereafter. Most of the old settlers moved to the city of Marion as the result of a natural gas boom there. Most of the other farming settlements showed a similar decline, although there were exceptions. In Gibson County the Lyles settlement continued to prosper, as did also the farmers of Lost Creek in Vigo County. As the result of the trend toward the cities by 1900 only 26.5 of the Negro population lived in country districts, while 73.5 per cent lived in communities of 2,500 or more.[43]

The most spectacular urban growth was in Indianapolis, where the number of Negroes leaped from 498 in 1860 to 2,931 in 1870; to 6,504 in 1880; to 9,133 in 1890; and 15,931 in 1900. The last figure represented 27.7 per cent of the entire colored population of the state and 9.4 of the total population of the city. By 1900 the only Northern cities in which the number of Negroes exceeded those in Indianapolis were Philadelphia, New York, St. Louis, Chicago, Kansas City, and Pittsburgh, in that order. On the other hand, Indianapolis had a larger number than Cincinnati, Cleveland, or Boston. The only city in the entire list with a higher ratio of Negroes to whites was Kansas City, with slightly more than 10 per cent. In New York and Chicago, although the total number of Negroes was much larger, they constituted less than 2 per cent of the whole.[44] In view of these figures it is not surprising that Indianapolis

[43] U. S. Bureau of the Census, *Negroes in the United States* (*Bulletin 8*, 1904), 244; Tucker, *Randolph County*, 133-34; Whitson (ed.), *Grant County*, 1:355.

[44] Bureau of the Census, *Negroes in the United States* (*Bulletin 8*, 1904), 230-31, 269-71. In 1900 the total number of Negroes and the percentage of the total population which they represented in the principal cities in the North were as follows:

Boston	11,591	2.1	Kansas City	17,567	10.7
Chicago	30,150	1.8	New York	60,666	1.8
Cincinnati	14,482	4.4	Philadelphia	62,613	4.8
Cleveland	5,988	1.6	Pittsburgh	17,040	5.3
Indianapolis	15,931	9.4			

was not only the principal center of Negro activities in the state but that it also took an important place in the cultural and political progress of the entire Negro population of the North.

In Evansville, which was the second largest city in the state in 1900, with a population of 59,007, Negroes numbered 7,515, or over 12 per cent of the whole. Some of the smaller towns in the southern counties had an even higher proportion of colored residents. In Rockport in Spencer County they constituted over 19 per cent; in Mount Vernon in Posey County over 17 per cent; in Jeffersonville in Clark County over 16 per cent; in Princeton in Gibson County 13 per cent; in New Albany in Floyd County over 9 per cent; and in Madison in Jefferson County over 7 per cent.

In Richmond in the eastern part of the state, where so many of the early Negro settlers had come, there continued to be a sizable number. In 1900 they constituted more than 5 per cent of whole. On the opposite side of the state, in Terre Haute, Negroes made up 4 per cent of the total. In the northern part of the state fairly large numbers of colored people moved into some of the cities as the result of the natural gas boom during the last years of the century. In 1900 they made up more than 3 per cent of the total in Muncie, Anderson, and Marion. However, in the two largest cities in the north, Fort Wayne and South Bend, the number of Negroes remained inconsequential, while the great influx into the steel cities in the Gary area which was to occur during and after the first World War had not even begun in 1900.[45]

45 *Twelfth Census* (1900) :*Population*, pt. 1 :615-16.

9
ATTAINMENT OF CITIZENSHIP
AND SUFFRAGE

"WHEREAS THE CAUSE OF LIBERTY and human rights continues to prevail, and

"Whereas, we desire and need equality before the law in order to secure protection: . . .

"Resolved, That we are happy to witness the great change that is being made in the sentiments of the people of the United States; so that not only hatred on account of color or race is rapidly disappearing, but that mean, low black laws are being erased from almost every statute book of the different States of the Union, and laws enacted in their stead built upon truth, justice and liberty. . . ."[1]

The quotation above, from resolutions adopted at a meeting of the Indiana Colored Baptist Association in August, 1867, is an expression of the spirit of optimism that prevailed among Indiana Negroes in the years immediately following the Civil War, a period in which Northern Negroes, as well as Southern, felt that they were standing on the threshold of a new era. At the end of the war all of the old disabilities remained in force in Indiana, but the next few years were years of progress in the fields of legal and political rights. In spite of the fact that they had played a part in winning a Union victory and had relieved white men of military service, many of the men of the Twenty-eighth Regiment were legally ineligible to return to Indiana at the war's end because they had first come into the state in violation of the exclusion article of the Con-

[1] Indianapolis *Daily Journal*, August 28, 1867.

stitution. But nullification of this article was to be one of the first gains in the new era.[2]

Leaders among Indiana Negroes did not sit back and wait for the state legislature to confer rights previously denied but sought through organized efforts and appeals to public opinion to exert pressure upon the lawmakers. The most important efforts were the annual state conventions of colored people, but such occasions as Emancipation Day celebrations and Thanksgiving Day sermons were used not only to express thanks for progress already made by their race but to urge further gains. The first postwar convention met in Indianapolis in October, 1865, with about two hundred persons, representing about thirty counties, in attendance. The delegates discussed means of securing the repeal of the ban on Negro testimony and also prepared to ask the legislature for educational benefits and political rights. A resolution was adopted praising "the noble part our people have taken in the suppression of the late rebellion," and claiming for them "equal rights with other men before the laws." Another resolution declared that rights guaranteed in the Declaration of Independence and Constitution had long been "flagrantly, wickedly and most inhumanely violated, by the degenerate sons of noble sires; and that we hereby, in vindication of Republican principles, call upon the Federal and State Governments to *repeal* the unwholesome and tyrannical laws, which have bereft us of the rights guaranteed other American citizens, and which, by the founders of our institutions, were understood to be

---

[2] In a speech at Richmond in October, 1865, Oliver P. Morton pointed out that Indiana was scarcely in a position to demand that the former Confederate states confer legal and political rights upon the freedmen in view of the fact that Indiana retained all of the old disabilities in her own laws. Speaking of the Twenty-eighth he said: "We got credit on our own state quota for every man who went out. Yet according to the Constitution and law of Indiana, more than one-half of the men in that regiment have no right to come back again, and if they do come back they are subject to prosecution and fine; and any man who accepts them, or employs them, is also liable to punishment." Indianapolis *Daily Journal*, October 2, 1865.

guaranteed by the Constitution to *all men,* alike, regardless of color."[3]

The first concrete gain in the attainment of legal equality was the modification of the law on Negro testimony at a special session of the legislature in November, 1865. Governor Morton again asked repeal of the law which he characterized as a "stigma upon the humanity and the intelligence of the State," but even with his prodding it was impossible to secure outright repeal. Instead, a measure was passed which declared that "all persons of competent age, without distinction as to color or blood," should be competent witnesses, *except* that Negroes who had come into the state in violation of Article XIII of the Constitution should not testify in cases involving white persons.[4]

In consequence of the partial removal of the ban on testimony a Negro testified in a case involving a white man in Morgan County in January, 1866, and the Negro defendants won their case. But when a Negro boy who had come into the state after 1850 sought to prosecute a white man for beating him, an Indianapolis judge dismissed the case because all the witnesses were colored and hence incompetent to testify in the case. However, the efforts to limit the rights of persons who had come into the state contrary to Article XIII were short lived since that notorious feature of the 1851 Constitution was declared invalid by the Indiana Supreme Court in the winter of 1866.[5]

---

3 *Ibid.,* October 25, 1865.

4 *Ibid.,* December 25, 1865; Indiana *House Journal,* 1865 (special session), p. 35; *Laws of Indiana,* 1865 (special session), p. 162. The white supremacists regarded even this as going too far. A minority report in the Senate reiterated that the constitutions of the United States and of Indiana were written for white men and that the measure was contrary to the spirit of our government—and that it was "but the camel's nose, whose admission within the window of civil rights and privileges we must prevent, if we would retain our possessions as our fathers intended." Indiana *Senate Journal,* 1865 (special session), pp. 278-79.

5 *Morgan Gazette* reprinted in Indianapolis *Daily Journal,* January 31, 1866; *ibid.,* January 5, 1866. The rights of persons who had come into

The futility of Article XIII as a check on immigration was being demonstrated daily as more and more Negroes moved into the state. Moreover, recent actions by the Federal government threw doubts upon its constitutionality. In the special session of 1865 there were efforts made both to initiate an amendment to remove the article from the Constitution and to repeal the law for the enforcement of the article, but both failed. In the House a committee recommended the adoption of the latter measure, whereupon a Negrophobe member offered a substitute to enforce the exclusion article more effectually by "making it obligatory on the Governor to see that the laws be faithfully executed, and if need be, call out the militia for the enforcement of the same."[6]

What the legislature refused to do was accomplished by the judiciary. Early in 1866 a case came before Judge Charles H. Test of the circuit court in Lafayette in Tippecanoe County involving the right of a Negro who had come into the state after the adoption of Article XIII to bring a suit for wages for labor he had performed. The judge held that the suit could be maintained and that the [Thirteenth?] Amendment to the Constitution of the United States "abrogated so much of our State Constitution as denies the colored man the right to reside or make contracts within this State."[7]

the state in violation of Article XIII were finally established by the Supreme Court in 1869. In a trial in Wayne County over a contract for the sale of real estate, the judge refused to admit the testimony of a mulatto who had entered the state in violation of the article on the grounds that the law of 1865 prohibited him from doing so. However, the Supreme Court decided that the limitation on testimony was void in view of the fact that Article XIII had already been found invalid (see immediately below). Turner *v.* Parry, 27 Ind. 163-67.

   6 Kettleborough, *Constitution Making*, 2 :75-76 ; Indiana *House Journal,* 1865 (special session), pp. 73, 208, 225, 430-31, 556-57.

   7Indianapolis *Daily Journal,* April 21, 1866. Judge Test must have been referring to the Thirteenth Amendment, since the Fourteenth Amendment had not yet been adopted. His application of the amendment, which merely abolished slavery, is not clear.

A few months later an opinion of the Indiana Supreme Court gave the *coup de grâce* to Article XIII. In this case a Negro named Jacob Smith sued a group of white men in the Marion County Court of Common Pleas for payment of a promissory note. The defendants sought to have the case dismissed on the grounds that Smith had come into the state in violation of the Constitution and therefore could not maintain a suit and that any contract made with him was void. The trial court ruled in favor of the defendants, but Smith appealed his case to the Supreme Court and won a victory. In an opinion which was indicative of the changing attitude toward Negroes in courts of law, Judge Robert Gregory held that Article XIII was void because Negroes were citizens of the United States. In determining the question of citizenship he passed over the dictum of Chief Justice Taney in the case of Dred Scott, decided on the eve of the Civil War, holding that although that opinion had never been overruled, it was "now disregarded by every department of the government." He mentioned with approval the dissent of Justice Curtis in the Dred Scott case and cited an opinion given by Attorney General Edward Bates in 1862 in which Bates had said that a "free man of color, if born in the United States, is a citizen of the United States." Gregory relied most heavily on the recently passed Civil Rights Act of April 9, 1866, which declared: "that all persons born in the United States and not subject to any foreign power, excluding Indians not taxed, are hereby declared to be citizens of the United States." Gregory insisted that Congress had the right to pass the law, that it was merely declaratory so far as it defined citizenship, and that "so far as disabilities had been grafted on slavery, or had grown out of the relation of master and slave, article thirteen of the Constitution of the United States, abolishing slavery, confers express powers on congress 'to enforce this article by appropriate legislation.' "[8]

8 Smith *v.* Moody and others, 26 Ind. 299-307; Indianapolis *Daily Journal*, November 2, 1866. In spite of Gregory's assertion, there was

After the Supreme Court decision Governor Morton asked the 1867 session of the legislature to delete Article XIII from the Constitution. Although controlled by Republicans the legislature took no action on his recommendation but did repeal the law of 1852 for the enforcement of Article XIII.[9]

The fact that they were at last recognized as citizens was hailed with joy by Negroes and helped strengthen their devotion to the land of their birth. Moses Broyles, in a Thanksgiving Day sermon preached soon after the Supreme Court decision, declared that in past years he would have felt some reluctance in expressing thanks for the prosperity of the nation in view of the oppressed condition of the colored population, but now, he said: " . . . I think that I speak the sentiments of our people generally when I say that we love this Government above all others. This is our native land. It is the only land that we know anything about by experience; and notwithstanding we have been oppressed here, yet whatever blessings we have enjoyed, and are still enjoying, have come to us in this country, and most of us expect that all the blessings we shall enjoy in this life will be in America. Yes, America is our home; and I think that we feel as much of national pride in its prosperity as any other people. . . ." But, he continued, "We want to enjoy rights and privileges in a government that we have helped to build up and sustain; yea, that we have helped to rescue from the very jaws of destruction. If we suffered every wrong in time of slavery, we want to enjoy every privilege of a free people in time of liberty.

considerable doubt as to the right of Congress to pass the Civil Rights Act. President Andrew Johnson had vetoed it on the grounds that it was an invasion of powers reserved to the states, but Congress had overridden his veto. The provisions concerning citizenship were later incorporated into the Fourteenth Amendment.

[9] *Laws of Indiana,* 1867, p. 233. Article XIII was not finally deleted from the Constitution until 1881. For a further account of the protracted efforts to amend the Constitution see below, 249-50.

. . . These are natural desires, which beat high in the heart of every true patriot. . . .

"We should not be blamed, then, for being like other people. . . . We want access to the public schools for our children. We want the privilege of casting our votes for those who make and administer the laws we must obey. . . .

" . . . we do not want to pour out any vengeance upon our former oppressors. We wish to let the past go. But while we leave the past and press forward, we want our white friends to do likewise. If we hold no malice against them for formerly oppressing us willingly, we trust that they will not hold so much prejudice against us, because we were oppressed against our choice."[10]

Broyles's sermon was not only an expression of thanks for gains already made but a plea for the elimination of remaining disabilities. Resolutions adopted by a state convention of Negroes earlier in November, 1866, were even more explicit. While tendering thanks to the Supreme Court for its "able and just" decision in the Smith case, the delegates declared: "That loving this, our native land, with all the ardor and devotion of true patriots, and proud of the high position our land occupies among the nations of the earth, we do hereby most solemnly agree that we demand that all disabling laws, words and clauses, which mark distinction between men on account of race or color, be stricken out of our statute books, and we pledge our property, our lives, and our sacred honor to the maintenance and perpetuity of the country *when this is done.*"[11]

With the recognition of citizenship already attained the delegates at this convention devoted most of their efforts to

---

10 Indianapolis *Daily Journal,* December 3, 1866. In an Emancipation Day address in January, 1867, the Reverend Whitten Lankford of the Bethel A.M.E. Church in Indianapolis expressed satisfaction that "Indiana, the last State in the Union to do justice by its colored inhabitants, has at last pronounced the thirteenth article of the Constitution and legislation in pursuance thereof null and void." *Ibid.,* January 2, 1867.

11 *Ibid.,* November 8, 1866. Author's italics.

a demand for the conferral of political rights. They adopted resolutions, prepared a petition to the legislature, and drew up a statement to the people of Indiana, all of them asking for suffrage as a matter of right. In them they tried to answer the objections that were usually made by the opponents of suffrage, especially the fears expressed by white politicians that political rights meant social equality. They declared: " . . . we recognize a wide distinction between political equality and social equality; we regard political equality as a right, and social equality as a privilege, and we denounce the attempts of certain political leaders to identify them with each other. . . ."[12]

The appeal to the white voters stated: "We are aware that it is objected that we are too illiterate and ignorant to have a voice in deciding the great questions of State and National interest. But while we claim that we are equally as intelligent as thousands of other citizens of the State who do vote, we hold that virtue and patriotism are more essential qualifications in the voter than intelligence. If we have virtue and intelligence enough to fight on the right side, certainly we will not vote on the wrong side.

"We are not asking for social equality. . . . Such equality can not be brought about by legislation, but depends upon culture, and is a matter of taste. Because men go to the polls and vote on equal terms is no reason that they should associate together, unless they choose to do so."[13]

Recognition of citizenship and nullification of Article XIII had been attained with relative ease, not because of the importunities of the colored population, but because white leaders in the Republican party, including members

[12] Indianapolis *Daily Journal*, November 8, 1866. The petition to the legislation was couched in humble terms and said in part: "Though, believing, as we do, that the right of suffrage is ours by right, and ours by inheritance, we will wait with patience the sure and inevitable results and certainties of future human events, which are full of promising omens." *Ibid.*, November 10, 1866.

[13] *Ibid.*, November 12, 1866.

of the judiciary, had taken the initiative. But Republican leaders were at first exceedingly reluctant to espouse the cause of Negro suffrage because they regarded it as politically dangerous.

Negro suffrage had begun to emerge as a political issue as soon as it became apparent that the Civil War would result in the emancipation of the slaves. Indiana Democrats feared that suffrage would be a consequence of emancipation and prepared to fight it with every weapon at their command.[14] Their position on the question was entirely clear, but that of the Republicans was equivocal and subject to change. At first the latter denied any intent of conferring voting rights, insisting that the question of suffrage belonged to each state and that Negroes were not ready for political rights. Later, in an effort to protect the civil rights of freedmen in the South and to perpetuate the Republican party in power in that region, they sought to impose Negro voting upon the former Confederate states but not those in the North. Finally, they forced the adoption of the Fifteenth Amendment and began to seek to win the votes of Indiana Negroes. Both Democrats and Republicans regarded the suffrage question as of importance principally because of its bearing upon the political future of the South. At the war's end the number of potential Negro voters in Indiana was so small that neither party was concerned with it.

In June, 1865, the Indianapolis *Journal,* which was the principal Republican paper and which usually expressed the views of Oliver P. Morton, decried a proposal for granting freedmen the right to vote. Instead it urged a constitutional amendment under which a state's representation in Congress would be based, not on its total population, but on its voting population. This would mean that the representation

---

[14] An editorial in the Indianapolis *Daily Sentinel,* March 14, 1865, warned that having carried the Thirteenth Amendment through Congress the Republicans were preparing for the "coming issue," Negro suffrage. Chief Justice Salmon P. Chase was quoted as saying: "The black man has been emancipated. *It now remains to arm him with the ballot.*"

of the Southern states would be reduced if they did not confer suffrage on the Negroes but it did not compel them to do so. This suggestion foreshadowed a provision which was later incorporated into the Fourteenth Amendment.[15]

The only important Republican in Indiana ready to take a stand in favor of Negro suffrage at this time was George W. Julian, member of Congress from the part of the state which had been the heart of the antislavery movement. Julian's attitude alarmed nearly all the politicians in the party, who regarded the introduction of the issue as premature. Oliver P. Morton, who had a personal grudge against Julian, and the Indianapolis *Journal* began a campaign to discredit him. In September Morton made a speech in Richmond, principal city of Julian's district, in which he declared that Negroes were as yet not qualified to vote. He attacked a proposal which Charles Sumner had made to enfranchise Negroes and to disfranchise whites who had aided the rebellion, warning that this would lead to Negro domination and race warfare. Instead he endorsed the proposal for apportioning representation according to the number of voters. In his message to the legislature in November Morton said: "The subject of suffrage is, by the national Constitution, expressly referred to the determination of the several States, and it can not be taken from them without a violation of the letter and spirit of that instrument."[16]

Because of the possibly adverse effect of the suffrage issue on the Northern electorate an effort was made to keep that question out of the political campaign of 1866.[17] In Indiana

[15] Indianapolis *Daily Journal*, June 2, July 7, 21, 1865.

[16] *Ibid.*, October 2, 1865; George W. Julian, *Political Recollections, 1840-1872* (Chicago, 1884), 263-70; Indiana *House Journal*, 1865 (special session), pp. 37-38.

[17] When it was rumored that the Congressional Joint Committee on Reconstruction was considering a recommendation of Negro suffrage, a group of Republican congressional members from New York, Illinois, and Indiana warned against permitting the issue of Negro suffrage in any form to be injected into the coming campaign. The opposition was strong enough to put a quietus on the issue for the time being. John

it was constantly repeated that the question of the voting privilege was reserved to the states. In February the Indianapolis *Journal* assailed Thaddeus Stevens for insisting upon Negro suffrage and asserted: "This violent effort to enfranchise the negro is utterly distasteful to the American people. . . . And as certain as the planets move in their orbits, just so certain it is that the people of Indiana, if called upon next October to vote on the question of negro suffrage, would vote overwhelmingly against it."[18]

In spite of Republican protestations to the contrary Democrats insisted that Republicans were trying to foist Negro suffrage upon the voters of Indiana and that the Fourteenth Amendment, which conferred citizenship, would have the effect of conferring the ballot. To refute this Morton took pains to show that the proposed amendment did not confer suffrage. Instead, he said in a speech at New Albany, *"The principle enunciated by the amendment is this, that wherever there is a race of people who are deemed unworthy or unfit to receive and enjoy political rights they shall not be made the basis for conferring political rights and powers upon others."* In a speech at Anderson the Governor spoke against Negro suffrage and Negro equality.[19]

By the time of the opening of the 1867 session of the General Assembly Morton appeared to have modified his position to the point of advocating the enfranchisement

Mabey Mathews, *Legislative and Judicial History of the Fifteenth Amendment* (Johns Hopkins University *Studies in Historical and Political Science,* Series 27, nos. 6-7, Baltimore, 1909), 14.

[18] Indianapolis *Daily Journal,* February 10, 1866.

[19] *Ibid.,* July 19, September 24, 1866. The *Journal* repeatedly insisted that the only way to keep suffrage under the control of the states was to adopt the Fourteenth Amendment. Its adoption would be "assurance that the people of Indiana can keep this question in their own hands and forever be at liberty to decide it for themselves." *Ibid.,* September 1, 1866. Republican candidates hotly denied any intention of conferring the right to vote upon Indiana Negroes. For example, the candidate for the office of state treasurer protested: "I am opposed to conferring the right upon the negroes in the State of Indiana. Let no man here misunderstand me and report me in favor of negro suffrage." *Ibid.,* July 3, 1866.

of Southern Negroes, but not those of the states which had remained loyal to the Union. In his last message to the legislature before that body elected him to the Senate of the United States he asserted that, although the question of voting normally belonged to the states, the only way of assuring loyal governments in the South was to confer the vote upon the Negroes in those states. This soon became the official Republican position. The state platform of 1868 declared that it was necessary to extend suffrage to Negroes of the South because of the "continued rebellious spirit" of that section, but that " . . . the question of suffrage in all the loyal States belongs to the people of those States under the Constitution of the United States." A similar declaration was incorporated into the national platform by the convention which nominated Ulysses S. Grant for the presidency.[20] The platform of the Indiana Democrats, on the other hand, made no distinction between the "loyal" and the "rebellious" state but said simply: "We are opposed to conferring the right of suffrage on Negroes. We deny the right of the general government to interfere with the question of suffrage in any of the States of the Union."[21]

Throughout the campaign of that year Republicans concentrated upon the necessity for punishing treason and insuring loyal governments in the South. No mention was made in Indiana or elsewhere of the possibility of a constitutional amendment which would have the effect of enfranchising northern Negroes. In September the suffrage issue was raised in a debate between Republican Governor Conrad Baker and Democratic Senator Thomas Hendricks, a well-known advocate of white supremacy. Baker was quoted as saying: "I have always said that in the loyal States negro suffrage was a question for the people of those States, . . . and that they had a right to settle the question as they thought best. I stand here today, and I say that

[20] Indiana *House Journal*, 1867, pp. 47-52; Indianapolis *Journal*, February 21, 1868.

[21] Indianapolis *Journal*, January 9, 1868.

you still have this right, and I should resist with all the power I have, personally and politically, any attempt on the part of Congress to interfere with suffrage in the State of Indiana."[22]

The election of 1868 was scarcely past before a movement was under way in the Republican-controlled Congress for a constitutional amendment guaranteeing Negro suffrage. Four days after the election dispatches from Washington to the New York newspapers began to quote a "Radical Senator" to the effect that a suffrage amendment would be introduced when Congress reconvened in December. The decision to push through an amendment was due to the narrowness of the margin of the Grant victory and to the fear that the Southern whites, if they gained control of their state governments once more, would amend state constitutions so as to disfranchise Southern Negroes. Nevertheless, as late as January 5, 1869, the Indianapolis *Journal* raised practical and moral objections to the proposed amendment, questioning whether the requisite three fourths of the states could be prevailed upon to ratify it. Furthermore, in the face of both state and national platforms of the Republicans in 1868, it asked: " . . . would it not be an act of bad faith in the Republican Party to attempt to force it upon the people in this manner?" Oliver P. Morton was quoted at the same time as saying that the proposed amendment was impractical since some Northern states had already voted down Negro suffrage, "and I suppose it would be out of order for the legislature of those States to accept the proposed amendment against the will of the people."[23]

And yet within a matter of a few days the same Morton, in a most remarkable *volte face,* emerged as a leading advo-

22 Indianapolis *Journal*, March 15, 1869.

23 Mathews, *Fifteenth Amendment*, 20-21; Indianapolis *Journal*, January 5, 1869. Proposals for Negro suffrage had recently been rejected in several Northern states including Connecticut, New York, and Ohio. It was believed that efforts of Republicans to change the suffrage requirements contributed to Democratic victories in some local elections in 1867.

cate of a constitutional amendment. Although not entirely satisfied with the wording of the proposed article, he urged speedy Congressional action in order to secure immediate ratification since most of the state legislatures were in session during the first months of 1869.[24]

Democrats accused Republicans of bad faith in so rapidly abandoning their election-year pledges. They pointed out that by inserting the plank which reserved suffrage to the Northern states into their platform they had taken the issue of Negro suffrage out of the campaign of 1868. The question had played no part in the election of the state legislatures which would now be asked to ratify the amendment. Thus the voters in the states were denied an opportunity of expressing their will on the subject. One of the strongest arraignments of the Republicans was in a speech of Senator Hendricks. He reminded members of the party of the plank which had been adopted less than a year before, and said, " . . . I simply ask honorable Senators now to make the pledged and plighted faith of their party to the country good and true, and not in the face of the nation and humanity to give it the lie. . . .

"I ask honorable Senators, upon this question of submission for ratification, what that plighted faith of a great party to the people did mean! Was it an evasion? if so, your party is unworthy of a Nation's support. Was it a trick and a fraud? Then you are not only unworthy of a Nation's support, but worthy of the condemnation of virtuous manhood everywhere and in all ages. . . ."[25]

In spite of such protests the amendment was pushed through Congress before the end of February, making it possible to submit it to the legislature of Indiana before its

[24] Instead of a prohibition against denying the right to vote because of race, color, or previous condition of servitude, Morton would have preferred a positive conferral of the right to vote. He foresaw that the purpose of the amendment might be circumvented by literacy or educational rquirements.

[25] Indianapolis *Daily Sentinel*, February 1, 1869.

biennial session came to an end early in March. It looked as though the action of Indiana might be crucial since it was apparent that it was going to be difficult to secure the ratification of the necessary number of states. In view of this fact Democrats in the Assembly were determined to block a favorable vote and thus compel the issue to be taken to the voters. An editorial in the Indianapolis *Sentinel* declared that by eliminating the suffrage question from the 1868 campaign Republicans had gained control of the legislature by false representations and urged Democrats, who opposed the amendment, "to resort to any measure to defeat its ratification, until the people have had opportunity to pass upon it."[26]

Although the Republicans had majorities in both houses, Democratic strategists hoped to block favorable action on the amendment by resigning in large enough numbers to prevent a quorum from being present when the vote was taken. The state Constitution explicitly stated that a quorum consisted of two thirds of each house. Before the amendment came up for consideration seventeen Democratic Senators, out of a total membership of fifty, and thirty-seven Representatives, out of a total of one hundred, submitted their resignations, thus blocking not only action on the suffrage amendment but on other important matters, such as appropriations and taxes.[27]

The Democrats had ample grounds for accusing the Republicans of betraying their campaign pledges, and perhaps they were correct in assuming that a majority of Indiana voters were opposed to Negro suffrage. In an effort to stir

26 Indianapolis *Daily Sentinel,* March 3, 1869.

27 Indiana *House Journal,* 1869, p. 893; Indianapolis *Journal,* March 5, 1869; Indianapolis *Daily Sentinel,* March 5, 1869. A typical letter of resignation from one of the senators to the Governor declared that the reason for the resignation was "for the purpose of securing to the people of Indiana, and particularly to my own constituency, the right to express their voice on the adoption or rejection of the Constitutional Amendment, enforcing negro suffrage, which is proposed to be adopted by the present Legislature without such expression of the people." *Ibid.*

up popular opposition to the amendment the Democratic members of the legislature prepared an Address to the People of Indiana, which contained the same appeals to racial prejudice which the party had used in the pre-Civil War period. The preamble declared: "We believe the Government was formed *for* white men, in the *interest* of white men, as well as we *know* it was created *by* white men, by whom the colored people were looked upon as an inferior and subordinate race." The address declared that the movement for the amendment was due to the narrow margin of Republican victory in 1868, which had resulted in this scheme for winning additional votes by "placing in the hands of those whom they hope to control—an ignorant, irresponsible and depraved race—this glorious right to found, uphold and direct the government." Following the resignation of the Democratic legislators a mass meeting was held in Indianapolis to protest the proposed amendment. Thereafter similar meetings were held in Evansville, Terre Haute, New Albany, Columbus, and other cities. All of them adopted resolutions condemning the Republicans for their perfidious actions and deploring "Negro equality."[28]

Since enactment of necessary legislation had been precluded by the mass resignations, it was necessary to call a special session and to hold special elections to fill the vacant seats. All the men who resigned were triumphantly re-elected, but whether this was a significant test of popular opinion on suffrage is open to question. The men whom the caucus had designated to resign were, of course, from districts which were normally solidly Democratic. There does not seem to have been any strenuous effort by Repub-

[28] Indianapolis *Daily Sentinel*, March 6, 15-17, 22, 1869. Resolutions adopted at Evansville, which sounded like an echo from the past, declared that the "introduction of the negro element into our political system would result in discord, anarchy, and a war of races, and that the only true line of policy, as a measure of safety to both races, is to *colonize the negro* and retain the political power solely in the hands of the white race." Evansville *Courier* reprinted in *ibid.*, March 11, 1869.

licans to capture the seats, and the number of votes cast was not heavy.[29]

Meanwhile, the failure to secure a vote in favor of ratification of the Fifteenth Amendment at the regular session of the Indiana Assembly caused some consternation among the Radicals in Congress, but Senator Morton was equal to the challenge. As an admiring contemporary biographer remarked: "The means by which he obtained the ratification of three more States illustrates his fertility of resources and his eminent qualities of leadership."[30] Since the former confederate states, Virginia, Mississippi, and Texas, had not yet been readmitted to the Union, Morton offered as an additional requirement for readmission that they ratify the Fifteenth Amendment, although all three states had already fulfilled all the conditions which Congress had previously said would be prerequisites for readmission. The proposal was adopted at Morton's urging, and he was also responsible for a measure which compelled Georgia, which had at first rejected the Fifteenth Amendment, to reverse its action and ratify. Under duress the four states finally cast their votes in favor of the hated article.[31]

Morton was also largely instrumental in thwarting a second attempt by Indiana Democrats to prevent the vote

[29] Indianapolis *Journal,* March 29, 1869.

[30] Charles M. Walker, *Sketch of the Life, Character, and Public Services of Oliver P. Morton* . . . (Indianapolis, 1878), 145.

[31] William Dudley Foulke, *Life of Oliver P. Morton* (2 vols. Indianapolis, 1899), 2:117-25. In the debate over Morton's proposal Senator Trumbull of Illinois, a Republican, objected that it was breaking faith to impose the additional requirement upon the three states. But Morton insisted that the amendment must be adopted to thwart the Indiana Democrats, since the latter had thought that without their approval the Fifteenth Amendment would fail, but that if the votes of the three Southern states were counted the vote of Indiana would not be necessary. Because the Georgia legislature had rejected the Fifteenth Amendment and had also expelled its Negro members, the bill introduced by Morton compelled the legislature to reconvene and seat the Negro members and ratify the amendment before Georgia senators and representatives would be seated in Congress.

cf that state from being included in those which ratified the amendment. At the special session which convened in April, 1869, it was agreed by members of both parties that necessary financial legislation should be passed before the suffrage amendment was taken up. When the way had been paved for consideration of the latter measure, Democrats again attempted to forestall action by resigning in sufficient numbers to make a quorum impossible. This time their tactics failed because of the advice given the Republicans by Morton, who arrived from Washington just as the Democrats were preparing to bolt. Although the constitutional provision that a quorum consisted of two thirds of each house had always been interpreted as requiring the presence of two thirds of the full membership, at a secret caucus the resourceful Morton insisted the sensible interpretation was that a quorum consisted of two thirds of the actual membership at any given time. Hence, if the Democrats resigned, a quorum would consist of two thirds of the members that remained after the resignations. The Republicans followed this advice and went ahead and voted on the amendment in spite of the resignations of the Democrats. Although the Democrats and a part of the Republican press expressed doubts as to the legality of the proceedings, in view of long-established precedents as to the nature of a quorum, the vote of the Indiana General Assembly was certified to the Secretary of State in Washington as a legal act of ratification, and Indiana was counted as one of the states ratifying the Fifteenth Amendment.[32]

As a practical matter this ended efforts to block the enfranchisement of Negroes in Indiana, since the ratification of the Fifteenth Amendment had the effect of nullifying the parts of the Indiana Constitution which limited suffrage

[32] Foulke, *Morton*, 2:113; Indiana *House Journal*, 1869 (special session), pp. 508-10, 604-5; *Senate Journal*, 1869 (special session), pp. 4, 17-19, 384-85, 474-76; *Brevier Legislative Reports,* compiled by Ariel and William Drapier, 11(1869):239-40; *Laws of Indiana*, 1869 (special session), p. 128.

to white persons. However, political reverberations over
the manner of the ratification continued. In their 1870 platform Democrats protested the counting of Indiana among
the states which had ratified and declared their "unalterable
opposition to its ratification." That year they gained control
of the state legislature for the first time since the Civil
War, though to what extent this outcome reflected popular
disapproval of the high-handed conduct of the Republicans
at the last session it is impossible to judge. In the session
in 1871, Democrats introduced resolutions to the effect that
the "pretended ratification" of the Fifteenth Amendment
was null and void, but the Republican minority insisted
that ratification was valid and "a finality and incapable of
recision or withdrawal." Furthermore, they added: "Political equality is right, unless the Declaration of Independence is wrong," and that it was "too late for any political
party to file a special demurrer to the methods or manner
by which this grand result was accomplished."[33]

In spite of the adoption of the Fifteenth Amendment,
which made void the part of the suffrage article which
disfranchised Negroes, and in spite of the court decision
voiding Article XIII, these racial distinctions, though meaningless, remained in the Constitution of Indiana for years.
The long delay in removing them was due in part to indifference and in part to the difficulty of amending the Constitution, which required that proposed amendments be
passed by two successive sessions of the legislature, which
met only every two years, and then be submitted to the
voters for ratification by a majority of the electorate. In
1873 articles were adopted by both houses deleting the racial
distinctions, but no action was taken on them in 1875, with
the result that the proposals were dead. In 1877 a fresh
start was made, and a series of amendments was proposed,
including provisions for the removal of those dealing with

[33] Indianapolis *Journal,* January 10, 1870; Indiana *Senate Journal,*
1871, pp. 255, 300, 328-32; Indiana *House Journal,* 1871, pp. 522-23.

Negroes, and these were again voted on favorably by the session which met in 1879. Thus the way was cleared for submission of the amendments to the voters in the regular township elections in the spring of 1880. The results of these elections showed that the total number of votes cast in favor of the amendments, which included several articles besides those dealing with Negroes, was greater than the number against, but many persons who voted for township officers failed to vote at all on the amendments since they were on separate ballots. The state Supreme Court therefore ruled that the amendments were not ratified, holding that the vote cast did not meet the requirement of the Constitution of an affirmative vote of a "majority of the electors," since the votes cast for the amendments did not constitute a majority of the votes cast in the township elections. The court ruled that a majority of the electorate— that is, persons voting in those particular elections—had not voted in favor of the amendments, and that they had been neither ratified nor rejected.

The decision necessitated submitting the amendments once more to the voters. This was done at a special election in March, 1881, called solely for this purpose. At this time a majority of those voting voted affirmatively, and the amendments were at last declared adopted. In consequence, the old Article XIII dealing with Negro exclusion and the parts of the suffrage article which dealt with color were finally erased.[34]

[34] Kettleborough, *Constitution Making,* 2:117-23, 130-46, 156-64, 167-76, 202-7; The State *v.* Swift, 69 Ind. 505. After the adoption of the amendments discussed above the only racial distinction remaining in the Indiana Constitution was the word "white" in the militia article (Article XII, section 1). There were repeated efforts in the state legislature before 1900 to pass an amendment deleting the word, but because of technicalities and the lengthy and cumbersome method of amending the Constitution, all of them failed. It was not until 1936 that an amendment removing the word "white" was finally adopted. In spite of the Constitution some of the militia laws dropped the word "white" and some colored companies were organized. See for example *Laws of Indiana,*

Even before the adoption of the Fifteenth Amendment some Indiana Negroes had begun to evince an interest in politics and to pledge support to the Republican party in the hope of winning Republican support for Negro suffrage. Colored conventions frequently adopted resolutions praising individual Republican leaders and expressing thanks to Congress for measures in behalf of their race. In the split which developed between President Andrew Johnson and the Radical Republicans the sympathies of the Negroes were with the latter. In 1866 a convention meeting in Indianapolis, after praising Thaddeus Stevens and the Radicals, declared: " . . . we have lost confidence in the accidental profligate representative of J. Wilkes Booth, who disgraces the Presidential chair. . . ." In an Emancipation Day celebration in 1867 Negroes marched in a parade carrying banners which displayed such slogans as "Abraham Lincoln— he lives in our memory," and "We would vote the way we shot !"[35]

While ratification of the Fifteenth Amendment was pending, a Negro in Greencastle wrote a letter to the Indianapolis *Journal* (which sounded as though it might have been inspired by a white politician) in which he expressed the gratitude of Indiana Negroes to Oliver P. Morton and predicted that Negroes would flock to the Republican party "as naturally as water flows downward." Although the exigencies of national politics, rather than concern for the Negroes of Indiana, had forced Republicans to support the Fifteenth Amendment, once that step was taken they lost

1889, p. 325; *ibid.*, 1895, pp. 102-3; *Report of the Adjutant General of the State of Indiana*, 1893-94, p. 36.

[35] Indianapolis *Daily Journal*, November 9, 1866; January 2, 1867. During the summer of 1867 at the request of Tennessee Republicans two Indiana Negroes, James S. Hinton of Indianapolis and a Reverend Mr. Williams from Henry County, were sent by the Indiana State Committee to Tennessee to work for the party among the newly enfranchised freedmen. On their return to Indianapolis the two men addressed a gathering of Negroes at which they urged that Indiana Negroes be given the same rights as those in Tennessee. *Ibid.*, August 12, 17, 1867.

no time in cultivating Negro votes. As early as 1869 the Indianapolis *Journal* was happily predicting that ratification of the suffrage amendment would mean six to eight thousand more Republican votes in Indiana.[36]

When the news came that the Fifteenth Amendment was at last a part of the Constitution there were rejoicings and celebrations among the colored people throughout the state —at Terre Haute, Logansport, Lafayette, Shelbyville, North Vernon, Kokomo, and elsewhere. The most imposing event took place in Indianapolis, where various colored fraternal organizations arranged a parade and speechmaking. In the procession were floats decorated with banners displaying such sentiments as: "Oliver P. Morton, the Friend of the Colored People," and "We Stand by the Party Who Stood by Us." There was an array of speakers, both white and colored, who urged the newly enfranchised voters to support the Republican party. Among them was the Reverend Moses Broyles, who advised the members of his race, "above all to stick to the party of freedom, the party of liberty. Vote a straight Republican ticket at the next election, without any scratching." A white speaker warned the Negroes not to forget the Democratic record of hostility toward them, nor the benefits which had come to them through the Republican party. He recalled the epithets which white men sometimes applied to Negroes and declared: "If you *do* forget these things then you are *coons*. Then you are ourangoutangs. If you do forget it, then my prayer will be that God will strike you dead."[37]

---

[36] Indianapolis *Journal,* June 25, October 20, 1869.

[37] *Ibid.,* April 2, 8, 18, 21-22, 29, 1870. Local Republican conventions had already begun to invite Negroes to participate in their activities. The first example which the author has discovered was in Tippecanoe County, where a resolution was adopted that since the Fifteenth Amendment had been adopted and "the black man having been thereby made a voter, the colored citizens of Tippecanoe County, twenty-one years of age and over, are entitled to participate in the action of this Convention on equal terms with its white members." A similar resolution was adopted a few days later in Putnam County. *Ibid.,* February 7, 16, 1870.

The Republican state platform of 1870 declared: "We rejoice in the ratification of the Fifteenth Amendment . . . and we extend to the colored man a helping hand to enable him in the race of life to improve and elevate his condition."[38] Throughout the campaign of that year meetings of various kinds were held in an effort to arouse the interest of the new voters. All the speakers carried the same message: the benefits which the Negroes had received from the Republicans, the hatred of Democrats for colored men, the debt of gratitude which Negroes owed to Republicans. On the eve of the fall election, the first in which Negroes participated in Indiana, the Indianapolis *Journal* published the following appeal. It is doubtful if many of the newly enfranchised voters were sufficiently literate to read it, but it embodies the arguments that Republicans were to use with success for decades in winning the colored vote.

"TO COLORED MEN.

"Before casting your vote to-day it would be well for you to reflect a moment on past events. Who passed laws in Indiana that prohibited colored men from voting? Democrats. Who put an article in the Constitution of Indiana prohibiting colored people from coming to this State and punishing white men who would give them work? Democrats.

"What court decided that provision of our State Constitution void? The Republican Supreme Judges of Indiana.

"Who decided that the colored man had no rights which a white man is bound to respect? The Democratic Judges of the Supreme Court of the United States.

"Who passed the Thirteenth Amendment, giving freedom to the slaves? Republicans.

"Who passed the Fourteenth Amendment giving you civil rights? Republicans.

[38] *Ibid.*, February 23, 1870.

"Who passed the Fifteenth Amendment giving you the right to vote? Republicans.

"Who opposed all these? Democrats.

"Whom will you please if you vote the Reform [Democratic] ticket? Democrats. . . .

"Will you thus repay the Republicans for what they have done for your race? Will you join hands with your enemies to defeat your friends?"[39]

---

[39] Indianapolis *Journal,* October 11, 1870.

10
EQUAL PROTECTION OF THE LAWS?

"No STATE SHALL MAKE or enforce any law which shall abridge the privileges or immunities of citizens of the United States; nor shall any State deprive any person of life, liberty, or property, without due process of law; nor deny to any person within its jurisdiction the equal protection of the laws." This section of the Fourteenth Amendment was the heart of the Reconstruction program of the Radical Republicans and was intended by its framers primarily as a protection to the civil rights of Negroes. In the twentieth century, as the result of judicial interpretation, the last clause especially has become the constitutional foundation for outlawing segregation and eliminating racial discrimination. However, in the nineteenth century the guarantees of "due process" and "equal protection of the laws" were ideals which fell short of attainment by Indiana Negroes. Removal of racial distinctions in the state Constitution and laws did not insure equality of treatment, and even the enactment of positive guarantees did not put an end to discrimination.

In the years immediately after the Civil War Negroes concentrated their efforts upon securing educational and political rights. The question of denial of the use of transportation facilities, hotels, restaurants, etc. was approached with caution since Negro leaders were aware of the deep-seated prejudice which much of the white population felt toward anything which smacked of "social equality." They felt that they would weaken their position in the fight for schools and suffrage if they attacked other forms of discrimination.[1] Occasionally one of the more militant members of the race protested against unequal treatment. A delegate to the Colored Convention of 1866 was reported as "throwing a bombshell" into the meeting when he introduced a resolution "requiring men to work for black men, as they do for white men in barber shops, bath rooms, etc." An excited discussion followed, but the presiding officer adjourned the convention before action was taken on the proposal. At the convention in Terre Haute the following year a resolution along the same lines was adopted, but in 1871 when a resolution was offered demanding "equality in hotels, railroad cars and barber shops," it was tabled after a debate.[2]

One gain which was made in the postwar years was the right of colored men to equal treatment on the street cars in Indianapolis. The street car company had a rule that colored women might ride inside the cars but that colored men must stand on the front platform, even though they were required to pay full fare. One Negro brought charges

[1] The type of prejudice with which colored persons had to contend is shown by an editorial in the Indianapolis *Daily Herald*, July 18, 1867, which declared: "It must be remembered that the distinction of color in peoples was not made by man but by God. The Almighty is the author of the distinction . . . . He must have intended some great purpose in making white and black people; and, with the distinction of colors, he at the same time created feelings that attracted into one body those of like colors, and repelled those of a different color . . . . The antagonism of races is one of the most natural and universal of all sentiments.
"There is no instance in which it has been obliterated in a people or even mitigated."

[2] Indianapolis *Daily Journal*, November 9, 1866; October 8, 1867; March 24, 1871. In the summer of 1865 a group of colored Masons, who were going by rail from Indianapolis to Shelbyville for the funeral of a deceased member, were refused admission to the passenger coach and compelled to ride in the baggage car although they paid full fare. One of them wrote a letter to the Indianapolis *Daily Journal*, exclaiming, "Now, sir, in the name of humanity and justice, how long are these things to exist, that colored men are to pay full fare, the same as white people, and then be treated thus, because some Copperheads are disposed to object to their presence?" *Ibid.*, August 23, 1865.

of assault and battery after a conductor put him off a car because he attempted to occupy an inside seat. At the trial in the Marion County Circuit Court in 1867 it was shown that the conductor was merely acting in accordance with the instruction of the company which employed him. The judge ruled that: "The company is a common carrier, and its obligation is to carry all persons who conduct themselves in a decent and orderly manner." He asserted that the company had no right to discriminate on the basis of sex or color and that the regulation had no legal force.[3]

The judge cited no authority in his opinion, which was a somewhat remarkable one in view of the fact that the Fourteenth Amendment had not yet been adopted. The adoption of this amendment in 1868 aroused little interest among Indiana Negroes. Aside from reaffirming their citizenship, which had already been recognized, it had no immediate effect upon their condition. Both Negroes and whites thought of the guarantee of the amendment as applying principally to the freedmen of the South. In 1875 Congress adopted a Civil Rights Act which provided to all persons in the United States guarantees of full and equal enjoyment of accommodations and privileges in such places as inns, public conveyances, and places of public amusement, "applicable alike to citizens of every race and color, regardless of any previous condition of servitude." But this too was regarded as being primarily for the benefit of Southern Negroes.[4]

3 *Ibid.*, July 9, 13, 1867.
4 U. S. *Statutes at Large*, 18(1873-75) :pt. 3:335-37. In Indiana white politicians were primarily interested in the second section of the Fourteenth Amendment which was designed to compel Southern states to grant Negro suffrage or suffer a reduction in their representation. The amendment was ratified by the Indiana legislature after little debate. The 1874 state platform of the Democrats, adopted while the civil rights bill was under consideration in Congress, condemned the two Indiana senators, Morton and Pratt, for supporting the bill. The platform declared that the proposal of such a measure made it imperative that the American people decide at the ballot box "whether or not they will be coerced to

The act attracted little attention in Indiana, where Negroes rarely attempted to invade the places designated by custom and economic circumstances for the use of white persons. The attempt of a group of visitors to invoke the act created a furor in Indianapolis in 1877. The Negroes involved were a troupe of singers and musicians who were appearing at the local opera house in a production entitled "Out of Bondage." Their manager had made arrangements for them to lodge and take their meals at a hotel, but the waiters in the main dining room, acting on the instructions of their superiors, refused to serve them. Instead they were ordered to go to the ordinary, a room where the children and servants of guests of the hotel were customarily served. When repeated efforts to receive service in the regular dining room failed, the manager of the troupe brought suit against the proprietor. In the course of a hearing before a United States commissioner one of the lawyers representing the hotel insisted that there had been no violation of the Civil Rights Act, that the act guaranteed that colored people should have food and shelter, but that it did not prevent the hotelkeeper from stipulating where they should eat or sleep. He insisted that the Negroes wanted to be a "privileged aristocracy," and that although "only a few years ago these people were slaves under the lash, and have been freed through the efforts of their white friends, now they will not eat with children and servants." These arguments did not persuade the commissioner to quash the charges, and when he refused to do so, the defendants settled the case out of court, the terms of the settlement not being disclosed.[5]

the absolute social as well as political equality of the negro race with themselves." Indianapolis *Journal*, July 16, 1874.

[5] *Ibid.*, August 31, September 1, 3, 1877; Dunn, *Greater Indianapolis,* 1 :252-53. When another member of the troupe invaded an Indianapolis oyster house, the waiter attempted to charge him an exorbitant price and a white patron threatened the Negro when he objected. Later the proprietor of the place was quoted as saying that it was his policy to discourage colored patrons by charging exorbitant prices—that that was the

In 1883 the Supreme Court of the United States found the portion of the Civil Rights Act of 1875 referred to above to be unconstitutional. It held that the Fourteenth Amendment did not confer upon Congress the power to enact general legislation for the protection of civil rights. Furthermore, it held that, while the amendment made void state legislation which abridged the rights of citizens, it did not forbid discriminatory acts by private individuals. The decision was denounced by a national convention of Negroes meeting in Louisville, Kentucky, but it attracted surprisingly little comment in Indiana. An editorial in the Indianapolis *Journal,* while not critical of the decision, voiced regret that the issue of civil rights would now be reopened. It expressed the opinion that the only way in which colored citizens could secure relief from the effects of the decision would be by another amendment to the United States Constitution or through state legislation.[6]

In consequence of the decision Indiana and other Northern states adopted laws against discrimination on account of color.[7] Ironically the Indiana law was adopted by a legislature which was controlled by Democrats, who were traditionally opposed to enlarging the rights of Negroes. A Democratic senator from Marion County, W. C. Thompson, introduced "An Act to protect all citizens in their civil and legal rights, and prescribing penalties for the violation there-

"way in which we get even with the niggers." Indianapolis *Journal,* September 1, 1877.

[6] Civil Rights Cases, 109 U. S. 3; Indianapolis *Journal,* October 16, 1883.

[7] State civil rights laws were enacted by Northern states in the following years: Connecticut, 1884, 1905; Illinois, 1885; Iowa, 1884, 1892; Massachusetts, 1865, 1866, 1885, 1893, 1895; Michigan, 1885; Minnesota, 1885; Nebraska, 1885, 1893; New Jersey, 1884; New York, 1873, 1881, 1893, 1895; Ohio, 1884; Pennsylvania, 1887; Rhode Island, 1885; Wisconsin, 1895. No civil rights legislation was enacted in Maine, New Hampshire, and Vermont. Leslie H. Fishel, Jr., "The North and the Negro 1865-1900: A Study in Race Discrimination" (unpublished Ph. D. thesis, Harvard University, 1953), 433.

of." He defended the bill as necessary in view of the Supreme Court decision, which had said that this was a field in which only the states could act. The measure brought forth remarkably little debate on the floor. A few senators opposed it on the grounds that it was "class legislation." They insisted that since Negroes were already citizens there was no need to single them out for special privileges. The bill passed the Senate by a vote of 36 to 5, and in the House it was adopted without a dissenting vote after almost no discussion.[8]

The law, which was modeled closely after the Federal law of 1875, declared that all persons within the state were entitled to equal enjoyment of the accommodations of inns, restaurants, barber shops, theaters, public conveyances, and other places of public accommodation. Anyone denying, or aiding and abetting in the denial of, the full enjoyment of such accommodations "except for reasons applicable alike to all citizens of every race and color, and regardless of color or race," was subject to pay damages not exceeding one hundred dollars and also to be deemed guilty of a misdemeanor and subject to a fine of one hundred dollars and a thirty-day imprisonment. Another section of the act declared that no person should be disqualified as a juror because of race or color and made any officer who failed to summon a juror because of color subject to a fine and thirty days in prison.[9]

Members of both parties appear to have voted for the measure for reasons of political expediency. By supporting it Democrats hoped to win some Negroes from their allegiance to the Republican party. In practice the law proved to be ineffectual in accomplishing its stated purpose, and racial patterns remained unchanged by its passage. Few Negroes ventured into places that were regarded as being

[8] Indiana *Senate Journal*, 1885, pp. 37, 264, 267-68; Indiana *House Journal*, 1885, p. 1119.
[9] *Laws of Indiana*, 1885, pp. 76-77.

for white clientele, and when they did, proprietors had ways of refusing to serve the unwelcome patrons. Even when refused services Negroes rarely invoked the civil rights law, partly out of diffidence, partly because of the cost and unpleasantness of legal action. The maximum amount which could be collected under the act would scarcely cover the cost of the suit. A few suits were instituted by more aggressive members of the race, but they usually merely emphasized the futility of the law. It apparently was not until 1888 that a case was actually decided. It grew out of the fact that a Negro employee of an Indianapolis bank, while in the company of a group of white men, was refused service in a restaurant. He brought suit and was awarded sixty dollars in damages in a justice of the peace court, but the Superior Court of Marion County reversed the judgment since the Negro was unable to prove that the proprietor of the restaurant had been present when he was refused service or that the proprietor had instructed the waiter not to serve him.[10]

This decision discouraged other suits since it was seldom possible to prove that proprietors were responsible for the refusal of service, and the law did not make employers liable for the acts of their employees. In 1890 a group of five men which included J. T. V. Hill, the first colored lawyer in Indianapolis, brought suit when they were refused service in a "white" restaurant. In this case the proprietor admitted the truth of the complaint and paid damages of fifty dollars—ten dollars to each plaintiff.[11] This was a petty victory in a justice of peace court and did not constitute the significant test of the law which Negro leaders felt was needed. In 1894 a case arose which for a time seemed to present an opportunity of making a clear-cut test in the state Supreme Court. Because of the personalities

---

[10] Indianapolis *World,* June 23, 1888; *The Freeman* (Indianapolis) August 27, 1892.
[11] Indianapolis *World,* July 12, 1890.

involved it attracted wide attention and threatened to have political repercussions. It started when a white operator forcibly ejected a colored man from an elevator in an Indianapolis hotel, stating that it was a rule that no Negro rode in an elevator. Considerable excitement was generated by the fact that the Negro was Charles H. Stewart, publisher of a newspaper and prominent in Republican circles, and the incident occurred during a Republican convention in the hotel in which was located the state headquarters of the party.

Stewart brought suit for assault and battery against the elevator operator, but the judge of the police court dismissed the case. He declared that the hotel had a right to make its own rules, and that if there were any violation of civil rights involved, it was for a higher court to determine, but added: "I believe that the principal injury in the case was in the sensitive pride of the prosecuting witness." The handling of the case by the judge, who was a Republican, brought protests from the Indianapolis *News* as well as from the Negro press. The *News* predicted that Negroes would take political revenge against the Republicans. George L. Knox, publisher of the *Freeman* and one of the most influential Negroes in the party, also warned that there would be political consequences and insisted that Stewart's case must be taken to a higher court and won, that it involved an issue which affected every Negro in Indiana. A mass meeting of colored people was called, which adopted resolutions condemning the hotel for the outrage and denouncing the judge's handling of the case. Financial support was pledged to help Stewart take the case to a higher court in order to make a test of the civil rights law.[12] This intention was thwarted when Stewart's counsel, Robert B. Bagby, a Negro, for undisclosed reasons asked help of a white law firm, the members of which were also leading

[12] Indianapolis *World*, May 5, 12, 1894; Indianapolis *News* quoted in *ibid.*, May 5, 1894; *The Freeman*, May 5, 12, 1894.

Republicans. On their advice it was decided to file a suit for damages but not to invoke the civil rights law, which, of course, frustrated the intention of making this a case to test the law. The *Freeman*, pointing out this fact, demanded a test case: "If colored men of Indiana are to be thrown out of elevators, denied the hospitalities of hotels, restaurants, eating stands or the saving influences of Young Men's Christian Associations, because of the color of their skin, they the colored men of Indiana want to know it, but by a fair test under the law forbidding it as it stands upon the books."[13]

The Stewart case came to an abrupt end when the proprietor of the hotel where the elevator incident had occurred settled out of court, paying Stewart the sum of three hundred dollars and writing him a letter of apology in which he stated that the offending operator had been dismissed and that there would be no discrimination in the future. To emphasize the point of the settlement he added: "I recognize and believe in that cardinal principle of the Republican party, the equality of all men before the law."[14]

The civil rights act was never interpreted by the Indiana Supreme Court, but in 1895 a case arising under it did reach the Appellate Court, the next highest tribunal. One of the principals in the case was an eighteen-year-old colored boy, Preston Eagleson, a member of the Indiana University football team, who had gone with his teammates to the town of Crawfordsville for a game with Wabash College. When he was refused accommodations in a Crawfordsville hotel, a suit was brought in his behalf. The trial court awarded him one hundred dollars, and the Appellate Court sustained the decision since the evidence showed that he had been denied accommodations because of his color and for no other reason.[15]

13 *The Freeman*, May 26, 1894. For an account of discrimination in the Y. M. C. A., see Chapter XIV.
14 Indianapolis *World*, June 2, 1894.
15 Fruchey *v.* Eagleson by next friend, 15 Appellate Reports (Ind.),

This decision attracted little attention even in the Negro press and did not have the effect of enlarging appreciably the rights enjoyed by Negroes. The civil rights law remained on the books, but on the rare occasions when it was invoked it was given the narrowest interpretation possible.[16] When there was a clear-cut case of violation, the defendants frequently preferred to make a cash settlement out of court, thereby avoiding a decision which would cause publicity and perhaps bring them more colored patrons.[17] Proprietors who refused service to colored persons usually did so because they feared the effect which serving them would have upon their white patrons. Negro proprietors themselves sometimes discriminated against members of their own race out of anxiety for their white patronage. Even George L. Knox, who as publisher of the *Freeman* was a vigorous champion of civil rights, refused service to Negroes in the barber shop which he operated in an Indianapolis hotel. This policy of a wealthy and prominent member of the race,

88-104. The Appellate Court is a statutory court created to relieve the congestion in the Supreme Court. In most cases there is no appeal from its decision.

[16] In 1900 a colored woman hairdresser tried to use the elevator of an Indianapolis hotel to go to the room of a patron in order to dress her hair. When she was refused the use of the elevator, she brought suit under the civil rights act. The hotel company contended that since she was not a guest in the hotel, she had no right to use the elevator even though she was in the building on legitimate business. The judge of the Marion County Superior Court accepted this argument and ruled against the woman. Indianapolis *World*, February 17, 1900. In 1920 in a case appealed to the Appellate Court it was held that an ice-cream parlor was not an "eating place" within the meaning of the civil rights law and therefore to refuse to serve colored patrons in such a place was not a violation of the law. Chochos *et al. v.* Burden *et al.*, 74 Appellate Reports 242-45.

[17] In the summer of 1892 two colored women were denied accommodations at a watering resort in Daviess County. When they threatened to bring suit, the proprietor agreed to settle the case out of court. He was reported to have paid them $400 rather than allow the case to go to trial. *The Freeman*, August 27, 1892; Indianapolis *World*, November 26, 1892.

who claimed to be the political leader of the Negro population of Indianapolis, evoked criticism in Negro newspapers
throughout the country. The Indianapolis *World*, a rival of
the *Freeman*, declared that Knox had a right to choose his
patrons, but that "he must be told that he cannot discriminate
against his own people and at the same time demand their
support. A white man's 'nigger' has no place in the respect
of decent colored people."[18]

The number of suits brought under the civil rights law
is no index as to the amount of discrimination, and the
extent to which Negroes were barred from "white" establishments is difficult to judge. Of course, conditions varied
in different parts of the state. While a Negro might expect
service in a town in a northern county, he would not think
of venturing into a "white" restaurant in one of the Ohio
River towns. There is evidence that even in the northern
part of the state as well as in Indianapolis discrimination
was increasing rather than declining in the nineties. This
was no doubt due in part to increased immigration of
Southern Negroes in this decade. It also reflected developments in the South, where proscriptive race legislation and
Jim Crow-ism were reaching their zenith. Throughout the
North there was not only acquiescence among the white
population in the "Southern Way" of solving the race
problem but a tendency to imitate it in practice. An editorial
in the *Freeman* in 1894 declared: "Up to within the last
two or three years it had been the pride and boast of every
colored man who had his home in Indianapolis, that he
was a resident of the freest and most advanced city in the
North in the municipal recognition extended the Negro and
the rights and privileges freely and cheerfully given him

18 Indianapolis *World*, September 24, 1892. In New Albany there were
colored men who managed restaurants in which other colored men were
refused service except in the kitchen. In Crawfordsville there was a
barbershop which accepted colored patrons so long as a white man owned
it, but when the same shop was purchased by a Negro, he refused to serve
members of his own race. *Ibid.*, April 9, 1887; September 6, 1890.

in a civil way." But, the editorial warned, "Either the Negro of this city must bestir himself, keep his weather eye open or he'll wake up some morning to find himself reduced in the matter of civil privileges in the city of Indianapolis to the level of his brethren in many Southern cities, who are subjected to all sorts of humiliation without recourse or relief."[19] The fact that discrimination was practiced in spite of legislation prohibiting it was due not only to the attitude of the white population but also to the acquiescence of the Negroes in the treatment accorded them. The proddings of the Negro press had little effect upon the average Negro. The situation was summed up in an editorial in the Indianapolis *World* which said that when the proprietor of a public place refused service to a Negro, he proclaimed by his action: "I know I have no LAWFUL right to treat you this way, but I see by your color that you will offer no objection." To which the colored man, by his failure to object, replied: "Yes, that's true. I am of different color, although a CITIZEN in the LAW, so for this reason I will not trouble you to insist upon my rights."[20]

One symbol of racial prejudice which remained unchanged in the period after the Civil War was the legislation prohibiting mixed marriages. Indiana judges held that neither the adoption of the Civil Rights Act of 1866 nor the Fourteenth Amendment invalidated the Indiana law, and members of the legislature showed no disposition to modify the law, although Indiana and Nebraska remained the only states in the North to proscribe such marriages.

[19] *The Freeman*, May 5, 1894. There were increasing evidences of discrimination against Negroes in the northern part of the state. For example, in Kokomo in Howard County, where Negroes had been accepted to a greater degree than in most communities, in 1898 a group of white waitresses went on strike rather than serve the members of a troupe of colored singers who were in the city for an engagement at one of the white churches. Indianapolis *Journal* quoted in Indianapolis *World*, December 17, 1898.

[20] Indianapolis *World*, August 22, 1896.

In 1867 when an Indianapolis Negro was indicted for marrying a white woman, his counsel argued that the Indiana law was in conflict with the Civil Rights Act of 1866, which conferred citizenship upon Negroes and prohibited abridgment of their rights to make contracts. However, the judge ruled that because it entailed religious and moral obligations marriage was more than a civil contract and was subject to restrictions by the state in spite of the Federal law. The Negro was found guilty and sentenced to two years in prison and fined five thousand dollars.[21]

A different interpretation was given by a judge in Evansville, where a marriage between a white man, who had come to the United States from Holland, and a mulatto girl led to a riot and threats of lynching. The preacher who performed the ceremony as well as the man and the girl was arrested, but the judge ordered them released. He held that their marriage was lawful and that the Indiana law was made void by the Civil Rights Act. In another case which arose in the same county an indictment against a Negro for marrying a white woman was quashed on the grounds that the Indiana law was contravened not only by the Civil Rights Act but by the more recently adopted Fourteenth Amendment. However, the state Supreme Court reversed this decision. It held that the Fourteenth Amendment did not give the Federal government the power to invade the police powers of the states, and that neither it nor the Civil Rights Act had impaired or abrogated the Indiana law.[22]

Although there was little disposition on the part of mem-

21 Indianapolis *Journal*, November 12, December 5, 1867; January 27, 1868.

22 *Ibid.*, July 12, 1870; State *v.* Gibson, 36 Ind. 389-405 (1871). The opinion was handed down before the Supreme Court of the United States had had occasion to interpret the effect of the Fourteenth Amendment. The opinion of the Indiana court anticipated the line of reasoning that was to be followed by the United States Supreme Court with regard to the effect of the amendment upon Federal-state relationships.

bers of either race to intermarry with the other, the law, with its extreme penalties and implications of racial inferiority, was regarded as an affront by members of the colored race. The arrest of two colored ministers in Indianapolis in 1875 for performing marriages contrary to the law brought protests from Negro leaders. A mass meeting was held at the Second Baptist Church at which the arrests were condemned and plans were made to raise funds for the defense of the ministers. One of the speakers expressed the feelings of most persons present when he declared: "We do not want to marry white women, for we have as good women wrapped up in black skins as ever walked God's green earth; but we don't want to be singled out from the mass of citizens in the State and especially legislated upon."[23]

A state convention of colored men met the following month primarily to seek modification of the marriage law. Resolutions were adopted which asserted the belief that the law contravened the Fourteenth Amendment, even though the Indiana Supreme Court had held otherwise. The next legislature was asked to "remove these invidious distinctions," which the marriage law contained, but neither the next legislature nor subsequent ones took steps to change the law other than to modify slightly the penalties which it imposed. In 1884 when a Negro in Madison was sentenced to three years in prison for marrying a white woman, the Indianapolis *Journal* termed the sentence "outrageous" and declared that the law should be changed—"not that such alliances may be encouraged but that equal and exact justice be meted out to citizens of all classes."[24]

[23] Indianapolis *Journal*, August 31, 1875.

[24] *Ibid.*, September 22, 1875; *Statutes of Indiana containing the Revised Statutes of 1852 . . . and Subsequent Legislation* (2 vols. Indianapolis, 1876), 2:446-47, 473; *Revised Statutes of Indiana*, 1881, Sec. 2136. In 1879 William Nelson of Vigo County was sent to the state penitentiary for marrying a white woman. Colored people of the state, aroused over the extreme sentence, circulated petitions in which they condemned the

At the next session the only serious effort to repeal the law was made, when the Reverend James M. Townsend of Wayne County, the only Negro member, introduced in the House a bill for the abolition of all distinctions as to race in Indiana law. In a dramatic speech in behalf of his measure Townsend insisted that although few Negroes wished to intermarry with white persons, the present law on marriage had the effect of encouraging immorality and especially the licentiousness of white men toward Negro women. The law made it impossible for the children of unions of persons of mixed blood to be legitimatized. He declared: "A white man so low, so degraded and inferior enough to dishonor and degrade a colored woman, should be made by the laws honorable enough to marry the woman he has thus degraded." Townsend's white colleagues were unimpressed, and the bill was tabled without discussion.[25]

The number of prosecutions is no index as to the number of mixed marriages. Such unions usually went unnoticed unless brought to the attention of the authorities. Persons who wished to marry in spite of the law sometimes went to another state to have the ceremony performed.[26] But

law under which he was convicted as a "relic of pro-slavery legislation" and asked Governor James D. Williams to pardon Nelson, but there is no evidence that Williams acted upon the petition. Indianapolis *Leader,* November 29, 1879; Indianapolis *Journal,* August 20, 23, 1884.

[25] *Brevier Legislative Reports,* 22(1885) :282; Indiana *House Journal,* 1885, pp. 137, 243, 245, 913, 996-98.

[26] In 1885 when an affidavit was filed against an Indianapolis Negro charging him with marrying a white woman, he protested that he had not known that he was violating any law—that he had assumed that there was no prohibition since so many mixed unions existed in Indianapolis. He blamed his arrest on the fact that the man swearing to the affidavit had a personal grudge against him. Indianapolis *Daily Sentinel,* May 23, 1885. In 1894 when a white man and a colored woman were arrested on charges of fornication, the man, a German, insisted that he would like to marry the woman but was prohibited from doing so by law. The judge released the couple on a small bond with the understanding that they would go to Illinois and be married and return to Indianapolis. Indianapolis *World,* January 13, 1894.

even this method of evading the prohibition in Indiana law would have been outlawed by a measure introduced in the 1899 legislative session. A bill, which passed the Senate, would have made it a felony for a colored man to cohabit with a white woman or for a white man to cohabit with a woman with one eighth or more of Negro blood. Penalties of imprisonment of from one to ten years and fines ranging from one hundred to one thousand dollars were imposed. The Indianapolis *World,* organ of Negro Democrats, denounced the measure, which had been passed by a chamber in which Republicans were in a majority, as "an unmitigated outrage against the whole colored race," and sought to make political capital out of it. The bill died in a House committee, partly because of the private protests of Negro leaders, but as the *World* pointed out, if adopted it would have meant that: "A man and woman of different colors who . . . [might] have married in a state or country where such marriage is perfectly legal . . . [might], by emigrating to Indiana, become criminals and subject to degrading punishment." The attempt in the Senate to increase once more the legal disabilities against Negroes is evidence of the retreat of white Republicans from their earlier position as champions of equality and of the increase of racism which prevailed throughout the United States at the end of the century.[27]

In spite of the clause of the Indiana Constitution which stated that "every man, for injury done to him in his person, property, or reputation, shall have remedy by due course of law," and in spite of the guarantees of due process and equal protection of the Fourteenth Amendment, color was sometimes a factor in the administration of justice.

[27] Indiana *Senate Journal,* 1899, pp. 506, 626, 854, 942-43; Indiana *House Journal,* 1899, p. 1496; Senate Bill 376, Original Senate Bills, 1899 session (Archives Division, Indiana State Library) ; Indianapolis *World,* February 25, March 11, October 7, 1899.

To be sure important gains were made in the direction of equality before the law in the years following the Civil War. The first of these was removal of the limitation on the right of Negroes to testify in court and the next the invalidation of Article XIII of the state Constitution which had restricted the right to make contracts.[28] Another step was the admission of Negroes to jury service, although the number of Negro jurors remained insignificant. In spite of the fact that the Federal Civil Rights Law of 1866 prohibited discrimination on account of color in the selection of juries, no Negro seems to have been called in Indiana until after the ratification of the Fifteenth Amendment. The conferral of political rights was apparently interpreted as making Negroes eligible for jury duty. The first instance seems to have occurred in Marion County in April, 1870, when, at the suggestion of the defense attorney, four Negroes were called to serve on a jury which was to try the case of another Negro charged with grand larceny. The first Negro juror in Vincennes was reported in August of the same year. These two instances caused no disturbance, but when two colored men who had been summoned to duty in Terre Haute sought to take their places in the jury box, the white jurors, both Republicans and Democrats, walked out. At this the judge dismissed the colored men. The first Negro juror was reported in South Bend in 1871, in Muncie in 1876, and in Shelbyville in 1879.[29]

The mere fact the inclusion of a Negro on a jury was considered sufficiently newsworthy to be mentioned is evidence that such jurors were a rarity in the seventies. But Negroes claimed that a new law passed in 1881 which gave a larger degree of discretion to jury commissioners in the matter of drawing up panels made possible the exclusion of

[28] Both of these matters are dealt with in Chapter IX.

[29] Indianapolis *Journal,* April 23, August 25, 1870; May 30, 1871; Terre Haute *Journal* quoted in *ibid.,* November 1, 1870; Indianapolis *Daily Sentinel,* March 24, 1879.

Negroes. Only two colored men were called to jury duty in Marion County in 1881. Discrimination in the choosing of jurors was expressly prohibited by the civil rights law enacted in 1885, which provided that no person was to be disqualified as a grand or petit juror because of race or color. Any officer charged with the selection or summoning of a jury who failed to summon a juror because of color was declared to be guilty of a misdemeanor and subject to a fine of one hundred dollars and thirty days in prison. However, the enactment of the law appears to have been a meaningless gesture, for the penalties were never invoked. In many places Negroes were seldom called to jury duty and in some communities never. In Evansville, for example, where the percentage of colored people was higher than in any other large city in the state, it was reported that a jury commissioner positively refused to summon Negroes.[30]

In some communities of the state, at least, a double standard of justice seems to have prevailed, with the result that white men committed crimes against Negroes with impunity or only nominal penalties, while Negroes were severely punished for crimes against white persons. This was especially true in the years after the Civil War when feeling against Negro immigration was running high in southern Indiana. Many acts of wanton violence against Negroes, even murder, were committed, but the guilty parties were seldom brought to justice.

A few examples will suffice. In 1867 an Evansville dispatch to the Indianapolis *Daily Journal* reported: "The negro stabbed on the wharf Monday morning died yesterday evening. There is no clue to the murderer and no effort to hunt him out. It was only a nigger." In 1868 in Spencer County a Negro threw a rock at a white man who had spoken insultingly to him, and in retaliation the white man shot and killed the Negro. A jury found the killer guilty

---

[30] Indianapolis *Leader,* January 7, 1882; *Laws of Indiana,* 1885, p. 77; Evansville *Bulletin* quoted in Indianapolis *World,* October 1, 1892.

of manslaughter and sentenced him to three years in prison. The *Warrick Herald,* published at Boonville in the adjoining county, declared that the shooting was murder, unprovoked and inexcusable. "If the murdered man had only been white then everybody would have been unanimous in the opinion of Jaynes' [the 'killer's'] total guilt; but as he was 'only a nigger,' there are many people of such violent prejudices against color, that they regard the murderer as a very gallant fellow, who did a noble act. The idea that such a crime is merely rebuked by three years' imprisonment is a libel on justice." When another Negro was killed by a white man in the same county, the Indianapolis *Daily Journal* reported: "We can learn of no reason except that the victim was a 'nigger' and this is a 'white man's government.' "[31]

In Indianapolis in 1869 an altercation between a white carpenter and a Negro workman ended in the former shooting and killing the Negro. A coroner's jury pronounced the act premeditated murder, but the jury before which the man was tried was divided as to his guilt. Seven members were in favor of a conviction for manslaughter with a two years' prison term, while the remainder favored acquittal. The judge finally discharged them without a verdict.[32]

While white men went free Negroes were sometimes sentenced on the flimsiest evidence, and even for crimes which they did not commit. A fantastic instance of this occurred in Evansville. During a river-front brawl between a group of whites and Negroes a white man plunged into the waters of the Ohio and disappeared. He was believed to have

[31] Indianapolis *Daily Journal,* June 27, 1867; July 9, 1868; *Warrick Herald* quoted in *ibid.,* March 24, 1869. In Sullivan County a Negro was shot to death by a white constable in what appeared to be an unjustifiable attack. Several days later the constable had not been arrested. In Ladoga in Montgomery County a Negro barber was shot to death by a white man in a dispute over the payment for a shave. The white man fled and was not apprehended. *Ibid.,* September 10, 1868; July 13, 16-17, 1869.

[32] *Ibid.,* September 7, October 18-19, 1869.

drowned, although his body was not recovered and his death was not proved. Nevertheless, four Negroes were brought to trial for manslaughter. At the trial they were denied competent legal counsel, and a strongly anti-Negro bias was reported to have prevailed throughout the proceedings. One important defense witness was not allowed to testify. The four were found guilty, one being sentenced to twenty-four years in prison, the others to shorter terms as accessories to the crime. About three years later it was learned that the supposed victim had not drowned but had swum away unscathed and was living in Paducah, Kentucky. Apparently he had been aware of the trial but had failed to come forward to announce that he was alive. After this discovery the man who was serving the twenty-four-year term was pardoned by the Governor, but the men who had received the shorter sentences were already free, having served their entire terms before the error was discovered.[33]

In later years instances of flagrant miscarriages of justice appear to have declined as Negroes became increasingly aware of their legal rights. In one case in the nineties in which two Indianapolis Negro boys were convicted of murdering a white man an appeal was taken to the Indiana Supreme Court. Although there were strong indications that the pair was guilty, the evidence was largely circumstantial. The high court ordered that they be given a new trial, holding that part of the evidence used in the trial should not have been admitted and that the judge had erred in his instructions to the jury.[34]

Although their treatment in courts of justice improved, there continued to be a widespread feeling among Negroes that members of their race were frequently victims of police brutality, and there is evidence that the feeling was not without foundation. In 1876 in Indianapolis a Negro, who

[33] Evansville *Journal,* reprinted in Indianapolis *Journal,* April 29, 1871; *ibid.,* May 2, 1871.
[34] Parker *et al. v.* the State, 136 Ind. 284-93 (1893).

was in the custody of three policemen who had been sent
to arrest him on a minor charge, was shot to death by one
of them when he started to run away. The policeman who
shot him was brought to trial for manslaughter but was
acquitted. An editorial in the Indianapolis *Journal* called
the shooting "legalized murder" and implied that the policeman had deliberately given the Negro an opportunity to try
to escape so as to have an excuse for shooting him in cold
blood. In another instance in the same city a policeman
shot and killed a Negro who resisted arrest in connection
with a petty theft. The officer was arraigned before the
mayor but was acquitted of wrong doing.[35]

From time to time Negroes protested against police
brutality. For example, in 1887 a mass meeting was held in
an Indianapolis church after a Negro boy had been shot
by a deputy sheriff. Resolutions were adopted which condemned the shooting as "cowardly and uncalled for" and
added: "whereas said outrage was on the line and similar
in its surroundings to several other outrages of the same
nature that have been perpetrated on other citizens of this
community, both black and white, without punishment to
the offenders; therefore be it

"Resolved, That we view with indignation and alarm this
growing evil, while at the same time we condemn the luke-
warm manner and passiveness with which the outrages have
been viewed and treated by the courts and officials of our
city and county in the past."[36]

On the other hand, there was an occasional record of a
policeman receiving a penalty for violent treatment of
Negroes. In 1880 in Terre Haute a jury awarded damages
of thirty-five dollars to a Negro who brought charges against
a policeman who had shot him when arresting him for a
petty offense. In 1892 an Indianapolis policeman handled

---

[35] Indianapolis *Journal*, March 3, 6, 17, April 17, 1876; July 15, 16,
1886.
[36] *Ibid.*, June 1, 1887.

a Negro roughly when making an arrest and then beat him with a club when he protested. For this display the policeman was charged with assault and battery and fined one dollar and costs. The fine was small but it represented a moral victory. A Negro newspaper rejoiced that "for once justice, or a semblance of justice has been done to a colored man." The action of the judge, it maintained, "serves to teach some of the guardians of the city, that, though a man may be under arrest and colored he is nevertheless a man."[37]

Although some of the incidents related above show a disregard for the principles of justice, they did not reflect the same utter contempt for due process as did lynchings. Lynchings were not examples of mere wanton violence or even of premeditated murder; they were organized actions in which groups deliberately defied legal procedures and took into their own hands the punishment of alleged crimes.

It should be emphasized that all victims of lynch law were not Negroes. In Indiana, particularly in certain counties, for more than a generation after the Civil War there were instances of mob justice dispensed by vigilance committees and night riders. The number of such outrages cannot be determined with complete accuracy, but the number of white persons who were lynched was far greater than the number of Negroes. However, the number of Negroes was much greater proportionately since Negroes constituted only about 2 per cent of the entire population of the state. At least twenty Negroes, and probably more, were lynched in the period from 1865 to 1903.[38] Most of the victims were

[37] Indianapolis *Journal*, April 22, 1880; Indianapolis *World*, August 20, 1892.

[38] According to the Indianapolis *Journal*, January 5, 1869, during the last six months of 1868 alone thirteen persons were lynched in the state, none of whom appears to have been a Negro. According to another source forty-one white persons were lynched in the period 1882-1903. James E. Cutler, *Lynch-Law: An Investigation into the History of Lynching in the United States* (New York, 1905), 180. The first ex-

accused of rape or murder, sometimes combined with robbery. But not one of them had been found guilty in a court of law or even indicted by a grand jury. Some of them were seized after they had been arrested and were in the custody of officers while on their way to jail. Others were taken out of jail and lynched. In nearly every case the officers of the law either acquiesced or made only a token show of resistance. No attempt will be made to describe all of these gruesome and depressing incidents, but enough examples will be given to show the general pattern.

The first occurred in 1871 in Clark County, which had the doubtful distinction in the postwar years of being the scene of more murder, violence, and general lawlessness than any other county in the state. After a family of white persons was found hacked to death in their beds, an intensive hunt for their murderers was begun by their neighbors. Finally a slow-witted Negro was discovered who could not account for his whereabouts on the night of the murder. (Later evidence indicated that he had actually been at a house of prostitution but was afraid to admit it.) Under threats of being hanged for lying, he finally confessed that, although he had not committed the murder, he was implicated, and named another Negro as the actual murderer and a second one as his accomplice. After his confession he and the other men whom he had named were jailed. In jail he alternately repudiated and confirmed his confession, but the story which he had told contained a number of implausible features. Aside from this confession the evidence against the trio was circumstantial and of dubious character, some of it perhaps "planted" by persons who wished to turn suspicion away from themselves. For these, or for other reasons, the grand jury failed to return an indictment, but before the three men were released a mob

ample of lynching of Negroes in Indiana after the Civil War which the author has discovered was the lynching in Evansville described in Chapter VIII.

stormed the Charlestown jail and carried them off. Preparations had been carefully made, and plans for the lynching
were common knowledge. A reporter for the Louisville
Courier Journal was given permission to stay at the jail all
night so that he would not miss any of the excitement.
About one o'clock a "well ordered" mob of masked men
approached the jail and battered down the doors while the
unprotesting sheriff watched. The three Negroes were
carried off to a woods outside the town where the one who
had been named as the actual murderer was first burned
with brands, after which all three were hanged. An inquest
was held following the lynching, but the coroner's jury,
after a short deliberation, returned a verdict that the three
men had met death by hanging at the hands of persons
unknown.[39]

In 1878 an especially horrendous lynching occurred in
Mount Vernon, in the extreme southwest of the state.
There a gang of Negroes had forced their way into the
place of business of a group of white prostitutes. The
following day four of the men who were suspected of being
involved were jailed. When an attempt was made to arrest
a fifth man, his father shot a deputy sheriff to death. The
son escaped but the old man was jailed. When news of the
arrests spread, a mob gathered outside the jail but was
persuaded to withdraw temporarily. However, when a
rumor was started that the Governor was sending a con-

---

[39] James M. Hiatt, *Murder and Mob Law in Indiana! The Slaughter
of the Park Family and the Lynching of the Negroes Taylor, Davis and
Johnson* (Indianapolis, 1872). In giving his charge to the grand jury
which investigated the case the judge remarked that during the period
in which he had held office sixteen persons had been hanged by mobs in
his judicial district. *Ibid.*, 3 After the lynching, other acts of violence
against Negroes in the vicinity were reported. The homes of the
widows of two of the victims of the lynching were burned. Louisville
Ledger quoted in Indianapolis, *Journal,* March 27, 1872. In September,
1872, another Negro was hanged by a group of vigilantes in Monroe
County for horse stealing. Again the coroner's jury returned a verdict
of death at the hands of persons unknown. *Ibid.,* September 23, 1872.

tingent of the militia to avert any disorder, a mob of about two hundred men armed with pistols rushed to the depot. Some of them hauled a cannon from the courthouse lawn and set it up opposite the railroad station, threatening to fire upon any militiaman who might alight, but these precautions proved unnecessary since no militia had been sent. Meanwhile plans for lynching the prisoners had been completed. At night a mob of masked men returned to the jail, overpowered the guards, and unlocked the doors. Inside the jail the old man who had shot the deputy sheriff was butchered and his body cut to pieces by relatives of the man he had shot. The other four Negroes were taken from their cells and marched to the town square, where they were hanged. Thereafter the mob dispersed, and apparently no effort was made to apprehend any of the participants.[40]

No other lynching of a Negro appears to have occurred until 1886. The next victim was a farm laborer in Greene County who was accused of murdering his employer and attempting to rape his wife. The man was arrested and jailed in Greene County but was taken to the jail in Vincennes when there were rumors that lynching was planned. The precaution was unavailing. A gang of masked men, carrying sledge hammers and other implements, appeared in Vincennes, marched to the jail, beat down the doors, and seized the Negro. A huge crowd witnessed the hanging in the courthouse square, and his body was left dangling as a grisly warning to other Negroes.[41]

During the late eighties and throughout the nineties the number of lynchings in the United States rose sharply, and outrages against Southern Negroes became a source of national shame. The spirit of mob rule infected Indiana, where lynchings, especially of Negroes, increased. Most of these examples of mob rule succeeded because officers of

---

40 Evansville *Journal* reprinted in Indianapolis *Journal*, October 12, 1878.

41 *Ibid.*, January 13-16, 1886.

the law made only a halfhearted resistance. When authorities showed determination, mobs were cowed. When a Negro was jailed in Marion in Grant County in 1885 on charges of raping a white girl, a mob threatened to storm the jail, but the sheriff and guards resisted. When the mob advanced in spite of warnings, shots were fired and one man was killed. As might be expected this had the effect of dispersing the mob.[42]

In 1894 an attempt at lynching a Negro who had confessed to the rape of a white farm wife in Boone County was thwarted. While the man was being taken from the jail to the courthouse, a mob momentarily seized him and also the sheriff who had him in custody. A free-for-all fight followed, but officers managed to retake the prisoner and escort him to the courthouse where he entered a plea of guilty and was sentenced in accordance with due process. A band of ten deputies then took him to the train; and there was no further show of violence.[43]

Although the Indiana press usually deplored lynchings, it sometimes seemed to inflame race feeling by its lurid reporting of crimes committed by Negroes, and no influential newspaper launched a crusade to arouse public opinion against mob law. Most local and state officials also failed to speak out, and the general public appeared apathetic or actually to condone outrages. It was not until 1899 that an Indiana governor asked for legislation to deal with the problem. He was stung into action by the fact that five white men were lynched in 1897 and a sixth in 1898 and even more by the fact that the governor of Georgia, the state which led the nation in the number of lynchings, cited the record of Indiana in condoning the record of his own state. In consequence Governor James A. Mount urged a law that would make the county in which a lynching or "white capping" occurred liable for damages in a civil suit

<hr />

42 Indianapolis *News,* July 14, 1885.
43 Indianapolis *World,* February 10, 1894.

and which would compel a sheriff who surrendered a prisoner to a mob to forfeit his office. He asserted: "It cannot be argued that the lax enforcement of law justifies a manifestation of contempt of courts and disregard for the law. Any county that can organize a sentiment to prevent lynchers from being punished can also organize against crime and punish criminals in a court of justice."[44]

The legislature responded by passing a law which not only provided that a sheriff who surrendered a prisoner should be removed from his office, but which also made it the duty of a sheriff to call upon the Governor to send militia if he had reason to believe that a lynching would be attempted. It also imposed the death penalty or long prison terms for persons who participated in a lynching. In recognition of the fact that local public opinion might make enforcement difficult, the act provided that action might be begun either by a regular indictment by a grand jury or by the filing of an affidavit with the state attorney general.[45]

Although the purpose of the law was admirable it proved unworkable as a means of stopping lynching or punishing the participants. The first violation of the law occurred the following year in Rockport, where three Negroes were taken out of jail and hanged in connection with the murder of a white barber. Two men confessed their part in the crime, but the third, who had an alibi, died protesting his innocence. The hangings were watched by thousands of spectators who cheered at the sight. The citizens of Rockport were reported as condoning the action of the mob as a "warning" to other lawless Negroes. A United States marshal in the town was quoted as saying that he was not surprised at the lynching in view of the fact that local Negroes had become "overbearing and lawless." He added that his fellow citizens had been forebearing in the face of an increase in crime by Negroes.

44 Indiana *Senate Journal*, 1899, pp. 16-17.
45 *Laws of Indiana*, 1899, pp. 500-2. The law defined lynching as any action by a mob which resulted in death.

Soon after the hangings it was reported that the state was preparing to take action against the sheriff and that the Governor was hopeful that some of the mob might be brought to justice, but the matter seems to have been dropped without charges being filed against any of the participants.[46]

A few weeks later another lynching, even more sadistic in its details, occurred in Terre Haute. This time the victim was another Negro, who apparently had shot to death a young white school teacher. Two hours after he was jailed he was dragged out by a mob which took him to the bridge over the Wabash River and hanged him. After he was dead, his body was taken down and burned in a huge bonfire, while thousands of people, including many women and boys, looked on. The authorities had taken no steps to stop the mob. The sheriff later said that he had intended to use every effort to protect the Negro, but that a "prominent businessman" had advised him not to try; therefore he had ordered his deputies not to shoot. The Governor, who had learned that a mob was gathering, had offered to send troops, but the Terre Haute authorities had replied that it was not necessary. After the lynching two other Negro prisoners were taken from the Terre Haute jail to Indianapolis to prevent a repetition of mob action. Meanwhile many Negro residents were fleeing from the city in terror.[47]

The Terre Haute lynching was the last one in which the state failed to take action. In January, 1901, a new governor, Winfield Durbin, had taken office, and to him belongs much of the credit for bringing a halt to the orgy of mob rule. Durbin not only recommended stronger legislation, he took action against a local official who failed to resist a

---

[46] Indianapolis *Journal*, December 17-18, 23, 31, 1900; Indianapolis *Sun* quoted in Indianapolis *World*, December 22, 1900.

[47] Indianapolis *Journal*, February 26-28, 1901. A mobbing almost occurred in the city of Brazil when a Negro coal miner protested to a white miner who admitted that he had participated in the Terre Haute lynching.

mob and more significantly, he used the state militia to quell a mob.

In 1902 a Negro lynching occurred in Sullivan County, where a mob of armed men forced the sheriff to surrender a colored man accused of assaulting two white women. Rumors that a lynching was planned had reached the office of the Governor, who prepared to send troops to the scene but rescinded his order when word came that the Negro was already dead.[48] As the result of his surrender of the prisoner the Governor and Attorney General declared that the sheriff had forfeited his office. The latter refused to be ousted and defended his conduct. His attorney declared: "He knew everybody in the mob. The sheriff had to face his best friends, men with whom he had lived and worked all his life." When he had threatened to shoot, several men had told him to go ahead, that they might as well be dead as to have their wives dishonored by Negro fiends, and the sheriff had not been willing to shoot his friends. At a prolonged hearing before the Governor several witnesses, some of whom admitted to having been members of the mob, defended the sheriff's conduct. Durbin was unmoved by this and declared that the office was vacant, and the man was not reinstated. The Governor insisted that the ouster would have a "salutary influence."[49]

Although his action may have caused other sheriffs to stiffen their resistance to mob threats, it did not reduce

[48] *Ibid.*, November 21, 1902. The Negro protested his innocence to the end. The crowd which lynched him was described as small and orderly. A few women bystanders clamored "to burn the brute," but his body was left hanging to a telephone pole.

[49] *Ibid.*, November 22, December 11, 1902; Indiana *House Journal,* 1903, p. 50. In 1901 the legislature had amended the law on lynching to provide that if a prisoner was taken from the custody of a sheriff, that was conclusive evidence of the failure of the sheriff to perform his duties and his office should at once be declared vacant. The sheriff was given the right of appeal to the Governor and might be reinstated if he persuaded the Governor that he had done everything in his power to prevent the lynching. *Laws of Indiana,* 1901, pp. 311-12.

racial tension. During the following months numerous minor incidents of mob violence and threats of lynchings were reported, while newspaper accounts of outrages against Negroes in other states may have fanned the flames of bigotry. On July 4, 1903, in Evansville one of the worst race disorders and orgies of mob rule in the history of the state broke out as the result of the fatal shooting of a white policeman by a Negro. The Negro was also seriously wounded in the gun battle with the officer but was taken to the jail in Evansville. As word of the killing spread, the situation in the city became increasingly ominous. A mob formed and made two attempts to storm the jail, but was repulsed both times by the guards. After they had withdrawn the second time, the sheriff took advantage of the respite to take the prisoner, under heavy guard, to the jail in Vincennes. That night a seething, howling, but disorganized mob of two thousand gathered outside the Evansville jail and demanded the surrender of the Negro, unaware of his removal. In an effort to dissuade them from their attempts to force an entry the sheriff permitted two groups to enter the jail to search for the prisoner in order to verify the fact that he was not there, but in spite of this the crowd continued to grow.

Meanwhile clashes between whites and Negroes were occurring in other parts of the city. After a number of individuals had been attacked on the streets during the day, Negroes began to arm and to go about in groups for protection. This led to reports that Negroes were preparing a general assault on the white population and caused part of the mob at the jail to leave and to go Negro hunting. Wherever a Negro was sighted, he was fired upon. While this was going on, a group of terrorized Negroes broke into a hardware store and seized arms and ammunition. Afterwards a gang of whites entered the same store and carried off more guns. A race war seemed imminent.

The sheriff had already called upon the Governor for aid, and a company of state militia had arrived and taken up their positions outside the jail. The mob, which the Governor later said had gathered "ostensibly seeking to avenge the murder of a policeman by a Negro, but actually engaged only in a senseless uprising against duly constituted authority," now began to hurl taunts and insults at the members of the militia. This situation continued for hours, with more and more acts of provocation on the part of members of the crowd. Finally someone threw a stone, knocking down one of the guards. A shot was fired, and then firing became general. Deputies at the jail windows joined the members of the militia in firing on the mob. The crowd melted away, but as they fled, some members fired on the guardsmen, wounding five of them. In the whole affray six persons were killed instantly, and five more died later. Between thirty-five and fifty were wounded.[50]

Additional units of the militia were rushed to the city, but they were not needed. After the shootings a revulsion of feeling swept the city. Most of the populace, frightened and appalled by the tragedy, stayed indoors, and for the next few days the streets were deserted. There was no diminution in racial bitterness. At one manufacturing plant all the colored laborers were driven away, while the men who worked on the drays and wagons around the railroad sheds had a similar experience. Many Negroes fled from the city. The country roads were dotted with those leaving on foot, while the steamboats on the Ohio River were crowded with others. Some of them went to Terre Haute, while a few were reported seeking work as far north as Anderson.[51]

In the Evansville City Court nine men who had been members of the mob were fined one hundred dollars each and sent to jail for thirty days for carrying weapons. Several other members of the mob and three Negroes were

[50] Indianapolis *Journal,* July 6, 7, 1903; Indiana *House Journal,* 1905, p. 57.
[51] Indianapolis *Journal,* July 7, 8; 1903.

later arrested on charges of riotous conspiracy in connection with the race disorders. A grand jury investigated the mob violence, but although sixty witnesses were examined, it was impossible to fix responsibility for the deaths which had resulted from the clash with the militia.[52]

Governor Durbin was criticized in some quarters for his part in the Evansville tragedy. Some critics held him responsible for the violence because he had not sent in a sufficiently large number of militiamen to overawe the crowd completely. There was also bitterness against the members of the militia for their part in the killings, although they had been provoked beyond endurance and one of their own members had been attacked by the mob. There were reports that some of the members of the company which had fired on the mob had been dismissed from their jobs, while firms which employed other members were said to be being boycotted. On the other hand, the conduct of the Governor and the militiamen was applauded. The Indiana conference of the ministers of the A.M.E. Church, which met a few days after the riot, adopted resolutions praising Durbin. President Theodore Roosevelt wrote him a long letter commending him for his attitude upon lynching. In the letter the President expressed concern over the growth of lynchings and particularly the increase in outrages against colored men—"on which occasions the mob seems to lay most weight, not on the crime, but on the color of the criminal." Roosevelt praised Durbin for resisting the mob spirit and for having "vindicated the majesty of the law."[53]

In recounting the measures taken at Evansville in his message to the next legislature Durbin declared: "Deplorable as was this tragedy, its effect as an object lesson has been most salutary," and subsequent developments seem to have

[52] Indianapolis *Journal*, July 8, 10, 11, 20, 21, 1903. Robert Lee, the Negro who had shot the policeman, was never brought to trial because he died of the gun wounds he received in the affray with the man he killed. *Ibid.*, July 9, August 1, 1903.

[53] *Ibid.*, July 12, August 9, 1903.

vindicated his judgment of the affair. Although the newspapers continued to report brawls between whites and Negroes and threats of lynchings, and although other evidences of race prejudice did not abate, the Indiana public appears to have lost its taste for lynchings. Memories of the price which the Evansville mobsters had paid no doubt deterred others. Although lynchings continued to occur in other Northern states as well as in the South, in Indiana for many years they were only a shameful memory.[54]

[54] Indiana *House Journal,* 1905, p. 57. A study of lynchings in the United States covering the period 1889 to 1918 which was made by the National Association for the Advancement of Colored People shows that there were no later lynchings in Indiana in that period. *Thirty Years of Lynching in the United States 1889-1918* (New York, 1919), 63-64, 85. The only lynching since 1903 which the author has discovered occurred in Marion in Grant County in 1930. See below, 393.

11
POLITICAL ACTIVITY

ATHOUGH AT FIRST JUBILANT over the attainment of suffrage, Negroes soon found that the right to vote did not open the way for the elevation of their race as they had expected. Exploited by white leaders and denied a significant share in party affairs many of them became disillusioned and easily corrupted. The new voters at first naturally turned to the party which claimed credit for emancipating their race and for conferring political rights upon them. Republican politicians in turn cultivated their votes and never let the race forget its indebtedness to the G.O.P., although they were reluctant to support Negro candidates for elective office or to share political patronage with them.

In the presidential campaign of 1872, the first in which Negroes participated, a pattern was established which was to prevail in subsequent contests. Efforts to arouse enthusiasm for the re-election of Grant started early. In April there was a parade—described as one of the largest ever held in Indianapolis—to celebrate the anniversary of the ratification of the Fifteenth Amendment. That night at a rally Godlove S. Orth, Republican member of Congress, delivered a much-publicized address, in which he recalled in the usual manner the past efforts of his party in behalf of the Negro and the attempts of the Democrats to block these efforts. He exhorted his listeners:

"Colored men of Indiana! Your duty to yourselves, to your race and your country is clearly marked and defined. . . .

"We are rapidly approaching another Presidential election, and for the first time in your lives you are permitted

(288)

to assist in selecting a Chief Magistrate of this great Republic." He called on his audience to study the history of the
Republican party—"its brilliant record, with not a single
spot to tarnish its fair escutcheon . . . ," and warned
against the restoration of the Democrats, which would mean
a turning back "to the days of those pestiferous and pernicious dogmas of the State rights and State sovereignty,"
and restoration to power of Southern rebels.[1]

During the summer there were numerous affairs such as
excursions and picnics, in which pleasure and politics—and
sometimes religion—were blended. As a Fourth of July
celebration, which was principally a Baptist affair, with
Moses Broyles serving as chairman, there was a railroad
excursion from Indianapolis to Greencastle, where a picnic
and political rally were held. Later a similar event at Mor-
ristown, which attracted about two thousand Negroes from
Indianapolis and Rush and Shelby counties, was sponsored
by the Bethel A.M.E. Church of Indianapolis. The Republican candidates for lieutenant governor and other state
officers accompanied the group and made speeches.[2]

The only factor to mar the prospect of a solid Negro vote
for Grant and the Republicans was the small contingent
heretofore noted as champions of their race who had joined
the Liberal Republican movement and were seeking to defeat
Grant. Horace Greeley, the Liberal Republican presidential
candidate, might be expected to win Negro votes because of
his long record as an abolitionist. But even more significance
was attached to the fact that Senator Charles Sumner of
Massachusetts, for many years the foremost friend of the
colored race in the government of the United States, had
written a letter advising Negroes to support Greeley. In
Indiana George W. Julian, who had supported Negro suffrage when other Republicans were afraid to espouse an
unpopular cause, had broken with the regular Republicans

[1] Indianapolis *Journal*, April 1, 2, 1872.
[2] *Ibid.*, July 3, August 2, 1872.

and was a candidate for congressman-at-large on the Liberal-Republican-Democratic ticket. The possible effect of the defection of the two men upon the colored vote caused concern among regular Republicans, who went to extreme lengths to discredit them. At numerous meetings of Negroes throughout the state similar resolutions, apparently inspired by the high command of the party, were adopted condemning Sumner and Julian. At the Methodist rally mentioned above a resolution was adopted expressing sorrow at Sumner's apostasy and condemning him for writing his "recent false, slanderous and malicious letter against President Grant for the purpose of influencing the votes of the colored people of this country." A meeting at the Second Baptist Church in Indianapolis took similar action, as did meetings at Terre Haute and Thorntown.[3]

In his home territory in eastern Indiana, where George W. Julian had been long known as a staunch friend of the Negro, strenuous efforts were made to discredit him. At a meeting at Cambridge City at which white speakers castigated Julian, resolutions were adopted by the colored faithful which praised Grant and assured "such deluded leaders as Sumner and Julian" that they had their pity and their prayers, but could not have their votes. Another parade and rally at Richmond, which attracted some three thousand Negroes from eastern Indiana, was admittedly held to refute claims which the Democrats were making that Julian could control colored votes in Wayne County.[4]

[3] Indianapolis *Journal,* August 2, 1872.

[4] *Ibid.,* August 17, 30, 1872. Of the Cambridge City meeting the *Journal* reporter remarked with satisfaction: "The number of colored voters who will probably follow George W. Julian in his treachery could be guessed by the contempt and derision which every mention of his name elicited." *Ibid.,* August 17. In his memoirs Julian recounted that the efforts to picture him as a traitor were so successful that at one meeting at which he spoke colored men came armed with revolvers, "breathing the spirit of war which Senator Morton was doing his utmost to kindle." Julian, *Political Recollections,* 342.

When the votes were in, it was found that Julian had suffered an overwhelming defeat, while throughout the country Negroes had rejected the leadership of Greeley and Sumner and had voted for Grant. It was ironical that they should have used their newly acquired political rights to repudiate men who were genuinely interested in their advancement.[5]

In shaping the political attitudes of Negroes in 1872 and for years thereafter Negro ministers played a conspicuous role. This was not surprising in view of the influential part which the churches played in all aspects of Negro life. Ministers had been prominent in the colored conventions which worked for the attainment of suffrage, and they were the leaders to whom their people naturally turned for guidance in the newly opened field of political activity. Without exception the ministers supported the Republican party and were in some cases bitterly partisan. A natural consequence was that white Republican leaders should try to reach colored voters through them. One of the most stalwart of colored Republicans was Moses Broyles of the Second Baptist Church in Indianapolis. Broyles constantly urged his followers to be unswerving in their political allegiance, and his church was frequently used for political meetings. Another Baptist minister, R. McCary, was one of the two colored delegates from Indiana to the Republican National Convention of 1872. Willis Revels of the African M.E. church did not display the same zeal for politics as Broyles, but he campaigned actively for Grant, and many other examples of the dual religious-political role of ministers could be mentioned.[6]

[5] Greeley was especially crushed at being repudiated by the Negro voters. He said: "I was an Abolitionist for years, when it was as much as one's life was worth even here in New York, to be an Abolitionist, and the Negroes have all voted against me." Julian, *Political Recollections,* 348.

[6] Indianapolis *Journal,* July 13, 1872. As late as 1894 the Reverend J. P. Thompson, pastor of the Blackford Zion Church in Indianapolis,

In 1874 the annual meeting of the Indiana Baptist Association, which was made up of colored ministers, adopted the following:

"That we fully realize and highly appreciate the religious and civil liberty that we enjoy at the present time, as compared with our condition fifteen years ago. We do not forget the party, who through Divine Providence, has been instrumental in our emancipation, and intellectual and moral elevation, and we shall labor to keep the Republican party in power as it is pledged to the Supplementary Civil Rights Bill."[7]

The entry into politics was accompanied in some cases by violence and fraud. The intense devotion of Negroes to Republicanism and the antipathy which some Democrats felt for Negroes led to physical clashes, while charges that Republicans bought Negro votes and brought colored floaters into the state were frequently made. Politics was blamed for a riot which occurred in 1868, even before Negroes could vote. On the night of a Democratic rally members of an organization of Democratic veterans who called themselves the "White Boys in Blue" clashed with a group of Negroes. The affair started when one of the White Boys attempted to beat up a Negro who insisted upon cheering for Grant instead of cheering for Seymour, as the White Boys tried to compel him to do. It ended up in a general riot in which some of the White Boys broke into a Negro grocery store, while others engaged in a free-for-all fight with a group of Negroes who had been attending services in a Baptist church.[8]

was quoted as saying from the pulpit: "I sometimes feel that I would rather die and go to hell, than be a Negro Democrat." Indianapolis *World*, May 5, 1894.

[7] *Minutes of the Seventeenth Anniversary of Colored Indiana Baptist Association* (1874), 20.

[8] Indianapolis *Daily Sentinel*, August 19, 28-29, September 1, 4, 8, 1868; Indianapolis *Journal*, August 20, 27, 29, September 2, 11, 1868. The captain of the White Boys was arrested but acquitted after a lengthy

At the municipal elections in Indianapolis in 1871 there were reports that Democrats were attempting to intimidate colored voters, but there were no disorders. Several clashes occurred during the campaign of 1872. One of the more serious was in Jeffersonville, where a fight between white Greeley Guards and colored supporters of Grant ended with the white guards riddling one of the Negro houses with bullets and breaking up the furniture.[9]

The worst outbreak of violence on an election day seems to have occurred in Indianapolis at the mayoralty election in May, 1876. There were several minor clashes during the day, and toward evening an affray broke out between bands of Negro Republicans and Irish Democrats which had to be quelled by police. During the melee one Negro was stabbed, two or three were shot, and several others were severely beaten. Witnesses to the fight insisted that the policemen who were trying to restore order shot at defenseless Negroes. Seven whites were arrested on charges of beating Negroes with clubs. When the Negro who had been stabbed died of his wounds, the Republican Central Committee pledged money to prosecute his assailant. The guilty person was never identified, although several witnesses were interrogated. Ultimately all of the cases against the rioters were dismissed.[10]

In the ensuing state and presidential elections that fall both parties took steps to restrain their more zealous members, and although there were the usual reports of fraud and vote buying, not a single fight was reported in Indianapolis. Thereafter there seem to have been no important race incidents in connection with elections in the capital city, but occasionally a disorder was reported in another community. For example, in the local elections of 1880 in Shelbyville white ruffians were reported to have attempted to prevent

trial. A colored boy who hallooed for Grant during a parade for Seymour was reported to have been beaten up. *Ibid.*, October 27, 1868.

[9] Indianapolis *Journal*, September 24, 1872.

[10] *Ibid.*, May 2-5, 10, 1876.

Negroes from voting. One man was indicted by a Federal grand jury, but the case appears to have been dismissed.[11]

While Republicans accused Democrats of intimidating Negro voters, Democrats countered by insisting that Republicans imported Negro voters from outside the state and bought Negro votes. The Republicans, of course, denied these charges and accused the Democrats of encouraging ineligible aliens to vote and forging naturalization papers. Among all of the charges and countercharges it is impossible to arrive at the facts, but it seems probable that there was an element of truth in all the accusations. Before the adoption of adequate registration laws and the secret ballot, vote buying was relatively easy, and Indiana voters, regardless of color, had a reputation for being susceptible to being bought.

As early as 1871 the Evansville *Courier* claimed that Negro voters were being imported by the Republicans for the purpose of carrying a municipal election. During the presidential campaign of 1872 Republicans were accused of bringing colored voters from Kentucky to some of the towns in southern Indiana and sending some of them as far north as Indianapolis. On election day there were reports that Democrats were displaying placards offering rewards for the spotting of illegal voters.[12]

There were the usual charges of the use of "floaters" in the spring elections of 1876. A grand jury in Indianapolis afterwards indicted several persons for illegal voting and for perjury in swearing as to the eligibility of voters. Testimony at the trial of one white Republican henchman showed that he kept a boarding house at which as many as forty Negroes had been lodged just prior to the election.[13]

11 Indianapolis *Journal,* October 9, 1876; April 6, May 21, 1880.

12 Evansville *Courier* quoted in *ibid.,* March 22, 1871; *ibid.,* October 7, 9, 1872.

13 The defendant was found guilty of perjury and sentenced to three months in prison. Indianapolis *Daily Sentinel,* June 14-17, 1876. The local government was in the hands of the Democrats at this time, and the persons indicted were all Republicans. The Indianapolis *Journal,*

There were rumors of elaborate plans for the importation of Negro voters before the fall elections of 1876. As early as September strange Negroes, who had been brought in for voting purposes, were reported in Indianapolis. Dispatches from Kentucky said that word was being passed among Negroes that there was "lots of money in Indiana and lots of colored help wanted over there this fall"—to insure the election of Benjamin Harrison as governor. Hundreds of Negroes were reported to have passed through Louisville from southern Kentucky and even Tennessee en route to Indiana. There was said to be a noticeable decline in the number of Negroes around the tobacco warehouses in Louisville and the wharves of nearby Portland as the result of their temporary stay in Indiana. It was also charged that a reunion of Union veterans which was held in Indianapolis in September was in part a device for paying the expense of bringing in colored veterans from Kentucky with the understanding that they would remain until after the October and November elections. But, regardless of the truth or falsity of the allegations, the Republican efforts were not enough, for Harrison was defeated in his try for the governorship and the state cast its electoral vote for the Democratic presidential candidate.[14]

The most famous charges of importation of Negroes was in connection with the North Carolina exodus of 1879, which is dealt with in another chapter. This alleged scheme for increasing the Republican vote differed from other attempts in that the immigrants from North Carolina were expected to settle permanently in Indiana instead of merely coming in for voting purposes.

June 17, 1876, remarked plaintively that the jurors, "strangely enough . . . seem unable to find any Democrat who has thus violated the law. That party spirit has ruled in this matter seems very probable."

14 Indianapolis *Daily Sentinel,* September 14, 20, 22, 1876. In the municipal election in Evansville in 1879, which resulted in a Republican victory, almost a thousand more votes were cast than in the previous election. Democrats attributed the outcome to the importation of Negro voters from Kentucky. *Ibid.,* April 8, 12, 1879.

Charges of vote buying continued throughout the eighties and reached their peak in the presidential election of 1888, which is generally regarded as having been the most corrupt of any national election, not only in Indiana but throughout the country. William W. Dudley of Indiana, chairman of the Republican National Committee, won lasting fame of a sort by his letter to county chairmen in Indiana in which he instructed them to "divide the floaters into blocks of five, and put a trusted man, with necessary funds, in charge of these five, and make them responsible that none get away."[15] There were estimates that there were several thousand "floaters" in the state. Although Negroes were not especially conspicuous in these irregularities, they had a share in them. An Indiana University professor, who wrote an eyewitness account of part of the events of election day in Bloomington, told of one Negro voter who had sung in a Democratic glee club during the campaign but who was "captured" by the Republicans on election day. He heard another Negro taunt the Democrats with, "Oh, we sing with you, but we don't vote with you!" The writer saw two other Negroes brought to the polls in a buggy and watched as a party worker placed Republican ballots in their hands. He saw the Negroes hand their ballots through a window, without the inconvenience of having to alight from the buggy.[16]

The events of 1888 were so scandalous that even the Republican governor, whose party was the principal, although not the only, offender, asked for legislation to insure the purity of the ballot box. By the time of the next national election Indiana had adopted the Australian ballot, and thereafter charges of vote buying declined. In 1890 there was a slight flurry over rumors of another scheme to colonize Indiana with Negroes from the South in order to assure a

[15] The notorious letter was published in Indianapolis *Daily Sentinel*, October 31, 1888.

[16] Richard H. Dabney, "Indiana Floaters," in *The Nation*, 47:412 (November 22, 1888).

Republican victory. But if there ever was actually such a plot it did not materialize.[17]

In later elections Republicans followed the pattern of wooing the Negro vote which had been set in 1872. During every campaign colored Republican clubs were formed to whip up enthusiasm and get out the vote. Republican orators, white and black, continued to excoriate the Democrats as the party of treason and to stress the debt of gratitude which Negroes owed the G.O.P. In their appeal for Negro votes Republicans dwelt almost exclusively on their past record and offered nothing new. After 1870, except to ask for the removal of the word "white" from the militia article in the state Constitution, Republican state platforms contained no planks with an especial appeal to Negroes. After a few years the initial ardor which Negroes had felt when granted political rights began to cool. Active political workers became increasingly disgruntled over the fact that they received few rewards for their services to the party. Support of members of their race for public office and the extent of their share in the distribution of patronage, rather than any particular legislative program, became the criteria by which most Negroes measured their political status. Judged by these standards their position was weak. In spite of the increasing number of Negro voters, white leaders showed a reluctance to support Negroes for public office because they feared the effect upon white voters.[18]

17 *Republican Scheme of 1890 to Colonize Indiana with Negroes from North Carolina* (n. p., 1890).

18 In 1879 a Negro hoped to be nominated by the Republicans for one of the positions of city alderman in Indianapolis. He was unsuccessful and there were rumors that party leaders at the city convention had deliberately "counted him out," although he had actually received the number of votes necessary for the nomination. Indianapolis *Daily Sentinel,* April 7, 8, 1879. A Negro Republican candidate for constable in Peru was defeated by his Democratic opponent by 2,780 votes in 1882—a defeat of landslide proportions. It was said that only seventy-five white Republicans voted for him. Indianapolis *Leader,* April 15, 1882.

In 1880 the Indianapolis *Leader,* the only Negro newspaper in the state, began to strike a note which was to be
used increasingly, but unsuccessfully, by disgruntled Negro
Republicans. The *Leader* pointed out that although the total
colored population of Indiana was not large, in certain counties Negroes were sufficiently numerous that Republicans
could not be elected without their votes—"yet when these
men are elected to office they almost universally refuse to
confer any subordinate appointments upon colored men."
Negro workers were expected to be satisfied with appointments to sweep out offices or polish spittoons.

The Democratic Indianapolis *Sentinel* agreed that the Republicans were dependent upon the Negro vote for carrying
the state, but the Republican *Journal* denied this, asserting
that the number of Negroes in the North was not large
enough to affect the outcome in any state.[19]

Dissatisfaction with past Republican policies was dissipated somewhat in 1880 by the nomination and election of
the first Negro member of the state House of Representatives. He was James S. Hinton, a man who, as much as any
other, was regarded as the spokesman for his race in this
period. He had been a leader in the Negro conventions of
the post Civil War years and had been sent to Tennessee as
early as 1867 to work for the Republican party among the
newly enfranchised voters of that state. In 1872 he was
one of the two Negro delegates from Indiana to the Republican national convention, and in 1873 he had been chosen
by the state legislature as a canal commissioner, the first
colored man to be chosen by that body for any office.[20]

19Indianapolis *Leader,* May 1, September 11, 1880.
20 James S. Hinton was born in Raleigh, North Carolina, of free
parents, in 1834. About 1848 he came to Terre Haute, Indiana, where
he attended a subscription school. Later he attended a Quaker school in
Vigo County and the Greenville Institute in Darke County, Ohio. In
Terre Haute he was befriended by a white physician, who urged him to
study medicine and prepare to be a missionary to Liberia, but Hinton
soon abandoned this plan. He worked as a barber and taught school in

After Hinton's nomination for the legislature the *Leader* felt that the Republicans had fulfilled their obligations to the colored voters, declaring: "The colored people of this country are honor bound to support the Republican ticket in the coming contest," and warning of the disastrous consequences if the Negro-hating Democrats should triumph. On the eve of the election it cried: "A Negro vote a Democratic ticket! No, never. God forbid! Go hungry; let the wintry wind pinch your scantily clothed person; deny yourself the necessaries of life—but don't, for the love you owe your families and the allegiance due your race, dishonor and degrade yourself by voting in favor of the worst political organization ever smiled upon by Heaven's beneficent sun."[21]

In 1882 Negroes again received recognition in the nomination of another acknowledged and respected leader, Dr. Samuel A. Elbert of Indianapolis, for state representative, but he and the rest of his party went down to defeat before a Democratic upsurge.[22] Although the nominations of Hinton and Elbert were pleasing, there were increasing doubts among the more thoughtful members of the race as to the

Terre Haute and in 1862 came to Indianapolis. During the Civil War he served as a recruiting officer for the Massachusetts Fifty-fourth. In Indianapolis he engaged in the real estate business and became prominent in Masonic and political circles. He was also a trustee of Wilberforce University. After his one term in the legislature, during which he did nothing outstanding, he did not seek public office again, but remained a recognized leader in all Negro affairs until his death in 1892. J. E. Land, *Indiana's Representative Men in 1881* (Indianapolis, 1881), 24-25; *A Biographical History of Eminent and Self-Made Men of the State of Indiana* (2 vols. Cincinnati, 1880), 1:District 7:93-94.

[21] Indianapolis *Leader,* September 4, October 2, 1880.

[22] Elbert's career as a physician is discussed elsewhere in this book. He was active in Republican politics for many years. In the McKinley campaign of 1896 he headed a national group of Negroes. As a reward for his services he was offered the post of consul at the port of Bahia in Brazil but declined it, apparently because he thought he was entitled to a more attractive appointment. Indianapolis *World,* July 3, August 21, 1897.

sincerity of the Republicans' claim of being the especial champion of the Negro. The abandonment of Southern Negroes by the Hayes administration had caused misgivings, and under Arthur there was increasing dissatisfaction. In 1883 a national convention of colored people meeting in Louisville refused to endorse the Arthur administration, and some delegates began to talk of forming a third party. The decision invalidating the Federal Civil Rights Act, which was handed down in 1883 by a Supreme Court made up of Republican appointees, caused further alarm.

While there might have been dissatisfaction with the G.O.P., few Negroes thought of leaving that party to join the Democrats. In fact, for many years, a Negro who voted the Democratic ticket was regarded as an oddity, to be treated with ridicule or contempt. In 1871 a member of the race who voted a Democratic ballot in Indianapolis was reported to have received an "egg salute," while the only colored man who voted the ticket in Michigan City was carried off to the lockup, dead drunk. The Democratic organization does not appear to have made much of an effort to cultivate Negro voters, although the Indianapolis *Sentinel* occasionally twitted them about their blind devotion to Republicanism. It asserted that most of the colored voters in Indianapolis were "as abject slaves to the Republican party as they were to their old masters before the war." By 1878 there was a colored Democratic club in Indianapolis. One of the earliest leaders among colored Democrats was J. T. Mahorney, who had been active in the Negro convention movement, serving as president of one of the state conventions and as a delegate to a national convention. He was also a leader in the Knights of Labor and the colored Masons.[23]

In 1884 any tendency that Negroes might have had to stray from the fold was checked by the fearsome pictures

---

[23] Indianapolis *Journal*, May 3, 8, October 7, 1878; Indianapolis *Daily Sentinel*, April 7, 1879.

which white Republicans drew of the consequences which a Cleveland victory would have for their race. Although the state of Indiana as a whole went Democratic that year, one Negro, the Reverend James M. Townsend of Richmond, was elected to the state House of Representatives from a district which was a Republican stronghold. Townsend was a man of many talents and a sincere and dedicated leader of his race. He had served in the famous Massachusetts Fifty-fourth Regiment during the Civil War, attended Oberlin College, and taught school before becoming a minister in the A.M.E. church. As a member of the legislature he tried unsuccessfully to secure the abolition of all distinctions based on race in Indiana law.[24]

Although many Negroes had been genuinely alarmed over the election of Cleveland, the first Democratic president since the Civil War, they soon found that change in administration made little change in racial policies. In the realm of patronage Cleveland followed the example of his Republican predecessors in appointing Negroes as ministers to Haiti and Liberia and as recorder of deeds in the General Land Office. He actually named more Northern Negroes to minor offices than had his predecessors, who had tended to disregard them because of their numerical insignificance.

[24] Townsend was born in Gallipolis, Ohio, in 1841. His parents were devout members of the African M.E. Church, and while he was still in his teens he started preaching. After the Civil War he attended Oberlin College for two years, then came to Evansville, Indiana, where he served as principal of a colored school for four years. He continued his studies and returned to the ministry, holding pastorates in Richmond, Terre Haute, and Indianapolis. He also served as secretary of the Parent Home Missionary Society and went as a delegate to the Ecumenical Conference in London, England. In 1883 he was awarded the degree of Doctor of Divinity by Wilberforce University. Meanwhile, he had returned to Richmond where he served as minister until 1889, when he went to Washington as recorder of deeds in the General Land Office during the Harrison administration. He preferred the ministry and soon gave up the post and returned to Richmond. He left once more, this time to go to Quinn Chapel in Chicago, but again returned to Richmond where he died in 1913. *The Freeman* (Indianapolis), January 5, May 18, 1889; Richmond *Palladium,* July 21, 1913.

Among the first Negro postmasters north of the Mason-Dixon line was William H. Roundtree, who received the appointment at Lyles Station in Gibson County from Cleveland in 1885. Several other Indiana Negroes received minor Federal appointments, while a Democratic state legislature enacted the civil rights law of 1885, in part as a bid for the Negro vote. The Indianapolis *Sentinel* hopefully said that Negroes were drifting into the Democratic party as they began to realize that the Republicans merely used them to win elections and then took all of the offices themselves. By this time there was little difference between the political parties so far as their policy toward Northern Negroes was concerned, so Republicans continually held up the plight of Southern Negroes before Northern voters and warned: "The colored man who votes for a Democrat is making the tyranny in the South more crushing to his people."[25]

The presidential campaign of 1888 saw the first serious effort in Indiana to induce the Negro voters to break away from the Republican party. Because of their traditional repugnance to the name "Democrat" they were not urged to affiliate with that party so much as they were urged to be "independent" and to increase their political strength by dividing their votes between the major parties. The argument was, of course, that so long as the Republicans were sure of their votes they would treat them with indifference, but if their votes were divided, both parties would bid for Negro support. This type of appeal was developed in the columns of a new Negro newspaper, the *Freeman,* which was launched in Indianapolis in July, 1888. Its editor, Edward E. Cooper, who had been a Republican, now openly espoused the Democratic cause, although he later returned

25 Indianapolis *Recorder,* April 15, 1933; Indianapolis *Daily Sentinel,* April 1, 1885; Indianapolis *Journal,* October 14, 1886. Although there were as yet few signs of political independence among Negroes, a colored Democratic club was active in the municipal campaign of 1887 in Indianapolis, and that year the colored Indianapolis *World,* heretofore always Republican, endorsed the Democratic candidate for mayor. Indianapolis *World,* September 17, October 1, 1887.

to the Republican fold. The *Freeman* tried to show that although the Republicans could not carry the state without Negro votes, they were ingrates who did not give the Negroes the rewards they deserved. "How much longer," it asked, "are the colored voters expected to do the voting and be rewarded with promises?" In reply to Republican assertions that the colored vote was "all right," i.e., "safe," it declared: "Not a colored man from Indiana had a voice in the last National Republican Convention, and yet the white bosses think the Negroes are all right. . . .

"The colored Republican leaders in this city are a sick looking set, as they are allowed neither a voice in the management of affairs, or office or boodle."[26]

In July a national convention of colored men, including delegates from fifteen states, who styled themselves Independents, met in Indianapolis. Prominent among them were Peter H. Clark, Negro educator from Cincinnati, who was elected president of the group, and T. Thomas Fortune of New York, another journalist who temporarily left the Republican fold, and Milton J. Turner, recorder of deeds in the Cleveland administration. Charles E. Sheldon of Evansville was the temporary chairman. All of the speakers at the conclave struck the same note, urging Negroes to develop political independence. One of them declared that Negroes had been subservient to one party long enough and that a black face should no longer be a Republican badge. If Negroes had any debt to the Republican party, it had long since been discharged. Peter H. Clark said that the Negro had been servile so long that one of independent mind was thought to be either driven to cast the ballot as he did, or to have been bought. While urging independence the convention adopted a resolution endorsing the Cleveland administration and pledging support to Cleveland in his campaign for re-election. An editorial in the *Freeman* hailed the convention as marking the beginning of a new emancipation for the Negro and the death of his political serfdom. It

26 *The Freeman,* July 21, August 4, 1888.

added: "Colored men must learn to respect each other's opinions and differences of opinion, cease longer to follow the blind leadership of ignorance and gratitude."[27]

The *Freeman's* estimate of the strength of the "independent" movement was exaggerated, but the fact that the Republicans took pains to discredit the movement suggests that they had misgivings about the Negro vote. The Indianapolis *Journal* described the convention as a "trap for colored voters" and insisted that many of the delegates held appointments under the Cleveland administration and that the Democratic party furnished the funds to bring them to Indianapolis, which was probably true. It declared: "Not a single delegate was admitted who stands well with his own people in the ward and precinct in which he resides." The Negro *World* adopted the same note.[28] In a letter to the *Journal* the Reverend James M. Townsend insisted that the motives of the independents were purely mercenary. He asserted that every outrage that had ever been perpetrated upon the Negro in the history of the United States was "chargeable to Democracy," while every civil and political right which he enjoyed had been made possible by the Republicans. He insisted that so long as the Negro vote was suppressed in the South, Northern Negroes must be Republicans. Of the recent convention he said: "Let those gentlemen come and hold their convention, if they choose; but colored men of Indiana, you who have any self-respect or love of race, set your faces as flint against such double-dealing, and say to those who would have you make peace with the enemy: 'What pledges do you bring for our safety and well being? You have none, and we will not allow you to decoy us into the enemy's camp, there to be more foully dealt with than before.' "[29]

27 *The Freeman*, July 28, 1888.
28 Indianapolis *Journal*, July 14, 19, 26, 30, 1888; Indianapolis *World*, July 28, 1888.
29 Indianapolis *Journal*, July 25, 1888. The Douglass Republican Club

Although in the end the new political movement attracted few voters, it enlivened the campaign. Even the women, though without the vote, took part. A Frances Cleveland Club was organized, while the Republicans, not to be outdone, formed a Caroline Harrison Club. Colored Republicans heaped abuse upon the Democratic supporters, whom they regarded as renegades. At a mass meeting in Indianapolis a minister of the A.M.E. church from New York pleaded for a Republican victory. He declared that he did not believe that a colored man could really be a Democrat. Germans, Italians, Irish, or Frenchmen might change their politics, but not Negroes. They simply could not bring themselves to join the party which was still the party of slavery.[30]

Colored Republicans did not confine their attacks to verbal onslaughts. The *Freeman* claimed, as the campaign grew warmer, that it was "unsafe for a colored man to attempt to deliver a Democratic speech, unless he is liberally protected by officers of the law." It was reported that Charles E. Sheldon of Evansville had received a letter warning him that he would be killed if he tried to speak in Princeton, while several men in Indianapolis also received threatening letters. There were several minor acts of violence such as smashing the windows of the house of a colored Democrat who displayed Cleveland's picture. The *Freeman* complained that acts of lawlessness of this sort were not rebuked in the Republican press, and pointed out that "the most intolerant

of Greene County adopted the following resolution: "Resolved that we denounce and condemn the proceedings of the recent independent colored convention in session in Indianapolis, and that we lift up our voices against such an inconsistent and ungrateful action on the part of our race." *Ibid.*, July 31, 1888.

30 *The Freeman*, July 21, 28, August 11, 1888; Indianapolis *Journal*, August 31, 1888. At the Independent Convention Mrs. J. T. V. Hill of Indianapolis was introduced as the president of the Frances Cleveland Club. She made a little speech in which she promised the support of the women—"all the assistance which the home and fireside can give. We are not unmindful that we ladies, in common with you bear social ostracism and the sting of unkind expression."

and hot-headed class of participants in these riots are the Negroes themselves."[31]

The efforts of the Democrats to capture the negro vote met with little success. While Harrison's margin of victory was extremely narrow, and Democrats won control of the state legislature, most Negroes remained loyal to the Republicans, although, as suggested elsewhere, that loyalty was sometimes purchased with five dollar gold pieces.[32] The alliance with the G.O.P. continued unbroken throughout the nineties, but feelings of disillusionment and frustration mounted. The presence of a Republican administration in Washington did not improve the lot of Negroes in the South as the campaign orators had promised. Indeed the number of outrages in that region, particularly lynchings, rose to an all-time high under Harrison. The Lodge Federal elections bill, designed to protect the voting rights of Southern Negroes, failed to pass because Northern Republican senators joined Southern Democrats in opposing it. Very early in the new administration Northern Negroes began to express dissatisfaction with the small number of Federal appointments which they received. Even James M. Townsend, whom Harrison appointed as recorder of deeds, publicly expressed the opinion that Harrison did not show enough consideration to Negroes in such states as Indiana, Ohio, Michigan, and New York, where their votes had been indispensable to Republican victory. Townsend resigned his office after a few months, and was succeeded by another Indiana Negro, the Reverend Dolphin P. Roberts of Evansville. The only other colored man from the state to receive an appointment of any consequence was William D. McCoy,

31 *The Freeman*, September 29, November 3, 1888.

32 William Waldon, Negro Republican candidate for the Indiana House of Representatives from Indianapolis, went down to defeat when the Democrats elected their slate of candidates to that body. Waldon was much younger and less distinguished than any of the Negroes previously nominated for that office. He was an active party worker and prominent in several Negro fraternal organizations. Indianapolis *World*, June 2, 1888.

a young Indianapolis schoolteacher. McCoy was nominated for membership in the Indiana House of Representatives in 1890, but after he was defeated in the Democratic sweep of that year, he was appointed by Harrison as minister to Liberia. He and his bride arrived in the Negro republic in 1892, but the tropical climate proved too much for the American Negro, and he died after a few months.[33]

In spite of Negro grumblings white Republicans showed no disposition to give them any but the lowest offices in Indiana. In Evansville, where the Negro element was expected to be satisfied with the nomination of one of their members as constable, the Republican newspaper frankly declared: "Not one colored man out of a hundred is fit to hold office. They are ignorant through no fault of their own. . . . No matter how kindly Republicans feel toward colored people, they cannot hand the destinies of a community over to ignorant rulers." Lack of enthusiasm on the part of Negro voters which resulted from refusal of the party organization to reward them, probably contributed to the Republican defeat in 1890. A letter from a group of colored voters in Grant County, which had a sizable number of Negro voters, expressed the feelings of many members of the race:

"We are not asking to be made judges of the courts, nor to go to Congress nor to be elected county clerk, auditor, treasurer, etc., but we know we have among us colored men who are worthy of deputyships in some of the offices to which we have so many years helped to elect white Republicans. . . .

"Now that this matter has been carefully thought over, is it not plainly to be seen that we are only wanted for our votes to keep the Republicans in office?"[34]

33 *The Freeman,* October 23, 1890, supplement; January 9, 1892; Indianapolis *Journal,* July 20, 1890; Indianapolis *World,* April 22, June 24, 1893.

34 Evansville *Journal* quoted in Indianapolis *World,* April 19, 1890; *The Freeman,* November 1, 1890, supplement.

In spite of their disillusionment over the Republican party Negroes as a whole continued to be contemptuous of members of their race who called themselves Democrats. Republican politicians lost no opportunity to keep these feelings alive. During the 1890 campaign a Negro, John R. Lynch, formerly a Congressman from Mississippi, told a political rally in Indianapolis: "The colored man who says he is a Democrat admits that the meanest, dirtiest, most contemptible white man is better than he is"—a characterization which was widely publicized and which gave great offense to colored Democrats. During the local campaign of 1891 when a group of Negro Democrats tried to hold a meeting in Indianapolis, their speakers were driven from the platform by colored Republicans, and the meeting ended in a riot.[35]

In 1892, when the Republicans faced a difficult campaign for other reasons as well, the threat of a defection of Negro voters seemed more real than at any previous time. The only Negro candidate named for any office which carried any distinction was in Howard County, where a Baptist minister, Richard Bassett, was nominated and elected to the state legislature. In Indianapolis and Evansville, where Negroes were most numerous, they were ignored. In Evansville the Republican chairman refused to appoint Negroes to any kind of a post, while in Indianapolis the county chairman was reported to have said that Negroes were a detriment to the Republican party because their presence alienated white voters. He expressed repugnance at the mingling of white and colored party workers and was said to have delayed opening a county headquarters because he did not want "lazy coons" hanging about the place.[36]

Democrats sought to capitalize upon Negro discontent. The Evansville *Courier* declared that Negroes would never

[35] *The Freeman,* October 23, 1890, supplement; Indianapolis *Journal,* October 21, 1890; Indianapolis Daily *Sentinel,* October 27, 1892; Indianapolis *World,* July 9, 1892.

[36] Indianapolis *World,* April 2, August 20, 27, September 10, 1892; Evansville *Bulletin* quoted in *ibid.,* October 1, 1892.

be anything but political slaves "so long as they continue to humbly obey the orders of the white Republican bosses," and tried to show them the power they might exercise if they would show political independence. The Indianapolis *World*, formerly a Republican organ, but now in the Democratic column, used the following appeal:

"No sensible colored man ever claimed that the Democratic party has done any great things for the colored race neither has the colored people done anything for the Democratic party, and so we are about even. The colored people, however, have done much for the Republican party and hence that party is greatly in our debt. Since the ratification of the 15th. Amendment to Federal Constitution we defy any one to cite one thing the Republican party has done for the Negro."[37]

At the Democratic national convention an organization called the "National Colored Men's Tariff-Reform League" was formed, with James T. V. Hill of Indianapolis as temporary chairman. When this Democratic group announced a convention in the Indiana capital, Republicans regarded this attempt to challenge Benjamin Harrison in his home city as an affront. They decided to beat the Democrats at their own game and sent out a call to politicians in Washington, Philadelphia, Chicago, and Louisville to send colored Republicans to Indianapolis to break up the meeting. As the result of the Republican influx the Democratic meeting turned out to be a rather sorry affair. When word came that George L. Knox, leader of Indianapolis Negro Republicans, and a group of his followers were coming to invade the hall where they were meeting, the Democrats somewhat ignominiously adjourned. They later reconvened, but met under police protection and denied admission to Republicans who tried to storm the meeting. The Republicans then held a separate meeting at which their

[37] Evansville *Courier* reprinted in Indianapolis *World*, September 24, 1892; *ibid.*, October 8, 1892.

speakers denounced the attempt by a few "sore headed Democratic niggers" to give the impression that Negroes were deserting the Republican party.[38]

Before the end of the campaign Republican leaders became alarmed and took steps to minimize the defection of the Negroes. On the eve of the election the Republican county chairman sent out a circular to the colored ministers in Indianapolis asking them to encourage their congregations to take part in a Republican parade, while the ministers themselves were urged to preach sermons in behalf of the Republican cause. Tactics such as these, which would have occasioned no comment in the early days of Negro suffrage, were offensive to at least some of the clergymen.[39]

Headlines in the Indianapolis *Journal* confidently declared: COLORED VOTERS AS A UNIT WILL REMAIN TRUE TO HARRISON AND THE PARTY THAT IS THEIR ONLY FRIEND. Beneath was an article in which the Reverend James M. Townsend was quoted denying that there was any truth in the "much-talked-of disaffection of colored voters." He insisted: "I am in a position to know, and I affirm that the utmost unity prevails among the colored people of Indiana, and their votes will be cast for Benjamin Harrison and the Republican ticket." Townsend spoke as an active party worker. Probably the words of a young physician more accurately reflected the attitude of the average Negro: "We hurrah for Harrison others hurrah for Cleveland, I do not intend to contract laryngitis, nor bronchitis not any other 'itis' whooping for anybody any more. What has either of them done for us as compared with what they could and ought to have done?"[40] When the votes were in, it was found that the Democrats had carried the state. It

[38] Indianapolis *Journal*, October 18, 19, 1892; Indianapolis *Daily Sentinel*, October 18, 1892; Indianapolis *World*, October 22, 1892.

[39] Indianapolis *World*, November 5, 1892; Indianapolis *Daily Sentinel*, October 27, 1892.

[40] Indianapolis *Journal*, October 12, 1892; Indianapolis *World*, July 30, 1892.

was reported that hundreds of Negroes in Indianapolis had voted the Democratic ticket. While this may have been an exaggeration, indifference of Negroes toward the Republican cause (combined perhaps with the fact that vote buying was reduced because of the secret ballot) seems to have contributed to the outcome.[41]

On the whole the efforts to win the rank and file of Negroes to a permanent alliance with the Democrats failed, although a small group of leaders made vigorous efforts. The first statewide conference of an Indiana Democratic League of colored voters was held in Indianapolis in July, 1894. The following month a National Democratic League convention met in the same city, but only twenty-six delegates showed up. In 1896 Alexander E. Manning, who had recently become business manager of the Indianapolis *World*, served as president of the convention of the National League of Negro Democrats in Chicago. This meeting adopted a series of resolutions which denounced the Republican national platform as the work of plutocrats and endorsed the free and unlimited coinage of silver at the ratio of sixteen to one. A minority of the delegates refused to support the resolution on silver. During the campaign the *World* was one of the few Negro newspapers in the country to support bi-metallism. In its columns it carried on a debate on the money question with T. Thomas Fortune, the New York journalist, who, after supporting Cleveland, had returned to the Republicans.[42]

[41] In spite of the Democratic sweep the Reverend Richard Bassett was elected to the state House of Representatives from Howard County, a Republican stronghold. As a member of the legislature Bassett contributed little. Illness necessitated his absence from part of the session.

[42] Indianapolis *World*, August 15, 1896. Alexander E. Manning and James T. V. Hill, the first Negro lawyer in Indianapolis, were for many years the backbone of the colored Democratic movement in the state. Manning was born a slave in Virginia in 1856. He came to Indianapolis in 1882 as a steward for the New York, Lake Erie and Western Freight line. He was soon active in politics and was used by the Democratic State Committee to speak to colored voters throughout the state. Dur-

Negroes generally appear to have been indifferent to the monetary issue, and the Bryan campaign, which was primarily an agrarian one, had little appeal for them. The Republican national platform condemned lynching and employed the customary phraseology with regard to the right of every citizen to cast his ballot, but it made no recommendation as to how to stop lynching or the disfranchisement of Southern Negroes. The Negro question played no part in the national campaign, but an editorial in the *Freeman* sought to keep the local Negroes in line by warning them: "A vote for Bryan is a vote for the further impalement of the Southern Negro on the social and political crucifix."[43]

Although Negroes resisted Democratic efforts to woo them in national and state elections, the story in municipal politics in Indianapolis was somewhat different. In three successive elections large numbers of Negroes cast their votes for a Democrat, Thomas Taggart, thereby helping him to win an unprecedented number of terms as mayor. As county auditor and as Democratic state chairman Taggart had already won a personal following among Negroes, and in 1895 when he first ran for mayor a group of colored

ing Cleveland's second term he was frequently mentioned as a possibility for the post of minister to Liberia, but the appointment did not materialize. For more than thirty years Manning served as the official courier of the Democratic National Committee, traveling throughout the United States in the service of the party leaders. He attended every national convention during that period. During the first World War he was a member of the conciliation staff of the National Employment Bureau. For thirty-two years he was editor and publisher of the Indianapolis *World*. He died in 1925. *The Freeman*, December 22, 1894; August 22, 1896; Indianapolis *News*, January 26, 1925.

43 *The Freeman*, October 31, 1896. *The Freeman* had been a Democratic paper but in 1892 was purchased by the Negro Republican leader George L. Knox, and was thereafter strongly partisan on the G.O.P. side. Although no Negro had been named for a state office in 1894, in 1896, Gabriel Jones, an Indianapolis school teacher, was nominated and elected to the Indiana House of Representatives. As a member of the legislature he fought unsuccessfully for the enactment of a law guaranteeing colored children equal treatment in the schools. See below, 337-38.

Republicans formed an organization to support him. The Indianapolis *World* insisted that colored voters played an important part in his victory and had gained the respect of both parties by their show of independence. In 1897 there was again an organization of "independent" Negroes who supported Taggart. Two white newspapers commented on the part which they played in the Democratic victory. The Indianapolis *Journal* asserted that nearly one half of the Negro vote had gone to Taggart, while the Indianapolis *News* expressed the opinion that thereafter Negroes could not be regarded as chattels of the Republican party. Afterwards at the inauguration of the mayor, on the first occasion when a colored man had been invited to speak at such an affair in Indianapolis, Levi Christy of the Indianapolis *World* expressed gratification that Negro voters had thrown off their political bondage. In 1899 when Taggart was once again elected, he acknowledged his indebtedness to the colored voters by appointing a number of them to city jobs and by increasing their representation in the police and fire departments.[44]

The support of Taggart was merely a local and personal phenomenon and did not foreshadow any lasting desertion of the Republican party. His following was due in part to his own remarkable personal magnetism, in part to the fact that Negroes were dissatisfied with local white Republicans on a number of scores, and no doubt, as his enemies charged, to the money his followers spent on Negro votes. But his popularity was too widespread to be ascribed only to mercenary appeal. It grew out of the fact that he was practically the only politician of the period who systematically cultivated Negro voters and who acknowledged his indebtedness to them.

In spite of the large increase in the number of colored voters after 1870, Negroes had gained little in political

44 Indianapolis *World*, September 28, October 12, 1895; October 16, 23, 1897; September 30, 1899.

power by the end of the century. Except for the enactment of a civil rights law (accomplished under a Democratic legislature), no law had been passed which might be regarded as having been framed out of deference to the Negro vote. Measured in terms of elective and appointive offices Negroes had not received rewards commensurate with their numbers. The highest elective office to which they might aspire was membership in the lower house of the state legislature, an honor attained by only four Negroes, two of them from districts which were always solidly Republican. In Evansville and the other Ohio River towns and in Terre Haute, where Negroes held the balance of power, they were never elected to any office higher than that of constable and were given only the most menial of appointive jobs. In municipal politics in Indianapolis they fared a little better. Robert Bagby, John Puryear, and Henry Sweetland served on the city council, while small numbers of Negroes were admitted to the police and fire departments. In Kokomo, a city with a relatively small Negro population, J. A. Braboy was elected a city commissioner three times.

Negroes showed little interest in national political issues except those which had a distinct racial appeal. Although colored orators and newspapers might discuss the issues which divided the political parties, their interest in such matters as the tariff or bi-metallism seemed perfunctory. Indiana Negroes were aroused over the increasing number of outrages in the South and the movement to disfranchise Southern Negroes, but under Harrison and McKinley they became increasingly distrustful of the Republican party because of its acquiescence in conditions in the South. Their feelings of disillusionment and alarm over the future of their race were growing at the end of the century as the result of the aftermath of the war with Spain. Negroes had hailed the war to liberate Cuba and had enthusiastically volunteered for service because many of the Cubans were persons of "colored" blood. But as the fighting in the Philippines began more and more to assume the aspects of a race war, it became increasingly distasteful to Negroes. The Indianapolis *World* declared: "Negroes of America ought to stand as one man against the effort to conquer the Philippinos [*sic*] and force upon them an alien colonial government." Moreover racial prejudice in the United States seemed to be accentuated by the war. The subjugation of a colored people overseas seemed to sanction doctrines of white supremacy at home. Some of the opinions expressed by white Republicans to justify imperialism were similar to those used by Southern white Democrats to serve as an apology for their racial program.[45]

As Negroes became disillusioned with white Republican leadership, white politicians were also becoming indifferent to the Negro vote, taking it for granted or even regarding it as a liability to the party. In 1896 the Republicans began a long period of control of the state government in Indiana, during which the margin of their victories was large enough that they no longer felt it necessary to cultivate colored support. In 1898 and 1900 and thereafter Negroes were completely ignored in naming candidates for state office. In the Republican state convention of 1900 there were fewer Negro delegates than for many years.[46] The humanitarian interest in the advancement of the colored race, a heritage of the abolition movement which had infused the Republican party in an earlier period, was dissipated by the end of the century. In Indiana, as well as in the South, there was a "lily white" movement developing within the party. An editorial in the Indianapolis *News* on the subject of alleged buying of Negro votes by the Democrats in the 1899 mayoralty election was disparaging to both Southern and Northern Negroes. It asked: "Have they [Negroes] ever thought

[45] Indianapolis *World*, November 4, 1899. White soldiers sometimes referred to Filipinos as "niggers." The *World* quoted a letter from a soldier in which he said that hunting niggers [Filipinos] reminded him of hunting rabbits but added, "it is a great deal more fun hunting niggers than rabbits." *Ibid.*, June 10, 17, 1899.

[46] *Ibid.*, April 28, 1900.

that people who have not the courage to exercise their rights in the South, even in the communities where they have a heavy majority, and who are looked upon in the North as being particularly susceptible to the wiles of the scoundrels who purchase votes, must necessarily be regarded with some distrust by their white neighbors?" Then, having cast this slur upon colored voters, the editorial ended with the same argument that had been used when Negroes cast their first ballots, the debt that they owed to the white race:

"If the Negroes would only try to remember that it cost this country hundreds of thousands of precious lives, and millions of treasure, to make it possible for them to vote at all, they would, it seems to us, scorn to make merchandise of the privilege purchased for them at such a tremendous cost."[47]

47 Quoted in Indianapolis *World*, October 7, 1899.

12

EDUCATION 1865-1900

"WE PLEDGE OURSELVES to do all in our limited power to secure that intellectual and moral worth necessary to sustain a Republican form of Government; and for the encouragement of our race we will petition the Legislature of this State, at its next session to grant us access to the public school fund."[1] The foregoing resolution, adopted at the first colored convention in Indiana after the Civil War, showed the importance which Negroes attached to education and was at the same time a reminder that they were denied any share in the public school system.

After the war there was increasing pressure from white groups as well as Negroes for public schools for the colored population. But while the legislature delayed, Negroes themselves continued to provide some private schooling through their own efforts, as they had done during the prewar years. The need for educational facilities was made more acute by the immigration of former slaves, nearly all of whom were illiterate. Among the thousands of newcomers who flocked into the state the desire for schooling was second only to the desire for food and shelter. In view of the pitifully limited resources of these people their efforts to promote education were remarkable.

Nearly all of the schools for colored pupils were associated with the colored churches, although white church groups contributed financial assistance and advice. In 1866 the Plainfield Quarterly Meeting of Friends, which embraced the Indianapolis area, reported that there were four day

[1] Indianapolis *Daily Journal,* October 25, 1865.

schools for colored children in that city and five Sabbath schools. A report of A. C. Shortridge, superintendent of the Indianapolis schools, urging public schools for colored children, commented on the efforts which Indianapolis Negroes were making in their own behalf. Out of the 1,653 colored inhabitants listed in a census made in 1866, nearly three hundred were attending school. These schools, according to Shortridge, were "conducted and supported by themselves, and to a very limited extent, if at all, dependent on the charities of the public. The large proportion of colored children attending pay schools is very creditable to this people, and indicates an earnest desire for improvement. The ratio of school attendance to the total colored population is almost without precedent. Their schools are maintained under great disadvantages—without the generous sympathy of the public generally, with very moderate funds, with buildings unsuited to school purpose, with limited or no school apparatus, with uncomfortable school furniture, with insufficient textbooks, without classification, and with teachers unskilled in the art of imparting instruction. In our judgement [*sic*] humanity, justice, and sound public policy demand that this class of our citizens shall receive the benefits of our common school system."[2]

Apparently in response to Shortridge's plea the city gave the use of an old school building in the Fourth Ward, on the west side of the city, for a colored school. The Reverend Moses Broyles acted as principal, with G. W. Potter as his assistant. By May, 1867, an enrollment of one hundred and ten pupils was reported in spite of the fact that the school was maintained by tuition fees paid by the parents of the pupils. The first colored school in the eastern part of the city was opened at about the same time, under the sponsor-

2 Minutes of Plainfield Quarterly Meeting, 5th month 5, 1866 (MS in Archives of Friends Church, Plainfield) ; Indianapolis Public Schools, *Annual Report,* 1866, pp. 16-17, quoted in Heller, "Negro Education in Indiana," 99-100.

ship of the African M.E. church and a group of white Quakers. It was located in the mission which later became the Allen Chapel. The school was maintained on a tuition basis, the charge being $1.25 a month. The first teacher was Samuel A. Elbert, who had attended Oberlin College and who was later to become the first Negro in Indiana to receive an M.D. degree. In addition to the weekday school for children, there was also a Sunday school for adults in which many an ex-slave painfully learned to spell out his own Bible. A third school was taught by Rufus Conrad, the minister of the Second Christian Church, while there were several others of which no record survives.[3]

Not all of the persons in attendance at these schools were children. Many adults enrolled to learn the rudiments of reading and writing. The zeal for learning which was displayed by these older people caused the Indianapolis *Journal* to remark: "The desire of the enfranchised negro for knowledge is wonderful. The perseverance and success with which the adults apply themselves to the study of reading and writing excites surprise in all who have given the matter any attention. Hundreds of them who came to Indiana from slave States, where to read and write was a crime, have in two or three years made such progress as to enable them to read with facility, and write letters to their old friends who still live in the South."[4]

---

[3] Indianapolis *Daily Journal,* May 24, 1867; *History of Allen Chapel A.M.E. Church 1866-1944* (Indianapolis, n.d.), 12. By 1867 the Plainfield Quarterly Meeting reported that there were nine colored day schools within its limits, not all of which were necessarily in Indianapolis, since the meeting embraced counties to the west of the city. One of these schools had been in session for ten months of the year, another for seven, while the rest had lasted only one to three months. Out of 1,530 children of school age, 670 had attended school during the year. The Friends commented upon the eagerness of the new settlers, most of whom were almost destitute, for education and their willingness to pay the tuition of their children. Minutes of Plainfield Quarterly Meeting, 8th month 3, 1867.

[4] Indianapolis *Journal,* June 15, 1870.

Outside of Indianapolis there were similar efforts to establish schools through private efforts. In Evansville a group of philanthropic citizens donated a piece of land as a site for a colored school, while the city council appropriated funds for a building. After it was opened it was maintained through private contributions. In Gibson County subscription schools were started at Lyles Station and Sandhill soon after the Civil War. One was held in a church, the other in a private home. Tuition charges ranged from $1.00 to $1.50 a month for each pupil. In 1867 a school was started in Carthage in Rush County with the assistance of Quakers. The following year a schoolhouse was erected at the Walnut Grove settlement south of Carthage. In addition to these schools there were older ones which had been started in the prewar years and doubtless many others of which no record remains.[5]

While these valiant but inadequate efforts at providing for educational needs were going on, the movement for public assistance was advancing. Governor Oliver P. Morton, although unprepared to advocate political rights for Negroes at the war's end, strongly championed their right to education at the public expense. In his message to the special session of the legislature in the fall of 1865 he called attention to the article in the state Constitution which said that the General Assembly should provide for a system of common schools, "wherein tuition shall be without charge, and equally open to all." He asserted that the provision "would seem, in letter and spirit, to embrace all the children of the State without regard to *color*. Surely it cannot be denied that, as we have a colored population in our midst, it is our interest, independent of those considerations of natural justice and humanity which plead so strongly, to educate and elevate that population." Morton did not recommend admit-

5 Indianapolis *Journal*, September 7, 1867; Clift, "Negro in Vanderburgh, Posey, and Gibson Counties" (unpublished M.A. thesis, Indiana University, 1941), 17; "History of Carthage Friends Church" (typed copy, Indiana State Library), 5-6.

ting colored children to the same schools with whites, but urged separate schools as a concession to public opinion which opposed any mingling of the races. The House committee on education reported favorably on a bill under which township trustees would have been required to organize a school for colored children in any township in which there were fifteen or more such children. A minority report expressed opposition to any legislation for the benefit of the Negro on the oft-repeated grounds that: "Our Government was established by white men, for white men and women, and children, and their posterity." The minority insisted that Indiana must not hold out any inducements such as public schools or she would be overrun by Negroes, and warned that they intended to resist the school measure and to "fight every inch of the ground marked out for the elevation of the negro race in our midst."[6]

This point of view was assailed in an able speech on the floor by a delegate who urged: "All history shows that it is not good policy for a State to have in their midst an ignorant and illiterate people. Give them knowledge; it will make them better men and more devoted to the interests of the State." He cited the support which Negroes had given the Union cause during the recent war and demanded that justice be done them in the matter of education in order that the whites might "in a measure, repair some of the evils and, requite some of the wrongs that have been done them." But in spite of the fact that the House was controlled by Republicans, who claimed to be the especial friends of the Negro, the measure for colored schools was defeated.[7]

Before the next meeting of the legislature powerful pleas had come from educational groups. The Indiana State Teachers Association had adopted resolutions calling for state funds for colored schools, while members of the Indianapolis School Board and the superintendent of the Indian-

---

[6] Indiana *House Journal*, 1865 (special session), pp. 33-34, 116, 145.
[7] *Ibid.*, 510.

apolis schools prepared an appeal to the legislature in which they praised the efforts which the Negroes were already making in their own behalf and pointed out the injurious effects upon the community of depriving any portion of the population of educational opportunities. The report which the State Superintendent of Public Instruction presented to the legislature called attention to the increasing number of Negroes in the state and their changing status, citing the enactment of the Federal Civil Rights Act and the nullification of the exclusion article of the state Constitution by the Indiana Supreme Court. Since it was evident that the colored population was going to remain in Indiana, he insisted that the welfare of the state, as well as principles of justice, demanded that they be educated. He recommended legislation which would provide for separate colored schools in communities where the number of Negroes was large enough to make this practical and which would require the trustees to make other provisions in communities where there were fewer than fifteen colored children.[8] In his message to the General Assembly in 1867 Governor Morton repeated portions of his 1865 message on the subject of schools, but again that body, although controlled by members of his party, ignored his request. A measure for colored schools was introduced into the Senate but was defeated.[9]

The convention of the Indiana Colored Equal Rights League which met in Terre Haute in October, 1867, devoted most of its sessions to the school question. It condemned the legislature for its "indifferent and unjust refusal to vote us a proportionate amount of the public school fund of the State." And in view of the repeated rebuffs by the legislature

[8] Indiana Superintendent of Public Instruction, *Report*, 1865-66, p. 51. A convention of colored men meeting in November, 1866, asked that they be taxed "the same as other citizens" and receive their share of the school funds to educate their children. Indianapolis *Daily Journal*, November 8, 1866.

[9] Indiana *House Journal*, 1867, pp. 41-42; Indiana *Senate Journal*, 1867, pp. 523-24.

the convention urged further efforts on the part of Negroes themselves to solve their own problems. A resolution was adopted which proposed that Negroes voluntarily levy and collect a tax upon their own property to raise a school fund. Another resolution authorized a suit against the state authorities to compel a payment of "all the moneys due us from the Common School Fund of the State." However, there is no evidence that steps were taken to carry out either proposal.[10]

In his message to the legislature in 1869 Governor Conrad Baker renewed the plea made by his predecessor for a change in the school law, pointing out that only one other Northern state (Illinois) had failed to provide for the education of its colored citizens. During the regular session the House passed a measure, but the Senate failed to act.[11] Finally at the special session of that year (the same one at which the Fifteenth Amendment was ratified) an act was passed which required school trustees to organize separate schools for colored children where there was a large enough group to justify such a school. If there were not enough colored children in one district to support a school, several districts might be consolidated. However, if there was not a sufficient number of colored children within a "reasonable distance" to make a consolidated school practical, the trustees were permitted to "provide such other means of education for said children as shall use their proportion, according to numbers, of school revenue to best advantage." The act also put the property of white and colored owners on the same basis for the assessment and collection of school taxes.[12]

10 Indianapolis *Journal,* October 8, 1867.
11 Indiana *House Journal,* 1869, pp. 273, 512-13; Indiana *Senate Journal,* 1869, pp. 57-58.
12 *Laws of Indiana,* 1869 (special session), p. 41. Heretofore the property of colored persons had been exempt from the special school tax which was levied to pay the salaries of teachers, but their property had been subject to the regular property tax, part of which was used for the construction of school buildings.

The long-delayed legislation was greeted with joy by the Negro population. A meeting of the colored Indiana Baptist Association adopted a resolution expressing "pleasure and gladness" at the action of the lawmakers and promising to encourage colored people to use the educational opportunities which were offered them. At the same time the meeting took cognizance of reports that school trustees in some places had announced that they did not intend to open colored schools at once. Another resolution was adopted which declared: "We . . . demand that common schools be opened in every city and locality in the State, according to law, and if the course of keeping our children out of the common schools is carried out in those cities, we will seek redress in the courts."[13]

In the cities with the largest Negro population steps were taken to open separate schools at the next school term. During the summer of 1869 meetings were held in the colored churches in Indianapolis to inform the parents of what would be expected of them when their children started to school. Large numbers attended these meetings, and the colored population generally showed enthusiasm over the new opportunities for their children. Two colored schools were opened in September, 1869. During the first term about 250 children out of a total of 479 of school age were in attendance. In Evansville two schools were opened and were well attended in spite of the fact that most of the colored population was extremely poor. In Terre Haute a public school was held in the African M.E. church. In Vincennes, Connersville, Shelbyville, and in a few rural communities, such as Lost Creek Township in Vigo County, separate schools were also opened. On the other hand, in Logansport, in spite of the fact that there were twenty-six children of school age, school officials found technical reasons for refusing to open a school for them. By 1870 New Albany reported a colored school with an enrollment of two hundred, while several

13 Indianapolis *Journal,* August 28, 1869.

smaller schools were opened in other places. The State Superintendent of Public Instruction reported that in most counties officials had complied readily with the requirements of the school law and that colored parents had shown a strong desire to send their children to school. In some communities trustees were reluctant to provide for colored children. In most places where there were too few children to justify a separate school the children were simply denied any opportunity for an education.[14]

By 1873 the Superintendent reported that he knew of no county where separate schools had not been provided where the number of colored children was large enough to support a school. In many other places, where their numbers were smaller, they had been admitted to white schools. By 1875 almost seven thousand colored children, or about 68 per cent of those of school age, were enrolled in public schools, as compared with 76 per cent of the white children.[15]

After the adoption of the 1869 law various questions as to its meaning arose. One of them was what constituted a "colored child," since the law did not define the term. In New Albany two children were denied admission to a school for white children on the grounds that they were "colored," although it was shown that only one sixty-fourth of their ancestry was Negro. The county superintendent concurred in this ruling, but it was reversed by the State Superin-

14 *Ibid.*, August 12, September 6, December 29, 1869; A. C. Shortridge, "The Schools of Indianapolis," Pt. III, in *Indiana Magazine of History,* 8(1912) :127; Superintendent of Public Instruction, *Report,* 1869-70, p. 161, and 1877-78, pp. 36-39.

15 U. S. Commissioner of Education, *Annual Report,* 1873-74 (Washington, D.C., 1874), 100; Superintendent of Public Instruction, *Report,* 1875-76, pp. 20-22. In 1875 almost two thirds of the children enrolled were in nine counties. These counties with their colored enrollments were: Marion, 1,196; Vanderburgh, 537; Clark, 427; Vigo, 389; Floyd, 309; Spencer, 347; Wayne, 279; Jefferson, 278; Gibson, 245. In spite of the report of the State Superintendent, a colored convention meeting in Indianapolis in September, 1875, reported that in some places trustees still refused to establish colored schools. Indianapolis *Journal,* September 22, 1875.

tendent, who drew upon the state marriage law for a definition of a colored person. Since the law prohibited intermarriage between a white person and a person with one eighth or more of Negro blood, he concluded that a person with less than one eighth of Negro blood might attend a white school.[16]

A more serious question was the status of colored children in communities where they were too few to justify a separate school. In such places the law said that the trustee should provide "other means" of education without defining the means. This clause was interpreted variously. In some places, such as the city of Fort Wayne, colored children were admitted to white schools, but in other places they were refused admittance. The State Superintendent of Public Instruction reported that in some places the law resulted "in sending the colored children to a private school, in others in giving the children books to read, in others, in giving the money belonging to each child to the parents to spend as they please, but in many of them it results in nothing."[17]

[16] *Indiana School Journal* (organ of the State Teachers' Association and of the Superintendent of Public Instruction), 19(1874) :26-27. Prior to the adoption of the 1869 law and the Fifteenth Amendment a similar question had arisen in Ripley Township in Rush County. Here a man who was partially of colored blood but predominantly white sought to vote in an election. A Rush County judge, citing precedents in Ohio and Massachusetts courts, held that he was "white" within the meaning of the law and therefore entitled to vote. Thereupon the township trustees inquired of the State Superintendent of Public Instruction as to whether the man's children were entitled to attend the common schools, then exclusively for "white children." Since the law gave any person who had the right to vote in a general election the right to participate in school elections, the superintendent ruled that "children having a preponderance of white blood are entitled to the privileges of the common schools of Indiana." However, this ruling was not publicized and does not seem to have had any widespread effect. It was superseded by the later ruling in connection with the New Albany schools. *Ibid.,* 14(1869) : 422; Indianapolis *Journal,* October 6, 1869.

[17] Superintendent of Public Instruction, *Report,* 1875-76, p. 24.

In Lawrence Township of Marion County, where there was no separate school, the attempt of a colored man named Carter to enter two of his children and two of his grandchildren eventually resulted in an opinion of the Indiana Supreme Court as to the meaning of the law. When the children were refused admittance, Carter sought a mandate to compel the school officials to enroll them. The lawyers who represented him insisted that the refusal to admit the children was a violation of both the Fourteenth Amendment to the Constitution of the United States and of the clause in the Indiana Constitution (Art. I, sec. 23) which said: "The General Assembly shall not grant to any citizen, or class of citizens, privileges or immunities which, upon the same terms, shall not be equally open to all citizens." They also appealed to the part of the state Constitution which required a "general and uniform system of common schools, wherein tuition shall be without charge and equally open to all."

Carter won his case in the Marion County Superior Court, which held that since the adoption of the Fourteenth Amendment, conferring citizenship upon Negroes, the educational requirements of the state Constitution applied to Negroes. The judge did not attempt to rule on the question as to whether separate schools violated the Constitution but asserted that where separate schools were not provided colored children could not be refused admission to white schools.[18] This ruling was reversed in the highest state court in an opinion written by Chief Justice Samuel Buskirk. While admitting that since the adoption of the Fourteenth Amendment the state was required to make some provision for the education of Negroes, the judge made the provision of that amendment regarding "equal protection" virtually meaningless. He held that the amendment had not in any way affected the right of a state to regulate its own educational system and to classify students as it chose, according to age, sex, or color. In language reminiscent of Roger B.

18 *Indiana School Journal,* 19(1874) :344-46.

Taney and the pre-Civil War era he said that the framers
of the Indiana Constitution had not intended that document
to embrace Negroes and that the Fourteenth Amendment
did not compel the state to admit Negroes to white schools.
He pointed out that Carter's attorneys had not tried to prove
that the school trustee had denied the children all educational means whatever—merely that he had refused admission to a white school. But, Buskirk argued, in any case,
even if the trustee had made no provision whatever for
the education of the children, the children would not have
been entitled to attend the white school, "because the legislature has not provided for the admission of colored children
into the same school with white children in any con-
tingency." In the absence of legislative action the courts
were said to have no authority to admit colored children
regardless of the Fourteenth Amendment.[19]

The decision seems to have caused school authorities in
some places to expel colored children who had been attending
mixed schools.[20] The opinion was severely criticized and

[19] Cory *et al. v.* Carter (1874), 48 Ind. 327-66. In writing the opinion
Buskirk was attempting to follow the interpretation of the U. S. Supreme
Court the year before in the Slaughter House Cases (16 Wall 36), in
which a distinction had been made between the rights of United States
citizenship and state citizenship and in which the Fourteenth Amendment
had been given an extremely narrow meaning. The "separate but equal"
doctrine by which segregation was to be justified by the Supreme Court
in later years had not yet been enunciated. The key case, Plessy *v.* Fergu-
son (163 U. S. 537), was not decided until 1896. Although the Plessy
case concerned a state law requiring segregation in transportation facilities, the same principle was used repeatedly by the court in later years
in school cases. The court held that so long as the "separate" facilities
were substantially "equal" for members of both races, the segregation
laws did not violate the guarantee of "equal protection of the laws." In
the Indiana case, of course, there had been no attempt to show that
the means for education of Negro children were in any sense "equal"
to those for white children.

[20] For example, three colored children who had been attending a white
school in Greene County were expelled after the decision. As a result
the father of the children started a movement to raise funds to take an
appeal to the Supreme Court of the United States, but apparently the
attempt met with little success. Indianapolis *Journal,* April 12, 1876.

the soundness of the doctrines expressed was open to question, but it had the effect of bringing the inequities under the 1869 law to public attention. In 1877, on the recommendation of the State Superintendent of Public Instruction, the General Assembly amended the law. School authorities might still organize separate schools, but where there were no separate schools the amendment provided that "colored children shall be allowed to attend the public schools with white children." The law further provided that when a pupil attending a colored school could show that he had made sufficient advancement (by examination or otherwise) to be placed in a higher grade than that offered in the colored school, he was to be permitted to enter the advanced grade in a white school, and that no distinction should be made in that school on account of race or color.[21]

After the adoption of the 1877 law some communities which had maintained separate schools abandoned them. One example was Logansport, which reported that it had closed its colored school, "the pupils being admitted into the other schools on equal terms with the whites—a matter of economy as well as success." The counties with the largest colored populations retained segregation, and soon after the enactment of the new law the attorney for the Indianapolis school board gave an opinion that in towns and cities where separate schools were maintained colored children could not demand admission to white schools. The question of separate or mixed schools was left almost entirely up to the local authorities. In 1882 the state Supreme Court ruled that a trustee could not be compelled to establish a separate school in a township where there was not a substantial number of colored children, even though some white patrons might object to the presence of colored children in a white school.[22]

21 *Laws of Indiana,* 1877, p. 124; Superintendent of Public Instruction, *Report,* 1875-76, pp. 23-24.
22 Superintendent of Public Instruction, *Report,* 1877-78, p. 339;

In spite of this opinion in some places trustees insisted upon setting up one school which all colored children in the township were compelled to attend, regardless of the distance they had to walk and even though white schools might be much closer. In one township where there were already twelve white schools a trustee opened a colored school, forcing some children to walk three and one-half miles each way in order to attend school. The question of whether they could be compelled to attend the school was taken to the state Attorney General, who ruled that colored children should go to separate schools when they were "reasonably convenient," but that where they were required to walk "unreasonably" long distances, they should be permitted to go to the white schools. What constituted a "reasonable" distance was a matter to be decided by the trustee, but the Attorney General expressed the view that in the present case the distance was probably unreasonable.[23]

Although an occasional child might benefit from such a ruling, in many places, especially in rural areas, as a result colored children had to trudge long distances to a colored school, even though they might pass white schools on the way. Moreover, the schools which they attended were likely to be inferior to the white schools since the law contained no effectual guarantee that the segregated schools should be equal. For example, in a rural community near Indianapolis, the township trustee refused to permit a group of about ten colored children to attend a white school and set up a separate school in a building that could not be heated, with a teacher who had never qualified for a teaching cer-

Indiana School Journal, 22(1877):174; State, *ex rel.* Oliver *et al., v.* Grubb, Trustee, 85 Ind. 213-19.

23 James H. Smart, *Commentary on the School Law of Indiana* (Indianapolis, 1881), 200. In the case of two small children in Marion County who lived within a few feet of a white school but who would have to walk two and one half miles to a colored school, the State Superintendent ruled that they might attend the white school. *Indiana School Journal*, 27(1882):129-31.

tificate. He ruled that the children could attend classes until the weather became too cold and then finish the school term the next summer when warm weather returned. The State Superintendent repeatedly ruled that such arrangements did not meet the requirements of the law and that colored children were entitled to equal treatment. In 1883 an opinion was given that it was the duty of the trustee "to furnish colored children, as far as may be possible, school privileges for an equal length of time with the whites," and that a town school board had no right to give the white children the benefits of an eight-month term and the colored children only seven.[24]

This opinion may have done something to equalize the length of the school term, but glaring inequalities remained between the buildings for white and colored children and in the course of instruction. In Richmond the Rev. James M. Townsend threatened to institute a damage suit against the school board for refusing to allow colored children to attend the schools where German was taught. In order to avoid the suit the board agreed to make an addition to the colored school and to provide a teacher of German. This action did not have the effect of really equalizing the schools. A pupil tried to transfer to the white school on the grounds that the colored school did not provide the facilities which he needed. The school authorities refused to permit the transfer because the pupil had not passed an examination and did not have the certificate for admission as provided in the 1877 law. The case eventually reached the Indiana Supreme Court which upheld the refusal of the transfer. In its opinion the court admitted that the evidence showed that the colored school had few pupils and that the course of instruction was not the same as that offered in the white school. Nevertheless, while saying that there could be "no denial of educational privileges, no total exclusion from

24 *Indiana School Journal,* 28 (1883) :258; Indianapolis *Leader,* September 17, 1881.

schools, except for cause," the court held that "there may be rules and regulations for their government, and these rules and regulations courts are bound to respect." They refused to override the local authorities, leaving the question entirely in their hands.[25]

After this decision the State Superintendent reiterated once more that "every colored person of school age is entitled to receive instruction equal in amount and quality to that given to other children of the school corporation, of the same grade. . . ."[26] Nevertheless, differences continued to exist in the facilities for members of the two races which mere expressions of this sort did nothing to erase.

In Indianapolis the colored schools more nearly approximated equality in equipment and quality of instruction than did those in most places. Some separate schools were maintained, but after the adoption of the law of 1877 there were also some mixed schools. After 1878 the annual reports of the school board ceased to give separate enrollment figures for the members of the two races but lumped them both together. In 1879 and for several years thereafter there appear to have been four buildings designated for colored children, while elsewhere colored children attended mixed schools. In 1894 the superintendent of schools aroused a storm of protest among the colored population when he ordered the colored children in one of the mixed schools to be transferred to an all-colored school in order to make room for more white pupils. Since attending the colored school involved a longer walk for his daughter than did attending the mixed school, one colored parent tried to make a test case by refusing to accede to the transfer. A local judge ruled that the child had no choice but to attend the colored school when ordered to do so. As the result of this ruling some children were compelled to attend all-

25 Indianapolis *Leader,* January 1, 1881 ; State, *ex rel.* Mitchell *v.* Gray *et al.,* School Trustees, 92 Ind. 303-6.

26 *Indiana School Journal,* 29 (1884) :619.

colored schools rather than the schools nearest them, but in some districts mixed schools continued.[27]

In 1878 the opening of public night schools in Indianapolis gave many colored adults their first opportunity to attend school. During the first year there were 179 colored persons in attendance out of a total of 434. The superintendent was not entirely pleased with the results of the experiment in the white schools, where some of the pupils proved unruly. But "in the colored schools, so great was the anxiety of the pupils (mostly adults, often gray-headed) to learn that all that was necessary was to provide the opportunity." In 1895 an Industrial Training School was opened to which colored pupils were admitted on the same terms as white. Here they studied such subjects as sewing, cooking, typing, shorthand, and woodworking, free of tuition. In 1898 the first cooking class in the elementary schools was introduced in one of the colored schools, and two years later shop work for boys was introduced in the same school.[28]

From the time that colored schools were opened it became a matter of racial pride that they should be staffed with colored teachers, especially since teaching was one of the few occupations which an educated Negro might hope to

[27] Indianapolis Public Schools, *Annual Report*, 1878, pp. 125-43; *The Freeman*, September 29, 1894; Indianapolis *World*, July 13, 1895.

[28] Indianapolis Public Schools, *Annual Report*, 1878, pp. 80-81; Indianapolis *World*, February 23, 1895; Superintendent of Public Instruction, *Report*, 1899-1900, pp. 698, 705. Some years before some of the colored children of the city had begun to receive some elementary vocational training in special Saturday classes offered by the Indianapolis Free Kindergarten Society. The classes were organized to give underprivileged girls, white and black, some practical training in cooking and other household arts, but colored boys also asked admission in order that they might obtain training which would help them become cooks and waiters. These domestic training classes were conducted for many years under the sponsorship of the society until domestic science became a part of the regular curriculum of the Indianapolis Public Schools. Indianapolis Free Kindergarten Society, *Annual Reports*, 1882-1900, *passim*.

enter. In Indianapolis the school authorities appear to have attempted to accede in most cases to the wishes of the colored population. When the first schools were opened in 1869, two colored women were employed as teachers for one of the two schools. The second school was staffed at first by white teachers, since the school board demurred for some reason at hiring colored men and no other qualified women were available. The ban against men was soon dropped, and men usually served as principals of the schools. By 1902, 53 out of a total of 585 teachers in the elementary schools of the city were colored.[29] The faculties of the colored schools were usually entirely colored, but no colored teachers were ever used in the mixed schools.

No group except ministers enjoyed greater prestige among the members of their race than did the teachers, some of whom became outstanding members of the Negro community. Among these were three members of a remarkable family, Robert Bruce Bagby, Benjamin D. Bagby, and James D. Bagby, who served as principals of three of the schools. The parents of the three were born slaves in Virginia, but the father was able to purchase his freedom from his master, a tanner, who taught him his trade and later made him a partner in his business. In 1857 Bagby took his family, which then consisted of six sons, to the vicinity of Oxford, Ohio. From the father, who was a self-educated man, the sons received their first lessons in reading, writing, and geography. Four of them later attended Oberlin College, although Robert appears to be the only one who received a degree. In addition to serving as principals of the schools the three who settled in Indianapolis also started the first successful Negro newspaper in the city, the *Leader,* and were active in Republican politics. Robert Bagby was the first Negro member of the Indianapolis City Council. The fourth

29 Indianapolis Public Schools, *Annual Report,* 1902, p. 19. The first two colored teachers were Mrs. Lottie Douglass and Miss Susan Depew.

brother who attended Oberlin, Edwin Bagby, settled in Terre Haute, where he also became a school principal.[30]

The principal of the fourth colored school in Indianapolis for some years was Levi E. Christy, who had been born in Salem, Indiana, in 1851, but whose family moved to Xenia, Ohio, in 1865 because of the growing hostility toward Negroes in that part of Indiana. He attended public schools in Xenia and later night schools in Indianapolis and finally Wilberforce University. In 1885 he resigned his position in the Indianapolis schools to become editor and senior proprietor of a second Negro newspaper, the Indianapolis *World*. In the late nineties he left journalism to become a minister of the A.M.E. church.[31] William D. McCoy, another early principal, was a native of Cambridge City, Indiana, who had gone to Helena, Arkansas, during the Reconstruction years and there had attained the position of county superintendent of schools. In 1879 he came to Indianapolis to teach and was later appointed to the principalship of the largest colored school. In 1890 he resigned this position and was nominated as a member of the Indiana House of Representatives by the Republicans. Although he was defeated for that office, he was appointed by President Harrison as minister to Liberia, one of the highest posts open to a colored man in government service. McCoy was unable to endure the climate of that republic and died a few months after his arrival, although he was only about forty years old. In his will he bequeathed his estate, about fifteen hundred dollars, to the Indianapolis schools. The school board designated the money as a fund for the benefit of colored pupils and named the school which he had headed the William D. McCoy School.[32]

[30] *Ibid.*, 1878, p. 125; Indianapolis *Journal*, January 6, 1880.

[31] Irvine Garland Penn, *The Afro-American Press and Its Editors* (Springfield, Mass., 1891), 222-23.

[32] *The Freeman*, July 2, 1890; Indianapolis Public Schools, *Annual Report*, 1902, pp. 110-11. For earlier mention of McCoy see above, 306-7.

In Evansville there were three colored schools by 1887 with a staff of eighteen. One school was a twelve-room structure, but the other two had only two and three rooms. All colored children were required to attend these schools. They were far from adequate for a school population which numbered almost two thousand, and probably less than half of the children of school age were enrolled in them.[33] In Terre Haute the first colored school was opened in quarters in the African M.E. church in 1869 with one teacher. The following year a second teacher was added, and the third year the school was moved into a building formerly occupied by a white school. Although the school authorities asserted that it was equal to the schools provided for white children, enrollment grew slowly. As the result of the increase in Negro population after the immigration of 1879 described earlier, a second school was opened in 1884 and a few years later a third. In 1887 a colored critic described these schools as "simply abominable" and as greatly inferior to the white schools. In 1888 less than one third of the children of school age were enrolled in these schools. In 1889 the situation was improved somewhat by the opening of a new building for one of the schools. A policy of employing white teachers to staff it brought protests from the Negro population, so that the next year colored teachers were appointed to it. Thereafter faculties of all of the colored schools seem to have been colored.[34]

In some of the other cities with large colored populations in which separate school systems were maintained a rela-

[33] Indianapolis *World*, November 26, 1887; Superintendent of Public Instruction, *Report*, 1887-88, pt. 2:101.

[34] The principal of the first colored school was Zachariah M. Anderson. Other principals in the early years were John Sims, Edwin R. Bagby, Ernest Meyzeil, S. W. Stuart, Joseph Jackson, and Mrs. Adorah Knight. Superintendent of Public Instruction, *Report*, 1887-88, pt. 2:103; Terre Haute Public Schools, *Report*, 1871-72, p. 45; 1872-73, p. 33; 1874-75, pp. 31-32; 1891-92, pp. 147-49; Merle B. Shepard, "Negro Schools in Vigo County" (unpublished M.A. thesis, Indiana State Teachers College, 1948), 37-39.

tively low percentage of school children were enrolled. For example, in 1888 only 36 per cent of those of school age were enrolled in Mount Vernon in Posey County, 45 per cent in New Albany, 45 per cent in Jeffersonville, 50 per cent in Madison, and 56 per cent in Richmond.[35]

Although the colored population as a whole does not seem to have objected to the principle of segregation, they did protest against the obvious inequalities which existed in many places. The only serious effort to bring about the equalization of the schools through legislation was made in the 1897 session of the General Assembly when Gabriel Jones, a colored member from Marion County and a teacher himself, proposed to repeal the provision of the 1877 law regarding colored schools. As a substitute he offered the following: "that the children of colored parents shall be entitled to the same rights and privileges in the public schools of the state of Indiana as are offered therein to the children of white parents, and that there shall be no discrimination made against or preference shown to any child on account of his or her color, but every child shall have equal educational facilities, regardless of color." The House committee on education reported favorably on the Jones bill. On the floor an amendment that "nothing herein shall prevent the keeping of separate schools for colored children" was voted down, but other amendments were adopted which substituted for the original proposal a measure which would have permitted all colored children to attend the school nearest their place of residence and which would have made a school trustee who discriminated against a child because of color guilty of a misdemeanor and subject to a fine.[36]

The bill as amended passed the House, but strong enough opposition developed to prevent a vote on it in the Senate.

[35] Superintendent of Public Instruction, *Report*, 1887-88, pt. 2: pp. 29, 41, 58, 84, 108.

[36] House Bill 46, Original Indiana House Bills, 1897 Session (Archives Division, Indiana State Library) ; Indiana *House Journal*, 1897, pp. 489, 746, 751-54, 842, 1011, 1310.

Some white Republican leaders were reported to be dis-
pleased with Jones for proposing the bill. Opinion among
Negroes themselves was sharply divided. In the eyes of
most members of the race the strongest argument in favor
of separate schools was the fact that they offered employment to colored teachers. The measure which passed the
House did not expressly abolish all colored schools, but
many colored teachers viewed it as a threat to their positions.
A petition from thirty teachers in Indianapolis asked that
the bill not pass. It declared: "If such Bill becomes a Law,
we believe that it will be detrimental to the colored people
of the State; that it will deprive not only ourselves but many
colored men and women of their livelihood; and that it
will remove the opportunity that colored men and women
now have to strive after and obtain honorable employment
in our public schools." On the other hand, some Negroes
strongly urged the adoption of the bill. To counter the
teachers' petition another group, which included some of the
most highly educated Negroes in Indianapolis, sent another
petition in which they asserted that the colored people of
the community were overwhelmingly in favor of the measure
because "Indiana alone of all the northern states keeps up
this discrimination against colored children," and added:
"We ask no special or class legislation, but simply that the
class legislation on our statute books be removed."[37] In
spite of this argument the efforts of George L. Knox,
probably the most influential Negro Republican at that time,
were reported to have been decisive in killing the bill in the
Senate.[38]

[37] The petition continued: "The question of the employment of colored
teachers has no connection with the legislation. The schools are for the
children. Our only concern about teachers is that the best only be employed. The opposition to this measure on the part of any colored people
comes only from their interest in the employment of certain teachers, but
the number is so small and their motive so apparent, that no attention
should be paid to their clamor." Both petitions are appended to the
original House Bill 46 in the Archives.

[38] John W. Lyda, *The Negro in the History of Indiana* (Terre Haute,
1953), 87.

An accurate statistical measurement of the progress of Negro education before 1900 is impossible. The figures in the reports of the State Superintendent of Public Instruction are questionable for several reasons. One of their most obvious deficiencies arose from the fact that after 1879 the school reports in Indianapolis, where the number of colored pupils was greatest, usually lumped the members of both races together. In 1901, four years after a compulsory attendance law for children under fourteen had been adopted, the report of the State Superintendent shows that about 69 per cent of the colored children of school age (between six and twenty years) were enrolled in school, as compared with over 73 per cent of the whites in the same age group. However, these figures represent merely enrollment and not attendance, and no figures are available to show what proportion of the children attended regularly or the number of colored children who graduated from elementary schools. There is evidence that even as late as 1900 the number of colored persons who finished the eighth grade was extremely small.[39]

The failure of large numbers of colored children to avail themselves of the educational opportunities open to them was due to a variety of reasons. The most obvious one was the poverty of most of the colored population, which made it necessary for children to leave school and try to help supplement the family income. The lack of a tradition of schooling in Negro families also contributed to indifference, while the limited facilities and the dreary surroundings in most colored schools were discouraging. Many Negroes became disillusioned when they discovered that schooling had little economic value for members of their race since most occupations remained closed to them, regardless of their training.

[39] Superintendent of Public Instruction, *Report*, 1901-2, pp. 240-43. In 1904 it was reported that a total of only 133 colored pupils graduated from all of the district and graded schools of the state in one year. *Ibid.*, 1903-4, p. 267.

In spite of the fact that the number who finished school was small the proportion of the colored population who had received the rudiments of an education increased steadily. One index of this is the decline in illiteracy. In 1880, 35 per cent of the colored population of the state over the age of ten was classified as illiterate. By 1900 this figure had been reduced to 22 per cent. Although there remained a wide difference between the ratio of literacy among Negroes and the native white population, of whom less than 4 per cent were illiterate in 1900, the difference was decreasing. At the end of the century only 1.5 per cent of Negro children between the ages of ten and fourteen could not read and write.[40]

A few of the students who graduated from the elementary schools went on to the public high schools, which were still in their infancy in Indiana in the period when schools were first opened to Negroes. The Indianapolis High School (later Shortridge High School) was opened in 1865 and graduated its first class in 1869. Before it was ten years old it had opened its doors to colored students. The 1869 school law had applied only to elementary schools and had made no mention of high schools. Nevertheless, in the summer of 1872 a committee of Negroes headed by the Reverend Moses Broyles met with A. C. Shortridge, the superintendent of city schools, and asked that colored pupils be admitted to the high school. They insisted that to refuse them was contrary to both the state Constitution and the Fourteenth Amendment of the United States Constitution. In spite of the fact that the law gave him no authority to do so, Short-

---

[40] Superintendent of Public Instruction, *Report,* 1903-4, pp. 436-37. The 22 per cent of illiteracy compared favorably with the national average of 44.5 per cent of illiteracy for the entire Negro population of the United States in 1900. On the other hand the percentage of illiterates was higher in Indiana than in any of the other states in the east North Central division—Ohio, Illinois, Michigan, and Wisconsin. U. S. Bureau of the Census, *Negroes in the United States (Bulletin No. 8,* 1904), 148, 268.

ridge agreed to admit one colored student as a test. Accordingly, a girl was enrolled, and although one member of the School Board privately questioned Shortridge's action, her presence brought no objections from students or parents and she went on to graduate in the class of 1876.[41]

In 1877 the way was officially opened for the admission of colored students to the high schools by the change in the school law. The act of 1877 provided that when a child attending a colored school showed by examination or otherwise that he was prepared to be placed in a higher grade than that afforded by the colored school, he was to be admitted to a white school. This meant that school corporations had the option of admitting colored students to the white high schools or of establishing separate schools.

In Indianapolis colored students continued to attend the white high school. No accurate figures on their number are available since the school records did not indicate race, but their number was larger than in any other city. By 1887 nineteen had graduated, and the number steadily increased. By 1896 there were six colored members in the class which graduated at midyear. The opportunities for colored persons were enlarged in 1898 when several teachers in the school organized a free night school. In the statement of the purpose of the night school it was declared that it should be open "to any person of any race, color, age or sex, who is capable of doing work along high school lines."[42]

Elsewhere in the state the number of Negro students in attendance was so small that the graduation of a member of the race was regarded as a newsworthy event. For example, the first Negro students were graduated from high school in Shelbyville and Marion in 1888, in Columbus in

[41] Shortridge, "The Schools of Indianapolis," Pt. III, in *Indiana Magazine of History,* 8:128-29. The student was Mary Rann, the first Negro to graduate from an Indiana high school. Indianapolis *Daily Sentinel,* June 18, 1876.

[42] Indianapolis *World,* December 17, 1887; January 20, 1896; Indianapolis Public Schools, *Annual Report,* 1902, pp. 107-9.

1892, while none were graduated from the Fort Wayne High School until 1898.[43]

In the towns in the southern part of the state, although the number of Negroes who sought entrance was extremely small, they were not admitted to the white schools. Instead they were given special instruction in high school subjects by teachers in the colored elementary school. Sometimes the arrangements were on an individual basis, but in others there was a "high school department" in the elementary school building to which some of the teachers were assigned on a part-time basis. Before 1900 Evansville, New Albany, Vincennes, and Madison were listed as having separate high schools, although in no case did the school have a separate building of its own. By that date the Clark High School in Evansville had an enrollment of eighty pupils and four teachers; Scribner High School in New Albany had thirty-two pupils and two teachers; and Vincennes High School ten pupils and one teacher. None of these schools were accredited. The only commissioned high school for colored students before 1900 was the one in Madison, which received the rank in 1893. The school was housed in the same building with an elementary school but had a laboratory equipped for the teaching of chemistry and physics. The first student was graduated in 1897, and as late as 1904 only twenty-three students had been graduated.[44] The small enrollment and slow growth of the high schools the school authorities attributed principally to the poverty of the colored population. Nearly all colored pupils were compelled to leave school as soon as they could legally do so, at the age of fourteen. Even younger children were frequently

[43] Indianapolis *World*, November 12, 1887; February 20, 1892; March 26, 1898; Whitson (ed.), *Grant County*, 1:356.

[44] U. S. Commissioner of Education, *Annual Report*, 1899-1900, vol. 2: 2510; Superintendent of Public Instruction, *Report*, 1902-3, pp. 238-39. By 1904 colored high schools were also reported in Jeffersonville, Rockport, Princeton, Mount Vernon, and Corydon, but they had no separate buildings and usually only one teacher. *Ibid.*, 1902-3, pp. 263-67.

expected to earn the money for their own books and clothing and to help their parents. Of those who succeeded in finishing high school a very large percentage were self-supporting.

But neither the fact that the number who graduated from high school was extremely small nor the fact that they obtained their education against great odds served to remove the stigma attached to their color in some communities. In at least two instances white students refused to participate in commencement exercises with colored graduates. In Vincennes in 1886, before there was a regular colored high school, a Negro girl had completed her high school course by receiving individual instruction. But half a dozen white students protested when it was proposed that she should receive her diploma at the same commencement with them. In Washington in Daviess County a similar incident occurred. There a colored girl had made heroic efforts to receive a high school education, earning all of her expenses. As in the other case she had received individual instruction and had not attended classes with white students. When the school authorities suggested that she participate in the exercises with the other students, all but two of the white students objected, thus compelling the holding of two commencements.[45]

A small group of Negroes also attended various institutions of higher learning—colleges, universities, normal schools, and medical schools. Although they were few in number, they furnished much of the leadership of their race. A number of persons who had attended Oberlin College came to Indiana, especially in the years immediately following the Civil War. Among them were such men as the Rev. James M. Townsend, Dr. Samuel Elbert, the Bagby brothers, and

[45] Indianapolis *Journal*, June 17, 1886; Indianapolis *World*, May 3, June 7, 1890. Apropos the Vincennes incident the *Journal* remarked: "The good men and women who are wearing out their lives under tropical suns to spread the good news might come back and exert their influence, if they have any, on the people of Knox County. There is a field for practical missionary work."

other outstanding ministers and teachers. Several of the teachers in the Indianapolis schools had attended that institution.[46] A smaller number of Indiana residents attended Wilberforce University in Ohio, which was maintained by the African M.E. Church. A very few attended Howard University in Washington, D.C., but almost none attended the Negro colleges in the South.

The three state-supported institutions of higher learning in Indiana, Indiana University, Purdue University, and Terre Haute Normal School, admitted colored students, and few, if any, of the private colleges openly raised color barriers, but Negro students were rare in all of them. In two small private schools there were reports that white students objected to colored students, but in both cases the school authorities upheld the right of Negroes to enroll. In the first case a colored girl from Pennsylvania enrolled in a normal school at Danville in Hendricks County. Students from Kentucky and Missouri protested, but the faculty ignored them, and the girl continued in the school. In 1899 when two Negroes from Cass County, Michigan, entered Manchester College, a denominational school in northern Indiana, two students from Alabama objected. When the board of trustees upheld the right of the Negroes to attend, the Southerners withdrew from the college. One of the first Negroes to attend Indiana University was accepted by his white classmates as a member of the football team and also represented the university in a state oratorical contest.[47]

An early study of college-educated Negroes made at Atlanta University showed that only nine Negroes graduated from Indiana colleges between the Civil War and 1900. They were distributed as follows: four from Indiana Uni-

---

46 Indianapolis Public Schools, *Annual Report,* 1878, pp. 125-43.

47 Indianapolis *Journal,* September 22-23, 1880; Indianapolis *World,* February 23, 1895; December 2, 1899. The Negro student was Preston Eagleson who was also the first Negro to receive a Ph.D. degree from Indiana University. Conversation of the author with Eagleson's half-brother who is now a member of the faculty of Howard University.

versity, one from Purdue University, three from Butler College, and one from DePauw and Franklin colleges respectively.[48] Although the number of graduates probably was actually slightly higher than this, attendance by Negroes remained extremely small.

In spite of prejudice and financial obstacles a few persons also obtained medical degrees. The first member of the race to receive the M.D. degree in the state was Samuel A. Elbert, who came to Indianapolis in 1866 after two years at Oberlin and taught in the private school maintained by

[48] *The College-Bred Negro American* (*The Atlanta University Publications, No. 15*, Atlanta, 1910), 48-49. One of the first colored graduates from Indiana University was C. F. Williamson, who taught for a time in the Indianapolis schools and later became principal of the colored school in New Albany. George W. Lacey was the first colored graduate of Purdue, while D. R. Lewis received a degree in civil engineering in 1894 and Fred Stokes a degree in chemistry the same year. The first Negro graduate from Butler College was Gertrude Mahorney of the class of 1887. She was the only colored woman to receive a degree in Indiana before 1900 and one of eighty-two in the United States to receive a degree before that date. Her brother, J. T. Mahorney, Jr., of the class of 1889, was the second colored graduate from Butler. A third graduate from Butler was Ezra C. Roberts of the class of 1898. For three years he served as assistant editor of the college paper and was an outstanding college orator. After graduation he taught in the Indianapolis public schools until 1906 when he resigned to take a position at Tuskegee Institute in Alabama. Indianapolis *News*, June 16, 1906. A few Negroes graduated from the Terre Haute Normal College (now Indiana State Teachers College), the first being J. R. Lytle of Terre Haute in 1888. Negroes were admitted from the beginning to the institution founded in Indianapolis in 1882 by Eliza Blaker, which later became the Indianapolis Teachers College. Graduates taught in the Indianapolis schools and the kindergartens maintained by the Indianapolis Free Kindergarten Society. One of the first colored graduates was Mrs. J. T. V. Hill, who taught in the Indianapolis schools for forty years, retiring in 1932. Indianapolis *World,* April 5, 1890, June 9, 1894; Indianapolis *Recorder,* February 9, 1901; Indianapolis *Journal,* June 18, 1887; Indianapolis *News,* June 4, 1940; Kelly Miller, "The Education of the Negro," in U. S. Commissioner of Education, *Annual Report,* 1901, p. 826; Verner K. Howell, "A Forty-two Year Survey of the Negro Graduates from Indiana State Teachers College" (unpublished M.A. thesis, Indiana State Teachers College, 1945), 1.

Allen Chapel for a time. Becoming interested in medicine he was permitted by two white doctors to study in their office, and after this experience tried to gain admission to a medical school but found that he was barred from most of them because of his color. When Indiana Medical College opened in 1869 Elbert was allowed to attend classes through the intercession of one of the white doctors in whose office he was studying. However, although he paid tuition, he was not given the status of a regular student and was told that he would not be allowed to receive a degree. But Elbert protested that he had met the entrance requirements and paid his tuition and was entitled to earn a degree. He persisted until the faculty reversed its position. He received his M.D. in 1871, and after his successful fight several other Negroes were permitted to graduate from the school.[49]

About twenty years later another barrier to professional progress was overcome by Sumner Furniss, who was the first Negro to be admitted as an intern in the Indianapolis City Hospital. He was graduated in third place in his class at Indiana Medical College, the only Negro in a class of fifty-four. As the result of a competitive examination he received an appointment to the internship but found that some members of the hospital staff were opposed to permitting him to accept the post. The superintendent, while insisting that he had no personal prejudice because of color, expressed fear that all but charity patients would refuse to come to the hospital when it was known that there was a colored intern. Furniss was finally admitted, although he was requested to eat his meals in a room apart from the white staff members. His presence apparently brought no objections from patients, and in 1895 he began a long and successful practice which continued until his death in 1953.[50]

49 Indianapolis *Journal*, January 6, 1880.
50 Indianapolis *World*, April 7, June 9, 1894.

13

EARNING A LIVELIHOOD

"Our people in the North, while free from many out-rages practiced on our brethren in the South, are not wholly exempt from unjust discriminations. Caste prejudices have sufficient sway to exclude them from the workshop, trades and other avenues of remunerative business advancement."[1] This statement, part of an address to the nation adopted by a National Convention of Colored Men in Nashville, Tennessee, in 1879, reflected accurately the condition of Negroes in Indiana at that date. And in Indiana, as in most northern states, it appears that "caste prejudice" based on color was stronger in the economic realm in 1900 than it had been in 1879.

Most of the newcomers from the South who flocked into the state after the Civil War eventually moved into the cities and towns even though some of them worked as farm la-borers when they first arrived. Many of the younger gen-eration of the older farm communities of the state also moved cityward during the last part of the century. By 1900 only about 26 per cent of the Negro population (be-tween fourteen and fifteen thousand persons) remained in rural areas. Most of this group were farm laborers, for according to the census of 1900 only 1,043 farms in the state were operated by Negroes. Of these about two thirds were owned by the operators, while the remainder were farmed by tenants. Although a few prosperous Negro farmers remained in such communities as the Lyles settle-

[1] Quoted in Fishel, "The North and the Negro" (unpublished Ph.D. thesis, Harvard University, 1953), 125.

ment in Gibson County or Lost Creek in Vigo County, they were exceptional. Most Negro farmers were poor, and in general their condition compared unfavorably with that of the white farmer. Most of their farms were small, about fifty acres on an average, while the size of the average farm worked by a white man was nearly twice as large. Moreover the average income of the Negro farmer was only about half that of the white farmer.[2]

Desire to improve their economic condition was usually the primary motive causing rural Negroes to migrate, but in the cities they found most types of employment closed to them. This was due in part to the fact that a large proportion of them were former farm laborers without any particular skill. But even those who had a trade were seldom able to use it. The number of Negroes who were able to establish themselves in the skilled trades or industry was extremely small. A somewhat larger number were able to make a living in various service occupations, while a small group established themselves as independent businessmen. A few others entered government service or the professions. But the mass of Negroes of both sexes were found either in some form of domestic service or doing manual labor. Some of the jobs open to them were seasonal in character, and many did not offer steady employment. The result was that most of the Negroes in the cities lived a hand-to-mouth existence in poverty-stricken surroundings.

Census records show that most colored workers were listed simply as "laborers" with no particular occupation, which usually meant that they did any kind of manual work which presented itself. Among men such occupations as teamsters, whitewashers, hod carriers, waiters, porters, and janitors, were common. In the river towns some of them worked on the boats and docks. Most of the women who were employed were in domestic service. Some were cooks or maids,

[2] U. S. Bureau of the Census, *Negroes in the United States* (*Bulletin 8,* 1904), 190, 296-97, 332-33.

while others were laundresses or women who did cleaning by the day.

A resolution adopted at the first statewide convention of colored men after the Civil War in Indianapolis had asked that African youths be taught trades in order that they might become "useful members of society."[3] But the hopes expressed in this resolution were doomed to disappointment, for one of the conspicuous failures of Negroes throughout the North was their inability to gain an entrance into the ranks of skilled laborers. In an oration which he delivered in 1880 the Negro leader, Frederick Douglass, thus described their plight: "It is easier to get a colored lad into a lawyer's office to study law, than into a blacksmith-shop to hammer iron." He added: "The effects of being ruled out of all respectable trades at the North, has compelled the colored people there to crowd the cities, lanes and allies [sic]—and live by work which no other class of people will do. This work being occasional, coming at intervals, and never long continued exposes them to the ten thousand evils of enforced idleness and poverty."[4]

A study made after the census of 1890 showed only 2,287 Negro men out of a total Negro population of over forty-five thousand in Indiana as engaged in trades which could in any sense be classified as skilled. Of these by far the largest group, 699, were barbers. The other trades which engaged the largest numbers were as follows: miners and quarrymen 185; iron and steel workers 162; engineers and firemen 154; carpenters and joiners 133; brickmakers 130; railroad employees 128; saw and planing mill men 124. There were only 15 machinists and 14 printers.[5] In some fields,

[3] Indianapolis *Daily Journal,* October 26, 1865.

[4] Quoted in Fishel, "The North and the Negro, 1865-1900," 158.

[5] *The Negro Artisan (Atlanta University Publications No. 7,* Atlanta, 1902), 125. The distribution of other trades was as follows:

Telegraph and telephone operators _____ 2   Glass workers _____ 56
Blacksmiths and wheelwrights _____ 81   Harness makers _____ 5
Apprentices (Unclassified) _____ 24   Masons, stonecutters __ 92

such as carpentry, the number of Negroes appeared to be decreasing. A study made in Indianapolis in 1900 indicated that the only one of the building trades in which substantial numbers of Negroes were found was hod carrying.[6]

Almost none of the industries in Indianapolis employed Negroes. In 1900 there were only three colored moulders and two moulder helpers and five cupola tenders in the entire city. A total of 125 Negroes were employed as common laborers in the foundries, but most establishments had no Negro employees.[7] On the whole the number of skilled workers among Indianapolis colored laborers was declining rather than increasing at the end of the century. Some of the older generation who had acquired skills while still in slavery were dying out, and the younger men showed little disposition to acquire skills which they had no opportunity to use. Few Negroes were attending the industrial training school which the city maintained.

But although the occupational opportunities in Indianapolis were extremely limited one condition in that city probably caused Negroes to fare somewhat better than in many northern cities. This was the relatively small number of recent European immigrants compared with other cities of its size, which had the effect of reducing the competition for unskilled jobs. A few types of work were open to Negroes which were closed to them in most places. For example, Indianapolis was one of three cities in the North in which a few colored men worked as street railway em-

Butchers	12	Millers	12
Cabinetmakers	18	Painters	40
Carriage and wagonmakers	9	Plasterers	90
Coopers	11	Tailors	7
Textile mill operators	34	Woodworkers	39

[6] In 1900 twenty-five Negroes were listed as carpenters in Indianapolis, of whom five were contractors or boss carpenters, while twenty made a living at carpentry but could not be classified as fully skilled. There were thirty plasterers in the city at that date, whereas there had been ninety ten years earlier. *The Negro Artisan*, 105-6.

[7] *Ibid.*, 105.

ployees along with white men.[8] In the smaller cities the
opportunities were even more restricted. One exception was
in the mining towns of the western and southern parts of
the state. At the end of the century the number of Negroes
employed in the coal mines was on the increase.[9]

The failure of Negroes to gain an entry into the skilled
trades and industry was due in part to their own lack of
training, but it was primarily due to the attitude of white
employers and workers. Some employers who would otherwise have been willing to hire Negroes were reluctant to
do so because of the widespread feeling that white workers
would refuse to work with them. Whether prejudice was
as universal as it was represented cannot be determined since
few employers risked trouble by hiring Negroes. An occasional incident was reported which seemed to confirm the
prevalent theory. For example, when a Negro was employed
in the cutting room of an iron mill in Muncie, between one
hundred seventy and two hundred white workers went on
strike.[10]

Although only a small minority of workers belonged to
labor unions before 1900, the position of the unions on the
subject of Negro workers helped to set the general pattern.
The refusal of unions to admit colored members had the
effect of barring Negroes completely from some occupations.
This attitude had not prevailed at the end of the Civil War,
when for a short time it had appeared that workers of both
races might be able to unite for their mutual benefit. White
leaders in the National Labor Union, which was organized
in the postwar years, showed an interest in the recently

8 James S. Stemons, "The Industrial Color-Line in the North," in
Century Illustrated Magazine, 60(1900) :478. In 1900 the total number of
Negroes in the city was 15,931, the number of foreign-born persons,
17,122.

9 Sterling D. Spero and Abram L. Harris, *The Black Worker: The
Negro and the Labor Movement* (New York, 1931), 215. In 1890 there
were 185 Negroes employed in mines and quarries. By 1900 the number
had reached 399.

10 Indianapolis *Recorder*, June 22, 1901.

emancipated slaves and appointed a committee on the subject of colored workers in 1867. In 1869 and in subsequent years Negro delegates attended the conventions of the union. There was also an attempt to form a separate organization of colored workers affiliated with the National Labor Union. In 1869 a National Labor Convention of Colored Men met in Washington. This movement died out after a few years, partly because Frederick Douglass, whose influence was dominant in all Negro affairs, was doubtful of the wisdom of promoting a movement which might weaken the allegiance of the Negro to the Republican party, which he regarded as the truest defender of the interests of the race. At the second convention a committee was appointed to attempt to organize workers in several states, of which Indiana was one. There is no evidence that anyone from Indiana participated in any of the early labor conventions or that there was any union activity among the colored population of the state in that period.[11]

The rise of the Knights of Labor in the eighties first brought a few Indiana Negroes into the labor movement. The constitution of this organization, which embraced more workers than any earlier movement, declared that no distinction as to color should be made in its membership. The admission of Negroes into locals affiliated with the national organization was encouraged. Two chapters of colored members were organized in Indianapolis and one each in Evansville, Cementville (Clark County), Terre Haute, and Brazil and perhaps elsewhere. These locals embraced all kinds of workers without regard to occupation and were made up entirely of Negroes. There is no evidence of Negro membership in mixed locals. Even the names of the colored leaders are unknown except for J. T. Mahorney of Indianapolis. Mahorney, who had been a leader in the state conventions of colored people in the postwar years, was one

11 Charles H. Wesley, *Negro Labor in the United States 1850-1925* (New York, 1927), 159, 161, 176-77, 183.

of the first Negro leaders in the state to leave the Republican party, which he felt exploited the Negro voter. He sought, without much success, to arouse the members of his race to seek to improve their condition through unionization and independent political activity. Although it was claimed that the Knights were responsible for securing better pay for brick and mortar carriers in Indianapolis, a majority of whom were colored, the mass of Negroes remained indifferent to the movement. In 1887 there was apparently an effort by the Knights to form a Union Labor ticket in the local elections but the loyalty of the Negroes to the Republican party prevented the movement from gaining a following among them.[12]

The success of the Knights was limited and short-lived. By 1890 they had given way before the American Federation of Labor, which was made up principally of unions of skilled workers. Although the official policy of the new organization was to insist upon equal treatment of white and colored workers, the fact was that member unions, which enjoyed a large amount of autonomy, frequently barred Negroes. In Indiana there were a few Negro members in the United Mine Workers but probably none in any of the other A. F. of L. affiliates.[13]

[12] *Ibid.*, 254-55; Sidney H. Kessler, "Organization of Negroes in the Knights of Labor," in *Journal of Negro History*, 37(1952) :259; Indianapolis *Journal*, July 5, 1887; Indianapolis *World*, July 30, October 29, 1887.

[13] As late as 1897 the A. F. of L. national convention reaffirmed that all members were welcome without regard to color, sex, creed, race, or nationality. In 1900 Samuel Gompers suggested that Negroes be organized into separate unions, and in 1902 the convention adopted the following rule: "Separate charters may be issued to Central Labor Unions, Local Unions or Federal Labor Unions composed exclusively of colored members." This action officially permitted national unions to exclude Negro members, a practice that had prevailed in local chapters for years. In 1900 substantial numbers of Negroes were to be found in the following unions: Barbers', Carpenters', Carriage Workers', Stationary Firemen's, United Mine Workers', and Longshoremen's. However, many unions reported no Negro members. Wesley, *Negro Labor*, 257-59; *Negro Artisan*, 157-58.

On the whole the efforts at unionization among the colored population of the state were sporadic and temporary, and the most successful unions were independent ones. One of these was made up of colored hotel waiters who formed the Knights of the Temple of Industry of the Hotel Brotherhood in 1885 under the leadership of H. J. Poe. This was a secret organization which served as a fraternal and benevolent association as well as a labor union. It maintained an employment office for members and sponsored social affairs such as parades and concerts. By 1887 it had two hundred and forty members in Indianapolis. Branches were also established in several other cities, and a woman's branch, known as the Companion Sisters of the Hotel Brotherhood, was formed. In 1888 there was a movement to form a janitors' union patterned after the Hotel Brotherhood, but it does not seem to have met with much success.[14]

There was an active and successful hod carriers' union in Indianapolis which was made up mainly of Negroes, although there were a few white members. In 1900 of three hundred fifty Negro hod carriers in the city about two hundred belonged. The union was not affiliated with any national organization. Unions made up of Negro teamsters and shovelers also attained some success. The blacksmiths' union was open to Negroes, and a number belonged to it. J. K. Donnell, a Negro, was corresponding secretary in 1900. There was a union of colored plasterers for a time in the nineties, but nothing is known about its size or strength. Although there was no rule excluding them from the carpenters' union in Indianapolis, Negroes did not join. They claimed that they gained nothing from membership because white carpenters refused to work with Negroes even though they were union members. The situation in the bricklayers' union was much the same. Negroes were nominally eligible but did not belong.[15]

---

[14] Indianapolis *Journal*, August 4, 1887; *The Freeman*, August 11, 1888; March 30, April 27, 1889.

[15] *Negro Artisan*, 105-6; Indianapolis *Labor Signal*, October 21, 1892; Indianapolis *Recorder*, July 6, 1901.

On the whole the condition of the mass of Negroes was improved not at all by the unions, while their opportunities were sharply circumscribed by the refusal of most unions to admit them. The exclusive policies, which became more pronounced in the closing years of the century, caused bitterness and developed an antiunion bias among many Negroes. The race newspapers frequently assailed unions as responsible for the Negro's failure to rise in the economic realm. As early as 1890 *The Freeman* was deploring discriminatory practices, declaring: "It is poor economic policy to spoil a good machinist to make a poor coachman, or to force a natural born compositor into the awkward roll [*sic*] of table waiter."[16]

One of the anomalies in the situation was that although educational opportunities for Negroes were steadily increasing, their occupational opportunities were declining as the result of the policies of the unions. In consequence many colored men with capacities for other work were compelled to remain in domestic service. Another result of barring Negroes from industry was to cause a disproportionate number to try to enter the learned professions. The Indianapolis *World* pointed out that parents frequently sacrificed in order to send their children to school only to find that occupational opportunities were no greater for the educated than for the uneducated Negro. The result was idleness and demoralization among colored youth. In another editorial the *World* declared: "A broader industrial field for the employment of Negro talent would lessen the rough and tumble scramble which ensues every time a little clerkship becomes vacant or a new school year begins." Furthermore, it added, admission into industry would lessen the cutthroat competition for jobs which caused Negroes to resort to misrepresentation and treachery to secure insignificant positions and which lowered the esteem of the colored race in the eyes of dominant white groups.[17]

16 *The Freeman*, April 9, 1890.
17 Indianapolis *World*, August 23, 1890; May 11, 1895. Similar views

In view of the anti-Negro bias shown by unions it is not surprising that colored men showed no sympathy for white strikers or that they sometimes were willing to be employed as strikebreakers. This was evident during the Pullman Strike of 1894 after the American Railway Union, contrary to the advice of Eugene Debs, voted against the admission of Negro members. Alexander E. Manning, a former railroad employee, in a speech before a group of Negro Democrats, denounced the railway union for its exclusive policy and declared that the strikers deserved no sympathy at the hands of colored men. On the other hand, he said, Negroes could not consistently condemn George M. Pullman, who had employed thousands of their race. An editorial in the *World* struck the same note and added that "if a hand is taken in the conflict by him [the Negro] his influence will more than likely go toward Mr. Pullman."[18]

The extreme bitterness which many Negroes felt toward the white working class, and especially white unionists, was reflected in a speech before the Indiana Afro-American Conference in 1899 in which it was asserted: "The greatest enemy of the Negro is the trade unionism of the North. The door of every factory in every state, city and town is closed against your boy because he is black. The door of business houses, with few exceptions, are closed against your daughters, educated, pure and refined though they be because they are black." The speaker insisted that employers barred Ne-

were expressed in an article in the *Atlantic Monthly* in 1898 by the distinguished Negro, John S. Durham. He said: "Educational facilities are improving every year, and an already large class is rapidly becoming more numerous, half-educated, without financial resources, denied the work which it is capable of doing and detesting the work it is forced to do. It is remarkable that this class has not shown a greater disposition to vice and crime than is the case. . . .

"About one-tenth of the population are denied the opportunity to grow, as the other nine-tenths are invited, encouraged, forced by open competition, to grow. This abridgement of opportunity affects the character of the whole class." John S. Durham, "The Labor Unions and the Negro," in *Atlantic Monthly*, 81 (1898) :230-31.

18 Indianapolis *World,* July 14, 1894.

gro workers, not because of their own prejudices, but because of the pressure of the trade unions, which would boycott them if they employed Negro labor.[19] Employers were able to exploit this situation to their advantage. Strikes sometimes presented Negroes with opportunities for employment which were ordinarily denied them. For example, some colored carpenters in Indianapolis found periods of strikes by white union members advantageous to them as nonunion members. The practice of hiring Negro strikebreakers does not appear to have been widespread, but there were occasional instances of it. It seems to have been most common in the coal mines in spite of the fact that a few Negroes were members of the United Mine Workers. As early as 1880 it was reported that sixty Negro miners had been brought from Richmond, Virginia, for the purpose of breaking a strike at Coal Creek in Fountain County.[20]

In 1897 about seventy-five Negroes were brought from Kentucky during a lockout at a mine in Daviess County. The men were given rifles and ammunition by the operators as a matter of protection. After a time part of the Negroes became dissatisfied and returned to Kentucky, claiming that the conditions under which they were to work had been misrepresented to them. Both the State Labor Commissioner and the Republican Indianapolis *Journal* expressed disapproval of the employment of the Negroes, but the Indianapolis *World* defended the right of the Negroes to accept employment and the right of the capitalists to hire them. Two years later an attempt to use Negroes from Kentucky during a strike near Evansville led to violence.

19 *Ibid.,* July 29, 1899.
20 *Negro Artisan,* 105; Indianapolis *Daily Journal,* August 19, 1880. The operator of the mine was a Democrat, and his action in importing the Negroes was said to be a source of embarrassment to William H. English, the Democratic vice-presidential nominee, who was a resident of Indiana. The *Journal* pointed out that the Negroes were brought into the congressional district of Daniel Voorhees, who had recently conducted a Senate investigation of an alleged Republican plot to colonize that part of the state with Negroes during the exodus of 1879.

As a group of about thirty of the imported workers approached the mine they were fired upon by some of the strikers. Seven Negroes were wounded, two seriously, although all recovered. A grand jury investigated the shooting and returned some indictments, but no one was convicted. There was no evidence that the officials of the United Mine Workers were in any way involved.[21]

In 1900 a request for a wage increase led to a lockout in a brick and pipe company in Terre Haute, which threw thirty men out of work. After closing the factory the superintendent went to Indianapolis where he hired twelve colored workmen whom he took back to Terre Haute. With this group and a few others operations were resumed. The Negroes were marched to and from work under the protection of a bodyguard. Feeling over the situation was so strong that a letter signed by one hundred citizens of West Terre Haute asked the intervention of the Governor, warning that the continued presence of the Negroes was likely to precipitate a riot. No serious violence seems to have resulted, although the company continued to resist efforts of the State Labor Commission to settle the dispute. Conditions of this sort naturally had the effect of increasing racial tension. For example, after Negro strikebreakers were used in the coal mines near Linton, no Negro was allowed in the town. When a catering firm from Terre Haute brought Negro waiters to Linton to serve at a large banquet, there were threats of violence, and it was necessary to hurry them out of town.[22]

The prejudice which barred colored workers from labor unions also barred them from "white collar" positions and occupations, such as selling, in which they would meet white patrons. The Negro press persistently urged the employment of colored salespeople and the boycotting of stores

21 Indiana Labor Commission, *First Biennial Report* (1897-98), 17-19; *Second Biennial Report* (1899-1900), 78; Indianapolis *World*, December 11, 1897.

22 Indiana Labor Commission, *Second Biennial Report*, 123-25; Indianapolis *Journal*, July 13, 1903.

which refused to hire them, but with little success. The employment of Negroes was rare. In 1889 one Indianapolis establishment which sold women's apparel hired a colored saleswoman—the only one in the city—but dismissed her after a few weeks because white customers objected to her.[23] In fact opportunities for colored women outside domestic service or related fields were almost nonexistent. The only skilled field in which Negro women were listed in considerable numbers was that of dressmaking and millinery. In 1890 there was only one colored stenographer in the whole state.[24]

A few persons found employment in government service. The development of the merit system of hiring Federal employees opened new opportunities for positions which offered greater remuneration and security than most of those to which Negroes could aspire. Some of the most highly educated members of the race were glad to accept routine positions. For example, William H. Furniss, a college graduate from Massachusetts, who had himself headed a Negro college in the South during Reconstruction, became a postal clerk in Indianapolis in 1890. He later became head of the special delivery and messenger services. Several other educated Negroes were employed as postal clerks or in the railway mail service. By the end of the century there were seventeen mail clerks and carriers in Indianapolis. Colored mail carriers were also found in a few other cities including Marion, Anderson, Frankfort, and Terre Haute. A few Negroes were employed in other Federal departments, principally the Bureau of Internal Revenue.[25]

Occasionally a Negro found employment in city and county government. These positions were usually of uncertain duration because they were involved in political patronage

[23] Indianapolis *World,* September 21, 1889; *The Freeman,* October 19, 1889.

[24] *Negro Artisan,* 125.

[25] *The Freeman,* January 11, 1890; Indianapolis *Recorder,* December 21, 1901; *ibid.,* Victory Progress Edition, July 7, 1945, sec. 1, p. 17.

but considerable prestige was attached to them. As early as the seventies Indianapolis began to hire a few colored policemen. The number fluctuated but probably never exceeded a dozen. Most distinguished was Ben Thornton, who was a member of the department for twenty-five years and attained the rank of detective. He was a leader in the Negro community, prominent in fraternal affairs, and owner of several pieces of real estate.[26] There were instances of colored policemen in other cities in the state, but they were rare. In Indianapolis there were also some colored firemen, and a clerkship or two was usually assigned to Negroes in each city administration.[27]

Although the mass of Negroes were wage earners, most of whom barely eked out an existence, a small middle class of business and professional men was developing. Many of the former were persons who had followed such occupations as that of carpenter, cook, barber, coachman, or teamster, and who were able to acquire their own businesses. Negro-owned businesses were usually found only in the towns with large colored populations since their customers were usually, although not always, colored.

One trade, regarded as especially the province of Negroes, in which it was customary for a colored man to have white customers, was that of barber. A number of men who achieved success in other fields started as barbers, while a few who remained in the trade acquired considerable wealth. The outstanding example was George L. Knox of Indianapolis. He had been born a slave but had come to Indiana during the Civil War. As a barber in Greenfield and Indianapolis he prospered until in the eighties he became proprietor of the barbershop in the Bates House, a leading hotel. With a staff of fourteen barbers his shop was considered

---

[26] *The Freeman*, March 16, 1889; Indianapolis *World*, June 23, 1900. Thornton was born a slave in Virginia in 1849. During the Civil War he escaped and attached himself to a Union soldier who brought him to Indiana.

[27] Indianapolis *Recorder*, December 21, 1901.

one of the finest in the country. With his earnings from this enterprise Knox bought *The Freeman,* a newspaper which he published until 1926. He was a prominent Republican, although he never held public office, and one of the most influential members of his race.[28]

There were a few examples of Negroes who were successful as contractors and builders on a small scale. One was J. H. Baptist, who had come from Virginia in 1876 and served as a butler in the house of John C. New for a time. He later turned to the trade of carpenter and set up his own business, which by 1888 employed between twenty and thirty men. Another success story was that of Anderson Lewis, who had been born a slave in Kentucky and had come to Indianapolis to seek work after emancipation. At first he encountered prejudice because of his color but finally persuaded a German blacksmith to give him a job. After working for nine years as a journeyman he was taken into a partnership by his employer. After the death of the first partner Lewis formed a partnership with another white man, this time an Irishman. The firm of O'Brien and Lewis expanded to include carriage making and repairing as well as blacksmithing. Still another prosperous business was that of O. A. Webb, who began by hauling coal and wood and developed a coal and teamster business which was one of the larger ones in the city.[29]

In addition to these ventures there were several other coal yards, transfer businesses, saloons, restaurants, and ice houses in Indianapolis at the end of the century which were operated by Negro proprietors. Several women were successful cateresses on a small scale. There was also one drug store, one men's clothing store, and one or two women's millinery establishments owned by Negroes. Another type of business which is dealt with more fully in another chapter was the race newspaper. In 1900 three weeklies, *The*

[28] *The Freeman,* January 5, 1889.
[29] *Ibid.,* August 4, 1888; January 11, 1890; Indianapolis *Journal,* January 6, 1880.

Indianapolis World, The Freeman, and the *Indianapolis Recorder,* were operating successfully. By that date there were also three colored insurance agencies and two colored building and loan associations in Indianapolis.[30] Outside of Indianapolis the opportunities for colored enterprises were more limited. In other communities there were a few small barbershops, hair dressing establishments, saloons, and restaurants. An exceptional case was that of J. A. Braboy of Kokomo. He was a native of Indiana, who had been raised in Franklin County, and who had enlisted in the Union Army at the age of seventeen. After the war he returned to Indiana and worked as a barber in several towns before settling in Kokomo. There he became the successful proprietor of a music and furniture store, in which he sold pianos, organs, and sewing machines. He was a member of the Kokomo City Council and prominent in the Christian Church of that city.[31]

Several Negroes earned a livelihood as musicians, a field in which there was less prejudice than in most. The best-known group of colored entertainers in the state was the family of Henry Hart. Hart was himself an accomplished

[30] *The Freeman,* August 4, 1888; Indianapolis *World,* December 31, 1892; Indianapolis *Press,* February 20, 1900; Indianapolis *Recorder,* December 21, 1901. The most renowned Negro-owned business in Indianapolis, The Walker Manufacturing Company, was not established until 1910, and does not fall within the scope of this volume. The founder of this remarkable enterprise, Mrs. C. J. Walker, was born in Louisiana, left an orphan at seven, was married at fourteen, left a widow at twenty with a child to educate. She went to St. Louis, where she worked as a laundress to earn money to send her daughter to public school. While in St. Louis she discovered the formula for a hair dressing which was to make her a fortune. She came to Indianapolis in 1910 and began the manufacture of the preparation. By 1915 it was the largest business in the state owned by a colored person, employing more than five thousand agents throughout the country. In 1915 Mrs. Walker moved to New York, but Indianapolis remained the headquarters of her business. Both in Indianapolis and New York she was identified with many philanthropic activities for Negroes and was noted for sponsoring Negro artists and writers.

[31] Indianapolis *World,* May 28, 1892.

violinist, who also knew other instruments, and who taught his daughters. One of them played the harp, the other the piano. The trio played at many social functions in Indianapolis and at summer resorts in the northern part of the state. One daughter, Myrtle, who was at one time the only colored harpist in the United States, studied for three years in Chicago and played in the British exhibit at the World Columbian Exposition in Chicago in 1893, as well as giving recitals in other cities. In addition to the Hart group there were several other small colored orchestral groups.[32]

By 1900 there was a small group of colored physicians and lawyers, most of whom were concentrated in Indianapolis because opportunities for practice in smaller towns were too limited to afford a living. The first colored M.D. in the state was Samuel A. Elbert. Born in Maryland of free parents in 1832, he had been forced by the death of his father to go to work as a field hand at the age of nine and did not have an opportunity to learn to read and write until he was twenty-two. As a young man he worked as a house servant in Baltimore, New York, and Cincinnati. During the first year of the Civil War he "joined" the Union Army as the servant of a group of white officers. He later returned to Ohio and attended Oberlin before coming to Indianapolis in 1866. His efforts to secure a medical education have been recounted elsewhere in this book. After receiving his degree from Indiana Medical College he began a long and successful career as a physician and benefactor and leader of his race. In 1872 he was appointed a member of the Indianapolis Board of Health. In 1879 he took the lead in attempting to care for the destitute immigrants from North Carolina who poured into Indianapolis during the exodus of that year. He was always active in Republican politics and was nominated for the state legislature in 1882 but was defeat-

32 *Ibid.*, July 27, 1895; December 5, 1896; Indianapolis *Press*, February 20, 1900; Indianapolis *Recorder,* December 21, 1901.

ed.[33] Like Elbert many of the other early physicians had no opportunities for schooling until they were grown and obtained their medical education after they were mature men. In Evansville was Dr. George Washington Buckner, who had been born a slave in Kentucky. He attended public schools in Indianapolis, the Indiana Normal School at Terre Haute, and the Eclectic Medical College in Indianapolis, from which he graduated in 1890. In 1913 he was appointed minister to Liberia by President Wilson. J. H. Ballard was born in Virginia but grew up in Illinois and attended Oberlin College in Ohio before coming to Indiana in 1872. He taught school for a time, attended Meharry Medical College in Nashville, Tennessee, and returned to Indiana, where he unsuccessfully attempted to build up a practice in Jeffersonville. He later taught school in Vincennes and did postgraduate work in medicine in Chicago. He finally settled in Indianapolis in the nineties and practiced successfully for a number of years.[34] Another doctor of the same generation was Wesley Robbins, who was born in Randolph County and attended Union Literary Institute as a young man. After graduating from the Eclectic Medical College he began practice in Indianapolis in 1884.[35]

Dr. Sumner Furniss, who, as noted elsewhere, was the first Negro to be admitted as an intern in the Indianapolis City Hospital, belonged to a younger generation. He began practicing in the nineties and remained a leader of the

[33] Indianapolis *Journal,* January 6, 1880; July 10, 1902. Of Elbert's six children, one son, James B., also began a career in medicine. The boy graduated from the Indianapolis High School at the age of sixteen and from the Indiana Medical College before he was twenty-one. He went to Memphis, Tennessee, to begin practice, but returned to Indianapolis after a short time because of race troubles in Memphis. His promising career was cut off when he died of consumption at the age of twenty-five. *Ibid.,* November 19, 1892; May 9, 1894.

[34] Folder marked "Racial, Vanderburgh County" in papers of Indiana Writers' Project, Work Projects Administration (Indiana State Teachers College, Terre Haute). *The Freeman,* December 22, 1894.

[35] Indianapolis *World,* December 31, 1892.

Negro community until his death in 1953. In addition to his medical work he was prominent in cultural and civic affairs. He became the first president of the Negro Y. M. C. A. and later a member of the Indianapolis City Council as well as attaining the highest rank of any Negro Mason.[36] For a few years a brother, Dr. Henry Furniss, who had been trained at Howard University, was associated in practice with him in Indianapolis. In 1898 Henry Furniss was appointed as consul to Bahia by the McKinley administration. In 1906 he was appointed as minister to Haiti, the last Negro to receive that appointment.[37] Dr. Joseph H. Ward, who began practicing in Indianapolis in the nineties, soon became one of the leading physicians as well as one of the figures most prominent in civic affairs, a position which he retained for more than half a century.

At the end of the century there were about ten Negro physicians in Indianapolis, five in New Albany, three in Evansville, and two each in Anderson and Muncie. Except for their names little is known about most of them.[38] There was about an equal number in the legal profession, although the requirements for practicing law were less strict than for medicine. The majority of colored lawyers, like their white contemporaries, gained admission to the bar by private study.

36 *Ibid.*, April 7, 1894; Indianapolis *News*, January 24, 1945; Indianapolis *Star*, January 19, 1953.

37 Indianapolis *News*, March 3, 1900; *The National Cyclopaedia of American Biography* (40 vols. and current vols. New York, 1898—), 442-43; Franklin, *From Slavery to Freedom*, 424. In 1904 Henry Furniss was married in London, England, to a German wife. He later settled in Hartford, Connecticut. The parents of the two brother physicians were both highly educated Negroes from Massachusetts. Sumner Furniss was named after Senator Charles Summer of Massachusetts. During Reconstruction the family moved to Mississippi, where William Furniss, the father, served as assistant secretary of state and later as head of Alcorn College for a short time. Later the family moved to Indianapolis, where, as already noted, the father became a postal clerk.

38 Indianapolis *Recorder*, December 21, 1901.

The first Negro to be admitted to practice in Indianapolis was James T. V. Hill, who was born in Chillicothe, Ohio, in 1855. He came to Indianapolis as a young man and worked as a mail clerk and barber to earn money to attend Central Law School, from which he graduated in 1882. For many years, until his death in 1928, he was a civic leader. He was one of the first Negroes to be active in the affairs of the Democratic party.[39] In 1894 Isador Blair, who had been born in Maryland but who had received his training in law at the University of Michigan, opened an office in Indianapolis, where he practiced for about ten years. Octavius Royall, a graduate of the law school of Howard University, who began to practice in the city about the same time, remained until about 1903.[40] James H. Lott, who also came to Indianapolis in the nineties, remained and practiced law for many years, becoming one of the leading men in the community. In Evansville one of the few colored lawyers was J. H. Scott, who was said to be the first Negro in the state to try a case before a Federal court.[41] Most of the other lawyers were men like Robert Bagby and Alexander Manning, who were admitted to the bar after studying privately and for whom the law was merely a part-time occupation which they followed in addition to some other work.

In addition to the doctors and lawyers there were a few Negroes in teaching and the ministry, whose work is dealt with elsewhere. Taken together this group of professional people and the businessmen and government employees constituted only a tiny fraction of the entire Negro population. But they exerted an influence out of proportion to their numbers, for it was from them that nearly all of the leadership of the Negro community came.

[39] Indianapolis *News,* February 20, 1928.
[40] *The Freeman,* September 26, 1896; Indianapolis *Recorder,* January 19, 1901.
[41] *The Freeman,* May 14, 1892.

14
SOCIAL ORGANIZATION

In 1870, AT THE TIME of the ratification of the Fifteenth Amendment an obscure Negro wrote a letter to the Indianapolis *Journal* expressing his views as to the manner in which the members of his race should use their newly acquired political rights. He concluded by saying: "There is another great question that will come up in Church and State, and we may as well meet it now; that is the social mingling of the white and colored people. I speak for myself. I have read the Bible through five times, and I find nothing left on record as evidence that God will condemn either party for mingling or not mingling. But, according to the custom of the American people, it is certainly best not to mingle. We can live united in all great national affairs, when properly administered, and live socially separate."[1]

This attempt to allay the fear of the white population of "social equality" was an accurate prophecy of the pattern which was to be followed. There was to be almost no "mingling" of the races, and although some colored men might chafe at the barriers which cut them off from the white society, few attempted to cross those barriers. Instead of entering the white man's social world the Negroes

[1] Indianapolis *Journal*, February 22, 1870. The writer of the letter was Peter W. H. Johnson, who described himself as a man sixty years old who had lived in North Carolina thirty-eight years and in Indiana twenty-two. Johnson's phraseology bears a rather remarkable similarity to that employed by Booker T. Washington in his famous Atlanta speech in 1895 in which he used the metaphor of the hand: "In all things that are purely social we can be as separate as the fingers, yet one as the hand in all things essential to mutual progress."

attempted to create a replica of it. Separate schools were provided by law, but separate churches, fraternal organizations, benevolent institutions, recreational groups, and race newspapers developed without legislative sanction and in spite of civil rights legislation.

In the realm of religion almost complete separation of the races prevailed, and probably no institution played so important a role in shaping the attitudes and conduct of Negroes as did their churches. Among Methodists, who were most numerous before the Civil War in Indiana, the African M.E. organization had been established for many years. Among the Baptists, who became the most numerous denomination, some colored churches had been in existence before 1865, and in the postwar years separate churches became almost universal except in a few communities in northern Indiana or in rural communities where there were too few Negroes to support a church. In many places the colored churches were established with the help of white persons. A white Baptist historian says of the movement: "Their [Negroes'] withdrawal from the white churches was usually amicable, although social pressure was undoubtedly a factor in it."[2]

On the subject of separate churches, as on the subject of schools, there were differences of opinion among Negroes. Not only the ministers but the rank and file of the race seem to have favored their own institutions, but a few persons objected. In 1871 at an Equal Rights Convention a resolution was offered which said: "That we oppose all class distinctions in Church, State or School, and believe that separate Church and school organizations are inimicable to the best interests of our people." This resolution gave rise to a spirited debate in which some colored ministers spoke in favor of separate churches. One lay delegate from Morgan County said he preferred to attend a colored church but was compelled to attend a white church because there were

2 Cady, *Baptist Church in Indiana*, 251.

too few colored people in his community to maintain a church. The controversial resolution was tabled after another delegate admonished the convention to stick to the business for which it had been called and leave the settlement of such questions to the ecclesiastical organizations.[3]

As the result of the migration of Southern Negroes the number of Baptists showed a remarkable increase. In 1867 there were fifteen colored Baptist churches in the state, with a total membership of less than one thousand. Ten years later there were fifty-three churches with a membership of almost three and one-half thousand. By 1887 the number of colored Baptists had reached 5,565. Second Baptist Church in Indianapolis grew rapidly, reaching a membership of 650 by 1876. It played an important part in the life of the colored people of the city, largely because of its pastor, Moses Broyles, who was not only an acknowledged leader among Negroes but who also enjoyed the confidence of the white leaders of the city. After Broyles's death in 1882 the church faced a troubled period in which membership declined and debts mounted until it temporarily lost the use of the church edifice. Its fortunes began to revive when the Reverend J. W. Carr assumed the pastorate in 1887. By the end of the century it had a membership of more than 1,700.[4]

Although many of the newcomers from the South joined the Second Church, others preferred to organize their own congregations. Some of the new churches were started in the rural areas outside the city but were later moved into Indianapolis as the colored population moved cityward. Among these was the Olivet Church, which was started as the Lick Creek Church southeast of Indianapolis, and Mt. Zion church, which was first located southwest of the city. By the end of the century there were about fifteen Baptist churches in Indianapolis.[5]

[3] Indianapolis *Journal,* March 23, 24, 1871.
[4] Stott, *Indiana Baptist History,* 263-64; Broyles, *Second Baptist Church,* 34-41; *The Freeman,* September 22, 1889; Indianapolis *World,* June 3, 1893.
[5] Broyles, *Second Baptist Church,* 55-56; Dunn, *Greater Indianapolis,*

In Evansville, which ranked next to Indianapolis in
Negro population, the Liberty Baptist Church, organized in
1865, came to rival the Second Indianapolis Church in size,
with a membership of 1,700 in 1898. By the end of the
century there were five colored Baptist churches in Evansville, while every other city in the state which had a Negro
settlement had one or more churches. Several rural churches
survived, among which those at Lyles Station in Gibson
County and Lost Creek Township in Vigo County were the
most prosperous.[6]

Although outnumbered by the Baptists after the Civil
War, the African Methodist Episcopal Church continued to
grow and to exert great influence. According to the census
of 1890 there were fifty-one churches in thirty counties,
with a total membership of 4,435. Marion County alone
had 1,053 members. Bethel Church, the oldest colored
church in Indianapolis, continued to be the largest A.M.E.
church in the state, with a membership of six hundred in
1900. Allen Chapel, the second A.M.E. church in the city,
was organized principally by new arrivals from the South.
It was started as a Sunday School for adults with the aid of
a group of white Quakers, but was soon brought under the
jurisdiction of the Indiana A.M.E. conference as a mission
and later a station. Other churches of this denomination
were Simpson Chapel, founded in 1874, Barnes Church,
founded in 1887, and Wayman Chapel, which later became
St. John's Church, founded in 1898.[7]

1:574-75. The Reverend M. W. Turner, who came from North Carolina,
finding no church of his choice in Indianapolis, joined with fourteen other
persons from North Carolina to form the First Free Will Baptist Church
in 1881. A few other Free Will Baptist churches were founded in towns
in the southern part of the state. Indianapolis *Recorder*, May 20, 1933.

[6] Stott, *Indiana Baptist History*, 263-64; *Minutes of Indiana Baptist
Association* [Colored], 1873-1901, *passim;* Indianapolis *Recorder*, December 21, 1901.

[7] *Eleventh Census* (1890): *Report on Statistics of Churches*, 552;
*Minutes of Sixty-third Session of the Indiana Annual Conference of the
African Methodist Church* (1901), 40; *Allen Chapel, 1866-1944, passim;*

Outside of Indianapolis the largest A.M.E. church was the one at Evansville. There were also large churches at Mount Vernon and New Albany in the southern part of the state, while in the eastern part the oldest and largest was the church at Richmond. For many years it was under the guidance of the Reverend James M. Townsend, who was the second Negro to be elected to the Indiana House of Representatives. Townsend later left a position in Washington to which he was appointed during the Harrison administration to return to Richmond, where he continued his successful career as an evangelist. He left again to become pastor of the Quinn Chapel in Chicago but resigned in 1896 to return to Richmond. In the north there were large and well-established churches at Lafayette, Muncie, and Marion, while in Terre Haute in the west there were two churches, Allen Chapel and Second Church. By 1900 nearly all the churches were found in the cities and towns, most of the rural churches founded in the period before the Civil War having disappeared. Notable exceptions, as with the Baptists, were the churches at Lyles Station in Gibson County and Lost Creek Township in Vigo County.[8]

Although most of the colored Methodists belonged to the A.M.E. church, a smaller number were adherents of the African Methodist Episcopal Zion Church, which differed principally from the other organization in not recognizing a separate order of bishops. Largest church of this denomination was Jones Chapel in Indianapolis founded in 1872 by a group from New Albany. A second church was organized in Indianapolis in 1886, while other churches were found in Evansville, Jeffersonville, and Corydon. There were also several Methodist congregations which were not affiliated with either of the colored organizations.[9]

Indianapolis *Recorder*, December 17, 1932; February 18, March 4, May 13, 1933.

[8] *Minutes of Sixty-third Session of Indiana Conference A. M. E. Church* (1901), 29-37.

[9] Dunn, *Greater Indianapolis*, 1:603; Indianapolis *Recorder*, December

Together Baptists and Methodists had a near monopoly on the membership of colored persons. This was due in part to the fact that these denominations were dominant in the Southern states from which most Indiana Negroes came and to the fact that these denominations were tireless in their efforts to win and hold converts, while other Protestant groups indulged in little proselytism among Negroes. A few colored members were found in the congregations of the Disciples of Christ (Christian) church. In 1866 a group of white members helped in the establishment of a separate colored church in Indianapolis, which came to be known as the Second Christian. Some of the professors and students at Northwestern Christian University (now Butler University) taught in the Sunday School in the early years. The membership grew slowly in spite of assistance of white sponsors, but the church survived and after a few years became well established.[10]

The Ninth Presbyterian Church which had been organized in 1872 dissolved in 1881 and was organized as a colored Presbyterian Church. It had little support among the colored population and at one time disbanded but was revived in the eighties and continued to grow.[11] The handful of colored Episcopalians in Indianapolis at first attended St. Paul's Church along with the white communicants. Later a mission church, known as St. Philip's, was organized, and in 1892, the Reverend I. B. Jack, a native of St. Vincent's Island in the West Indies, took charge. However, it was not until after 1900 that a successful church was established.[12]

21, 1901; *Eleventh Census* (1890) : *Report on Statistics of Churches,* 561. In 1890 the total membership of the A. M. E. Zion Church in Indiana was 1,339.

[10] Perry W. Swann, "History of the Christian Churches in Marion County, Indiana" (unpublished M.A. thesis, Butler University, 1938), 10-11; Broyles, *Second Baptist Church,* 35-37; Indianapolis *Recorder,* January 7, 1933.

[11] Dunn, *Greater Indianapolis,* 1:587; *The Freeman,* August 11, 1888; February 16, 1889.

[12] Indianapolis *World,* April 21, 1888; December 24, 1892; Indianapolis

Regardless of denomination no other group enjoyed greater prestige among Negroes than did the ministers, who took a prominent part in the fight for educational and civil rights and who served as political mentors as well as furnishing moral and spiritual leadership. Within their ranks were men who varied greatly in ability, education, and morals. Some of them were born into slavery; many had only the rudiments of a formal education; others attended such institutions as Oberlin, Wilberforce, or De Pauw. A typical example was Johnson Mitchem, born in Harrison County, Indiana, in 1826, whose total school attendance was thirty-three days. As a youth he lived in several places in southern Indiana, making a living chopping wood, as a farm hand, and working on the steamboats on the Ohio River. In 1858 he was converted to Methodism, became a Bible scholar, and later was a licensed preacher. He held pastorates in several communities in Illinois, Michigan, and Indiana, and compiled a vast amount of historical material concerning the A.M.E. church in Indiana. When he died in 1896, he left the bulk of his property to Wilberforce University.[13] On the other hand Alexander Smith, who served in the Bethel church in Indianapolis in the nineties, attained a divinity degree after years of struggling. The son of an Ohio farmer, he spent his boyhood working in the fields and did not finish common school until he was twenty-one. He was then enabled to attend Oberlin for one year through the generosity of a white friend. Thereafter he became a stonecutter, a trade from which he earned money to attend Wittenberg College for two years. After spending some

Recorder, December 31, 1932. Membership of Negroes in the Roman Catholic Church was rare in Indiana before 1900 but there were a few examples. There was probably less racial discrimination in the Catholic Church than in any of the Protestant denominations. The Indianapolis *World,* which had a Protestant staff, declared editorially (December 22, 1900) of the Catholic Church: "It is the one religion that has received the Negro into full fellowship without distinction as to 'race, color or previous condition of servitude.'"

[13] Indianapolis *World,* September 14, 1895; December 26, 1896.

time as an itinerant preacher he finally went to Wilberforce, where he received a B.D. degree in 1887.[14]

For some others educational opportunities were more easily attainable. The family of Abraham L. Murray, who was pastor of the Allen Chapel in Indianapolis, moved to Greencastle during the eighties so that he was enabled to attend De Pauw for four years. T. W. Henderson, who also served at the Bethel church, was born in North Carolina in 1845 and grew up among white Quakers who gave him his early education. Through the efforts of these white benefactors he later attended Oberlin. After the Civil War he served as teacher, preacher, and agent of the Freedmen's Bureau in Missouri. Later he moved to Kansas, where he not only held pastorates but started the first Negro newspaper in the state and helped care for immigrants during the exodus of 1879.[15]

Not all of the members of the clergy were selfless in their devotion to their congregations. Some of them were like the A.M.E. preacher, of whom the presiding elder candidly confessed: "Brother Shelton has not accomplished anything, neither spiritually nor financially." On the other hand, there were men like the Reverend Charles Williams, pastor of the humble little flock of the South Calvary Baptist Church in Indianapolis, who bought property in 1882 in his own name for a meeting place for the church, allowing the members to pay him for it. The final payment to him was not made until 1909, three years before his death.[16]

Some colored preachers won the respect not only of their own race but also of the white population. Among them were men like James Townsend, Moses Broyles, and Samuel Smothers. Smothers, who as a young man had headed the Union Literary Institute, in the years after the Civil War served as a minister of the A.M.E. church in several

[14] *The Freeman,* July 2, 1892.

[15] Indianapolis *World,* September 14, 1895; July 31, 1897.

[16] *Minutes of Sixty-third Session of Indiana Conference A. M. E. Church,* 33; Indianapolis *Recorder,* July 8, 1933.

Indiana cities. While he was preaching in Kokomo, a group of his neighbors, white and colored, urged that he become a candidate for the legislature. At a meeting in his honor a white teacher characterized him as "a man we all love; not because he is (colored) [*sic*] but because he is a man and a Christian minister whom we all have known . . . and respect, regardless of color. . . . His culture and religious qualifications fit him to preach to any congregation, white or colored, learned or unlearned, rich or poor."[17]

At the other extreme were preachers who won their reputations principally through buffoonery and dramatics. Colored camp meetings were frequently regarded as carnivals where white persons went to laugh at the antics of colored clowns. The conduct of such ministers was deplored in a report made at an annual A.M.E. conference, which urged ministers, as representatives of their church and their race, "to cultivate most earnestly habits of cleanliness, decency and sobriety." It urged: "Members of the great A.M.E. Church forever discard, the loud and boisterous laugh, the senseless jest and the disposition to do or say something that will make you appear funny. The part of the funny man is in perfect keeping with one in the Negro minstrel business, but does not comport with the dignity that should hedge a Methodist minister round about."[18]

Next to his church the group to which the average Negro was most strongly attached was his lodge or fraternal organization. Although all Americans have had a reputation for being "joiners," Negroes seemed to outdo their white fellow countrymen in enthusiasm for secret societies. Colored Masons continued to enjoy greater prestige and fur-

17 Indianapolis *World,* February 13, 1892.

18 *Minutes of Sixty-third Session of Indiana Conference A. M. E. Church,* 59. An example of such a camp meeting was held at North Vernon in 1880. It attracted an attendance estimated at five thousand. Forty railroad coaches brought in excursionists, and it was reported that there were more intoxicated persons in town than at any time in five years. Indianapolis *Journal,* August 3, 1880.

nish more race leadership than any other fraternity although their membership was smaller than that of some of the newer groups. By 1892 there were twenty-four lodges in the state, and during the next decade the number grew to sixty-eight, with a total membership of almost one thousand.[19] In 1888 Prince Hall Grand Chapter of the Order of the Eastern Star, the women's counterpart of the Masons, was organized with six member chapters in Indianapolis, Greencastle, Mount Vernon, and Terre Haute. By 1895 there were twenty-two chapters in the state.[20]

The largest fraternal organization of colored persons in the United States was the United Brothers of Friendship and the Sisters of the Mysterious Ten, which claimed more than two hundred thousand members by the eighteen nineties. Although it was primarily an organization of Southern Negroes, there were fifty-one chapters in Indiana in 1892, with a membership of about three thousand. Among its benevolent activities was the maintenance of a home for widows and orphans near Louisville.[21] Another group which had a membership of more than one hundred thousand, as well as a juvenile division, was the Knights and Daughters of Tabor. Originally a band of Illinois Negroes who formed a society to help liberate slaves, after emancipation

[19] Some of the Masonic chapters which had been founded before the Civil War disbanded as the result of the movement from the rural areas to the cities. The following men served as Grand Masters in Indiana between 1856 and 1900: John G. Britton, James S. Hinton, John W. Harrison, John Brooks, Edward Roberts, William Waldon, William Russell, Charles E. Bailey, Henry A. Rogon, Charles H. Lamer, W. T. Floyd, J. H. Walker, W. F. Teister, D. W. Caine. In rare instances colored men were members of white lodges. In 1875 Greensburg Lodge initiated John W. Thurman, who maintained membership in the lodge until his death in 1896 and served as Junior Deacon for six years. Grimshaw, *History of Freemasonry among the Colored People*, 215-16, 304; Indianapolis *World*, August 20, 1892; Indianapolis *Recorder*, December 21, 1901; *ibid.*, Victory Progress Edition, July 7, 1945, Sec. 1, p. 13.

[20] Lyda, *Negro in the History of Indiana*, 84; Indianapolis *World*, July 20, 1895.

[21] Indianapolis *World*, June 11, 1892; *The Freeman*, August 27, 1892.

it became a benevolent order similar to other lodges. In Indiana there were about two thousand members.[22] The Independent Sons of Honor and its women's branch, the Daughters of Honor, seem to have centered in Indiana, although there were also chapters in Louisville and its environs. At the annual meeting which was held in Indianapolis in 1892 ten railroad coaches of delegates came from Louisville.[23]

Like the Masons the Odd Fellows maintained a separate organization of colored members. In the seventies groups of this order began to be organized in Indiana, three chapters being formed in Indianapolis. The leading figure in the organization for many years and the first district master of Indiana was Benjamin T. Thornton, who also enjoyed prestige among his race as the only colored detective on the Indianapolis police force. A chapter of the women's order, the Household of Ruth, was also formed in 1875 and other chapters thereafter.[24] There were also colored branches of the Knights of Pythias. The first permanent lodge in the state was organized in 1897. By 1901 there were ten chapters in Indiana. Dr. J. H. Ward of Indianapolis was the first Grand Chancellor, and Will. H. Porter and George P. Stewart were also prominent in the early history of the body.[25]

These fraternal organizations filled a number of needs. Around them centered much of the social and recreational

[22] Indianapolis *World*, June 25, 1892.

[23] Indianapolis *Journal*, August 5, 1869; *The Freeman*, August 11, 1888; August 13, 1892.

[24] Indianapolis *World*, August 26, 1893. English Odd Fellowship had been introduced into the United States in 1806, but the application of a colored group for a charter was refused by the American parent group in 1842. Thereupon the rejected group petitioned Victoria Lodge in Liverpool, England, and were granted a charter. This chapter, the Philomathean Lodge of New York City, founded 1843, became the parent body of other colored chapters in the United States. *Ibid.*

[25] Indianapolis *Recorder*, December 21, 1901; *ibid.*, Victory Progress Edition, July 7, 1945, Sec. 1, p. 17.

life of their members, and the annual meetings, with their railroad excursions, parades, and merrymaking were events long remembered. The sense of brotherhood and of "belonging" which came with the initiation and oaths of secrecy, as well as the uniforms and insignia, were good for the morale of a people who, as individuals, were accustomed to being looked down upon. Many Negroes belonged to more than one of these orders, and men who sought to speak as political leaders of the race were nearly always prominently identified with fraternal affairs. Moreover, the organizations gave a promise of much-needed security against the hazards of sickness and death through such benevolent activities as the care of sick members, payment of death benefits, and care of widows and orphans.

In addition to the work of the fraternal organizations there were other charitable and philanthropic activities for colored persons, most of which were maintained through the help of white persons. One of the most important was the Colored Orphans Home in Indianapolis, which was begun soon after the Civil War under the sponsorship of the Western Yearly Meeting of Friends. Donations came principally from white persons, but the largest single gift was the bequest of a colored man, John Williams of Washington County, whose brutal murder has been recounted elsewhere. Before his death Williams had made a will in which he asked that his property be used for the education of the colored race in Indiana. His executor, William Lindley, a Quaker, turned over the sum of $5,750, which had been realized from the sale of Williams' property, to the Orphans' Home. The home was opened in 1871 under the operation of a board of managers made up of women of the Society of Friends and a board of directors of men of different denominations. Several hundred children were cared for by the home in the period before 1900, many of them being placed in foster homes.[26] A large kindergarten for colored

[26] Minutes of Plainfield Quarterly Meeting, 8th month 6, 1870; 8th month 5, 1871; Trueblood, "Story of John Williams," in *Indiana Maga-*

children was maintained by the Indianapolis Free Kindergarten Society. Although the members of the sponsoring society and the principal of the kindergarten were white women, some of the kindergartners were colored women, and the mothers of the pupils were organized into a Mothers' Club, which helped to support the institution. The kindergarten society also operated a nursery where working mothers might leave their small children.[27]

The Alpha Home for Aged Colored Women in Indianapolis was the first institution of its kind in the United States. The idea of an establishment where needy women could be cared for without having to accept public charity was first conceived by a colored woman and was taken up by various colored groups, but the home was made possible principally through the gift of a house and lot presented by a white woman, Mrs. Paulina T. Merritt. The original structure, which accommodated only five or six women, was opened in 1886. It was maintained by contributions, especially from colored church groups and fraternities. Until his death in 1892 James S. Hinton was chairman of the board of directors of the home.[28]

In addition to these institutions, which were entirely for Negroes, there were a few institutions, both public and private, in which members of both races were cared for. Some Catholic institutions, such as the Evansville Home for the Aged and the St. Vincent's Orphan Asylum in Fort Wayne, had a few colored inmates. Catholic hospitals, including St. Mary's Hospital in Evansville and St. Joseph's Hospital in Fort Wayne, had a few colored patients. Negroes were also cared for in the Indianapolis City Hospital and the Evansville City Hospital. There were a few colored

zine of History, 30:151-52. Indianapolis Year Book of Charities, 1888-89, Appendix, xlii. See also above, 225.

27 Indianapolis World, June 27, 1894.

28 Indianapolis Journal, June 29, 1886; First Annual Report of the Alpha Home for Aged Colored Women (1902), 15-17; Indianapolis World, November 12, 1892.

children in the Soldiers' and Sailors' Orphans' Home in Knightstown, a state institution.[29]

Although members of white society felt an obligation to do philanthropic work for Negroes and there was a limited amount of interracial co-operation in the maintenance of benevolent institutions, white members were unwilling to share the benefits of the Indianapolis Young Men's Christian Association with Negroes. There was no rule barring colored members, but no colored members were admitted although several had applied. This policy caused the Indianapolis *World* to denounce the Y. M. C. A. as a "caste institution" and to add bitterly: "We suppose there would be no objection to the admission of a Chinaman or a dago, but the discrimination is solely against the Negro." The matter came out in the open in 1888 when the president rejected the applications for membership of two or three Negroes. When there were protests he defended his action by pointing out that the churches of the city barred colored members. The controversy led to an attempt to amend the constitution of the organization so as to limit membership to white persons, and several young men announced their determination to withdraw if colored members were admitted. The fight against the proposed amendment was led by two clergymen, one of whom, Dr. Joseph Jenckes of St. Paul's Episcopal Church, pointed out that there were colored members in his church. The amendment was tabled with the understanding that the policy of tacitly excluding Negroes would continue. The *World* branded these proceedings "a burning shame and an eternal disgrace to the fair name of Indianapolis" and asserted that the men who supported exclusion were "hypocrites of the deepest dye." A few months later one Negro, whose application had been

---

[29] *Eleventh Census* (1890): *Report on Crime, Pauperism, and Benevolence*, pt. 2:901-2.

on file for a long time, was admitted to membership, but the organization remained closed to Negroes generally.[30]

As a result of this discriminatory policy a colored branch of the Y. M. C. A. was organized. The moving spirit was a young physician from Tennessee, Dr. Henry L. Hummons, who enlisted the support of a friend, Dr. Dan H. Brown. After some preliminary meetings in various colored churches a group styling themselves the "Colored Young Men's Prayer Band" was organized in 1900. In 1902 it was admitted as a branch of the state Young Men's Christian Association. In later years, as the Senate Avenue Branch of the Y. M. C. A., it attained national fame because of its Monster Meetings, which were forums at which distinguished Negro and white speakers were presented.[31]

In the fields of recreation and entertainment there was no intermingling, but Negroes patterned their pleasures after those of white society. They celebrated the same holidays, organized the same types of clubs and entertainments, and enjoyed the same sports. One exception to the general pattern was the emancipation celebrations, gala events which belonged peculiarly to Negroes. In the years following the Civil War the first of January was always the occasion for ceremonies commemorating Lincoln's final proclamation on January 1, 1863. In later years September 22, the date of the preliminary proclamation, was celebrated with parades and picnics. The anniversary of emancipation in the West Indies continued to be observed with similar festivities.[32]

[30] Indianapolis *World,* November 19, 1887; April 21, September 15, 1888.

[31] Indianapolis *Recorder,* Victory Progress Edition, July 7, 1945, Sec. 1, p. 13. During 1901-2 the Prayer Band met in the Flanner Guild, which had been opened in a frame building given by a white philanthropist, Frank W. Flanner, in 1898 as a social service center for Negroes. For a short time the Prayer Band directed the activities of the guild. They helped establish a program of playground activities and classes in sewing and cooking. In later years this institution, known as Flanner House, achieved a national reputation as a social service center for Negroes. *Ibid.,* Sec. 4, p. 29.

[32] For accounts of emancipation celebrations see Indianapolis *Journal,*

With the exception of these affairs the accounts of the social events described in the Negro press differed very little from those described in the other newspapers of the day, although the attempts to imitate white affairs sometimes struck a ludicrous note.

For at least two or three years a Colored Fair was held in Indianapolis in late August preceding the regular state fair. The first occasion of this sort was planned by a colored group known as the Marion County Agricultural Association in 1879. Apparently it was a huge success. There were exhibitions of horses and pacing and trotting races in addition to displays of needlework, lace, baked goods, preserves, and so forth made by colored women. The fair was attended by a group of five hundred people from Louisville as well as colored people from all over Indiana. A similar fair was held the following year but was less successful.[33]

In the cities and towns countless clubs were organized, some of them purely recreational, others with a cultural purpose. For example, in Indianapolis in the winter of 1888-89 alone there were found, among others, a Douglass Literary Society, a Bethel Literary Society, a Parlor Reading Circle, a debating society in the Second Christian Church, and a colored dramatic company. There were numerous musical groups. In 1889 there was one called the Ermina Opera Company, which was made up of young ladies trained in both music and elocution. In 1890 the Metropolitan Club, a young men's social group, sponsored a concert at the A.M.E. church at which there were orchestral and vocal numbers. In the nineties annual music festivals were started at the Bethel Church in which an orchestra and chorus composed of local talent as well as soloists from other cities participated.

August 2 and December 31, 1867; August 5, 1869; December 30, 1870; January 2, 1872; September 23, 1880; August 3, 1887.

[33] Indianapolis *Journal*, August 26, 1879; Indianapolis *Daily Sentinel*, May 23, August 26, 27, 1879; Indianapolis *Leader*, August 30, 1879.

Colored people showed the same interest in sports which the rest of the American public was beginning to manifest in the late nineteenth century. The fame which colored baseball players were to win in the twentieth century was foreshadowed by the enthusiasm for that game. Shortly after the Civil War two amateur teams were reported in Indianapolis—the Eagles composed principally of barbers from the shop in the Bates House and the Mohawks, made up mostly of barbers from other establishments. By 1887 there were two professional teams, the Indianapolis Browns and the Black Diamonds. Several other cities with large colored populations also had teams. In baseball, as in other activities, racial lines were sharply drawn. In 1888 John W. Fowler, a graduate of Oberlin, who had acquired a reputation for his prowess in baseball, was hired, sight unseen, to play on a team in Lafayette. When the manager and players saw him he was rejected at once because of his color. In Kokomo, which had a reputation for being less race conscious than most Indiana cities, the baseball team refused to have a colored member and refused to play against a team with such a member.[34]

Exclusion from the white man's society caused humiliation and bitterness, but the creation of separate organizations and institutions stimulated race consciousness and pride. A conspicuous example of this was the Negro press. The newspapers fought all forms of discrimination and demanded the elimination of racial barriers, but they were the products of the situation against which they inveighed, and the very fact that they existed promoted race consciousness. Indianapolis, with its large Negro population, offered a promising field for Negro journalism.

Before the Civil War there had been no Negro newspaper in Indiana. In 1870 there were only ten such papers in the entire United States, but by 1880 there were thirty. One

[34] Indianapolis *Daily Herald*, July 27, 1867; Indianapolis *Journal*, August 4, 1887; Indianapolis *World*, August 25, 1894.

of these was the Indianapolis *Leader,* a weekly which first appeared in August, 1879, and which continued publication until 1885. It was the joint enterprise of the three Bagby brothers, Robert, Benjamin, and James, who in addition to serving as principals of the public schools in Indianapolis, also started this first Negro newspaper. The youngest of the three, James, served as business manager, while the others contributed articles and editorials. Like most Negro papers of the period it was bitterly partisan in support of the Republican party, although whether it received financial support from Republican sources is not clear.[35]

In 1882 a second paper, called at first *The Colored World,* later the Indianapolis *World,* began publication. Various persons were associated with the undertaking, but the most important personality was Levi E. Christy, who was also a teacher in the Indianapolis schools. In 1885 Christy left teaching to become editor and senior proprietor of the paper. For a time Edward E. Cooper was joint editor. The *World* soon became one of the outstanding Negro papers in the country. It was given credit for introducing many new Negro writers to the reading public. It was also unusual in maintaining its own print shop and thereby giving employment and training to colored printers. Although Republican in politics during its early years the *World* was more restrained and less blindly partisan than many Negro newspapers. It presented news on national questions and about the condition of Negroes in all parts of the country as well as local news. A contemporary historian said of the paper and its editor: "As an editor, Mr. Christy is cool and conservative, and demands for the Afro-American the same chances and opportunities accorded to other American citizens. He appeals to the reason and better judgment, rather than to the passions or emotions."[36]

[35] Penn, *Afro-American Press,* 112; Indianapolis *Journal,* January 6, 1880; *The Freeman,* January 11, 1890.

[36] Penn, *Afro-American Press,* 222-23.

The *World* showed signs of political independence before 1888, and during the Harrison campaign it became increasingly critical of Republican policy. After its principal rival, *The Freeman,* became an out-and-out Republican paper, Christy's organ leaned more and more to the other side. Christy finally openly avowed his conversion to the Democratic faith and campaigned for Democratic candidates. In 1893 R. W. Thompson, a Democrat, became managing editor, although Christy remained publisher. It is probable that the paper was subsidized by the Democratic party to a limited extent. A few years later, when Christy left the field of journalism to become a minister of the A.M.E. church, Alexander E. Manning, who had long been identified with Democratic politics, became manager. W. Allison Sweeney, who had been associated for some years with *The Freeman,* left that paper to join the *World.* Under the direction of Manning and Sweeney the paper assumed a livelier and more militant tone on race questions.[37]

In the meantime *The Freeman* had begun publication in 1888. Its founder was Edward E. Cooper, formerly of the *World,* a man of ability and enterprise, but unscrupulous. Cooper had been born in the South but had come North in his youth. In 1876 he took a position as a hotel waiter in Philadelphia at the time of the Centennial Exposition. He later came to Indianapolis and attended school, working for his room and board and selling books to earn his expenses. He was one of the early graduates of the Indianapolis High School, the only Negro member in a class of sixty-five. After working in the United States Railway Mail Service

---

[37] R. W. Thompson later became a strong Republican. He maintained a news agency for the Negro press which was subsequently moved from Indianapolis to Washington, where it was known as the National Press Bureau. The agency was partially subsidized by money from Booker T. Washington and Tuskegee University. August Meier, "Booker T. Washington and the Negro Press," in *Journal of Negro History,* 38(1953):67. Although Manning remained an active Democrat, the *World* in later years gave support to Republican candidates.

for a few years he became associated with the *World*. In 1887 he gave up his interest in that paper, and in 1888 launched his own publication, *The Freeman*. The new venture, which styled itself "the first and only illustrated journal of the Afro-American race," immediately acquired a wide circulation. The paper was not local in outlook but was designed to appeal to Negroes everywhere. In addition to dealing with matters of current interest Cooper tried to present the past history of the colored race. The tone of the paper was dignified and its literary quality high. I. Garland Penn, whose book on the Afro-American press appeared while *The Freeman* was in its infancy, declared: "Success with it has been simply phenomenal. . . . The white journals of the country, without hesitation, term it the leading paper of the race." Concerning its merits he added: "As a literary paper it keeps pace with the educational and literary progress of the race. As an illustrated paper it portrays the Afro-American as he is, and not as so often represented by many of the white journals."[38] Although he had been a Republican and later returned to the Republican fold, Cooper proclaimed that his paper was to be politically "independent." The masthead declared: "The Freeman is an Independent Weekly Newspaper which bravely tells the Truth without fear or favor. It is published in the interest of the Negro, and is Fearless in the Advocacy of his Rights." Editorially the paper decried the long subserviency of Negro voters to the Republican party and urged political independence. It insisted: "A division of the Negro vote is essential to the ultimate solution of the Race Problem: It should divide, however, on questions which involve Principle."[39] Cooper enthusiastically supported Cleveland in 1888 and was critical of the Harrison administration, but

[38] Penn, *Afro-American Press*, 336-37, which quoted the *National Leader* as saying of *The Freeman*: "though in its infancy it has taken first rank in illustrated newspaperdom. We consider it the *Harpers' Weekly* of the colored race."

[39] *The Freeman*, July 21, 1888.

in 1890 he urged the defeat of Indiana's Democratic congressmen who had voted against the Federal elections bill.

Although *The Freeman* appeared to be a brilliant success, its publisher became entangled in various financial and legal difficulties which forced him to sell the paper in 1892. The purchaser was George L. Knox, owner of the largest barbershop in Indiana and a power in the Republican party, who had previously brought suit against *The Freeman* for the foreclosure of a mortgage. Cooper continued to work on the paper as manager for a few months under the new regime but later went to Washington as manager of the *Colored American*.[40] The change in ownership brought an abrupt reversal in the political attitude of *The Freeman*. Knox announced at once that henceforth the paper would be Republican. The *World* raised the question as to "whether the transfer [of owners] is not a fake resorted to to enable the Freeman to get its hand into the bar'l of the Republican central committee," but concluded that the purchase had been a bona fide one. Under Knox the editorial opinion was usually Republicanism of the more orthodox and uncritical variety. W. Allison Sweeney, who had been on the staff under Cooper, remained as editor. Sweeney was a native of Michigan, who had attended public schools in Ann Arbor. As a young man he displayed a taste for literature and early gained a reputation as an orator, stumping Michigan for the Republicans in 1872. Before coming to Indianapolis he had had experience on race papers in Detroit and West Virginia. He was regarded as an uncompromising champion

40 Indianapolis *World,* June 4, 1892; September 16, 30, 1893. Cooper was a complex and contradictory and not altogether admirable figure. His changing political attitudes seem to have been determined largely by motives of personal advantage. However, as editor of the *Colored American* he won praise from Negro leaders and was regarded as having powerful influence in shaping Negro opinion. The *Colored American,* like many other Negro newspapers, received some financial support from Booker T. Washington until its demise in 1904. Indianapolis *World,* April 7, 1900; Meier, "Booker T. Washington and the Negro Press," in *Journal of Negro History,* 38:75.

of civil rights. Later, Elwood Knox, son of the owner, became managing editor.[41]

In 1897 a new paper, the Indianapolis *Recorder,* appeared. Its publishers were William H. Porter and George P. Stewart, who had had some earlier journalistic experience. The masthead declared the *Recorder* to be: "A Negro Newspaper Devoted to the Best Interests of the Colored People of Indiana." It was Republican in politics but not bitterly partisan. Unlike the *World* and *Freeman,* which gave much coverage to national questions and Negroes in other parts of the United States, the new paper contained more local and state news and devoted more space to personal mention of Indiana Negroes. The formula was apparently a success, for the *Recorder* continued to prosper long after its rivals had ceased publication.[42]

Various race organizations, as well as the newspapers, attempted to carry on the fight for equal rights. Early examples were the Negro conventions of the post Civil War years. Thereafter for a time these separate racial movements tended to die out as Negroes looked to political activity, and especially to the Republican party, as the instruments for obtaining equal treatment. But toward the end of the century it had become obvious that reliance upon this method was entirely inadequate as both political parties appeared to be indifferent to the Negro. This led to a movement for an organization dedicated solely to the advancement of the

[41] Indianapolis *World,* June 4, 1892; May 26, 1894; *The Freeman,* September 26, 1896. As noted above, Sweeney later joined the staff of the *World.* Still later he went to Chicago where he became editor of the *Conservator.*

[42] The Indianapolis *World* ceased publication in 1924, *The Freeman* in 1926. The Indianapolis *Recorder* continues publication and is today the only Negro paper of any consequence in Indianapolis. Following the death of George P. Stewart, his son, Marcus Stewart, became editor of the *Recorder.* In addition to the papers mentioned, there were many ephemeral publications of which even the names have been lost. Usually they were political sheets which lasted only for the duration of a campaign.

colored race. In 1887 T. Thomas Fortune of New York sounded the cry for a league of American Negroes, an idea which was immediately endorsed by the Indianapolis *World*. In 1890 a national organization, the Afro-American League, was formed in Chicago. Its objects, as stated in the constitution, included more equitable distribution of school funds, resistance to lynch law, punishment of the perpetrators of lynching, and prosecution of civil rights cases in the courts.[43]

Indiana Negro leaders were sympathetic toward the organization, and a state Afro-American League with a membership of one hundred was soon formed. James S. Hinton was named president and Allison Sweeney chairman of the executive committee. Neither the state nor national organization showed much vitality and the movement died out after a short time. In the late nineties there was an attempt to revive it. A meeting styling itself a "Convention of Representative Afro-Americans of Indiana," attended by ministers and other leaders from all parts of the state was held in Indianapolis in 1899. Papers were read on subjects relating to race problems in the North and South, and delegates were elected to attend a national meeting of a revitalized Afro-American Council in Chicago.[44] The Chicago meeting was not much of a success, but in February, 1900, there was another attempt to form a permanent local organization in Indianapolis, and in August of that year the city was the scene of a convention of the National Council to which about one hundred and fifty delegates from all parts of the United States came. The meeting was held at a time when racial bigotry appeared to be rapidly increasing not only in the South but also in the North. Indiana itself had been the scene of lynchings in recent months, while on the very eve of the convention race disorders were reported in New York City and in Akron, Ohio, in the Western Reserve district, which had once been a stronghold of abolitionism.

[43] Indianapolis *World*, June 11, 1887; *The Freeman*, January 18, 1890.
[44] *The Freeman*, January 11, 1890; Indianapolis *World*, July 29, 1899.

Apropos of these events and the condition of the Negro generally the Indianapolis *News* expressed the opinion: "The generation that fought the Civil War to free the slave is not yet dead, and yet the black man is being disfranchised everywhere in the old slave states; he is falling away in consideration in the North; he is treated with a harshness that denies the fact that he is equal before the law. . . . In recent years there has been a growing hostility toward the black man. He has continually had fewer friends and more enemies."[45]

The delegates to the Afro-American Council took cognizance of the fact that the position of their race appeared to be deteriorating and condemned the attempts to abridge their rights. None of them proposed any sort of a program of action to put an end to the anti-Negro movement. Instead they adopted a resolution which rather wistfully declared: "We have faith to believe that revolutions never go backwards, and that the abiding sense of justice in the American people, North and South, will ultimately impel them to concede to us all that we contend for, and which is inherently ours, as it is theirs."[46]

[45] Quoted in Indianapolis *World*, September 1, 1900.
[46] *Ibid.*

15

EPILOGUE

To bring this study to a close in 1900 is somewhat arbitrary, as terminal dates for most historical studies are arbitrary. The year 1900 is as logical a stopping point as any. Although the number of Negroes in Indiana was to increase greatly after that date, by then racial patterns had been established in most areas as they were to remain for many years, and, in some cases, until the present.

The years between the Civil War and the end of the century were a period of substantial, if uneven, progress for the colored population, especially in the legal and political realms. Although equal treatment was not always maintained in practice, in the eyes of the law Negroes were recognized as citizens entitled to equal protection. While the adoption of the Fifteenth Amendment was bitterly resisted, once political rights were granted there was never any movement to take them away. Although some Negroes might be ignorant and venal and blindly partisan, and although white politicians might seek to exploit them, they voted openly and freely. The state, which before the Civil War had denied colored children any schooling at public expense, assumed responsibility for educating them and in theory, at least, for giving them the same schooling afforded white children. In spite of the fact that many communities maintained separate schools which were inferior to those for the white race, and in spite of economic conditions which prevented many colored children from taking advantage of the opportunities open to them, the race had made impressive progress in education by the end of the century.

In private relationships which were not regulated by law racial patterns changed less markedly. Economic opportunities did not keep pace with educational progress. Negroes continued to be barred from skilled occupations and, regardless of their qualifications and ambitions, were relegated for the most part to menial, unskilled, low-paying jobs. Socially there was almost no mingling of the races, and Negroes were denied accommodations in most public places which white patrons frequented in spite of the adoption of an innocuous civil rights law. In the social and economic realms there was evidence that barriers were hardening rather than relaxing at the end of the century and that race feeling was stronger than it had been a few years earlier.

The most striking change after 1900 was the great migration from the South, beginning during the First World War and continuing to the present. During the period from 1910 to 1920 the Negro population of the state increased by about 50 per cent. The rate of increase fell off slightly during the twenties but rose again during the thirties, until by 1940 there were 122,473 Negroes in the state or 3.3 per cent of the whole. The years of the Second World War and the postwar period saw the most spectacular increase. By 1950 Negroes numbered 175,785 or 4.4 per cent of the whole. The new arrivals headed for the industrial centers, by-passing the older Ohio River communities except for Evansville, and moving northward to Indianapolis and the newer cities in the extreme north, especially the steel centers in the Gary area. The last city, which did not even appear in the census in 1900, had reached a population of more than one hundred thousand by 1930, including 17,922 Negroes. By 1950 the number of Negroes had reached 39,326 or almost 30 per cent of the total population. However, the largest number continued to be found in Indianapolis, where by 1930 there were 43,967 Negroes or 12 per cent of the total. By 1950 the number had reached 64,091 or about 15 per cent of the whole. Meanwhile, the number of Negroes in some of the smaller cities in the southern counties had declined, and the movement from the farm to the city which had begun before 1900 continued until the Negro farmer had all but disappeared.

The great influx during the First World War led to a temporary increase in racial intolerance, one manifestation of which was the Ku Klux Klan, which was especially powerful in Indiana in the twenties. The last spectacular race disorder in the state occurred in 1930 in the city of Marion in Grant County, which had acquired a reputation for lax law enforcement. Two Negro youths, who had confessed to robbing and killing a white man and assaulting his young woman companion, were taken from the jail by a mob and hanged. Although race feeling was strong among much of the white population, the resort to mob violence was universally condemned, and the Marion incident was an isolated one. Probably most of the population of Indiana today would be startled to know that a lynching had occurred in the state so recently.

In the economic realm there was very real progress and a marked increase in material well-being for many members of the race. More and more Negroes found employment in industry, although in general only the menial and unattractive jobs were open to them. It still remained true that Negroes were the last to be hired and the first to be fired. No other group was so adversely affected by the Great Depression. But the industrial booms of the years of the Second World War and thereafter opened new opportunities for employment to thousands. However, the census figures of 1950 show that only about one eighth of Negro male workers were classified as craftsmen or foremen in industry, while the number in professional, managerial, and clerical positions was much smaller. The largest number remained in the unskilled categories whether in industrial or service jobs. Among women the largest group remained private household workers, with large numbers listed also as service workers and operatives in such businesses as laundries and dry cleaning establishments. Smaller numbers were found in manufacturing and clerical positions.

The economic position of some workers was strengthened by the rise of the Congress of Industrial Organizations, which, unlike most of the unions in the American Federation of Labor, not only admitted Negro members but actively fought against discrimination on all fronts. In some member unions Negroes attained positions of leadership, and through the activities of the C. I. O. some were able to exercise a more effective role in politics. In 1945 a noncompulsory Fair Employment Practices Act was adopted by the legislature. The preamble declared that it was "the public policy of the state to encourage all of its citizens to engage in gainful employment, regardless of race, creed, color, national origin or ancestry" and to discourage discrimination. The act authorized the State Labor Commissioner to make studies of discrimination, to receive complaints, and make recommendations, but no penalties were provided for noncompliance.

In the social realm Negroes continued to be a group apart. The civil rights act adopted in 1885 remained on the statute books without any strengthening amendments and was seldom invoked. The segregation of the races in such places as restaurants, hotels, and theaters remained almost complete until the years of the second World War, when a gradual relaxation of racial barriers began. Fortified by their stronger economic position and an increased awareness of their legal rights, Negroes gradually began to invade establishments heretofore regarded as exclusively for a white clientele, but proprietors continued to discourage their patronage. Although the old patterns have not changed rapidly, they are changing. Evidence of the persistence of racism in popular thinking is reflected in the fact that Indiana alone of Northern states east of the Mississippi retains in her laws a ban against interracial marriages, a law which was enacted before the Civil War.

In the field of education the school law of 1877, which provided for permissive but not compulsory segregation, remained unchanged for almost three quarters of a century. In the southern counties and in many of the cities throughout the state separate schools continued to be maintained. During the twenties, when the influence of the Klan was powerful, racial lines began to be more sharply drawn. For example, in Indianapolis, where heretofore there had been some all-colored and some mixed elementary schools, the school board ruled that all colored children must attend separate schools. In 1927 for the first time a colored high school was opened in the city, and thereafter colored students were excluded from the other high schools. It was not until 1949 that the state legislature adopted legislation banning segregation in public schools. The act provided for the completion of integration of pupils of both races by 1954 and provided that state funds should be cut off from any school system which practiced segregation or which discriminated on account of color in the hiring, upgrading, or tenure of teachers.

The unquestioning allegiance to the Republican party which had marked the entry of Negroes into politics continued well into the twentieth century. In spite of their increasing numbers Negro voters continued to be ignored for many years so far as elective offices were concerned. From 1897 to 1933 no Negro sat in the state legislature. During the late twenties defections from the Republican party began because of the close alliance of the leaders of that party with the Ku Klux Klan. The trend continued during the years of the Great Depression and the New Deal until a veritable revolution had occurred in Negro voting habits. A group which had been solidly Republican for generations became almost as solidly Democratic. The change that was taking place was reflected in the election of the first Negro Democrat to the General Assembly in 1932. Since that date there have been colored lawmakers at every session, some of whom have been generally recognized as being among the most able members. There has always been at least one member from Indianapolis while others have been elected from the industrial center of South Bend in the north and one from Evansville in the south. Most of them have been Democrats but some have been Republicans. The only Negro to serve in the state Senate is a Republican. Although in national elections in recent years most Negroes have voted for Democratic candidates, the vote is not solid. While Negro voters have continued to fail to receive elective offices in proportion to their numbers, their political strength and maturity have steadily increased, and their votes are cultivated assiduously by both parties. By the mid-twentieth century, in politics, as in education, patterns which had been established in the nineteenth century were drastically altered, while in the fields of occupations and social relationships, although they were changing, they were changing gradually.

INDEX

Teachers, Negro, 171, 172-73, 176-77n, 318-19, 330-31, 333-36, 338, 345n.

Teister, W. F., 376n.

Temperance societies, 148.

Tennessee, law concerning emancipation of Negroes, 56n; Negro migration from, 10, 32, 51, 224.

Terre Haute (Ind.), Negro population, 141n, 230n; Allen Chapel (A.M.E.), 155; Negro schools, 176, 336; Negro participation in politics, 314.

Terre Haute *Journal,* on abolitionists, 64n.

Terry, Eli, 102.

Test, Charles H., 234.

Thirteenth amendment, 204, 234, 239n.

Thomas, Cal, 43.

Thomas, Seth, 136.

Thompson, J. P., 291n-92n.

Thompson, John C., 178.

Thompson, R. W., 385.

Thompson, W. C., 259-60.

Thornton, Benjamin T., 360, 377.

Thornton, Henry, 41, 42n.

Thurman, Fountain, 135.

Thurman, John W., 376n.

Tipton, John, 52, 103n.

Tisdale, François, 26n.

Townsend, Rev. James M., 301, 343, 371, 374; legislator, 269, 301; political leader, 304, 306, 310; fights for equal school privileges, 331.

Trades, engaged in by Negroes, 142, 349-50n, 360-62.

Trail, William, 134, 172, 200.

Transportation, public, racial discrimination on, 255, 256-57.

Tucker, Ebenezer, 176, 177n, 181.

Tucker, John, 129-30.

Turner, Augustus, 142.

Turner, George, 6-7.

Turner, Rev. M. W., 370n.

Turner, Milton, J., 303.

Underground Railroad, 39-40; routes and stations, 40-41, 42-44, 52; agents, 41-44.

Union Army, enlistment of Negroes in, 192-203, 231-32n.

Union Literary Institute, Randolph County, 173-78n.

United Brothers of Friendship, 376.

United Mine Workers Union, 353, 357, 358.

United States Congress, petitions sent to, 8, 20; attitude toward colonization movement, 73-74. *See also* Legislation, Federal.

United States Constitution, interpretation of Art. IV, Sec. 2, 59n-60n. *See also* Fifteenth Amendment, Fourteenth Amendment, Thirteenth Amendment.

United States District Court for Indiana, decision concerning Negroes, 97-98.

United States Government service, Negroes in, 299n, 301-2, 306-7, 335, 359.

United States Senate, investigates 1879 Negro exodus from South, 215-23.

United States Supreme Court, decisions concerning Negroes, 112, 132, 235, 328.

Utica (Ind.), 226.

Vance, Zebulon B., 215n.

Vanderburgh, Henry, 6-7, 15, 27.

Vanderburgh County, Negro population, 210, 228, 230. *See also* Evansville.

Vaughan *v.* Williams, 110.

Vernon *Times,* on capture of fugitive slave, 108.

Vigo County, Negro population, 45, 46, 51, 134, 137, 228n, 229, 230; Negro schools, 172; value of land owned by Negroes, 140n. *See also* Terre Haute.

EMMA LOU THORNBROUGH, a pioneer in African American history, is Professor of History Emeritus at Butler University. Her many works on African Americans include *Since Emancipation: A Short History of Indiana Negroes, 1863–1963* and *T. Thomas Fortune, Militant Journalist.*